Readings in Educational Psychology

LEARNING AND TEACHING

Readings in Educational Psychology

LEARNING AND TEACHING

E. STONES

METHUEN & CO LTD
11 NEW FETTER LANE · LONDON EC4

First published in 1970
by Methuen & Co Ltd
11 New Fetter Lane London EC4
© 1970 by E. Stones
Printed in Great Britain
by Richard Clay (The Chaucer Press) Ltd
Bungay, Suffolk

SBN 416 13740 7 Hardback
    416 13750 4 Paperback

Distributed in the USA
by Barnes & Noble Inc

Contents

4 Some aspects of subject teaching

5 Programming teaching

Preface

This collection of readings has been compiled with the needs of readers at an intermediate stage in their study of educational psychology in mind. It assumes an acquaintance with the basic ideas in the field and a desire to read further and make direct contact with some original sources.

For reasons outlined in Section 1, the main criterion of selection of the papers was their coverage of the field of classroom learning with particular emphasis on the cognitive aspects. Within this general classification, papers which review research in a given area were often selected rather than journal articles reporting single experiments. The aim of the selection was to acquaint the reader with authoritative statements from leading workers in given fields which, while being research based, would also permit of a fuller treatment of the subject than would be possible from single research reports. Some direct reports of experiments are included, however, as are some more speculative model-building articles. Further criteria of selection were that the papers should not be too long and that they should be readable.

All papers have been edited and most shortened. To avoid producing a text peppered with marks indicating omissions and parentheses indicating editor's connecting matter, no indication is given in the body of the text when these emendations have been made. Almost all references have been omitted, but a selection from each paper and some additional key works have been brought together at the end of each section. A reader seeking more detailed reference can obtain this from the original paper.

I should like to stress, in conclusion, that the final selection of papers can only be considered as representative of work in the field rather than exhaustive.

Acknowledgements

The editor and publishers wish to thank the following for permission to reproduce material from the publications listed below:

Academic Press, Inc. and Dr R. Gagné for an extract from *Analyses of Concept Learning* by H. J. Klausmeier and C. W. Harris; American Psychological Association for *American Psychologist*, Vol. 18, 1963, *Journal of Educational Psychology*, Vol. 52, 1961 and *Psychological Review*, Vol. 56, 1949; Association for Supervision and Curriculum Development, Dr E. J. Amidon and Dr E. R. Powell for an extract from *The Supervisor: Agent for Change in Teaching* edited by J. Raths and R. R. Leeper; the editor of the British Journal of Medical Education for *British Journal of Medical Education*, Vol. 3, No. 2, 1969; Dr J. B. Brocklehurst for an extract from *Educational Review*, No. 19, June 1967; Department of Audiovisual Instruction, Washington, for *AV Communication Review*, Vol. 14, No. 1, 1966, and Vol. 15, No. 1, 1967; Educational Testing Service and A. S. Willmott for an extract from *International Newsletter – Educational Evaluation and Research*; Granada Publishing Ltd for *Speech and the Development of Mental Processes in the Child* by A. R. Luria and P. Ia. Yudovich; Granada Publishing Ltd and American Elsevier Publishing Company, Inc. for *Development in Learning: Contexts of Education* by E. A. Lunzer; Grune & Stratton, Inc. for *The Psychology of Meaningful Verbal Learning* by D. P. Ausubel; Harcourt, Brace & World, Inc. for *Language* by E. Sapir; Harvard Educational Review for *Harvard Educational Review*, Vol. 24, 1954, and Vol. 34, No. 2, 1964; Holt, Rinehart and Winston, Inc. for *Pygmalion in the Classroom* by R. Rosenthal and L. Jacobson; International Arts and Sciences Press, Inc. for *Soviet Education*, Vol. VII, No. 5, 1965, Vol. VIII, No. 6, 1966 and Vol. X, No. 3, 1968; Journal of Learning Disabilities and N. C. Graham for an extract from *Journal of Learning Disabilities*, Vol. 1, No. 11, 1968; The Journal of Teacher Education for

The Journal of Teacher Education, Vol. 13, 1962; Methuen & Co Ltd for *Aspects of Educational Technology* edited by W. Dunn and C. Holroyd; The M.I.T. Press for *Thought and Language* by L. S. Vigotsky; National Foundation for Educational Research for *Educational Research*, Vol. 9, No. 1, 1966 and Vol. 11, No. 3, 1969; National Society for the Study of Education for *Theories of Learning and Instruction* edited by E. R. Hilgard; Pergamon Press Ltd for *International Journal of Educational Sciences*, Vol. 1, 1967; Routledge & Kegan Paul Ltd and Humanities Press, Inc. for *Studies in the Nature and Teaching of History* edited by W. H. Burston and D. Thompson; Routledge & Kegan Paul Ltd and Stanford University Press for *Psychology in the Soviet Union* edited by B. Simon and *Educational Psychology in the U.S.S.R.* edited by B. Simon and J. Simon; Special Education for *Special Education*, Vol. 57, No. 4, 1968, and Vol. 58, No. 1, 1969; Sweet & Maxwell Ltd for *Programmed Learning*, Vol. 5, No. 2, 1968; UNESCO for *Teaching Machines in Programmed Instruction* by M. J. Tobin, paper read at UNESCO Seminar on Programmed Instruction, Varna, Bulgaria, August 1968; and University of Hull Institute of Education, Dr R. M. Beard and Dr R. R. Skemp for extracts from *Aspects of Education: The New Look in Mathematics Teaching* edited by F. Land.

SECTION I

Overview

A great problem facing the student of educational psychology is the difficulty of deciding exactly what it is. In the past there has been a lack of clarity and consensus which most authorities have sought to encompass by an encyclopedic eclecticism. The field of study spread wide and embraced subjects such as child development, mental hygiene, mental measurement and others, each of which generated its own sub-disciplines. A particular difficulty springs from the use of the same term to refer to clinical psychologists in child guidance work and to workers in the field of pedagogy. The work of the clinical educational psychologist has little relevance to the everyday work of the teacher, but the common use of the title *educational psychologist* generates confusion which leads to the assumption that it has. Another difficulty is created by the fact that at times the term *educational psychology* has embraced a strand of theory and practice which owes little if anything to experiment or scientific investigation and yet which confidently provides 'explanations' of aspects of children's behaviour and prescriptive formulas for educational practice. The distinguishing characteristics of this approach to educational psychology are its supremely confident assertions and complete lack of supporting evidence.

One field of study which does not lack scientific rigour, but which has not enthused students of education, is the laboratory study of learning. The study of animal learning is not without relevance to human learning but it is not in itself sufficient. Nor are the studies of rote learning in which generations of psychology students have acted as subjects. Yet they often form a quite substantial part of many courses on educational psychology.

One other aspect of educational psychology which formed the

staple of most texts and courses in the subject until recent years is the study of mental testing. Much attention was given to intelligence testing and theoretical models of the structure of the intellect. The preoccupation with this field of study was unfortunate, not because it was inappropriate but because it was accorded quite disproportionate attention.

In view of the extensive and ill-defined scope of the subject, any book which purports to deal with educational psychology is likely to be arbitrary and idiosyncratic in its selection of topics. This one is no exception. However, the papers which I have chosen relate to one central theme which is being increasingly seen as the main concern of the study of educational psychology, namely, the nature and conditions of classroom learning. Under this rubric I have chosen to focus particularly upon the cognitive aspects of classroom learning. I am conscious that other aspects of classroom learning are of considerable importance, for example social interactions, personality factors, individual differences, but to include sections dealing adequately with all these and other closely related topics would have resulted in an extremely lengthy or a very unrepresentative selection. In any case, I felt that the focus I have chosen, limited though it may be, is more likely than any other to give a student a clear idea of current concerns in the field of classroom learning and teaching.

It is perhaps worth remarking on the fact that the phrase *learning and teaching* is used rather than the single words *learning* or *teaching*. In reaction against older authoritarian views of teaching it became fashionable to refer to the children's learning and to de-emphasize the importance of the teacher's intervention in the process. The extreme case was the view of some advocates of discovery learning who saw the teacher more as an observer than a participant in the transactions of the classroom. In general the papers which follow espouse the view that there is such a discipline as *teaching*. The teacher is the key element in a given teaching system and it is the hope of several authors that eventually educational psychology will be able to equip him with a general theory or body of concepts relating to teaching as a science. As Ausubel points out in Section 2, this does not mean that we are to return to authoritarian drill and rote methods, but that we, as teachers, accept full responsibility for structuring a specific teaching system to optimize the children's learning. A theory of teaching would equip us to do that.

The context within which the papers chosen should be considered, therefore, is one concerning itself with those aspects of learning which are peculiarly human and particularly related to the class-room. Thus some aspects of the simpler types of learning, such as the acquisition of motor skills, are passed over in favour of the area of teaching which most concerns all teachers, that is, the building up of frameworks of concepts related to specific disciplines.

The most important consequence of focusing upon the higher forms of learning is that we are immediately involved in considerations of the role of language in this type of learning and the relationship of both to thinking. Therefore the first section of the book deals with the way in which these three phenomena interact. This section is the most theoretical and provides a context concerning the nature of human cognitive processes within which subsequent discussion about problems of classroom learning can be viewed.

The second section relates to the first in its concern with cognitive processes, but we are now concerned with how these processes may be influenced by the intervention of the teacher. This section also considers general problems of the relationship between research in the field of educational psychology and the problems of classroom practice. The main burden of this section, therefore, may be regarded as a discussion on the nature of a general theory of teaching relatable to specific disciplines but transcending them: a possible body of pedagogic principles rather than tips for teachers.

Section 3 deals with psychological problems as they impinge upon the teaching of different disciplines. We are therefore considering questions of a very practical nature. There is a real danger here that the contributions could be no more than specific hints, possibly useful in a very limited way but providing no real insight into the more fundamental aspects of teaching and learning. However, the extracts chosen avoid the danger and deal with likely areas of difficulty and misconception and suggest methods of ensuring true conceptual learning.

Section 4 is still very close to the problems of the classroom although the discourse is not related to the teaching of specific subjects. It treats of the processes of programming teaching. We could reasonably say that these papers are dealing with the finer details of the learning process.

Section 5 considers the problems of children who have learning difficulty. While there are special problems peculiar to such children, in fact many of the papers in the other sections are relevant to their needs.

Section 6 considers the main issues in the field of achievement testing. Here, again, we are not concerned with the bread-and-butter details of test construction so much as the psychological assumptions behind their construction and use. Some of the contributions suggest that a reappraisal of our principles and practices in testing would not be out of place.

Although the papers selected may be divided conveniently into the six sections discussed, it would be very unfortunate if they were to be considered as discrete units. In fact they are very closely interrelated. Thus, for example, one of the papers on reading in Section 3 is taken from a periodical which deals with matters relating particularly to Section 6. More generally, problems of programming, of evaluation, of ensuring adequate concept formation are all part of the teaching task. When we analyse a teaching task we are concerned to establish the nature of the concepts we wish the children to acquire. To ensure that the children are 'ready' to learn those concepts, we need to establish through the use of some diagnostic test their current level of knowledge in the field. We also need to arrange for suitable learning experiences, drawing on our knowledge of the processes of learning, and then we need to construct some sort of evaluative device to check whether our teaching objectives have been achieved. These activities demand reference to all the sections. It is my hope that the study of the papers in these sections will help the reader to approach the practical task in the classroom with somewhat more insight than he would otherwise have.

Thinking, language and learning

All teachers are concerned with children's thinking. Although part of a teacher's job may be concerned with non-cognitive aspects of children's learning, such as motor skills and affective or emotional behaviour, his main preoccupation is the effective development in children of increasingly complex and extensive modes of thinking.

Of course, problems connected with the other aspects of children's learning are not unimportant, but it would be impossible in the space available to cover the whole range of theory and hypothesis in all these fields. Therefore, this section focuses on problems of cognitive learning.

Cognitive learning is concerned with such things as the acquisition of concepts, of logical methods of thinking, of hypothesis forming and so on. In short the acquisition of knowledge and the ability to reason.

One of the greatest problems in school teaching and learning has been the relationship between language and cognitive learning. Because it is so easy to learn words quite divorced from the concepts they symbolize, that is to say 'parrot fashion', children often give the outward show of learning without having acquired the relevant concepts. As Vigotsky put it, their words conceal a conceptual vacuum.

However, language is crucial in the development of complex cognitive structures and without it it is very likely that man would be little more advanced than the anthropoid apes.

The papers in this section, therefore, are concerned with the processes of cognitive learning and language and their interrelationships. Together they provide a context for the discussions of teaching and learning in the classroom in the sections which follow. The opening contribution by Harlow raises the important question of the extent to which we have to learn to think. Liublinskaya reports on research which resembles that of Harlow but which is particularly concerned with the vital influence of language on concept formation and reasoning. Carroll takes up the question as to what we mean by concepts. Sapir, writing from a linguistic standpoint, gives a particularly lucid exposition of the relationship between language and concept formation. Luria and Yudovitch contribute to the discussion on concept formation but, in addition, also consider the effect of the acquisition of language on a child's ability to regulate his own behaviour. Vigotsky's contribution summarizes views, advanced more than thirty years ago although only recently made widely available, which have had a great impact on contemporary views on cognition and language. Piaget's paper deals particularly with reasoning and its development in young children. Gagné's contribution takes up the question of concept learning and the learning of principles.

Many of the papers cover similar ground from different standpoints. There is in some areas a good deal of agreement; but although many of the contributions draw extensively on empirical research, there is no body of received truth on this subject.

The field is still relatively unexplored and the problems are tremendously complex. However, the models being proposed, the hypotheses being advanced and the research findings reported should help educationists to understand more deeply both the problems and the possibilities inherent in the study of human learning.

---

1 Learning to think*

H. F. HARLOW

Helping children to acquire effective habits of thinking and reasoning is one of the prime jobs of a teacher. To what extent do children need to *learn* to think and to what extent are they born with certain powers

* Reprinted and abridged from H. F. Harlow, 'The formation of Learning Sets', *Psychological Review*, 56, 1949, pp. 51–65.

of reasoning? The author of this paper presents the view that all such functions must first be learned. In the present paper the author conceives of the acquisition of learning sets as 'learning to learn'. Elsewhere he also uses the expression 'learning to think'. Both seem legitimate titles and stress the extremely important advance in adaptive capacity which flows from this kind of learning. The experiments reported and the thesis advanced have been of seminal importance in the development of psychological thinking about the nature of human learning.

The variety of learning situations that play an important role in determining our basic personality characteristics and in changing some of us into thinking animals are repeated many times in similar form. The behaviour of the human being is not to be understood in terms of the results of single learning situations but rather in terms of the changes which are affected through multiple, though comparable, learning problems. Our emotional, personal and intellectual characteristics are not the mere algebraic summation of a near infinity of stimulus-response bonds. The learning of primary importance to the primates, at least, is the formation of learning sets; it is the *learning how to learn efficiently* in the situations the animal frequently encounters. This learning to learn transforms the organism from a creature that adapts to a changing environment by trial and error to one that adapts by seeming hypothesis and insight.

It is the purpose of this paper to demonstrate the extremely orderly and quantifiable nature of the development of certain learning sets and, more broadly, to indicate the importance of learning sets to the development of intellectual organization and personality structure.

The apparatus used throughout the studies subsequently referred to is illustrated in Fig. 1. The monkey responds by displacing one of two stimulus-objects covering the food-wells in the tray before him. An opaque screen is interposed between the monkey and the stimulus situation between trials and a one-way vision screen separates monkey and man during trials.

The first problem chosen for the investigation of learning sets was the object–quality discrimination learning problem. The monkey was required to choose the rewarded one of two objects differing in multiple characteristics and shifting in the left–right positions in a predetermined balanced order. A series of 344 such problems using 344 different pairs of stimuli was run on a group of eight monkeys. Each of the first thirty-two problems was run for fifty trials; the next 200 problems for six trials; and the last 112 problems for an average of six trials.

In Fig. 2 are presented learning curves which show the per cent of correct responses on the first six trials of these discriminations. The data for the first thirty-two discriminations are grouped for

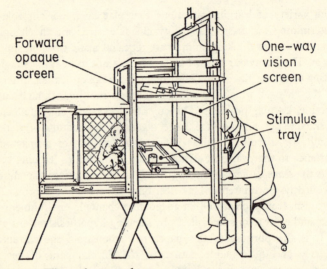

Figure 1. Wisconsin general test apparatus

blocks of eight problems, and the remaining discriminations are arranged in blocks of 100, 100, 56 and 56 problems. The data indicate that the subjects progressively improve in their ability to learn object-quality discrimination problems. The monkeys *learn how to learn* individual problems with a minimum of errors. It is this *learning how to learn a kind of problem* that we designate by the term *learning set*.

The very form of the learning curve changes as learning sets become more efficient. The form of the learning curve for the first eight discrimination problems appears S-shaped: it could be described as a curve of 'trial-and-error' learning. The curve for the last fifty-six problems approaches linearity after Trial 2. Curves of similar form have been described as indicators of 'insightful' learning.

We wish to emphasize that this *learning to learn*, this *transfer from problem to problem* which we call the formation of a learning

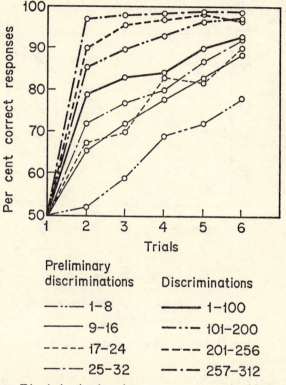

Figure 2. Discrimination learning curves on successive blocks of problems

set, is a highly *predictable, orderly* process which can be demonstrated as long as controls are maintained over the subjects' experience and the difficulty of the problems. Our subjects, when they started these researches, had no previous laboratory learning experience. Their entire discrimination learning set history was obtained in this study.

Through the courtesy of Dr Margaret Kuenne we have discrimination learning set data on another primate species. These animals were also run on a series of six-trial discrimination problems but under slightly different conditions. Macaroni beads and toys were substituted for food rewards, and the subjects were tested sans iron-barred cages. The data for these seventeen children produce learning set curves which are orderly and lawful and show progressive increase in per cent of correct responses.

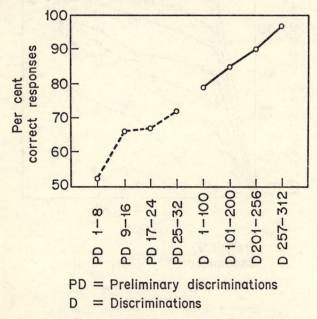

PD = Preliminary discriminations
D = Discriminations

Figure 3. Discrimination learning set curve based on Trial 2 responses

Learning set curves, like learning curves, can be plotted in terms of correct responses or errors, in terms of responses on any trial or total trials. A measure which we have frequently used is per cent of correct Trial 2 responses – the behavioural measure of the amount learned on Trial 1.

Figure 3 shows learning set curves measured in terms of the per cent correct Trial 2 responses for the 344-problem series. The data from the first thirty-two preliminary discriminations and the 312 subsequent discriminations have been plotted separately. As one might expect, these learning set curves are similar to those that have been previously presented. What the curves show with especial clarity is the almost unbelievable change which has taken place in the *effectiveness of the first training trial*. In the initial eight discriminations, this single paired stimulus presentation brings the Trial 2 performance of the monkeys to a level less than 3 per cent above chance; in the last fifty-six discriminations, this first training trial brings the performance of the monkeys to a level *less than 3 per cent* short of perfection. Before the formation of a discrimination learning set, a single training trial produces negligible gain; after the formation of a discrimination learning set, *a single training trial constitutes problem solution*. These data clearly show that *animals can gradually learn insight*.

In the final phase of our discrimination series with monkeys there were subjects that solved from twenty to thirty consecutive problems with no errors whatsoever following the first blind trial – and many of the children, after the first day or two of training, did as well or better.

These data indicate the function of learning set in converting a problem which is initially difficult for a subject into a problem which is so simple as to be immediately solvable. The learning set is the mechanism that changes the problem from an intellectual tribulation into an intellectual triviality and leaves the organism free to attack problems of another hierarchy of difficulty.

For the analysis of learning sets in monkeys on a problem that is ostensibly at a more complex level than the discrimination problem, we chose the discrimination reversal problem. The procedure was to run the monkeys on a discrimination problem for seven, nine or eleven trials and then to reverse the reward value of the stimuli for eight trials; that is to say, the stimulus previously correct was made incorrect and the stimulus previously incorrect became correct.

The eight monkeys previously trained on discrimination learning were tested on a series of 112 discrimination reversal problems. Figure 4 presents data on the formation of the discrimination reversal learning set in terms of the per cent of correct responses on Reversal Trial 2 for successive blocks of fourteen problems. Reversal Trial 2 is the first trial following the 'informing' trial, i.e. the initial trial reversing the reward value of the stimuli. Reversal Trial 2 is the measure of the effectiveness with which the single informing trial leads the subject to abandon a reaction pattern which has proved correct for seven to eleven trials, and to initiate a new reaction pattern to the stimulus pair. On the last forty-two discrimination reversal problems the monkeys were responding as efficiently on Reversal Trial 2 as they were on complementary Discrimination Trial 2, i.e. they were making over 97 per cent correct responses on

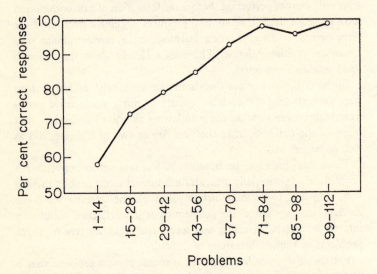

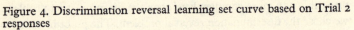

Figure 4. Discrimination reversal learning set curve based on Trial 2 responses

both aspects of the problems. The eight monkeys made from twelve to fifty-seven successive correct second trial reversal responses. Thus it becomes perfectly obvious that at the end of this problem the monkeys possessed sets both to learn and to reverse a reaction tendency, and that this behaviour could be consistently and immediately elicited with hypothesis-like efficiency.

This terminal performance level is likely to focus undue attention on the one-trial learning at the expense of the earlier, less efficient performance levels. It should be kept in mind that this one-trial learning appeared only as the end result of an orderly and progressive learning process; in so far as these subjects are concerned, the insights are only to be understood in an historical perspective.

Although the discrimination reversal problems might be expected to be more difficult for the monkeys than discrimination problems, the data of Fig. 5 indicate that the discrimination reversal learning set was formed more rapidly than the previously acquired discrimination learning set. The explanation probably lies in the nature

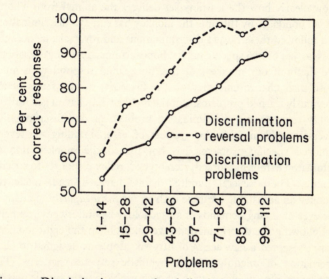

Figure 5. Discrimination reversal and discrimination learning set curves based on Trial 2 responses

of the transfer of training from the discrimination learning to the discrimination reversal problems. A detailed analysis of the discrimination learning data indicates the operation throughout the learning series of certain error-producing factors, but with each successive block of problems the frequencies of errors attributable to these factors are progressively decreased, although at different rates and to different degrees. The process might be conceived of as a learning of response tendencies that counteract the error-producing factors. A description of the reduction of the error-producing factors is beyond the scope of this paper, even though we are of the opinion that this type of analysis is based to an adequate theory of discrimination learning.

Suffice it to say that there is reason to believe that there is a large degree of transfer from the discrimination series to the reversal series, of the learned response tendencies counteracting the operation of two of the three primary error-producing factors thus far identified.

The combined discrimination and discrimination reversal data show clearly how the learning set delivers the animal from Thorndikian bondage. By the time the monkey has run 232 discriminations and followed these by 112 discriminations and reversals, he does not possess 344 or 456 specific habits, bonds, connections or associations. We doubt if our monkeys at this time could respond with much more than chance efficiency on the first trial of any series of the previously learned problems. But the monkey does have a generalized ability to learn *any* discrimination problem or *any* discrimination reversal problem with the greatest of ease. Training on several hundred specific problems has not turned the monkey into an automaton exhibiting forced, stereotyped, reflex responses to specific stimuli. These several hundred habits have, instead, made the monkey an adjustable creature with an *increased capacity* to adapt to the ever-changing demands of a psychology laboratory environment.

Following the discrimination reversal problem the eight monkeys were presented a new series of fifty-six problems designed to elicit alternation of unequivocally antagonistic response patterns. The first seven, nine or eleven trials of each problem were simple object–quality discrimination trials. These were followed immediately by ten right-position discrimination trials with the same stimuli continuing to shift in the right–left positions in predetermined orders. In the first seven to eleven trials, a particular object was correct regardless of its position. In the subsequent ten trials, a particular position – the experimenter's right position – was correct, regardless of the object placed there. Thus to solve the problem the animal had to respond to object–quality cues and disregard position cues in the first seven to eleven trials and, following the failure of reward of the previously rewarded object, he had to disregard object–quality cues and respond to position cues.

The learning data on these two antagonistic tasks are presented in

Fig. 6. It is to be noted that the object–quality curve, which is based on Trials 1–7, begins at a very high level of accuracy, whereas the position curve, plotted for Trials 1–10, begins at a level little above chance. This no doubt reflects the operation of the previously well-established object–quality discrimination learning set. As the series continues, the object–quality curve shows a drop until the last block of problems, while the position curve rises progressively. In the evaluation of these data, it should be noted that chance performance

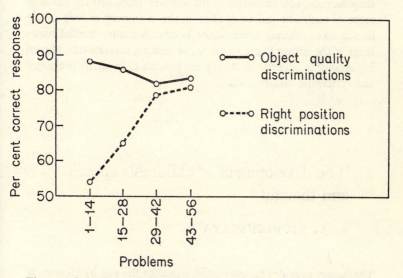

Figure 6. Learning set curves for problem requiring shift from object-quality discrimination to right-position discrimination

is 50 per cent correct responses for the object–quality discriminations and 45 per cent for the position discriminations, since each sequence of ten position trials includes an error 'informing' trial. It would appear that the learning of the right-position discriminations inter-feres with the learning of the object–quality discriminations to some extent. In spite of this decrement in object–quality discrimination performance for a time, the subjects were functioning at levels far beyond chance on the antagonistic parts of the problems during the last half of the series. We believe that this behaviour reflects the formation of a right-position learning set which operates at a high degree of independence of the previously established object–quality discrimination learning set.

Psychologists working with human subjects have long believed in the phenomenon of learning sets and have even used sets as explanatory principles to account for perceptual selection and incidental learning. These psychologists have not, however, investigated the nature of these learning sets which their subjects bring to the experimental situation. The determining experiential variables of these learning sets lie buried in the subjects' pasts, but the development of such sets can be studied in the laboratory as long as the human race continues to reproduce its kind. Actually, detailed knowledge of the nature of the formation of learning sets could be of such importance to educational theory and practice as to justify prolonged and systematic investigation.

2   The development of children's speech and thought*

A. A. LIUBLINSKAYA

This paper provides an interesting sequel to the one by Harlow. In situations resembling learning set experiments language is introduced systematically as a guide to children's reasoning.

In the paper the author makes reference to the first and second signalling systems. This is Pavlov's formulation. The first signalling system comprises the sense organs which provide us with information about the world around us. The second signalling system is language. Language symbolizes reality and thus acts as a signal of a signal, that is to say the second signalling system.

Liublinskaya stresses an aspect of learning which receives little attention elsewhere. She shows how the use of language enables children to *compare* things, which demands reasoning, whereas

* Reprinted and abridged from A. A. Liublinskaya, 'The Development of Children's Speech and Thought' in B. Simon (ed.), *Psychology in the Soviet Union*, Routledge and Kegan Paul, 1957, pp. 197–202.

children not using language discriminate between things at the perceptual level only (or at the level of the first signalling system).

The development of sensations, in particular of discriminatory sensitivity in children, is inseparably connected with the intervention of the second signal system. Long before the end of the first year of life, the infant's whole sensory apparatus is carrying out the complex function of analysing experience. At the age of 6 months the infant is capable of quite fine differentiation between stimuli from the outside world, and towards the close of the first year it is possible to establish a differentiated conditioned reflex with any analyser.[1] The introduction into perception of a word denoting the stimulus perceived – its colour or quality – causes a fundamental reorganization of the whole nature and nervous mechanism of the process of discrimination or differentiation. The development of the child's speech is possible only on the basis of the functioning of the first signal system. It is only on the basis of simple conditioned connections and a fine analysis of speech sounds that the connections of the second signal system can be formed. Then the child can master words as signals, which generalize a whole group of similar stimuli by abstracting the essential common features.

This view has been convincingly proved by research with children of pre-kindergarten and pre-school age. In children aged 1 year 1 month to 2 years 7 months a conditioned reflex was produced to the colour (in another case to the size) of a paper cap, under which the children found a sweet as reinforcement. With the experimental group the successful solution was accompanied by verbal designation of the distinguishing feature ('red' colour, 'small' size); with the control group, the differentiating feature was not named. The results were as follows:

(1) Initially, children in the experimental group required from nine to fifteen presentations for the formation of a temporary connection between the colour of the cap (or its size) and the corresponding food reinforcement. Children in the control group required two-and-a-half to three times as many presentations, the number rising to forty-five or fifty.

(2) The connection produced on the basis of food reinforcement

---

[1] i.e. any organ of perception.

and verbal accompaniment proved very persistent in the experimental group of children, and there was ready recovery after a five- to seven-day break. In the control group, the connections produced with such difficulty were extremely unstable and were found to be extinguished even on the following day.

(3) When the distinguishing feature (colour or size) was changed, children in the experimental group showed a quick, even immediate carry-over of the reflex to other objects, i.e. stimulus generalization. For example, after experiments with a red cap, the children lost no time in looking for the sweet under a red cup, a red box or a piece of red material. No transfer of reflexes was observed in children of the control group, in each new situation they had to produce the necessary conditioned connections anew. Here was a striking example of the role of a word as a signal, making possible abstraction and generalization both of an object and its features.

(4) The number of presentations was considerably reduced when conditioned connections had previously been formed to some one distinguishing feature. Thus children who knew the colour red needed only two to five presentations to form a connection to the colour yellow. The same reduction in the number of presentations was observed in the experiments with the control group, though, again, results were considerably less positive than for children of the same age in the experimental group.

(5) Both the speed with which connections are formed and their stability was found to increase somewhat with age. This is obviously a consequence of increased and varied experience, especially as concerns the child's verbal communication with those around him. Words become more efficient as signals for older children as compared with the younger ones. In the control group, abstraction of a factor on the basis of a sense-perception only, without a verbal denotation, was almost as difficult for the older children as for the younger.

In other investigations children were required to abstract the pattern (spots or stripes) from the colour of a butterfly's wings and to find a butterfly similar to the one given among a number shown to them. The experimental group were given a verbal label for the differentiating factor (the pattern), but the control group were not. Initially, however, neither group was given the verbal label, and at this stage children in both groups completely ignored the pattern on the butterfly's wings, being guided solely by colouring in choosing a pair. After the pattern had been denoted by fixed names ('spots', 'stripes', 'nets') even the younger members of the experimental group began to turn their attention away from colour and to compare patterns which were different in colour. The speed, accuracy and fineness of their distinctions was noteworthy; they were also able to explain their choices readily and intelligently, using various verbal labels, but always noticing exactly the features of the pattern, i.e. the essential identifying factor. Thus children described 'that butterfly' (the specimen) as having the same 'dots', 'fringes', 'crumbs', 'waves' etc., as the one they chose as being similar. In the reorganization of perceptual differentiation, which occurred on the introduction of language, there also emerged clearly the thinking process of comparison.

Results obtained with the control group confirm this conclusion; despite practice, even the older children could hardly distinguish the patterns. In control experiments carried out with an experimental and a control group, the children in the latter group made many mistakes, and did not understand their own rare correct solutions. Not one could explain his choice; to the question, 'How did you know that this was the butterfly to choose?' these children replied, 'I just knew', or 'I had a good look', etc.

The series of investigations showed that:

(1) The introduction of a word signalling the distinctive factor (colour, size, pattern) has decisive significance for its isolation and differentiation. Labelled with a word, such a feature becomes a powerful, really effective stimulus which acquires dominating significance in the complex of influencing stimuli. It becomes stronger still in the skills which the child uses in all his subsequent activity.

(2) An isolated feature designated by a word (for example, 'with spots' or 'red') acquires the significance of a generalized feature. The child begins to find it easy to isolate an analogous feature (colour, size, pattern) in any other object. This is of decisive importance for the improvement of the child's orientation in the environment.

(3) The introduction of language into the process of visual discrimination re-structures the whole activity of the analyser and the whole process of sense perception. There is no doubt that this is related also to other aspects of sensitivity. Simple differentiating –

discriminating – turns into a reasoning operation, that of comparing. The child learns to isolate common and distinguishing features in two similar stimuli. This confirms Pavlov's view that the second signal system 'builds' the first. To know how to compare is to master a thought-process essential for knowledge of any subject.

(4) Not every sign whereby the child orients himself in his differentiating activity is reflected in the second signal systems, is verbalized, i.e. perceived by the child. This was clearly illustrated by the experiments in choosing butterflies by their patterns. These had to do with the complex changing relationships between the first and second signal systems, which exist at different levels of child development and in adults, when phenomena of diverse content are reflected.

(5) When children compare two similar patterns and distinguish between them, without applying a word to the differentiating feature, this does not lead to any noticeable change in the actual process of visual perception. In spite of training, the child learns essentially nothing, and his sensitivity scarcely improves during the period of instruction.

Further investigations traced the role of words in the functioning of the motor analyser, i.e. in the substitution, mastery and abstraction of action by the small child. Sechenov considered that an essential part in the development of the small child's thinking is played by his muscular sense evolving as kinaesthetic perception in the solution of problems of movement. We investigated the influence of language on changes in kinaesthetic perceptions. Results showed how the use of language enables a young child's specific actions to become generalized and abstracted from the single concrete situation with which they were originally associated. It was demonstrated that an action, when generalized in language, becomes an early form of problem solving for the child. The enormous significance of this is easily understood. The word denoting an action makes possible its abstraction and generalization. The action is thereby reflected in the child as an object of knowledge, as a means of solving new, strange problems; this is done 'on the spot', because the child applies the known action to the solution of all analogous problems.

A fundamental role is played by the verbal designation of objects perceived by the child. Language is distinct from all other signals in that it signalizes a whole group of objects in a generalized way by abstracting their common features. This makes perception intelligible. The process is well illustrated in an investigation carried out by Lukina. A child aged 12 to 14 months connected the word 'ribbon' only with the ribbons on her bonnet, and did not relate the word to the ribbon by which a celluloid parrot dangled before her eyes. In another case, the familiar word 'cup' was the 'name' of one cup only – a small, pink cup with white spots. When a large white cup, to which the child did not yet relate this word, was placed before him, and he was asked 'Where is the cup?', the child waved his hands about and looked at his mother with a puzzled air; his perceptual knowledge did not yet have a generalized character. In such cases a word is a signal of the first system. Only as his experience becomes richer does the child relate one and the same word to many different objects of the same kind.

What takes place during this time? How does the child's knowledge of his environment change?

(1) Above all, converting a word into a signal of the second system means changing the reflection of the object itself. Initially, every cup is perceived by the child as a new and special object, whereas later he perceives any cup as a representative of a whole known group of objects: in the particular he sees the general. Later, he will be able, on this basis, to isolate the particular.

(2) There is, then, a change in the meaning of a familiar word. Initially, the word is connected with one concrete object, having a number of particular characteristic features which belong to it alone (e.g. white spots on a pink cup); the same word later signalizes features common to a multitude of objects which, though different in many ways, constitute a single group. While at first the word 'cup' signalizes a combination of features belonging to the object fortuitously as well as essentially, later the word signalizes the essential feature of the object, irrespective of changes in secondary features. This essential feature, found in the concrete and single instance, remains unchangeable and common for all objects of the same kind, and is the means of distinguishing them from other similar classes of objects. Only at this stage has the word acquired for the child that 'comprehensive' character distinctive of signals of the second system, which 'cannot be compared either quantitatively or qualitatively with

the conditioned stimuli of animals' (Pavlov), i.e. with signals of the first system. So the content of a word which the child has known for a long time changes; it becomes broader, more interesting, rich, exact and elastic.

3   Words, meanings and concepts*

J. B. CARROLL

All teachers in our schools spend most of their time doing their best to teach concepts. Probably a large number of them would have very hazy ideas as to what the word *concept* meant. In this paper the author presents a lucid account of the nature of concepts and makes suggestions which should help teachers to tackle the teaching of concepts in a more insightful and systematic way.

The teaching of words, and of the meanings and concepts they designate or convey, is one of the principal tasks of teachers at all levels of education. It is a concern of textbook writers and programmers of self-instructional materials as well. Students must be taught the meanings of unfamiliar words and idioms; they must be helped in recognizing unfamiliar ways in which familiar words may be used; and they must be made generally aware of the possibility of ambiguity in meaning and the role of context in resolving it. Often the task that presents itself to the teacher is not merely to explain a new word in familiar terms, but to shape an entirely new concept in the mind of the student.

Whether the teaching of words, meanings and concepts is done by the teacher, the textbook writer or the programmer, it is generally done in an intuitive, unanalytic way. The purpose of this article is to sketch, at least in a first approximation, a more analytical approach to this task.

* Reprinted and abridged from J. B. Carroll, 'Words, Meanings and Concepts', from *Harvard Educational Review*, 34 (2), 1964, pp. 178–90.

There is, in the first place, an unfortunate hiatus between the word 'meaning' and the very word 'concept' itself. *Meaning* and *concept* have usually been treated as quite separate things by different disciplines. *Meaning*, for example, has been considered the province of a somewhat nebulous and insecure branch of linguistics called *semantics*. *Concept* is almost anybody's oyster: it has continually been the concern of the philosopher, but has received generous attention from psychology. While the meanings of these two terms can be usefully distinguished in many contexts, it is also the case that a framework can be made for considering their intimate interconnections.

Second, there is a gap between the findings of psychologists on the conditions under which very simple 'concepts' are learned in the psychological laboratory and the experiences of teachers in teaching the 'for real' concepts that are contained in the curricula of the schools. It is not self-evident that there is any continuity at all between learning 'DAX' as the name of a certain geometrical shape of a certain colour and learning the meaning of the word 'longitude'. Even if such a continuity exists, it is not clear how the relative difficulty or complexity of concepts can be assessed.

Third, a problem related to the second arises when we ask whether there is any continuity, with respect to psychological 'processes', between the inductive, non-verbal type of learning studied in the psychological laboratory under the guise of 'concept learning' and the usually more deductive, verbal–explanatory type of teaching used in the classroom and in typical text materials.

In an effort to fill these gaps, we will sketch out a framework for conceptualizing problems of Meaning and Concept. For reasons that will eventually become clear, we must start with the notion of Concept.

THE NATURE OF CONCEPTS

In a totally inorganic world there could be no concepts, but with the existence of organisms capable of complex perceptual responses, concepts become possible. In brief, concepts are properties of organismic experience – more particularly, they are the abstracted and often cognitively structured classes of 'mental' experience learned by organisms in the course of their life histories. There is evidence that animals other than human beings behave with regard to concepts in this sense, but we shall confine our attention to human organisms. Because of the continuity of the physical, biological and social environment in which human beings live, their concepts will show a high degree of similarity; and through language learning, many concepts (classes of experience) will acquire names, that is, words or phrases in a particular language, partly because some classes of experience are so salient and obvious that nearly every person acquires them for himself, and partly because language makes possible the diffusion and sharing of concepts as classes of experience. We use the term 'experience' in an extremely broad sense – defining it as any internal or perceptual response to stimulation. We can 'have experience of' some aspect of the physical, biological or social environment by either direct or indirect means; we can experience heat or light or odour directly, while our experiences of giraffes or atoms, say, may be characterized as being indirect, coming only through verbal descriptions or other patterns of stimuli (pointer readings etc.) that evoke these concepts.

One necessary condition for the formation of a concept is that the individual must have a series of experiences that are in one or more respects similar; the constellation of 'respects' in which they are similar constitutes the 'concept' that underlies them. Experiences that embody this concept are 'positive instances' of it, experiences that do not embody it may be called 'negative instances'. A further necessary condition for the formation of a concept is that the series of experiences embodying the concept must be preceded, interspersed with, or followed by other experiences that constitute negative instances of the concept. As the complexity of the concepts increases (i.e. as there is an increase in the number of interrelations of the respects in which experiences must be similar in order to be positive instances), there is a greater necessity for an appropriate sequencing of positive and negative instances in order to insure adequate learning of the concept. At least this is true when the concept has to be formed from *non-verbal* experiences only, i.e. from actual exemplars or referents of the concept as contrasted with non-exemplars. But concept learning from verbal explanation, as will be noted below, must, as it were, put the learner through a series of vicarious experiences of positive and negative instances. For example, in telling a child what a lion is, one must indicate the range of positive and negative instances – the range of variations that could be found in real lions and the critical respects in which other animals – tigers, leopards etc. – differ from lions.

We have been describing what is often called the process of abstraction. We have given a number of *necessary* conditions for the formation of a concept; exactly what conditions are *sufficient* cannot yet be stated, but in all likelihood this will turn out to be a matter of (a) the number, sequencing or timing of the instances presented to the individual, (b) the reinforcements given to the individual's responses and (c) the individual's orientation to the task. The evidence suggests that the learner must be oriented to, and attending to, the relevant stimuli in order to form a concept. The public test of the formation of a concept is the ability to respond correctly and reliably to new positive and negative instances of it; we do not wish to imply, however, that a concept has not been formed until it is put to such a test.

The infant acquires 'concepts' of many kinds even before he attains anything like language. One kind of concept that is acquired by an infant quite early is the concept embodied in the experience of a particular object – a favourite toy, for example. As the toy is introduced to the infant, it is experienced in different ways – it is seen at different angles, at different distances and in different illuminations. It is felt in different positions and with different parts of the body, and experienced with still other sense modalities – taste, smell. But underlying all these experiences are common elements sufficient for the infant to make an identifying response to the particular toy in question – perhaps to the point that he will accept only the particular specimen that he is familiar with and reject another specimen that is in the least bit different. The acceptance or rejection of a specimen is the outward sign of the attainment of a concept – as constituted by the class of experiences associated with that particular specimen. The experiences themselves are sufficiently similar to be their own evidence that they constitute a class – a perceptual invariant, therefore, together with whatever affective elements that may be present to help reinforce the attainment of the concept (pleasure in the sight, taste, smell and feel of the toy, for example).

Even the concept contained in a particular object represents a certain degree of generality – generality over the separate presentations of the object. But pre-verbal infants also attain concepts which from the standpoint of adult logic have even higher degrees of generality. A further stage of generality is reached when the infant comes to recognize successive samples of something – e.g. a particular kind of food – as equivalent, even though varying slightly in taste, colour, temperature, etc. Because the different samples of food are about equally reinforcing, the infant gradually learns to overcome the initial tendency to reject a sample that is experienced as not quite the same as one previously experienced. That is, what seems to be initially a negative instance turns out to be a positive instance because it provides the same reinforcement as the earlier instance – the reinforcement being in this case a 'sign' that the new experience is to be taken in the same class as former ones. An even higher stage of generality is achieved when the child will accept and make a common response to any one of a number of rather different stimuli – for example, any one of a number of different foods. In adult terms, he has attained the concept of 'food' in some elementary sense. The explanation of this phenomenon may indeed draw upon the usual primary reinforcement theory (the equivalence of different foods in satisfying a hunger drive) but it also depends upon various secondary reinforcements, as when the parent punishes the child for eating something not considered 'food', like ants or mud. This is an elementary case in which culture, as represented by parents, provides signs as to what the positive and negative instances of a concept are.

Direct experience, i.e. the recognition of experiences as identical or similar, allows the infant to attain concepts that in adult language have names such as redness, warmth, softness, heaviness, swiftness, sweetness, loudness, pain etc. In some cases, the infant's concepts of sensory qualities may be rather undifferentiated. For example, because big things are generally experienced as heavy and strong, and small things are generally experienced as light-weight and weak, the infant's concept of size may not be adequately differentiated from his concepts of weight and strength. Without any social reinforcement to guide him, his concept of 'redness' may range over a rather wide range of the colour spectrum, and if he happens to have been born into a culture which pays little attention to the difference, say, between what we would call 'red' and 'orange', his concept of 'redness' may remain relatively undifferentiated even after he has learned a language – just as it has been demonstrated that different varieties of blue are not well coded in everyday English.

Furthermore, we can infer from various investigations of Piaget that the child's concepts of size, weight and other physical attributes of objects do not contain the notion of 'conservation' that his later experiences will teach him. For all the infant or young child knows of the physical universe, objects can change in size, weight etc., in quite arbitrary ways. It is only at a later stage, when the child has had an opportunity to form certain concepts about the nature of the physical universe that his concepts of size, weight and number can incorporate the notion of constancy or conservation that mature thinking requires. Experience with objects that can expand or contract through stretching or shrinking gives the child a concept of size that can properly explain the fact that a balloon can be blown up to various sizes. Indeed, this explanation may involve the concepts of 'expansion' and 'contraction'. At a still later stage, the child may learn enough about the relation of heat to expansion to explain why it is necessary to have seams in concrete roads, or why one allows for expansion in the building of large bridges. And it will be relatively unlikely that even as an adult he will learn enough about the concept of size to understand the concept of relativity – that the size of a body is relative to the speed at which it is travelling and the system in which it is measured.

Thus, concepts can in the course of a person's life become more complex, more loaded with significant aspects. Concepts are, after all, essentially idiosyncratic in the sense that they reside in particular individuals with particular histories of experiences that lead them to classify those experiences in particular ways. My concept of 'stone' may not be precisely your concept of 'stone' because my experiences with stones may have included work with pieces of a peculiar kind of vitreous rock that you have seldom seen. To a large extent how I sort out my experiences is my own business and may not lead to the same sortings as yours.

Nevertheless, I can specify the way I sort out my experiences by noting the *critical attributes* that differentiate them. I can specify what sensory qualities and attributes are necessary before I will classify an experience as being an experience of what I call a stone. But it is not even necessary for a person to be able to specify such attributes. A child who has learned a certain concept – who has learned to recognize certain experiences as being similar – may not necessarily be able to verbalize what attributes make them similar; he may not even be aware of the fact that he has attained a certain concept, since it may be the case that only his behaviour – the fact that he consistently makes a certain response to a certain class of stimuli – indicates that he has formed a concept. Such would be the case, for example, for the classic instance where the child is afraid of the barber because he wields instruments (scissors) that look like those of the doctor whom he has already learned to fear, and because he wears a similar white smock.

Indeed, this last instance exemplifies the fact that concepts may include affective components. Because concepts are embodied in classes of experiences they include all the elements of experiences that may occur in common – perceptual and cognitive elements as well as motivational and emotional elements. My concept of 'stone' may reflect, let us say, my positive delight in collecting new varieties of minerals, whereas your concept may reflect the fact that you had unpleasant experiences with stones – having them thrown at you in a riot, or finding lots of them in your garden.

It has already been suggested earlier that since man lives in an essentially homogeneous physical and biological environment and a partially homogeneous social environment, it is inevitable that a large number of concepts arrived at by individual people should be the same or at least so nearly identical in their essential attributes as to be called the same; these concepts we may call *conceptual invariants*. We can be sure that throughout the world people have much the same concepts of *sun, man, day, animal, flower, walking, falling, softness* etc., by whatever names they may be called. The fact that they have names is incidental; there are even certain concepts that for one reason or another (a taboo, for example) may remain nameless.

It is probably when we enter into the realms of science and technology and of social phenomena that the concepts attained by different people will differ most. In science and technology concepts vary chiefly because of differences, over the world, in the levels of scientific and technological knowledge reached; and in the social sphere they will differ chiefly because of the truly qualitative differences in the ways cultures are organized. Nevertheless, within a given community there will be a high degree of commonality in the concepts recognized and attained, in the sense that there will be relatively high agreement among peoples as to the attributes that are criterial for a given concept. For example, even though types of families vary widely over the world, the concept of *family* within a given culture is reasonably homogeneous. At the same time, differences in intellectual and educational levels will account for differences in the sheer number of concepts attained by individuals within a given culture.

WORDS AND THEIR MEANINGS

In the learning of language, words (and other elements in a linguistic system, including phonemes, morphemes and syntactical patterns) come to be perceived as distinct entities, and in this sense they form one class of perceptual invariants along with the perceptual invariants that represent common objects, feelings and events. The child must learn to perceive the various instances of a given sound or word as similar, and eventually to differentiate the several contexts in which a given sound or sound pattern is used.

Many words or higher units of the linguistic system come to stand for, or name, the concepts that have been learned preverbally. Certainly this is true for a long list of words that stand for particular things or classes of things, qualities and events. For the English language, these categories correspond roughly to proper and common nouns; adjectives; and verbs of action, perception and feeling. It is perhaps less clear that 'function words' like prepositions and conjunctions, or grammatical markers like the past tense sign can represent concepts, but a case can be made for this. For example, prepositions like *in, to, above, below, beside, near* correspond to concepts of relative spatial position in a surprisingly complex and subtle way; and conjunctions like *and, but, however, or* correspond to concepts of logical inclusion and exclusion, similarity and difference of propositions, etc.

The processes by which words come to 'stand for' or correspond to concepts can best be described in psychological terms. Without going into the details here, we can only say that in every case there is some sort of reinforcing condition that brands a word as being associ-ated with a given concept. This is true whether the word is learned as what Skinner calls a *mand* (as when a child learns the meaning of *water* as a consequence of having water brought whenever he says 'water') or as a *tact* (as where the child is praised or otherwise re-inforced for saying 'water' when he sees or experiences water), because in either case the word is paired contiguously with the con-cept *as an experience*. The connection between a word and the con-cept or experience with which it stands in relation must work in either direction: the word must evoke the concept and the concept must evoke the word.

As a physical symbol, a word is a cultural artifact that takes the same, or nearly the same, form throughout a speech community. It is a standardized product on which the speech community exercises a considerable degree of quality control. Not so with concepts, which as we have seen may vary to some extent with the individual, depend-ing on his experiences of the referents of the words. Society does, however, maintain a degree of 'quality control' on the referential meaning of words. The conditions under which the use of words is rewarded or not rewarded – either by successful or unsuccessful communication or by direct social approval or disapproval – can be looked upon as constituting the 'rules of usage' of a word, and these rules of usage define the *denotative meaning* of a term. Thus, there is a rule of usage such that the noun *mother* can be used only for a certain kind of kinship relation. One thinks of denotative meaning as something that is socially prescribed. Connotative meaning, how-ever, banks heavily on those aspects of concepts that are widely shared yet non-critical and perhaps affective (emotional) in content. 'Mother' as a noun might evoke various emotional feelings depend-ing upon one's experience with mothers.

Perhaps it is useful to think of words, meanings and concepts as forming *three* somewhat independent series. The words in a language can be thought of as a series of physical entities – either spoken or written. Next, there exists a set of 'meanings' which stand in complex relationships to the set of words. Those relationships may be de-scribed by the rules of usage that have developed by the processes of socialization and communication. A 'meaning' can be thought of as a standard of communicative behaviour that is shared by those who speak a language. Finally, there exist 'concepts'; the classes of experience formed in individuals either independently of language processes or in close dependence on language processes.

The interrelations found among these three series are complex: almost anyone can give instances where a word may have many 'meanings', or in which a given 'meaning' corresponds to several different words. The relationships between societally-standardized 'meanings' and individually-formed 'concepts' are likewise complex, but of a somewhat different nature. It is a question of how well each individual has learned these relationships, and at least in the sphere of language and concepts, education is largely a process whereby the individual learns either to attach societally-standardized words and meanings to the concepts he has already formed, or to form new concepts that properly correspond to societally-standardized words and meanings. A 'meaning' of a word is, therefore, a societally-standardized concept, and when we say that a word stands for or names a concept it is understood that we are speaking of concepts that are shared among the members of a speech community.

To the extent that individual concepts differ even though they possess shared elements, misunderstandings can arise. My concept of 'several' may correspond to the range 'approximately three to five', where yours may correspond to 'approximately five to fifteen'. Speech communities may differ, too, in the exact ranges in which they standardize meanings. The word *infant* seems to include a higher age range in Great Britain (in the phrase 'infants' schools') than it does in the United States, and in legal contexts the word may even refer to anyone who has not attained some legal age like 21 years.

The fact that words vary in meaning according to context has given rise to one form of a 'context theory of meaning' which seems to allege that the meaning of a word is to be found in its context; this is only true, however, in the sense that the context may provide a *clue* as to the particular meaning (or standardized concept) with which a word is intended to be associated. In fact, the clue usually takes the form of an indication of one or more elements of a concept. For example, in the phrase *A light load* the context suggests (though it does not determine absolutely) that *light* is to be taken as the opposite of heavy because loads vary more importantly in weight than in their colour, whereas the context in *A light complexion* suggests the element of colour because complexions can vary in colour but only very improbably in weight. It is not surprising that normal language texts have been found to have redundancy, for the elements of concepts suggested by the words in a sentence are often overlapping.

CONCEPT FORMATION RESEARCH

We are now in a position to inquire into the possible relevance of concept formation research to the learning of the meanings and concepts associated with words in a language.

Practically all concept formation research since the days of Hull has been concerned with essentially the following task: the subject is presented with a series of instances which are differentiated in some way; either the task is finding out in what way the several instances match up with one of a small number of names, or (in the simpler case) it is one of discovering why some instances are 'positive' (i.e. instances of the 'concept' the experimenter has in mind) or 'negative' (not instances of the 'concept'). Typically the stimulus material consists of simple visual material characterized by a number of clearly salient dimensions – e.g. the colour of the figures, the geometrical shape of the figures, the number of figures, the number of borders, the colour of the background etc. Occasionally the critical characteristics of the concept are not clearly in view – as in Hull's experiment where the critical stroke elements of Chinese characters tended to be masked by the rest of the figures, or as in Bouthilet's experiment where the critical feature was the inclusion of letters found in the stimulus word. Sometimes the critical elements are semantic elements of words, as in Freedman and Mednick's experiment in which the task was to find the common semantic element in a series of words such as *gnat, needle, stone* and *canary*.

Thus, there are two elements to be studied in any concept-formation task: (1) the attributes which are criterial to the concept – their nature and number, the number of values each attribute has and the discriminability of these values, and the salience of the attributes themselves – that is, whether the attributes command attention and are readily perceivable, and (2) the information-

articulation of the word; nor the visual perception on the part of the hearer of this articulation; nor the visual perception of the word 'house' on the written or printed page; nor the motor processes and tactile feelings which enter into the writing of the word; nor the memory of any or all of these experiences. It is only when these, and possibly still other, associated experiences are automatically associated with the image of a house that they begin to take on the nature of a symbol, a word, an element of language. But the mere fact of such an association is not enough. One might have heard a particular word spoken in an individual house under such impressive circumstances that neither the word nor the image of the house ever recur in consciousness without the other becoming present at the same time. This type of association does not constitute speech. The association must be a purely symbolic one; in other words, the word must denote, tag off, the image, must have no other significance than to serve as a counter to refer to it whenever it is necessary or convenient to do so. Such an association, voluntary and, in a sense, arbitrary as it is, demands a considerable exercise of self-conscious attention. At least to begin with, for habit soon makes the association nearly as automatic as any and more rapid than most.

But we have travelled a little too fast. Were the symbol 'house' – whether an auditory, motor or visual experience or image – attached but to the single image of a particular house once seen, it might perhaps, by an indulgent criticism, be termed an element of speech, yet it is obvious at the outset that speech so constituted would have little or no value for purposes of communication. The world of our experiences must be enormously simplified and generalized before it is possible to make a symbolic inventory of all our experiences of things and relations and this inventory is imperative before we can convey ideas. The elements of language, the symbols that ticket off experience, must therefore be associated with whole groups, delimited classes, of experience rather than with the single experiences themselves. Only so is communication possible, for the single experience lodges in an individual consciousness and is, strictly speaking, incommunicable. To be communicated it needs to be referred to a class which is tacitly accepted by the community as an identity. Thus, the single impression which I have had of a particular house must be identified with all my other impressions of it. Further, my generalized memory or my 'notion' of this house must be merged with the notions that all other individuals who have seen the house have formed of it. The particular experience that we started with has now been widened so as to embrace all possible impressions or images that sentient beings have formed or may form of the house in question. This first simplification of experience is at the bottom of a large number of elements of speech, the so-called proper nouns or names of single individuals or objects. It is, essentially, the type of simplification which underlies, or forms the crude subject of, history and art. But we cannot be content with this measure of reduction of the infinity of experience. We must cut to the bone of things, we must more or less arbitrarily throw whole masses of experience together as similar enough to warrant their being looked upon – mistakenly, but conveniently – as identical. This house and that house and thousands of other phenomena of like character are thought of as having enough in common, in spite of great and obvious differences of detail, to be classed under the same heading. In other words, the speech element 'house' is the symbol, first and foremost, not of a single perception, nor even of the notion of a particular object, but of a 'concept', in other words, of a convenient capsule of thought that embraces thousands of distinct experiences and that is ready to take in thousands more. If the single significant elements of speech are the symbols of concepts, the actual flow of speech may be interpreted as a record of the setting of these concepts into mutual relations.

The question has often been raised whether thought is possible without speech; further, if speech and thought be not but two facets of the same psychic process. The question is all the more difficult because it has been hedged about by misunderstandings. In the first place, it is well to observe that whether or not thought necessitates symbolism, that is speech, the flow of language itself is not always indicative of thought. We have seen that the typical linguistic element labels a concept. It does not follow from this that the use to which language is put is always or even mainly conceptual. We are not in ordinary life so much concerned with concepts as such as with concrete particularities and specific relations. When I say, for instance, 'I had a good breakfast this morning,' it is clear that I am not in the throes of laborious thought, that what I have to transmit is hardly more than a pleasurable memory symbolically rendered in the grooves of habitual expression. Each element in the sentence defines a separate concept or conceptual relation or both combined, but the sentence as a whole has no conceptual significance whatever. It is somewhat as though a dynamo capable of generating enough power to run an elevator were operated almost exclusively to feed an electric doorbell. The parallel is more suggestive than at first sight appears. Language may be looked upon as an instrument capable of running a gamut of psychic uses. Its flow not only parallels that of the inner content of consciousness, but parallels it on different levels, ranging from the state of mind that is dominated by particular images to that in which abstract concepts and their relations are alone at the focus of attention and which is ordinarily termed reasoning. Thus the outward form only of language is constant; its inner meaning, its psychic value or intensity, varies freely with attention or the selective interest of the mind, also, needless to say, with the mind's general development. From the point of view of language, thought may be defined as the highest latent or potential content of speech, the content that is obtained by interpreting each of the elements in the flow of language as possessed of its very fullest conceptual value. From this it follows at once that language and thought are not strictly coterminous. At best language can but be the outward facet of thought on the highest, most generalized, level of symbolic expression. To put our viewpoint somewhat differently, language is primarily a pre-rational function. It humbly works up to the thought that is latent in, that may eventually be read into, its classifications and its forms; it is not, as is generally but naïvely assumed, the final label put upon the finished thought.

Most people, asked if they can think without speech, would probably answer, 'Yes, but it is not easy for me to do so. Still I know it can be done.' Language is but a garment! But what if language is not so much a garment as a prepared road or groove? It is, indeed, in the highest degree likely that language is an instrument originally put to uses lower than the conceptual plane and that thought arises as a refined interpretation of its content. The product grows, in other words, with the instrument, and thought may be no more conceivable, in its genesis and daily practice, without speech than is mathematical reasoning practicable without the lever of an appropriate mathematical symbolism. No one believes that even the most difficult mathematical proposition is inherently dependent on an arbitrary set of symbols, but it is impossible to suppose that the human mind is capable of arriving at or holding such a proposition without the symbolism. The writer, for one, is strongly of the opinion that the feeling entertained by so many that they can think, or even reason, without language is an illusion. The illusion seems to be due to a number of factors. The simplest of these is the failure to distinguish between imagery and thought. As a matter of fact, no sooner do we try to put an image into conscious relation with another than we find ourselves slipping into a silent flow of words. Thought may be a natural domain apart from the artificial one of speech, but speech would seem to be the only road we know of that leads to it. A still more fruitful source of the illusive feeling that language may be dispensed with in thought is the common failure to realize that language is not identical with its auditory symbolism. The auditory symbolism may be replaced, point for point, by a motor or by a visual symbolism (many people can read, for instance, in a purely visual sense, that is, without the intermediating link of an inner flow of the auditory images that correspond to the printed or written words) or by still other, more subtle and elusive, types of transfer that are not so easy to define. Hence the contention that one thinks without language merely because he is not aware of a coexisting auditory imagery is very far indeed from being a valid one. One may go so far as to suspect that the symbolic expression of thought may in some cases run along outside the fringe of the conscious mind, so that the feeling of a free, non-linguistic stream of thought is for minds of a certain type a relatively, but only a relatively, justified one. Psycho-physically, this would mean that the auditory or equivalent visual or motor centres in the brain, together with the appropriate paths of association, that are the cerebral equivalent of speech, are touched off so lightly during the process of thought as not to rise into consciousness at all. This would be a limiting case – thought riding lightly on the submerged crests of speech, instead of jogging along with it, hand in hand. The modern psychology has shown us how powerfully symbolism is at work in the unconscious mind. It is therefore easier to understand at the present time than it would have been twenty years ago that the most rarefied thought may be but the conscious counterpart of an unconscious linguistic symbolism.

One word more as to the relation between language and thought. The point of view that we have developed does not by any means preclude the possibility of the growth of speech being in a high degree dependent on the development of thought. We may assume that language arose pre-rationally – just how and on what precise level of mental activity we do not know – but we must not imagine that a highly developed system of speech symbols worked itself out before the genesis of distinct concepts and of thinking, the handling of concepts. We must rather imagine that thought processes set in, as a kind of psychic overflow, almost at the beginning of linguistic expression; further, that the concept, once defined, necessarily reacted on the life of its linguistic symbol, encouraging further linguistic growth. We see this complex process of the interaction of language and thought actually taking place under our eyes. The instrument makes possible the product, the product refines the instrument. The birth of a new concept is invariably foreshadowed by a more or less strained or extended use of old linguistic material; the concept does not attain to individual and independent life until it has found a distinctive linguistic embodiment. In most cases the new symbol is but a thing wrought from linguistic material already in existence in ways mapped out by crushingly despotic precedents. As soon as the word is at hand, we instinctively feel, with something of a sigh of relief, that the concept is ours for the handling. Not until we own the symbol do we feel that we hold a key to the immediate knowledge or understanding of the concept. Would we be so ready to die for 'liberty', to struggle for 'ideals', if the words themselves were not ringing within us? And the word, as we know, is not only a key; it may also be a fetter.

Language is primarily an auditory system of symbols. In so far as it is articulated it is also a motor system, but the motor aspect of speech is clearly secondary to the auditory. In normal individuals the impulse to speech first takes effect in the sphere of auditory imagery and is then transmitted to the motor nerves that control the organs of speech. The motor processes and the accompanying motor feelings are not, however, the end, the final resting point. They are merely a means and a control leading to auditory perception in both speaker and hearer. Communication, which is the very object of speech, is successfully effected only when the hearer's auditory perceptions are translated into the appropriate and intended flow of imagery or thought or both combined. Hence the cycle of speech, in so far as we may look upon it as a purely external instrument, begins and ends in the realm of sounds. The concordance between the initial auditory imagery and the final auditory perceptions is the social seal or warrant of the successful issue of the process. As we have already seen, the typical course of this process may undergo endless modifications or transfers into equivalent systems without thereby losing its essential formal characteristics.

The most important of these modifications is the abbreviation of the speech process involved in thinking. This has doubtless many forms, according to the structural or functional peculiarities of the individual mind. The least modified form is that known as 'talking to one's self' or 'thinking aloud'. Here the speaker and the hearer are identified in a single person, who may be said to communicate with himself. More significant is the still further abbreviated form in which the sounds of speech are not articulated at all. To this belong all the varieties of silent speech and of normal thinking. The auditory centres alone may be excited; or the impulse to linguistic expression may be communicated as well to the motor nerves that communicate with the organs of speech but be inhibited either in the muscles of these organs or at some point in the motor nerves themselves; or, possibly, the auditory centres may be only slightly, if at all, affected, the speech process manifesting itself directly in the motor sphere. There must be still other types of abbreviation. How common is the excitation of the motor nerves in silent speech, in which no audible or visible articulations result, is shown by the frequent experience of fatigue in the speech organs, particularly in the larynx, after unusually stimulating reading or intensive thinking.

All the modifications so far considered are directly patterned on the typical process of normal speech. Of very great interest and importance is the possibility of transferring the whole system of speech symbolism into other terms than those that are involved in the typical process. This process, as we have seen, is a matter of sounds and of movements intended to produce these sounds. The sense of vision is not brought into play. But let us suppose that one not only hears the articulated sounds but sees the articulation themselves as they are being executed by the speaker. Clearly, if one can only gain a sufficiently high degree of adroitness in perceiving these movements of the speech organs, the way is opened for a new type of speech symbolism – that in which the sound is replaced by the visual image of the articulations that correspond to the sound. This sort of system has no great value for most of us because we are already possessed of the auditory-motor system of which it is at best but an imperfect translation, not all the articulations being visible to the eye. However, it is well known what excellent use deaf-mutes can make of 'reading from the lips' as a subsidiary method of apprehending speech. The most important of all visual speech symbolisms is, of course, that of the written or printed word, to which, on the motor side, corresponds the system of delicately adjusted movements which result in the writing or typewriting or other graphic method of recording speech. The significant feature for our recognition in these new types of symbolism, apart from the fact that they are no longer a by-product of normal speech itself, is that each element (letter or written word) in the system corresponds to a specific element (sound or sound-group or spoken word) in the primary system. Written language is thus a point-to-point equivalence, to borrow a mathematical phrase, to its spoken counterpart. The written forms are secondary symbols of the spoken ones – symbols of symbols – yet so close is the correspondence that they may, not only in theory but in the actual practice of certain eye-readers and, possibly, in certain types of thinking, be entirely substituted for the spoken ones. Yet the auditory-motor associations are probably always latent at the least, that is, they are unconsciously brought into play. Even those who read and think without the slightest use of sound imagery are, at last analysis, dependent on it. They are merely handling the circulating medium, the money, of visual symbols as a convenient substitute for the economic goods and services of the fundamental auditory symbols.

The possibilities of linguistic transfer are practically unlimited. A familiar example is the Morse telegraph code, in which the letters of written speech are represented by a conventionally fixed sequence of longer or shorter ticks. Here the transfer takes place from the written word rather than directly from the sounds of spoken speech. The letter of the telegraph code is thus a symbol of a symbol of a symbol. It does not, of course, in the least follow that the skilled operator, in order to arrive at an understanding of a telegraphic message, needs to transpose the individual sequence of ticks into a visual image of the word before he experiences its normal auditory image. The precise method of reading off speech from the telegraphic communication undoubtedly varies widely with the individual. It is even conceivable, if not exactly likely, that certain operators may have learned to think directly, so far as the purely conscious part of the process of thought is concerned, in terms of the tick-auditory symbolism or, if they happen to have a strong natural bent towards motor symbolism, in terms of the correlated tactile-motor symbolism developed in the sending of telegraphic messages.

Still another interesting group of transfers are the different gesture languages, developed for the use of deaf-mutes, of Trappist monks vowed to perpetual silence or of communicating parties that are within seeing distance of each other but are out of earshot. Some of these systems are one-to-one equivalences of the normal system of speech; others, like military gesture-symbolism or the gesture language of the Plains Indians of North America (understood by tribes of mutually unintelligible forms of speech) are imperfect transfers, limiting themselves to the rendering of such grosser speech elements as are an imperative minimum under difficult circumstances. In these latter systems, as in such still more imperfect symbolisms as those used at sea or in the woods, it may be contended that language no longer properly plays a part but that the ideas are directly conveyed by an utterly unrelated symbolic process or by a quasi-instinctive imitativeness. Such an interpretation would be erroneous. The intelligibility of these vaguer symbolisms can hardly be due to anything but their automatic and silent translation into the terms of a fuller flow of speech.

We shall no doubt conclude that all voluntary communication of ideas, aside from normal speech, is either a transfer, direct or indirect, from the typical symbolism of language as spoken and heard or, at the least, involves the intermediary of truly linguistic symbolism. This is a fact of the highest importance. Auditory imagery and the correlated motor imagery leading to articulation are, by whatever devious ways we follow the process, the historic fountain-head of all speech and of all thinking. One other point is of still greater importance. The ease with which speech symbolism can be transferred from one sense to another, from technique to technique, itself indicates that the mere sounds of speech are not the essential fact of language, which lies rather in the classification, in the formal patterning, and in the relating of concepts. Once more, language, as a structure, is on its inner face the mould of thought. It is this abstracted language, rather more than the physical facts of speech, that is to concern us in our inquiry.

There is no more striking general fact about language than its universality. One may argue as to whether a particular tribe engages in activities that are worthy of the name of religion or of art, but we know of no people that is not possessed of a fully developed language. The lowliest South African Bushman speaks in the forms of a rich symbolic system that is in essence perfectly comparable to the speech of the cultivated Frenchman. It goes without saying that the more abstract concepts are not nearly so plentifully represented in the language of the savage, nor is there the rich terminology and the finer definition of nuances that reflect the higher culture. Yet the sort of linguistic development that parallels the historic growth of culture and which, in its later stages, we associate with literature is, at best, but a superficial thing. The fundamental groundwork of language – the development of a clear-cut phonetic system, the specific association of speech elements with concepts and the delicate provision for the formal expression of all manner of relations – all this meets us rigidly perfected and systematized in every language known to us. Many primitive languages have a formal richness, a latent luxuriance of expression, that eclipses anything known to the languages of modern civilization. Even in the mere matter of the inventory of speech the layman must be prepared for strange surprises. Popular statements as to the extreme poverty of expression to which primitive languages are doomed are simply myths. Scarcely less impressive than the universality of speech is its almost incredible diversity. Those of us that have studied French or German, or, better yet, Latin or Greek, know in what varied forms a thought may run. The formal divergences between the English plan and the Latin plan, however, are comparatively slight in the perspective of what we know of more exotic linguistic patterns. The universality and the diversity of speech lead to a significant inference. We are forced to believe that language is an immensely ancient heritage of the human race, whether or not all forms of speech are the historical outgrowth of a single pristine form. It is doubtful if any other cultural asset of man, be it the art of drilling for fire or of chipping stone, may lay claim to a greater age. I am inclined to believe that it antedated even the lowliest developments of material culture, that these developments, in fact, were not strictly possible until language, the tool of significant expression, had itself taken shape.

5 Language and mental development *

A. R. LURIA and F. Ia. YUDOVICH

The writings of the Soviet psychologist A. R. Luria have stimulated much thought and research in the field of human learning. In particular, his emphasis on the crucial influence of language on the development of mental processes in children has been an important contributory factor in the development of the current interest in the role of language in learning.

This paper presents an outline of Luria's position and also refers to the work of others in the field. Of particular interest is his discussion of the relationship between the two signalling systems. Language, he argues, radically modifies the principles of reinforcement and facilitates concept formation and abstraction generally.

Language, which incorporates the experience of generations or, more broadly speaking, of mankind, is included in the process of the child's development from the first months of his life. By naming objects, and so defining their connections and relations, the adult creates new forms of reflection of reality in the child, incomparably deeper and more complex than those which he could have formed through individual experience. This whole process of the transmission of knowledge and the formation of concepts, which is the

* Reprinted and abridged from A. R. Luria and F. Ia. Yudovich, *Speech and the Development of Mental Processes in the Child* (Trans. J. Simon), Staples Press, 1959, pp. 11–24.

basic way the adult influences the child, constitutes the central process of the child's intellectual development. If this formation of the child's mental activity in the process of education is left out of consideration, it is impossible either to understand or to explain causally any of the facts of child psychology.

Study of the child's mental processes as the product of his intercommunication with the environment, as the acquisition of common experiences transmitted by speech, has, therefore, become the most important principle of Soviet psychology which informs all research.

Since this principle has such decisive significance, and since it is central to our investigation, it is necessary to examine this question more fully.

It would be mistaken to suppose that verbal intercourse with adults merely changes the content of the child's conscious activity without changing its form.

Intercommunication with adults is of decisive significance because the acquisition of a language system involves a reorganization of all the child's basic mental processes; the word thus becomes a tremendous factor which forms mental activity, perfecting the reflection of reality and creating new forms of attention, of memory and imagination, of thought and action.

With the acquisition of such an 'extraordinary supplement' as the word, the most important factor emerging at the stage of man, there is introduced, in the words of Pavlov, 'a new principle of nervous activity . . . the abstraction and with this the generalization of the innumerable signals of the preceding system,[1] and, again . . . analysis and synthesis of these new generalized signals; on this depends man's infinite capacity for orientation in the environment, and, too, his highest form of adaptation – science'.

The word has a basic function not only because it indicates a corresponding object in the external world but also because it abstracts, isolates, the necessary signal, generalizes perceived signals and relates them to certain categories; it is this systematization of direct experience that makes the role of the word in the formation of mental processes so exceptionally important.

The mother's very first words, when she shows her child different

[1] The first signalling system (see p. 16).

objects and names them with a certain word, have an indiscernible but decisively important influence on the formation of his mental processes. The word, connected with direct perception of the object, isolates its essential features; to name the perceived object 'a glass', adding its functional role 'for drinking', isolates the essential and inhibits the less essential properties of the object (such as its weight or external shape); to indicate with the word 'glass' any glass, regardless of its shape, makes perception of this object permanent and generalized.

The word, handing on the experience of generations as this is incorporated in language, locks a complex system of connections in the child's cortex and becomes a tremendous tool, introducing forms of analysis and synthesis into the child's perception which he would be unable to develop by himself. For instance, when he acquires the word 'inkstand' (chernilnitsa) the child necessarily acquires also a form of systematization of perceived phenomena. He relates 'inkstand' to the groups of things related to colours (chern-, black), tools (-il-, the suffix for most Russian words designating tools) and containers (-nits-, the suffix for words designating these). As the word influences the child, therefore, it deepens and immeasurably enriches his direct perception, forms his consciousness.

This reorganization of perception – this transference of human consciousness from the stage of direct sensory experience to the stage of generalized, rational understanding – by no means exhausts the influence of the word in the formation of mental processes.

When he acquires a word, which isolates a particular thing and serves as a signal to a particular action, the child, as he carries out an adult's verbal instruction, is subordinated to this word. The adult's word becomes a regulator of his behaviour and the organization of the child's activity is thereby lifted to a higher, qualitatively new, stage. This subordination of his reactions to the word of an adult is the beginning of a long chain of formation of complex aspects of his conscious and voluntary activity.

By subordinating himself to the adult's verbal orders the child acquires a system of these verbal instructions and gradually begins to utilize them for the regulation of his own behaviour. Repeating the verbal indication of an object, he places it among other directly perceived things and makes it the object of his own complex active attention. When he establishes verbally the complex connections and relations between perceived phenomena he introduces essential changes in the perception of things influencing him; he begins to act according to verbally elaborated influences by reproducing the verbal connections reinforced by earlier adult instructions, and thereafter modifies them, isolating verbally the immediate and final aims of his behaviour, indicating the means of achieving these aims and sub-ordinating these aims to verbally formulated instruction. By these means the child advances to the stage of a new form of regulating his behaviour which gradually becomes, in Pavlov's words, 'a system, a unitary, higher form of self-regulation'. In sum, speech, the basic means of communication, becomes also a means of deeper analysis and synthesis of reality and, more fundamentally important, 'a higher regulator of behaviour'.

All this has a decisive significance for psychology. The fact that the word is included in the content of nearly all basic forms of human activity, that it participates in the formation of perception and memory, in stimulus and action, permits a new approach to an important region of mental activity. Perception and attention, memory and imagination, consciousness and action, cease to be regarded as simple, eternal, innate mental 'properties'. They begin to be understood as the product of complex social forms of the child's mental processes; as complex 'systems of functions' which appear as a result of the development of the child's activity in the process of intercourse; as complex reflective acts in the content of which speech is included, which, using Pavlov's terminology, are realized with the close participation of the two signal systems – the first signal system being concerned with directly perceived stimuli, the second with systems of verbal elaboration.

Only by understanding that the sources of all complex mental processes do not lie in the depths of the soul, but are to be found in complex forms of human social life and in the child's communication with people surrounding him, can we finally outgrow the prejudices which have been rooted for centuries in psychological science.

Soviet psychologists began to study the child's mental development in close connection with the development of speech three decades ago and there are a number of works dealing with this question.

L. S. Vigotsky was one of the first to express the view that speech plays a decisive role in the formation of mental processes, and that the basic method of analysing the development of higher psychological functions is investigation of that reorganization of mental processes which takes place under the influence of speech.

He investigated the development of understanding in children and reached the conclusion that characteristic forms of communication begin when there is generalization of several objects as a whole from direct impressions, and end when each process of analysis and synthesis of reality is defined by a word which distinguishes the necessary features and relates the perceived object to a definite category. Vigotsky and his colleagues undertook a whole series of experimental investigations: into the process of formation of active attention which begins to be built up by the directive participation of the word; into the process of development of memory which, with the mediation of the word, becomes progressively transformed into active, voluntary memorization; into the development of several other higher mental processes, the analysis of which invariably showed that their complex functional organization was built up with the closest participation of speech.

All these researches convinced Vigotsky of the great significance of speech in the formation of mental processes. Besides investigating the basic stages of development of complex mental processes through the organization of speech, he also arrived at the fundamental conclusion that human mental development has its source in the verbal communication between child and adult, that 'a function which is earlier divided between two people becomes later the means of organization of the child's own behaviour'.

Vigotsky's researches were followed by numerous other studies of the part played by the word as the basis of systems of connections which allow for further formation of the child's mental processes.

Towards the close of the thirties and the beginning of the forties, G. L. Rosengardt undertook an interesting series of investigations which demonstrated the role of the word in the formation of perceptions and in memorization during the first two years of life. This and other similar research showed convincingly not only that the word is gradually excluded from other complexes perceived by the child, but also the decisively important fact that, under its influence, the young child's perception and memory acquire new features; by allowing him to distinguish the essential features of an object the word makes his perception of objects generalized and constant and creates new possibilities for the development of coherent, differentiated memory.

Further research underlined the essential role played by speech in complex forms of child behaviour. The development of active forms of memorization, the earliest forms of the child's volitional behaviour and, in particular, the differentiation of motives of behaviour and the construction of complex conscious actions – all these have proved to be closely connected with those complex reorganizations of activity which appear in the process of generalization, and to stand in close relation to the development of the child's speech. Verbal processes, through generalization, enable the child to formulate aims and the necessary means for their achievement, to create an 'imaginative' play plan in subordination to which he can acquire complex forms of behaviour which are inaccessible to a direct attempt. Investigation of the genesis of higher forms of psychological activity once more demonstrated their complex composition and the role of speech in forming the child's consciousness.

Of recent years, Soviet psychologists and physiologists have not limited themselves to these questions but have also described changes in the course of nervous processes as a result of the participation of the second signal system.

A. G. Ivanov-Smolensky and N. I. Krasnogorsky long since attempted to show in practice the role of the word in the child's higher nervous activity. Their researches showed that the word can successfully replace unconditioned reinforcement, that with the aid of constant reinforcement of a conditioned signal through verbal instruction it is possible to form a new temporary connection, as successfully as by use of an unconditioned (food or defensive) reinforcement. Experiments undertaken by Ivanov-Smolensky's students also showed that the word can successfully replace a direct conditioned signal, that the reaction earlier obtained to the picture of a sparrow can easily and at once be obtained by substituting the word 'sparrow', the related word 'swallow' or the generalizing word 'bird'. Several other psychologists obtained similar data.

This work proved that the word can replace unconditioned or conditioned stimuli. Further research has underlined the essential fact that the word exercises a significant influence on the course of elaboration of temporary connections, hastening the process of elaboration, rendering the connections more stable and contributing substantially new features to their formation.

When elaborating differentiation in children of one and a half to two years, A. A. Lublinskaya noted that difficulties in differentiating strongly decreased when verbal labels were added to the differentiating signals. Children undergoing the experiment were able to differentiate four to five times more quickly than children in the control group and the differentiations elaborated with the participation of the word were more stable and generalized than those elaborated without it.

Special research has also shown that the experimenter's instructions not only significantly hasten the process of elaboration of new temporary connections and make them more stable but also essentially reorganize the natural course of these processes, for instance, by changing the natural relation of the strength of stimuli. It is well known that with the usual complex stimuli the leading role is played by the strong component, while the weak component of the complex retreats into the background and is inhibited by the strong one. But the word of the experimenter (or systems of previous connections evoked by the word) reinforce the weak component of the complex so that it changes into the strong, leading one, while the physically stronger component loses its leading significance.

It is interesting to note that in the usual experimental conditions the word has this effect with 4- to 5-year-old children, whereas in cases where the word of the experimenter revives stable old connections a change in the strength relations of stimuli occurs much earlier. Even more interesting is the fact that the child's speech itself begins to be progressively included in the formation of temporary connections and essentially changes this process.

Already in 1929 Vigotsky showed that every time the little child of 4 to 5 years of age is confronted with a problem which causes some kind of difficulty, there arises external speech, not directed to his interlocutor; the child states the situation that has arisen, takes from it 'verbal copy' and then reproduces those connections of his past experience which may help him out of present difficulties. Vigotsky attempted to show that this was not affective 'egocentric speech', about which Piaget was then writing, but the inclusion of speech to mediate behaviour by the mobilization of verbal connections which help to solve a difficult problem. His observations showed that the child first speaks aloud, to himself, but that his speech gradually dies away, passes into a whisper and finally becomes internal speech; and that the child of 7 to 8 years begins to solve complex problems with the aid of systems of internal verbal connections, which have arisen earlier in the course of verbal intercourse but have since become converted into his own individual mechanisms, enabling him to include verbal connections in the organization of his activity.

A period of twenty years elapsed before the data obtained by Vigotsky were checked and proved by new research. N. P. Paramonova, analysing the process of formation of motor reactions in the normal pre-school child, showed that the inclusion of his own speech as a means of organizing his activity, itself represents a complex and developing process. In the case of the child of 3 years, the elaboration of temporary connections by the method of verbal reinforcement is not yet mediated by his own speech, which gradually dies away, and proceeds slowly; but with the child of 4 to 5 years the process substantially changes. The appearance of the signal, accompanied by reinforcement, first calls forth questions from the child ('Do I have to press on this one?') and afterwards produces positive repetitions ('This red one! I have to press this!'); this shows that the connections elaborated have achieved their generalized verbal formulation.

These verbal repetitions are preserved for some time, but in the 6- to 7-year-old child they die away and vanish. What is characteristic here is the fact that, with the appearance of verbal formulations – in other words with inclusion of the child's own speech in his orientation to the signals presented – the very process of elaboration of new connections changes. Connections which were previously elaborated gradually, which needed permanent reinforcement and were extinguished when it was removed, begin now to be elaborated quickly, sometimes 'on the spot', become stably reinforced, cease to be in need of permanent reinforcement and begin to show those features of 'self-regulation' which Pavlov regarded as the essential peculiarity of human higher nervous activity.

The direct participation of the child's own speech in the process of elaboration of new connections is, according to these findings, well established in the child of 5 to 6 years. However, other research has shown that this participation of speech in the elaboration of new connections can be essentially disturbed by injuries to the brain and also by abnormal development; above all by that form of mental retardation which results from acute organic disease of the brain in early childhood.

In such cases the processes of higher nervous activity are so imperfect and the very speech of the child so defective – so poor are his connections, so immobile his dynamics – that the participation of speech in the formation of new connections becomes impossible and these are elaborated without the requisite participation of the abstracting and generalizing function of the word. It is precisely because of this that the mentally retarded schoolchild does not show those features of swift, mobile and stable elaboration of new connections which, as has just been pointed out, are characteristic features of the realization of this process when there is full-value participation of the two signal systems. The process of elaborating new connections becomes slow and gradual, continues for a long time to depend on permanent reinforcement, remains stable only because of the strictly determined discipline of the experiment, is easily inhibited by complication of the conditions and is not reflected in any kind of coherent verbal formulation.

Observations of mentally retarded children permit us to approach the problem of the role of speech in the formation of temporary connections from another angle; to study how the child's behaviour differs when the abstraction and generalization of speech plays no part in its formation.

Investigations of mentally retarded children belong to a new region of study where different methods are used to throw light on the role of speech in the formation of complex aspects of mental activity; this research is concerned with the data of psychopathology.

About thirty years ago the German psychopathologist K. Goldstein and his colleague, the psychologist A. Gelb, expressed the view that the acquisition of speech allowed man to rise above direct, visual perception to analysis of its data, to the relation of perceived objects to certain categories, so enabling him to organize his behaviour, not according to the visually perceived situation, but according to a deeper 'categorized' reflection of the world. They therefore connected freer, 'categorized' behaviour with acquisition of the word; very similar views were advanced by the well-known English neurologist H. Head.

After prolonged research they advanced the hypothesis that this complicated structure of 'abstract' or 'categorized' behaviour, which is a characteristic human feature, falls to pieces in cases of special verbal disorder – aphasia – which arise as a result of disturbances in the normal functioning of the cortex. They connected this disturbance of speech with the patient's return to more primitive and concrete behaviour. In the case of such patients, the possibility of advancing from the direct perceptional field is excluded and what should be an abstract 'categorized' operation becomes a simple reproduction of visual situations well established in the patient's previous experience.

This material provides a valuable illustration of the role of the word in the organization of complex mental processes and indicates the tremendous damage to human behaviour as a result of its loss. Research into the changes in mental processes in states of aphasia has contributed substantially to our understanding of the dependence of complex mental processes on speech; after these investigations it is difficult to deny that many of those higher psychological functions which have so often been discussed as manifestations of innate properties in fact result from the inclusion in activity of that tremendous formative factor, the word.

The data of psychopathological research, accumulated by Gelb, Goldstein, Head and other neurologists abroad, find a clear explanation in the psychology of higher nervous activity; in particular in Pavlov's finding concerning the interaction of the two signal systems and their participation in the formation of every human activity. Closely related data, which permit of an approach to the same question from another angle, have been obtained by psychologists who have investigated the peculiarities of mental processes in deaf-mutes.

The time has long since passed when the deaf-mute child was regarded as differing from his normal counterpart only by the absence of hearing and speech. Research carried out abroad, and by Soviet psychologists, has shown the changes that take place in the deaf-mute's perceptual processes because of his undeveloped speech; excluded from speech communication because of his defect in hearing, he does not possess all those forms of reflection of reality which are realized through verbal speech. The deaf-mute who has not been taught to speak indicates objects or actions with a gesture; he is unable to abstract the quality or action from the actual object, to form abstract concepts, to systematize the phenomena of the external world with the aid of the abstracted signals furnished by language but which are not natural to visual, practically acquired experience. The psychological research of Vigotsky and others and the educational observations of teachers of deaf-mutes show how great a degree of underdevelopment of complex perceptual processes accompanies all deaf-muteness, and how much effort must be spent to restore these serious defects in complex psychological processes by continuous teaching of verbal speech.

All this rich and many-sided research contributes important material towards elucidation of the part played by speech in the formation of the child's mental activity and lays a sound foundation for further studies of this kind.

6 Thought and word*

L. S. VIGOTSKY

This paper is taken from the book by Vigotsky first published in Russian in 1934 shortly after his death. The appearance of an English edition in 1962 provided a major contribution to contemporary discussions on the relationship between language and thinking and on the problems of cognition generally. The paper which follows is an

* Reprinted and abridged from L. S. Vigotsky, 'Thought and Word' in L. S. Vigotsky, *Thought and Language* (Trans. E. Hanfmann and G. Vakar), M.I.T. Press, 1962, pp. 119–53.

abridged version of the last chapter in the book and it summarizes some of the most important of Vigotsky's ideas. Of particular interest are his views on the nature of the relationship between language and thinking, and on the way in which word meanings evolve.

The meaning of a word represents such a close amalgam of thought and language that it is hard to tell whether it is a phenomenon of speech or a phenomenon of thought. A word without meaning is an empty sound; meaning, therefore, is a criterion of 'word', its indispensable component. It would seem, then, that it may be regarded as a phenomenon of speech. But from the point of view of psychology, the meaning of every word is a generalization or a concept. And since generalizations and concepts are undeniably acts of thought, we may regard meaning as a phenomenon of thinking. It does not follow, however, that meaning formally belongs in two different spheres of psychological life. Word meaning is a phenomenon of thought only in so far as thought is embodied in speech, and of speech only in so far as speech is connected with thought and illumined by it. It is a phenomenon of verbal thought, or meaningful speech – a union of word and thought.

Our experimental investigations fully confirm this basic thesis. They not only proved that concrete study of the development of verbal thought is made possible by the use of word meaning as the analytical unit but they also led to a further thesis, which we consider the major result of our study and which issues directly from the first: the thesis that word meanings develop. This insight must replace the postulate of the immutability of word meanings.

The discovery that word meanings evolve leads the study of thought and speech out of a blind alley. Word meanings are dynamic rather than static formations. They change as the child develops; they change also with the various ways in which thought functions.

If word meanings change in their inner nature, then the relation of thought to word also changes. To understand the dynamics of that relationship, we must supplement the genetic approach of our main study by functional analysis and examine the role of word meaning in the process of thought.

Let us consider the process of verbal thinking from the first dim stirring of a thought to its formulation. What we want to show now is not how meanings develop over long periods of time but the way they function in the live process of verbal thought. On the basis of such a functional analysis, we shall be able to show also that each stage in the development of word meaning has its own particular relationship between thought and speech. Since functional problems are most readily solved by examining the highest form of a given activity, we shall, for a while, put aside the problem of development and consider the relations between thought and word in the mature mind.

The leading idea in the following discussion can be reduced to this formula: The relation of thought to word is not a thing but a process, a continual movement back and forth from thought to word and from word to thought. In that process the relation of thought to word undergoes changes which themselves may be regarded as development in the functional sense. Thought is not merely expressed in words; it comes into existence through them. Every thought tends to connect something with something else, to establish a relationship between things. Every thought moves, grows and develops, fulfills a function, solves a problem. This flow of thought occurs as an inner movement through a series of planes. An analysis of the interaction of thought and word must begin with an investigation of the different phases and planes a thought traverses before it is embodied in words.

The first thing such a study reveals is the need to distinguish between two planes of speech. Both the inner, meaningful, semantic aspect of speech and the external, phonetic aspect, though forming a true unity, have their own laws of movement. The unity of speech is a complex, not a homogeneous, unity. A number of facts in the linguistic development of the child indicate independent movement in the phonetic and the semantic spheres. We shall point out two of the most important of these facts.

In mastering external speech, the child starts from one word, then connects two or three words; a little later, he advances from simple sentences to more complicated ones, and finally to coherent speech made up of series of such sentences; in other words, he proceeds from a part to the whole. In regard to meaning, on the other hand, the first word of the child is a whole sentence. Semantically, the child starts from the whole, from a meaningful complex, and only later begins to master the separate semantic units, the meanings of words, and to divide his formerly undifferentiated thought into those units.

The external and the semantic aspects of speech develop in opposite directions – one from the particular to the whole, from word to sentence, and the other from the whole to the particular, from sentence to word.

This in itself suffices to show how important it is to distinguish between the vocal and the semantic aspects of speech. Since they move in reverse directions, their development does not coincide, but that does not mean that they are independent of each other. On the contrary, their difference is the first stage of a close union. In fact, our example reveals their inner relatedness as clearly as it does their distinction. A child's thought, precisely because it is born as a dim, amorphous whole, must find expression in a single word. As his thought becomes more differentiated, the child is less apt to express it in single words but constructs a composite whole. Conversely, progress in speech to the differentiated whole of a sentence helps the child's thoughts to progress from a homogeneous whole to well-defined parts. Thought and word are not cut from one pattern. In a sense, there are more differences than likenesses between them. The structure of speech does not simply mirror the structure of thought; that is why words cannot be put on by thought like a ready-made garment. Thought undergoes many changes as it turns into speech. It does not merely find expression in speech; it finds its reality and form. The semantic and the phonetic developmental processes are essentially one, precisely because of their reverse directions.

The second, equally important fact emerges at a later period of development. Piaget demonstrated that the child uses subordinate clauses with *because, although*, etc., long before he grasps the structures of meaning corresponding to these syntactic forms. Grammar precedes logic. Here, too, as in our previous example, the discrepancy does not exclude union but is, in fact, necessary for union.

In adults the divergence between the semantic and the phonetic aspects of speech is even more striking. Modern, psychologically oriented linguistics is familiar with this phenomenon, especially in regard to grammatical and psychological subject and predicate. For example, in the sentence 'The clock fell', emphasis and meaning may change in different situations. Suppose I notice that the clock has stopped and ask how this happened. The answer is, 'The clock fell.' Grammatical and psychological subject coincide: 'The clock' is the first idea in my consciousness; 'fell' is what is said about the clock. But if I hear a crash in the next room and inquire what happened, and get the same answer, subject and predicate are psychologically reversed. I knew something had fallen – that is what we are talking about. 'The clock' completes the idea. The sentence could be changed to: 'What has fallen is the clock'; then the grammatical and the psychological subject would coincide. In the prologue to his play *Duke Ernst von Schwaben*, Uhland says: 'Grim scenes will pass before you.' Psychologically, 'will pass' is the subject. The spectator knows he will see events unfold; the additional idea, the predicate, is 'grim scenes'. Uhland meant, 'What will pass before your eyes is a tragedy.' Any part of a sentence may become the psychological predicate, the carrier of topical emphasis; on the other hand, entirely different meanings may lie hidden behind one grammatical structure. Accord between syntactical and psychological organization is not as prevalent as we tend to assume – rather, it is a requirement that is seldom met. Not only subject and predicate, but grammatical gender, number, case, tense, degree etc., have their psychological doubles. A spontaneous utterance, wrong from the point of view of grammar, may have charm and aesthetic value. Absolute correctness is achieved only beyond natural language, in mathematics. Our daily speech continually fluctuates between the ideals of mathematical and of imaginative harmony.

Behind words, there is the independent grammar of thought, the syntax of word meanings. The simplest utterance, far from reflecting a constant, rigid correspondence between sound and meaning, is really a process. Verbal expressions cannot emerge fully formed but must develop gradually. This complex process of transition from meaning to sound must itself be developed and perfected. The child must learn to distinguish between semantics and phonetics and understand the nature of the difference. At first he uses verbal forms and meanings without being conscious of them as separate. The word, to the child, is an integral part of the object it denotes. Such a conception seems to be characteristic of primitive linguistic consciousness. We all know the old story about the rustic who said he wasn't surprised that savants with all their instruments could figure out the size of stars and their course – what baffled him was how they found out their names. Simple experiments show that preschool children 'explain' the names of objects by their attributes. According to them, an animal is called 'cow' because it has horns, 'calf' because its horns are still small, 'dog' because it is small and has no horns; an object is called 'car' because it is not an animal. When asked whether one could interchange the names of objects, for instance call a cow 'ink', and ink 'cow', children will answer no, 'because ink is used for writing, and the cow gives milk'. An exchange of names would mean an exchange of characteristic features, so inseparable is the connection between them in the child's mind. In one experiment, the children were told that in a game a dog would be called 'cow'. Here is a typical sample of questions and answers:

'Does a cow have horns?'

'Yes.'

'But don't you remember that the cow is really a dog? Come now, does a dog have horns?'

'Sure, if it is a cow, if it's called cow, it has horns. That kind of dog has got to have little horns.'

We can see how difficult it is for children to separate the name of an object from its attributes, which cling to the name when it is transferred like possessions following their owner.

The fusion of the two planes of speech, semantic and vocal, begins to break down as the child grows older, and the distance between them gradually increases. Each stage in the development of word meanings has its own specific interrelation of the two planes. A child's ability to communicate through language is directly related to the differentiation of word meanings in his speech and consciousness.

To understand this, we must remember a basic characteristic of the structure of word meanings. In the semantic structure of a word, we distinguish between referent and meaning; correspondingly, we distinguish a word's nominative from its significative function. When we compare these structural and functional relations at the earliest, middle and advanced stages of development, we find the following genetic regularity: In the beginning, only the nominative function exists; and semantically, only the objective reference; signification independent of naming, and meaning independent of reference, appear later and develop along the paths we have attempted to trace and describe.

Only when this development is completed does the child become fully able to formulate his own thought and to understand the speech of others. Until then, his usage of words coincides with that of adults in its objective reference but not in its meaning.

[There now follows a lengthy discussion on the nature of inner speech which, while of great interest, is not central to the main theme of this section. Vigotsky then moves on to a review and final comment.]

We have come to the end of our analysis; let us survey its results. Verbal thought appeared as a complex, dynamic entity, and the relation of thought and word within it as a movement through a series of planes. Our analysis followed the process from the outermost to the innermost plane. In reality, the development of verbal thought takes the opposite course: from the motive which engenders a thought to the shaping of the thought, first in inner speech, then in meanings of words and finally in words. It would be a mistake, however, to imagine that this is the only road from thought to word. The development may stop at any point in its complicated course; an infinite variety of movements to and fro, of ways still unknown to us, is possible. A study of these manifold variations lies beyond the scope of our present task.

Our investigation followed a rather unusual path. We wished to study the inner workings of thought and speech hidden from direct observation. Meaning and the whole inward aspect of language, the side turned towards the person, not towards the outer world, have been so far an almost unknown territory. No matter how they were interpreted, the relations between thought and word were always considered constant, established for ever. Our investigation has shown that they are, on the contrary, delicate, changeable relations between processes, which arise during the development of verbal thought. We did not intend to, and could not, exhaust the subject of verbal thought. We tried only to give a general conception of the infinite complexity of this dynamic structure – a conception starting from experimentally documented facts.

To association psychology, thought and word were united by external bonds, similar to the bonds between two nonsense syllables. Gestalt psychology introduced the concept of structural bonds but, like the older theory, did not account for the specific relations between thought and word. All the other theories grouped themselves around two poles – either the behaviourist concept of thought as speech minus sound or the idealistic view, held by the Wuerzburg school and Bergson, that thought could be 'pure', unrelated to language, and that it was distorted by words. Tjutchev's 'A thought once uttered is a lie' could well serve as an epigraph for the latter group. Whether inclining towards pure naturalism or extreme idealism, all these theories have one trait in common – their antihistorical bias. They study thought and speech without any reference to their developmental history.

Only a historical theory of inner speech can deal with this immense and complex problem. The relation between thought and word is a living process; thought is born through words. A word devoid of thought is a dead thing, and a thought unembodied in words remains a shadow. The connection between them, however, is not a pre-formed and constant one. It emerges in the course of development, and itself evolves. To the Biblical 'In the beginning was the Word', Goethe makes Faust reply, 'In the beginning was the deed.' The intent here is to detract from the value of the word, but we can accept this version if we emphasize it differently: In the *beginning* was the deed. The word was not the beginning – action was there first; it is the end of development, crowning the deed.

7   The genetic approach to the psychology of thought*

J. PIAGET

In any discussion of children's thinking a contribution by Piaget is essential. The paper which follows presents some of the essential aspects of his views on the problem. In particular the ideas of re-

* Reprinted and abridged from J. Piaget, 'The Genetic Approach to the Psychology of Thought', *Journal of Educational Psychology*, **52**, 1961, pp. 151–61.

versibility, assimilation, accommodation and equilibration are discussed and their interrelationships explored.

The synoptic nature of the paper and the characteristic Piagetian style do not make for some easy reading. However, it is well worth close attention.

From a developmental point of view, the essential in the act of thinking is not contemplation – that is to say, that which the Greeks called 'theorema' – but the dynamic aspect.

Taking into consideration all that is known, one can distinguish two principal aspects:

(1) The formal viewpoint which deals with the configuration of the state of things to know – for instance, most perceptions, mental images, imageries.

(2) The *dynamic* aspect, which deals with transformations – for instance, to disconnect a motor in order to understand its functioning, to disassociate and vary the components of a physical phenomenon, to understand its causalities, to isolate the elements of a geometrical figure in order to investigate its properties etc.

The study of the development of thought shows that the dynamic aspect is at the same time more difficult to attain and more important, because only transformations make us understand the state of things. For instance: when a child of 4 to 6 years transfers a liquid from a large and low glass into a narrow and higher glass, he believes in general that the quantity of the liquid has increased, because he is limited to comparing the initial state (low level) to the final state (high level) without concerning himself with the transformation. Towards 7 or 8 years of age, on the other hand, a child discovers the preservation of the liquid, because he will think in terms of transformation. He will say that nothing has been taken away and nothing added, and, if the level of the liquid rises, this is due to a loss of width etc.

The formal aspect of thought makes way, therefore, more and more in the course of the development to its dynamic aspect, until such time when only transformation gives an understanding of things. To think means, above all, to understand; and to understand means to arrive at the transformations, which furnish the reason for the state of things. All development of thought is resumed in the following manner: a construction of operations which stem from actions and a gradual subordination of formal aspects into dynamic aspects.

The operation, properly speaking, which constitutes the terminal point of this evolution is, therefore, to be conceived as an internalized action reversible (example: addition and subtraction etc.) bound to other operations, which form with it a structured whole and which is characterized by well defined laws of totality.

So defined, the dynamics intervene in the construction of all thought processes; in the structure of forms and classifications, of relations and serialization of correspondences, of numbers, of space and time, of the causality etc.

Any action of thought consists of combining thought operations and integrating the objects to be understood into systems of dynamic transformation. The psychological criterion of this is the appearance of the notion of conservation or 'invariants of groups'. Before speech, at the purely sensory-motor stage of a child from 0 to 18 months, it is possible to observe actions which show evidence of such tendencies. For instance: From 4–5 to 18 months, the baby constructs his first invariant, which is the schema of the permanent object (to recover an object which escaped from the field of perception). He succeeds in this by coordinating the positions and the displacements according to a structure, which can be compared to what the geometricians call 'group displacements'.

When, with the beginning of the symbolic function (language, symbolic play, imagery etc.), the representation through thought becomes possible, it is at first a question of reconstructing in thought what the action is already able to realize. The actions actually do not become transformed immediately into operations, and one has to wait until about 7–8 years for the child to reach a functioning level. During this preoperative period the child, therefore, only arrives at incomplete structures characterized by a lack in the notion of combinations and, consequently, by a lack of logic (in transitivity etc.).

At about 7–8 years the child arrives at his first complete dynamic structures (classes, relations and numbers), which, however, still remain concrete – in other words, only at the time of a handling of objects (material manipulation or, when possible, directly imagined). It is not before the age of 11–12 years or more that operations can be applied to pure hypotheses.

The fundamental genetic problem of the psychology of thought is hence to explain the formation of these dynamic structures. Practically, one would have to rely on three principal factors in order to explain the facts of development: maturation, physical experience and social interaction. But in this particular case none of these three suffice to furnish us with the desired explanations – not even the three together.

MATURATION

First of all, none of these dynamic structures are innate, but they form very gradually. (For example: The transitivity of equalities is acquired at approximately $6\frac{1}{2}$–7 years, and the ability of linear measure comes about only at 9 years, as does the full understanding of weights etc.) But progressive construction does not seem to depend on maturation, because the achievements hardly correspond to a particular age. Only the order of succession is constant. However, one witnesses innumerable accelerations or retardations for reasons of education (cultural) or acquired experience. Certainly one cannot deny the inevitable role which maturation plays, but is determined above all by existing possibility (or limitation). They still remain to be actualized, which brings about other factors. In addition, in the domain of thought, the factors of innateness seem above all limitative. We do not have, for example, an intuition of space in the fourth dimension; nevertheless we can deduce it.

PHYSICAL EXPERIENCE

Experiencing of objects plays, naturally, a very important role in the establishment of dynamic structures, because the operations originate from actions and the actions bear upon the object. This role manifests itself right from the beginning of sensory-motor explorations, preceding language, and it affirms itself continually in the course of manipulations and activities which are appropriate to the antecedent stages. Necessary as the role of experience may be, it does not sufficiently describe the construction of the dynamic structures – and this for the following three reasons.

First, there exist ideas which cannot possibly be derived from the child's experience – for instance, when one changes the shape of a small ball of clay. The child will declare, at 7–8 years, that the quantity of the matter is conserved. It does so before discovering the conservation of weight (9–10 years) and that of volume (10–11 years). What is the quantity of a matter independently of its weight and its volume? This is an abstract notion corresponding to the 'substance' of the pre-Socratic physicists. This notion is neither possible to be perceived nor measurable. It is, therefore, the product of a dynamic deduction and not part of an experience. (The problem would not be solved either by presenting the quantity in the form of a bar of chocolate to be eaten.)

Secondly, the various investigations into the learning of logical structure, which we were able to make at our International Centre of Genetic Epistemology, lead to a unanimous result: one does not 'learn' a logical structure as one learns to discover any physical law. For instance, it is easy to bring about the learning of the conservation of weight because of its physical character, but it is difficult to obtain the one of the transitivity of the relationship of the weight:

$$A = C \text{ if } A = B \text{ and } B = C$$

or the one of the relationship of inclusion etc. The reason for this is that in order to arrive at the learning of a logical structure, one has to build on another more elementary logical (or prelogical) structure. And such structures consequently never stem from experience alone, but suppose always a coordinating activity of the subject.

Thirdly, there exist two types of experiences:

(1) The physical experiences show the objects as they are, and the knowledge of them leads to the abstraction directly from the object (example: to discover that a more voluminous matter is more or less heavy than a less voluminous matter).

(2) The logicomathematical experience supposes to interrelate by action individual facts into the world of objects, but this refers to the result of these actions rather than to the objects themselves. These interrelations are arrived at by process of abstractions from the actions and their coordinates. For instance, to discover that ten stones in a line always add up to ten, whether they are counted from left to right or from right to left. Because then the order and

the total sum have been presented. The new knowledge consists simply in the discovery that the action of adding a sum is independent of the action of putting them in order. Thus the logico-mathematical experience does not stem from the same type of learning as that of the physical experience, but rather from an equilibration of the scheme of actions, as we will see.

SOCIAL INTERACTION

The educative and social transmission (linguistic etc.) plays, naturally, an evident role in the formation of dynamic structures, but this factor does not suffice either to entirely explain its development, and this for two reasons:

First, a certain number of structures do not lend themselves to teaching and are prior to all teaching. One can cite, as an example, most concepts of conservation, of which, in general, the pedagogs agree that they are not problematic to the child.

The second, more fundamental, reason is that in order to understand the adult and his language, the child needs means of assimilation which are formed through structures preliminary to the social transmission itself – for instance, an ancient experience has shown us that French-speaking children understand very early the expression *quelques unes de mes fleurs* [some of my flowers] in contrast to *toutes mes fleurs* [all my flowers], and this occurs when they have not yet constructed the relation of inclusion:

Some A are part of all B;
therefore A < B

In conclusion, it is no exaggeration to maintain that the basic factors invoked before in order to explain mental development do not suffice to explain the formulation of the dynamic structures. Though all three of them certainly play a necessary role, they do not constitute in themselves sufficient reason and one has to add to them a fourth factor, which we shall try to describe now.

This fourth factor seems to us to consist of a general progression of equilibration. This factor intervenes, as is to be expected, in the interaction of the preceding factors. Indeed, if the development depends, on one hand, on internal factors (maturation), and on the other hand on external factors (physical or social), it is self-evident that these internal and external factors equilibrate each other. The question is then to know if we are dealing here only with momentary compromises (unstable equilibrium) or if, on the contrary, this equilibrium becomes more and more stable. This shows that all exchange (mental as well as biological) between the organism and the environment (physical and social) is composed of two poles: (a) of the *assimilation* of the given external to the previous internal structures, and (b) of the *accommodation* of these structures to the given ones. The equilibrium between the assimilation and the accommodation is proportionately more stable than the assimilative structures which are better differentiated and coordinated.

It is this equilibrium between the assimilation and accommodation that seems to explain to us the functioning of the reversible operations. This occurs, for instance, in the realm of notions of conservation where the invariants of groups are not accounted for by the maturation and the physical experience, nor by the sociolingual transmission. In fact, dynamic reversibility is a compensatory system of which the idea of conservation constitutes precisely the result. The equilibrium (between the assimilation and the accommodation) is to be defined as a compensation of exterior disturbances through activities of the subject orientated in the contrary direction of these disturbances. This leads us directly to the reversibility.

Notice that we do not conceive of the idea of equilibrium in the same manner as the 'gestalt theory' does, which makes great use of this idea too, but in the sense of an automatical physical equilibrium. We believe, on the contrary, that the mental equilibrium and even the biological one presumes an activity of the subject, or of the organism. It consists in a sort of matching, orientated towards compensation – with even some overcompensation – resulting from strategies of precaution. One knows, for instance, that the homeostasis does not always lead to an exact balance. But it often leads to overcompensation, in response to exterior disturbances. Such is the case in nearly all occurrences except precisely in the case of occurrences of a superior order, which are the operations of reversible intelligence, the reversible logic of which is characterized by a complete and exact compensation (inverted operation).

To apply these notions to children's reasoning we see that every new problem provokes a disequilibrium (recognizable through types of dominant errors) the solution of which consists in a re-equilibration, which brings about a new original synthesis of two systems, up to the point of independence.

During the discussion of my theories, Bruner has said that I have called disequilibrium what others describe as motivation. This is perfectly true, but the advantage of this language is to clarify that a cognitive or dynamic structure is never independent of motivational factors. The motivation in return is always connected to structural (therefore cognitive) determined level. The language of the equilibrium presents that activity, that permits us to reunite into one and the same totality those two aspects of behaviour which always have a functional solidarity because there exists no structure (cognition) without an energizer (motivation) and vice versa.

8 The learning of principles*

R. M. GAGNÉ

In this paper a leading American psychologist expounds his views on one of the most important aspects of human learning. In the course of the discussion he considers some of the problems created by conflicting connotations of the word *concept* and suggests a method of resolving the difficulty. In his suggestions he puts forward his views on the learning of principles which provide an extremely useful and convincing model of school learning.

It would surely be agreed by all investigators of learning processes that 'conceptual learning', as opposed to other, presumably simpler, forms of learning, constitutes by far the major portion of the learning associated with what is supposed to go on in schools. Most of us have, in fact, fallen into the habit of using the word *conceptual* in a pretty

* Reprinted and abridged from R. M. Gagné, 'The Learning of Principles', in H. J. Klausmeier and C. W. Harris, *Analyses of Concept Learning*, Academic Press, 1966, pp. 81–95.

broad sense to refer to the kind of behavioural change that is often verbal in its expression, but actually is a change in the symbolic or representational capabilities of the human learner. Thus, we tend not to think of acquiring capability to tie a shoelace or print a letter as conceptual. However, we do think of the performance of answering the following question as conceptual: 'What must I do if my shoelace becomes untied?' Bartlett,[1] however, reminds us that these two categories may not be so entirely different as we sometimes like to think.

Beyond these specific classes of human activity, we are also used to referring to the *content* of school subjects as conceptual, without necessarily considering the nature of behavioural change that may be involved. Thus, we often refer to the body of knowledge called physics as 'the concepts of physics', or the body of knowledge called genetics as 'the concepts of genetics'. If forced to say what we mean by the concepts of physics, we are inclined to reply by naming such things as mass, energy, work, gravitation and atom. In the case of genetics, the entities named might be genes, chromosomes, DNA, RNA and perhaps many others. We speak of students learning the concepts of physics and the concepts of genetics, by which we surely mean to imply that what is learned is conceptual.

When *concept* and *conceptual* are used in these ways, it seems to me very important to recognize that they are being employed in a most general, rough and imprecise manner. There is nothing wrong with this, because such imprecision is often required for communication in the English language. Conceptual in this sense refers to the general class of human activities that we infer to require internally stored symbolic or representational processes, as opposed to those that seem to require routine or habitual processes.

The requirements of ordinary everyday communication, however, are by no means the same as the requirements of scientific inquiry. In conversation, we may be satisfied to speak of the *particles* of matter; but a physicist would demand to know how such particles were defined, whether there were different varieties and what observations were required in studying them. Similarly, the investigator who approaches concepts scientifically is bound to want to know what

[1] F. C. Bartlett, *Thinking: An experimental and social study*, Allen and Unwin, 1958.

operations define them and whether one kind can be distinguished from another.

Eventually, I intend to talk about *principles*. The reason I lead up to it in this fashion, though, is this: If I am speaking conversationally, I have absolutely no objection to talking about the concepts of physics or the concepts of meteorology, or any other subject. I would not even insist that one speak of the principles of physics or the principles of meteorology, since the word *principle* in this conversational sense might be more restrictive in meaning. In contrast, though, if you invite me to study conceptual kinds of learning as a scientific investigator, the first thing that is apparent – strikingly so – is that there are several different kinds of things which may be referred to as concepts. And operating with this point of view, I should insist that in so far as they can be given precise scientific meaning, a concept and a principle are very different things indeed.

I am not at all confident that I could distinguish *all* of the behavioural entities that might be called by the name *concept*. But in order to proceed with the job of saying more about principles, I shall first need to distinguish these, at least, from concepts in their scientific meaning.

THE SCIENTIFIC MEANING OF CONCEPT

Despite differences in the language used to describe a concept, there is considerable agreement among research psychologists as to what this word means. Let me give some examples.

Berlyne believed that a concept is formed when overt behaviour comes to depend on certain properties of a stimulus pattern while disregarding other properties. 'It means forming what logicians and mathematicians call an "equivalence class" of stimulus situations, which share some characteristics but are distinct in other respects, and performing the same response to all members of the class.'

Kendler defined concept learning as the acquisition of a common response to dissimilar stimuli. But he also went on to say that concepts are associations, and that they function as cues or mediators of learned behaviour. This conception of the concept is basically similar to that of Osgood who emphasized the acquisition of a mediating process that can be 'detached' or 'abstracted' from the stimulus objects with which it may initially have been associated. From a somewhat different point of view, Carroll defined a concept as an abstraction from a series of experiences which defines a class of objects or events.

Although these examples of the definition of a concept are not exhaustive, they nevertheless derive from a sample of research people who are prominent in this field, and therefore cannot with wisdom be ignored. All these definitions have some general properties in common, and I judge these to be as follows:

(1) A concept is an inferred mental process.

(2) The learning of a concept requires discrimination of stimulus objects (distinguishing 'positive' and 'negative' instances).

(3) The performance which shows that a concept has been learned consists in the learner being able to place an object in a class.

The common examples of concept learning which would presumably be acceptable to each of these investigators might include the following: learning *chair* as a class of objects; learning *red* as a property of objects detachable from particular objects; learning classes of direction or position, such as *up*, *down*, *middle*, *right* and *left*, as classes of position or movement not invariably associated with particular positions or movements.

From the standpoint of the investigator of behaviour, therefore, the notion of a concept as an 'inferred process which enables the individual to classify objects' is both prominent and widely accepted. The next question is, according to such a definition, what could possibly be the meaning of the 'concepts of physics', the 'concepts of mathematics', the 'concepts of biology'.

Certain examples can perhaps be considered. In physics, for instance, one deals with lengths, times, distances and directions, and each of these needs to be learned as a concept, in rather precise form, by the beginning student of physics. One also deals with many classes of objects in physics – levers, gases, liquids, conductors, resistance, waves, lenses and many, many others. These could certainly be called concepts in accordance with the definition previously given. One might even include such concepts as force, volume, density, rotation, particle, frequency, refraction. Although these latter terms appear to have a somewhat greater degree of abstractness than the ones mentioned earlier, they can without too much of a strain be considered as concepts in the sense of classifiers of sets of objects or events. Similar examples could readily be given for mathematics and biology.

A physicist, or a physics teacher, would perhaps agree that what we have called concepts might be so designated, if one wants. However, he is likely to protest that they are somewhat trivial, and do not begin to include what he means by the concepts of physics. What about Newton's second law? What about potential energy? Work? Universal gravitation? Archimedes' principle? Heat? The structure of the atom? Similarly, were we to apply the suggested definition of a concept to mathematics, we should undoubtedly find that it failed to include many things the mathematician would like to think of as concepts of mathematics, such as integers, rational numbers, irrational numbers, functions and many others. In biology, it seems doubtful that this definition of concept could include such things as reproduction, mitosis, homeostasis, evolution and messenger and coding functions of cell components. All these concepts appear to be altogether too complex to be viewed as object classifications. They will not fit the definition derived from experimental studies of behaviour.

The implication of this discussion is, then, that one cannot generalize from scientific or laboratory findings about concept learning to all of the varieties of content which may be found in school subjects. Certain fundamental classifications of objects and events do, in fact, seem to fit the conception of concept derived from experimental studies. These should by no means be ignored, because they do have to be learned in order to proceed with the study of these subjects. But the concepts of physics (as an example) include a great many instances of capabilities to be learned which, even superficially, appear to involve more complex kinds of behaviour than are implied by a definition based on object classification.

PRINCIPLES

The next question is, then, how can these more complex capabilities be defined? How can one distinguish the kind of learning situation in which the capability acquired is simply one of being able to classify objects or object properties, and the kind of learning situation in which these apparently more complex entities, sometimes called concepts, are involved?

The clue to the added complexity may come from a consideration of the criterion performance in each case. As has been said, the performance that reflects the learning of a concept is one of identifying a class of things, or any member of the class. If the concept is a *radius* of a circle, we expect the student to be able to answer questions such as 'Show me a radius' or 'Draw a radius' when confronted with any drawing of a circle; in addition, we expect him to be able to 'pick out a radius' when confronted with drawings of circles containing a number of internal lines, some of which are radii and some not. We do not necessarily expect him to answer the question 'What is a radius' by means of a verbal definition, nor do we necessarily expect him to be able to tell us why a particular line is a radius. The performance for a concept, in other words, is simply one of identifying an object, or distinguishing it from other objects. It is an operation very close to 'stimulus discrimination', except that what is distinguished is a class, rather than a specific object.

An entity such as *work*, however, doesn't have this point-at-able quality. We do not think of asking a student to point to objects or situations in order to tell us which is work and which isn't. We may ask him to define work, to be sure, and this possibility will be discussed in a moment. Mainly, however, the performance that goes along with knowing what *work* is, is one of *demonstrating* that some particular situation involves work. *Demonstrating* involves more than pointing at, or *identifying*. That is why we say we are dealing with a capability that is more complex than is the case with a simple concept. My suggestion has been that this more complex learned capability be called a *principle* (or *rule*). In accordance with this idea, *work* is a *principle*. One would speak of *demonstrating* a principle, whereas one can ask for *identifying* a concept.

The principle of work under discussion here is

$$\text{work} = \text{force} \times \text{distance}.$$

That is, the work done is the product of the force acting on a body and the distance through which the body moves while the force is acting on it. What must the student do to demonstrate this principle? The answer is, he must identify not one, but several concepts and their proper sequence. To get *work*, he must identify a member of the class *force* (a concept), a member of the class *distance* (another concept) and an instance of the class *product* or *multiply* (a third concept). Their sequence must also be identified, in order to obtain the product (this would be more readily evident were division the concept involved rather than multiplication). In other words, the situation is more complex because there is not one concept, but several. Demonstration of a rule involves the simpler performance of identifying each concept and the sequence that relates them. There are many ways of saying this. For example, one could say a *principle is a relationship among two or more concepts*. This is all right, so long as it is understood by being referred back to performances.

Perhaps I need to clarify the meaning of 'demonstrating a principle'. I do not mean to imply by this a single measure of performance such as the question which verbally says to the student 'Demonstrate work in the following situation' and then describes the situation. Instead, it seems to me that there are a number of different questions that might be asked in order to determine whether a student has learned a principle. One might say 'What is the work done in pushing a body of 1,000 grams a horizontal distance of 30 centimetres' or 'Show how to calculate the work done by a force of 50 pounds pushing a trunk along a floor for 10 feet'. Any of these questions may be considered to reflect what is meant by 'demonstrate'.

Returning to the main thread of the argument, the distinction between a concept and a principle, the ideas of Berlyne may have both relevance to and compatibility with the present description. According to Berlyne, there are two types of concepts, or mediators, that occur in chains of thought. One is called situational, because it represents some aspect of a situation, whereas the other is transformational and represents an operation. It may be noted that, in these terms, concepts of *force* and *distance* occurring in the principle of work are situational mediators, whereas *multiply* is obviously a transformational mediator. It is possible to suppose that a principle must include both a situational concept and a transformational concept. I have not followed this line of thinking very far but it is a very appealing notion at first glance. And, of course, it is quite consistent with the idea that a concept is typically a single mediator, whereas a principle is composed of several mediators in a sequence or chain.

It would appear, then, that principles can be distinguished from what have previously been called concepts in two ways. First, the performance required to demonstrate that a concept has been learned is simply an identification, that is, a choice from a number of alternatives; a principle, in contrast, must be demonstrated by means of performances that identify its component concepts and the operation relating them to one another. Second, this means that the inference to be made about mediating processes is different in the two cases. A concept is a single mediator that represents a class of stimuli (or objects), whereas a principle is a sequence of mediators each of which is itself a concept.

Naturally enough, these two kinds of differences imply a third – namely, the difference in conditions required for learning the concept and the principle. To summarize briefly, learning a concept is a matter of presenting a variety of positive instances of the class together with the common response, and contrasting these with negative instances of the class. Thus the concept *three* may be learned by a child who makes the response 'three' to several different sets of objects, let us say, three marbles, three dots and three tables, while he is negatively reinforced for making this response to sets of objects numbering two or four or five.

Learning a rule such as 'three plus two equals five' requires quite a different set of learning conditions. First, it requires that the child already know the concepts contained in this sequence, namely, three, two, plus, equals and five. (Note that I do not speak here of learning the verbal sequence 'three plus two equals five', but the principle of which the verbal statement is merely a representation.) Second, it requires that these concepts be reinstated by him in the proper sequence. There are several ways of accomplishing this latter event, perhaps the simplest being by means of verbal instructions which name the component concepts in the proper sequence. Alternatively, if one is fond of 'discovery learning', the correct sequence may be hinted at or partially prompted, using the technique often referred to as 'guided discovery'. Finally, in order to promote recall, and also to determine whether the principle has truly been learned, the child may be asked to demonstrate that two plus three equals five, in any of the specific ways previously mentioned.

To complete the examples previously mentioned, it is evident that *radius* as a concept is learned under a different set of conditions than is a principle such as *work*. To learn *radius*, the student is presented with a number of different drawings of circles having straight lines within them. Some of these straight lines are radii, while some are not. He learns to point to the correct ones, and it is shown that he can point to a new and different radius that he has not seen before. For the principle of work, the conditions are quite different. First, one must make sure that he does, indeed, know what is meant by 'force', 'distance', 'equals' and 'multiply'. Verbal cueing may then be provided by the statement 'the work done is equal to the distance a body is pushed times the force acting on it'. This is followed by an example, such as 'How much work is done on a block of wood pushed 2 feet by a force of 10 pounds ?', and, perhaps, by one or two more. The determination that the student is able to apply the rule to one or more specific problems constitutes evidence that the rule has been learned. (Whether the student can state the principle in formal terms is a different matter, which may be of some importance for other purposes.)

In summary, a principle (or rule) is composed of two or more concepts having an ordered relationship to each other. A principle has been learned when it can be shown that a problem involving specific concepts can be solved by identifying these concepts correctly and placing them in the correct ordered relationship with each other; in other words, by 'applying the rule'.

CONCEPTS BY DEFINITION

It seems to me to be quite important to maintain as clear as possible a distinction between a concept and a principle, and I have tried to show why. An additional reason is that there is a strong tradition in experimental psychology relating concept to discrimination learning, and there are good theoretical reasons for keeping this relationship clean and unfuzzy. Within such a tradition, the principle becomes a kind of learned capability which goes a step beyond the concept in complexity, and, therefore, in theoretical sophistication.

Unfortunately, I have to face the fact that things are not this simple, and, in fact, in danger of being a little fuzzy. The difficulty arises from the fact that the term *concept* is used by educators, psychologists and others to include something other than just 'classes of concrete objects or object-qualities'. Even if I call *work* a principle, others will insist on calling it a concept. What about an *uncle*? Could this concept possibly have been learned by means of a set of contrasting examples? I am forced to agree that it cannot. Another example is a concept such as *mass*, encountered in physics. One of the main reasons why this concept gives beginning students so much trouble, I venture to guess, is that in contrast to many other concepts in physics (such as force, distance, liquid, gas) it cannot be learned by means of the direct observational method previously described. The concept *weight* can be acquired in this way, and therein lies a difficulty that bothers many physics teachers.

It appears, then, that many concepts must be learned, not by direct observation (contrasting concrete examples), but *by definition*. *Mass* can be learned by means of the definition 'that property of an object which determines how much it will be accelerated by a given amount of force'. *Uncle* can be learned via the definition 'brother of a parent, or husband of a sister of a parent'.

But what is being learned when one undertakes to acquire such concepts by definition? I should like to say that what is being learned is a *principle*, in accordance with what has been described previously. *Mass* is learned when one is able to demonstrate that the principle relating the concepts *force* and *acceleration* depends upon *mass* in an inverse way (the greater the mass, the smaller the acceleration). *Uncle* is learned when one is able to demonstrate specific examples of the relationships involving the concepts brother, parent, and husband sister, parent.

It should be pointed out that some experimental investigations of concepts have dealt with this kind of concept – the *concept by definition*, rather than with the more basic kind, the *concept by observation*. One of the best-known examples occurs in the work of Bruner, Goodnow and Austin. These investigators studied the acquisition of conjunctive concepts (e.g. 'all cards with three red circles'), disjunctive concepts (e.g. 'cards having red figures, *or* circles, *or* three figures') and relational concepts (e.g. 'cards having the *same* number of figures and borders'). It would appear that conjunctive concepts could be learned by contrasting positive and negative instances, since what are being combined are simply stimulus attributes. In other words, these are *concepts by observation*. Disjunctive concepts and relational concepts are quite different, however, since they require the combining of concepts. In other words, learning them requires learning a rule – they are *concepts by definition*. In the study cited, the latter two categories of concept were found to be considerably more difficult to learn than conjunctive concepts, under a particular set of learning conditions.

Another excellent example of the learning of concepts by definition (that is, by rule) is in the work of Shepard, Hovland and Jenkins. These investigators arranged stimulus objects having the dimensions triangle–square, large–small and black–white in various combinations so that some figures had to be sorted into a pile on the right, others into a pile on the left. The complexity of the classification that was to be learned could thus be varied. A Type I classification, the simplest, could be represented by such a rule as 'all circles on the left; triangles on the right', in other words, there were two *object classes*. A more complex rule was required for a Type II classification, such as, 'small triangles and large circles on the left; large triangles and small circles on the right'. Other more complex classifications were employed in addition. The results leave no doubt that there are marked differences in ease of learning of a concept of the simple Type I sort and those which are more complex.

Other examples can be cited of studies investigating the learning of concepts which are rule-like. The key to the difference between the two varieties, concepts by observation and concepts by definition, appears to be, in Berlyne's terms, that the latter require both transformational and situational concepts, whereas the former involve only one of these.

Differences between these two varieties of concepts can probably be established by experiment, as has been suggested. This does not, however, solve the semantic problem that there *are* two types, both called concepts. I confess I do not know how to change people's highly practised language habits, even though I know they should be changed. The best I can do here is to summarize the following conclusions:

(1) There are two types of learned capabilities called concepts.

(2) One is a concept by observation, the simpler type, whose learning conditions require contrasting presentation of positive and negative instances.

(3) The other is a concept by definition, which is in a formal sense the same as a principle. It is a combination of simpler concepts, and is typically learned by human beings via verbal statements that provide the cues to recall of component concepts and to their correct ordering.

RESEARCH QUESTIONS RELATED TO PRINCIPLE LEARNING

If one is clear about this distinction between a concept and a principle, one is in a good position to ask some questions about factors in the learning situation that affect the acquisition of principles.

The prerequisites of principle learning

It is hypothesized that principles are learned when previously learned concepts are combined in some particular order. In order to enter into such a newly ordered relationship, the concepts themselves must be recalled. The student who hears for the first time the statement of the principle 'the cotangent is the reciprocal of the tangent', cannot be expected to learn anything from this statement unless he can, in fact, remember what a reciprocal is and what a tangent is. The problem is, how well or how vividly must these subordinate concepts be recalled, at the time of learning, in order for the learning to be most effective? Is there a difference in rate of learning the principle, depending on how recently the component concepts have been recalled? This question may be related to the suggestion once made by Underwood regarding the importance of *contiguity* of concepts in complex learning. At any rate, the basic approach to investigation seems clear. Variations in the recency of recall would be related to the rapidity of principle learning under standard learning conditions, or alternatively, to the number of principles successfully acquired.

Another characteristic of component concepts that might be systematically varied is their *generalizability*. It is apparent that concepts may be more or less 'narrow' with respect to the class of specific instances they include. Thus, the concept 'number' is much more highly generalizable to a student of tenth-grade mathematics than it is to the student of third-grade mathematics. The specific instances that can be included as members of the class are much greater in the former case. How does this property of concepts affect the learning of principles in which these concepts are involved? The experimental approach suggested is one of deliberately varying the 'breadth' or 'generalizability' of concepts originally learned, and testing the effects of this variation in the subsequent learning of principles.

Individual differences in principle learning

Other kinds of prerequisites for principle learning may be conceived as more enduring characteristics of the individual learner. The *size of the store of concepts* available to the individual probably should be placed in this category. Studies too numerous to mention have demonstrated significant relationships between the size of vocabulary of individuals and their facility at meaningful learning. What is the psychological meaning of such a relationship? The particular hypothesis suggested here is that principle learning using typical printed text presentation of material will be more rapid in those individuals who have a greater store of relevant concepts. Testing such a hypothesis would, of course, require that individual differences in availability of relevant concepts be carefully measured – just any old vocabulary test would not necessarily do the job.

The conception of principle learning described here suggests still other kinds of individual differences that would bear looking into. For example, if the facility of principle learning is affected by the recall of component concepts, then individual differences in such *recall* might show a significant relationship. It has also been pointed out that the method of teaching principles to human beings usually involves verbal statements that provide cues to the desired ordering. Are there differences among individuals with respect to their ability to respond to such cues to sequence, or perhaps to 'hold in mind' such sequences when verbally cued? Still another individual difference pertains to generalizability again. As stated previously, one can think of a deliberate manipulation of the breadth of concepts which make up a principle. The additional possibility, however, is that individuals may vary in the amount of self-generated generalization that occurs when a concept is acquired. If this could be measured with suitable controls, it might turn out to be an important kind of individual variation related to principle learning.

Conditions of principle learning

Some of the conditions relevant to the learning of principles have already been mentioned, namely, those prerequisites that precede the act of learning itself, whether they are conceived as previous learning occasions, or as states within the learner. The remaining set of conditions centres upon the event of combining and ordering the concepts that make up the principle. By far the most common way of bringing this about is with the use of verbal statements, whether printed or oral.

There are some intriguing research problems here, which may be summed up in the question 'What is the most effective way to use words to guide the learning of principles ?' Certain active lines of research can be identified which bear upon this question. First, one thinks of the work on programmed instruction that is more or less specifically oriented to this problem, including work on cueing and prompting, size of step and response requirements. Second, there is the somewhat scattered but nevertheless important research on learning by discovery. Broadly speaking, this area of investigation deals with the amount and kind of cueing provided by words in principle learning. Discovery learning may be said to occur under conditions in which minimal cueing is given, whereas reception learning takes place when words are used to state the principle fully. Various intermediate amounts of cueing represent 'guided discovery'. The question of the effectiveness of different kinds and amount of guidance in discovery continues to be an important one for research.

There is also an interesting research problem, not as yet very well investigated, which may be stated as 'What kind of word or symbol ordering will produce the most effective principle learning ?' Most printed texts use English sentences. Although these are effective for some communication purposes, they are not the only possibilities, as the works of Virginia Woolf and James Joyce demonstrate. In mathematics and some forms of science, English sentences get to be altogether too space-consuming, and possibly also time-consuming for the learner. Over a period of years, the advocates of symbolic logic have recommended this form of symbolic communication as a means of cueing the learning of principles. From the standpoint of research, it is evident that we have as yet too few experimental results on this problem of how words and symbols may be used to guide the learning of principles.

SUMMARY

In its common meaning, the word *concept* refers to a broad class of inferred representational capabilities of the learner. In this sense, we speak of the concepts of biology, for example, as the entire set of knowledge components of an academic subject. This usage contrasts markedly with the meaning of concept as a technical term derived within a context of experimental studies of learning. In the latter sense, concept means an inferred process enabling the learner to identify classes of objects, object–qualities or events, despite variations in the particular stimuli used to form these classes.

Technically speaking, *concepts* are distinguishable from *principles*. The former are inferred as capabilities when the learner is able to identify an object class. The latter, however, require that the individual *demonstrate* one or more particular instances of application of the principle. The more complex performance associated with the principle leads accordingly to an inference of a more complex form of internal processing. A single mediator can be inferred to represent a class such as *radius* or *middle*; but a principle such as 'square the numerator' seems to demand a *sequence* of mediations, each of which is itself a concept. The principle, then, is a capability that makes possible the demonstration of a sequence of behaviour, each element of which may involve a concept.

Many concepts (such as *red*, *circle* or *liquid*) may be learned by methods requiring the observation of differences among stimuli that represent a class and stimuli that do not (negative instances). These have been extensively studied by experimental means; they may be called 'concepts by observation'. Other concepts (such as *mass*, *uncle*, *work*) require conditions of learning which are different from these

observational techniques. These may be called 'concepts by definition', since they are usually learned, in the human being, by means
of a carefully constructed sequence of instruction involving verbal
communication. In other words, learning of these latter concepts is
indistinguishable in a formal sense from learning principles.

Principles are learned under conditions that have two major
requirements: (1) the component concepts of which they are composed must be previously learned and readily recallable; and (2) a
communication, usually verbal, must be made to the learner indicating the correct sequence of these components.

These two conditions of principle learning suggest a number of
research questions which have as yet not received adequate answers.
For example, does the recallability of component concepts affect
principle learning? Does the generalizability of these concepts have
an effect on learning and transfer of principles? What sorts of individual differences may be related to principle learning, such as
differences in the availability and recallability of relevant concepts?
How can the communication of the correct sequence of concepts in
a principle be designed for most effective learning? What does this
have to do with discovery learning, and with 'learning guidance'?

There is much to be done in conducting scientific research on the
learning of principles as well as on the learning of concepts. It seems
evident that the planning and execution of such research will be
helped by the maintenance of as clear as possible a distinction
between principles and concepts, despite the blurring of this distinction produced by common language.

FURTHER READING

R. C. Anderson and D. P. Ausubel, *Readings in the psychology of
cognition*, Holt, Rinehart and Winston, 1965.

M. Annett, 'The classification of instances of four common class
concepts by children and adults', *British Journal of Educational
Psychology*, **29**, 1959, pp. 223–36.

D. E. Berlyne, 'Recent developments in Piaget's work', *British
Journal of Educational Psychology*, **27**, 1957, pp. 1–12.

R. Brown, *Words and things*, The Free Press of Glencoe, 1963.

J. Bruner *et al.*, *A study of thinking*, Wiley, 1956.

J. S. Bruner, 'The course of cognitive growth', *American Psychologist*, **19**, 1964, pp. 1–15.

J. Bruner *et al.*, *Studies in cognitive growth*, Wiley, 1966.

J. B. Carroll, *Language and thought*, Prentice-Hall, 1964.

J. P. de Cecco (Ed.), *The psychology of language thought and instruction*, Holt, Rinehart and Winston, 1967.

M. Donaldson and G. Balfour, 'Less is more: a study of language comprehension', *British Journal of Psychology*, **59** (4), 1968, pp. 461–71.

J. H. Flavell, *The developmental psychology of Jean Piaget*, Van Nostrand, 1963.

R. M. Gagné, 'Contributions of learning to human development', *Psychological Review*, **75** (3), 1968, pp. 177–91.

H. F. Harlow and M. K. Harlow, 'Learning to think', *Scientific American*, August 1949. Offprint no. 415.

P. Herriot, 'The experimental psychology of grammar and its relevance to children's language learning' in E. A. Lunzer and J. F. Morris (Eds.), *Development in human learning*, Staples, 1968, pp. 175–86.

J. McV. Hunt, *Intelligence and experience*, New York, Ronald Press, 1961.

B. Inhelder and J. Piaget, *The growth of logical thinking*, London, Routledge, 1958.

D. M. Johnson and C. A. O'Reilly, 'Concept attainment in children: classifying and defining', *Journal of Educational Psychology*, **55** (2), 1964, pp. 71–4.

H. J. Klausmeier and C. W. Harris, *Analyses of concept learning*, Academic Press, 1967.

M. M. Lewis, *Language thought and personality in infancy and childhood*, Harrap, 1963.

M. M. Lewis, 'Language and mental development' in E. A. Lunzer and J. F. Morris (Eds.), *Development in human learning*, Staples, 1968, pp. 144–69.

E. A. Lunzer, *The regulation of behaviour*, Staples, 1968.

E. A. Lunzer, 'Formal reasoning' in E. A. Lunzer and J. F. Morris (Eds.), *Development in human learning*, Staples, 1968, pp. 266–300.

A. R. Luria, *The role of speech in the regulation of normal and abnormal behaviour*, Pergamon, 1961.

G. A. Miller, 'The magical number seven, plus or minus two: some limits on our capacity for processing information', *Psychological Review*, **63**, 1956, pp. 81–97.

G. A. Miller, E. Galanter and K. H. Pribram, *Plans and the structure of behaviour*, Holt, 1960.

N. O'Connor, *Present day Russian psychology*, Pergamon, 1966.

E. A. Peel, 'Conceptual learning and explainer thinking' in E. A. Lunzer and J. F. Morris (Eds.), *Development in human learning*, Staples, 1968, pp. 304–25.

J. Piaget and B. Inhelder, *The early growth of logic in the child*, Routledge and Kegan Paul, 1964.

E. Stones and J. Heslop, 'The formation and extension of class concepts in primary school children', *British Journal of Educational Psychology*, **38** (3), 1968, pp. 261–71.

L. S. Vigotsky, *Thought and language*, M.I.T. Press, 1962.

Learning theory and teaching practice

Writing in 1899 in his book *Talks to Teachers* William James, a pioneer American psychologist, said: 'Psychology is a science and teaching is an art; and sciences never generate arts directly out of themselves.'

The fact that James himself made major contributions in the two fields did not prevent him from regarding them as two distinct disciplines. Until quite recently this distinction characterized research on learning. The result of this division was that the more scientific and prestigious research was conducted by psychologists in laboratory studies of animal learning or rote human learning only tenuously connected if at all with problems of classroom learning, while little research of a scientific nature was devoted to the study of human learning in the schools.

To some extent psychological research in the U.S.S.R. avoided this dichotomy and some of the leading Soviet psychologists have been closely interested in problems of pedagogy. Currently, however, educational psychologists in many countries are turning their attention to problems of classroom learning.

Some educationists, in reaction to earlier prescriptive pronouncements by 'method' experts on the principles of teaching, focus their attention exclusively on the learning of the child in the classroom.

Others are arguing for the need to develop a systematic body of knowledge on what might be called the psychology of teaching.

The papers in this section have been selected because they deal with general problems of the psychology of learning and teaching. The paper by Hilgard gives a broad perspective of research into learning and teaching. He considers that the dichotomy between experimental studies of learning and classroom practice needs to be broken down and he suggests approaches to this problem. Gage and Bruner consider that the study of the general methodology of teaching should be a central concern to educational psychologists. Kalmykova, taking a similar approach, outlines specific methods of conducting research into teaching and school learning.

Gal'perin outlines his approach to the teaching of mental skills in stages, which he has developed over a number of years of experimentation into problems of instruction. Talyzina also discusses Gal'perin's 'stages' but lays particular emphasis on the crucial importance of intervention by the teacher in the child's learning. Kersh and Wittrock review the literature in the field of discovery learning, an approach to classroom practice very different from that proposed by Talyzina. Carroll and Bogoiavlensky and Menchinskaia discuss general problems and approaches to the crucial aspect of classroom learning, the learning of concepts. Ausubel takes up two problems of overriding importance for classroom learning, the question of rote and meaningful learning, and the question of discovery and reception learning.

In the final paper, the authors discuss a method of investigating classroom events which gives interesting insights into a teacher's classroom behaviour and can give objective feedback to student teachers of their classroom performance.

Although most of the papers deal with key aspects of learning and teaching in broad perspective, they draw upon a considerable body of empirical research and are thus more than speculative. They provide a useful framework within which to consider more specific problems of learning and teaching.

1   A perspective on the relationship between learning theory and educational practices*

E. R. HILGARD

This paper can be regarded as a key-note article to this section. The author provides a clearly stated point of view on what should be the relationship between the findings from research into learning, and educational practice. The model which he provides should stimulate thinking by research workers and by practising teachers. The former might seek to discover the key areas in which work is needed at Hilgard's 'applied research' stages: the latter might question the extent to which his current practice is based on research findings. Other papers in this chapter provide pointers which should help to clarify both these issues.

STEPS ON THE ROAD FROM PURE-SCIENCE RESEARCH TO ESTABLISHED EDUCATIONAL PRACTICES

In order to avoid the sharp distinction between pure and applied research, I find it convenient to break up the stages from the 'purest' of research on learning to the most 'applied' research (that concerned with the adoption of an approved practice) into six steps according to their relevance to the educational enterprise. Three of these are placed within the 'pure-science' end of the continuum, three of them in the 'educational technology' end, as shown in Fig. 1. The steps are abstracted from what is, in fact, a continuum; any one investigator may work at once upon several of the steps, or in the areas in which the steps shade into each other. The roles become increasingly diverse as the steps become farther apart. While the diagram is self-explanatory, its two halves call for some added comments.

Pure-science research on learning

By pure-science research is meant that which is guided by the problems which the investigator sets himself, without regard for the im-

* Reprinted and abridged from E. R. Hilgard (Ed.), *Theories of Learning and Instruction*, National Society for the Study of Education, Chicago, 1964, pp. 405–15.

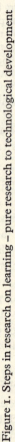

PURE RESEARCH

Not Directly Relevant	**Relevant Subjects and/or Topics**
Step 1	*Step 2*
Animal Mazes, Eyelid Conditioning, Pursuit Learning, etc.	Human Verbal Learning, Concept Formation, etc

TECHNOLOGICAL RESEARCH AND DEVELOPMENT

School-relevant Subjects and Topics	**Laboratory, Classroom, and Special Teacher**	**Tryout in 'Normal' Classroom**	**Advocacy and Adoption**
Step 3	*Step 4*	*Step 5*	*Step 6*
Mathematics Reading, Typing, etc.	Programmed Instruction; Language Laboratory, in Early Stages	Results of Step 4 Tried in Regular Setting	Manuals and Textbooks Prepared; Teacher Training Undertaken

Figure 1. Steps in research to technological development

mediate applicability of the results to practical situations. This does not mean that the investigator has no practical interests, or that he does not want his results used; it is only that he is patient and uses the methods and procedures appropriate to the topic on which he works. Within learning research we may divide the stages of relevance to learning into the following three, expanding somewhat the left three boxes of Fig. 1.

Pure-science research in learning

Step 1. Research on learning with no regard for its educational relevance, e.g. animal studies, physiological, biochemical investigations. Learning in the flatworm and learning in the rat with transected spinal cord classify here.

Step 2. Research on learning which is not concerned with educational practices but which is more relevant than that of Step 1 because it deals with human subjects and with content that is nearer to that taught in school, e.g. nonsense syllable memorization and retention. The principles being tested are likely to be theoretical ones, such as the relative importance of proactive and retroactive inhibition.

Step 3. Research on learning that is relevant because the subjects are school-age children and the material learned is school subject matter or skill, though no attention is paid to the problem of adapting the learning to school practices, e.g. foreign language vocabulary learned by paired-associate method with various lengths of list and with various spacing of trials.

These three steps of relevance all classify as pure-science research because the problems are set by the investigators in relation to some theoretical issues and do not arise out of the practical needs of instruction. Of course there may be bridges from any pure-science project to a practical one: perhaps drugs discovered in brain studies of rats may aid remedial reading, studies of interference may suggest intervals between classes or what should be studied concomitantly and language-vocabulary results in a pure context may guide language acquisition in schools. The main point is that the scientist has not committed himself to relevance. He may even disavow it, in line with a cult of pure science that seems to have been developing. According to this view, something is valuable precisely because it is remote from application; so long as it is precise, it does not matter how trivial it is. This is a faulty conception of pure science, and for the investigator to escape responsibility for the relevance of his work by falling back upon this 'pure science' is as likely to be a sign of weakness as of strength.

A further word on Step 3 is in order. The best work will be done at this stage by combining the skills of the subject-matter specialist with those of the experimenter upon learning. I have in mind combining the work of linguist and psychologist, as in the use of Hockett's linguistic analysis by Gibson, Gibson, Danielson and Osser,[1] and in the combination of experts in mathematical learning theory and linguists in the work of Suppes, Crothers, Weir and Trager.[2]

A brief characterization of the report by Suppes and others will be useful in showing some of the characteristics of Step 3 investigations. The authors consist of a logician sophisticated with respect to mathematical models, a psychologist whose work lies particularly in the field of mathematical learning and two linguists. The studies, which concern the teaching of the Russian language, used actual language students, working in the familiar setting of the language laboratory in one of the local junior high schools. The material to be studied was prepared with the aid of a linguist familiar with the structure of the Russian language, so that certain conjectures about linguistics could be studied at the same time that learning theory was being investigated. The discriminations called for were real ones – Russian words being spoken into the tape by someone fluent in Russian. Contrast this with the usual preparation of a list to be memorized in the laboratory! Without going into detail, let me indicate the kinds of things that come from such a study.

1. Linguists have offered some conjectures about which combinations of phonemes can be most easily identified and how easily allophones can be recognized. (An allophone is a phoneme that is acoustically a variant: the phoneme that is represented by the letter p in English is not equally explosive in s$p$eech, $p$each and to$p$most.

---

[1] Eleanor J. Gibson, J. J. Gibson, A. Danielson and H. Osser, 'A Developmental Study of the Discrimination of Letter-like Forms', *Journal of Comparative and Physiological Psychology*, LV (December 1962), pp. 897–906.

[2] Patrick Suppes, E. Crothers, Ruth Weir and Edith Trager, *Some Quantitative Studies of Russian Consonant Phoneme Discrimination*. Stanford, California: Stanford University, Institute for Mathematical Studies in the Social Sciences, Technical Report No. 49, 14 September 1962.

Hence these three p's are allophones.) The investigation gave evidence that most of the conjectures of the linguist were indeed correct. A native speaker has no trouble in hearing two allophones as the 'same' phoneme, but the student hearing a foreign language has a great deal of trouble, and in constructing a good program these details are important.

2. The effort to work up by small steps from the easier combinations to the more difficult ones, which seemed plausible enough from the theory of programming, turned out not to be advantageous. The students who received random presentations from the start did somewhat better than those who had the orderly progression from easy to difficult.

3. The mathematical model that proved to fit these data best was a two-stage model, as though learning took place in two jumps from no learning through an intermediate stage to mastery. What this means in terms of the underlying processes is not yet clear, it may mean that first comes a stage of discriminating the stimuli and responses, and then a stage of connecting them.

My reason for placing this investigation at Step 3 is that it is essentially a pure-science project, concerned with phoneme–allophone discrimination on the one hand, and mathematical models of learning on the other. Its relevance to classroom learning comes about because of its choice of subjects, laboratory conditions and subject-matter. It is close to the technology of instruction but is not yet designed to indicate just how Russian should be taught. The order of presentation (increasing difficulty v. random difficulty) is the most technologically relevant of the suggestions coming from the study, but this has to do with only a small aspect of learning Russian and requires more substantiation before it can be generalized. At the same time it is fairly obvious that experimentation closely related to the instructional task is likely to bear educational fruit more quickly than experiments classifiable with Steps 1 and 2.

Applied or technological research and development

We are ready to consider what happens on the right-hand side of Fig. 1, in the steps having to do with applied- rather than pure-science research. The steps may be described as follows:

Technological research and development

Step 4. Research conducted in special laboratory classrooms, with selected teachers, e.g. bringing a few students into a room to see whether or not instruction in set theory or symbolic logic is feasible, granted a highly skilled teacher.

Step 5. A tryout of the results of prior research in a 'normal' classroom with a typical teacher. Whatever is found feasible in Step 4 has to be tried out in the more typical classroom, which has limited time for the new method, and may lack the special motivation on the part of either teacher or pupil.

Step 6. Developmental steps related to advocacy and adoption. Anything found to work in Steps 4 and 5 has to be 'packaged' for wider use, and then go through the processes by which new methods or procedures are adopted by those not party to the experimentation.

It is evident that the mood has changed in the transition from pure-science research to technological research, although the distinction between Steps 3 and 4 may be slight under some circumstances, as indeed in the experiment by Suppes and others used in illustration of Step 3.

If one were to review the relationship between experimentation on learning by psychologists in its relation to education over the past several decades, it would be fair to say that too much of the research has rested at Steps 1 and 2 to be educationally relevant; educational psychologists, too, have tended to work at this end of the spectrum and then to jump, by inference, to Step 6, without being sufficiently patient about Steps 4 and 5. In this respect the introduction of programmed learning has been helpful, because of the serious concern both with the structure of subject-matter and with the individual learner for whom the program is designed.

It is fruitful to compare educational measurement with the psychology of learning according to the steps of Fig. 1. Educational measurements have been improved through the 'pure-science' researches in statistics, theory of scaling, factor analysis and so on; at the same time, the arranging of materials and the development of norms have been very careful, so that the better intelligence and achievement tests are well prepared and well accepted. Until the advent of the teaching machine there was little such processing of teaching materials, except for some rather spurious use of word counts in editing spellers and readers. A psychological speculation was for many years permitted to guide practice in the production of teaching materials, without the serious tryouts that would have been given to educational measurement materials. One consequence is that the prestige of educators who worked in the area of measurements was of high order among their psychological colleagues, while this has not been as true of those working in the field of learning. There are signs that this is now changing; what the steps of Fig. 1 say, among other things, is that there are important tasks to be done all along the way. Many indicators point to a much healthier situation today than a few years ago in that the attention of scholars is being attracted to all steps along the way from pure science to technological application.

A SET OF STRATEGIES FOR INTEGRATING THE PSYCHOLOGY OF LEARNING WITH THE TECHNOLOGY OF INSTRUCTION

Dividing the spectrum of pure and applied research into the six steps, three 'pure' and three 'technological', is descriptive of a problem, but it does not prescribe a program, except to invite good work all along the line. I wish to consider the same set of problems from a slightly different vantage point: the strategies that are involved with the aim of emerging with a scientifically based technology of instruction.

Strategy of discovery and invention

Discovery is the task of pure science, and the scientist in his laboratory must be free to perform this task in his own way. From the point of view of education, we need to make the approach in the spirit of pure science but need to direct it to relevant contents. There is no reason why we should not seek to have more experimentation on school children in the learning of subject-matters or necessary skills or the kinds of problem-solving that are likely to go on in school.

While assigning *discovery* to the pure-science end of our continuum of relevance, we must not overlook *invention*, which is by no means limited to scientists. Some promising advances in education have come about as the inventions of skilled teachers, and a technology of instruction needs to examine and conserve the values of these inventions. I think, for example, of the augmented Roman alphabet being tried out in England in order to gain the advantages of a purely phonetic reading and writing in English. This seems to be meeting with great success; I should call it an invention rather than a discovery. One might say the same of O. K. Moore's use of an electric typewriter with beginners in reading and writing. Pure scientists are inventive in the realm of ideas but not always in the realm of technologies. As one of my colleagues is fond of pointing out, an Einstein does not take out patents; an Edison does. We need both kinds, and this is an added reason why the psychologist whose work is to be relevant to education needs to be close to educators and teachers.

Strategy of development of methods, materials and procedures

At another level of science, this time applied science, we need those who will be concerned with the utilization of the discoveries and tested inventions from the investigations that have been described. This is not a matter of taking some principle and applying it in cookbook fashion to the subject-matter of schools. We have had too much of this in the past. For example, when Thorndike emphasized the significance of word counts as giving order to what is taught in reading, the very plausible notion that the more frequent words should be taught first became a fetish in the construction of some elementary-school readers. This was a scientific aid to textbook construction, to be sure, but the further steps in development were not taken. Whenever they *were* taken it was found that, in context, pupils could learn words that were considered too difficult on the basis of the frequencies from word counts. Now there is a kind of revolt against the artificiality that has crept into the substance of much of our reading material, and an effort is being made to revitalize it.

As soon as the more practical step is taken seriously, it becomes obvious that the psychologist cannot work alone. There is a structure to knowledge, so that later steps depend in part upon earlier ones. There are discriminations to be made. Theories gain their support from selected facts of a particular kind, so that what kinds of facts are taught may establish the readiness for theoretical interpretations. Much of this lies outside the psychology of learning and in the realm of the subject-matter – the mathematician, the physicist, the biologist and sociologist, the historian, the artist, the musician, the linguist. The serious interest being taken in the schools today by the scholars within the various disciplines is encouraging, but they can no more go it alone than the psychologists can go it alone. The emphasis upon the intellectual in education is fine, but it can easily produce, in new form, the old misunderstandings that gave rise to exaggerated theories of formal discipline. The subject-matter specialist is likely to think that his material is fundamentally so interesting that as long as it is arranged logically, and is comprehensible, the psychological problems will take care of themselves. This is no more true today than it ever was. This subject-matter expert has an essential role, but his collaboration with the learning expert is equally essential.

As long as the experimenter upon learning used artificial tasks, such as mirror-drawing, finger-mazes, pursuit rotors and lists on memory drums, he could suit his own convenience; once he decides to program symbolic logic or the Russian language or the appreciation of poetry, he has additional constraints upon him. He finds it necessary to collaborate not only with subject-matter experts but to make use of the experience of skilled teachers. One of the first lessons of program development is this: A good program is not developed out of the mechanics of program construction or out of familiarity with the psychology of learning; it is not developed out of subject-matter expertness, nor through the sheer artistry of an able teacher; it requires the collaborative effort contributed by the various expertnesses. Once a reasonably promising program is developed, it has to be tried out in a classroom, perhaps a laboratory-type classroom, but with real school children taught by a real teacher. Then, before the development is completed, it has to be tried out in a regular classroom, where other obligations also exist. A teacher has many responsibilities, and children have diverse interests; whatever is new has to be fitted in somehow within an existing set of classroom procedures. These steps are all rather foreign to the typical experimental student of learning, but they are essential if the educational program is to be sound. I would argue for a division of labour and prestige, so that those who take on the developmental task are recognized and honoured for the ingenuity they display, which must be at least equal to that of the pure scientist.

Strategy of innovation

In something as complex as a school system, we need another level of research strategy, which I shall call *the strategy of innovation*. The best of equipment may lie idle, the best of resources remain unused, the best techniques sabotaged, if there is not care in introducing the new methods or new materials to all concerned. Once the pure-science principles have been established and the applications validated in practice schoolrooms, the more widespread adoption is by no means guaranteed or, if the adoption is forced there is no assurance that the desired results will be forthcoming. Abstractly, the steps of innovation are clear enough: Provide (a) a sound research-based program, validated in tryout, (b) the program packaged in such a way as to be available, as in good textbooks, supplementary readings in the form of pamphlets, films, programs for teaching machines and guides for the teacher, (c) testing materials by which it can be ascertained if the objectives of the program have indeed been realized, with appropriate normative data on these evaluative instruments, (d) in-service training of the teacher to overcome the teacher's resistance to something new and to gain his enthusiastic acceptance of the program as something valuable as well as to train him in its use and (e) support for the program from the community, school boards, parents and others concerned with the schools.

It is my feeling that we have not done very well in appraising carefully our strategies of innovation. We have sometimes gone overboard for the novel and untried, just to keep up with the Joneses ('we have teaching machines, too'); at other times we have been very resistant. Commercialism and vested interests enter in unpleasant ways, sometimes supported, unfortunately, by fractions of the educational profession itself. Here, then, is a task calling for wisdom and sensitivity. The psychological contributions may come more from social psychology than from the psychology of learning, because the processes are those of social control and attitude change; but unless there is serious concern about the appropriate ways in which to bring innovation about, schools are likely to be the victims of whims, rather than the heirs of the best tradition we can establish through co-operative effort.

There are some specific suggestions that might be given considera-tion. It would be desirable, for example, for every school system, of whatever size, to have somewhere within it a school building, or at least a set of schoolrooms, devoted to in-service training of teachers and to innovation; these are on-going matters important at the com-munity level and cannot be left to teacher-training colleges or univer-sities. Both children and teachers could be rotated through these rooms in order to try out innovations before there is firm commit-ment to them. Thus, a few teaching machines or closed-circuit television projectors could be tried out without investing in them for a whole school system; teachers could have a voice in saying whether or not they wanted the new devices, or in selecting among various possibilities. Usually no harm would be done in waiting for a while if teachers were not ready, for methods imposed on teachers are un-likely to prove successful. Some of the innovations to be tried out might be those of successful local teachers themselves, here given the opportunity to show their colleagues how they do it in their own classrooms. Members of the school board and representatives of the parents could be brought in also to see things being tried out. The principles of tryout before acceptance, of choice by those who are to use the method, seem to me sound ones. If the new methods are indeed good, they will find acceptance.

The remarks that I have made reduce to this: In order to build a sound bridge from the experimental studies of learning to the class-room, we need a series of steps, for applied science consists of more than applying principles to practice. The main points are that in the research and development phases a collaboration is called for between psychologist, subject-matter specialist and teacher; beyond this, care-ful consideration has to be given to techniques of innovation. If we achieve success in integrating these phases, we will move towards that improvement of education which will be satisfying to us all.

2   Psychological conceptions of teaching*

N. L. GAGE

This paper considers the possibilities opening up for research and development in teaching as a result of the new realization of their importance and the increased provision of research workers and materials in education. Gage argues that, equally as important as new research tools, is the nature of our conception of teaching and the realization of its importance as a subject for study. He takes up the question raised earlier of the relationship between learning and teaching and proposes a way of looking at the problem which is likely to be more fruitful than laying exclusive or even dominant stress on either.

THE NEED FOR NEW CONCEPTIONS OF TEACHING

In this paper I wish to talk about the conceptions of teaching that will inevitably lie close to the heart of all research and development in education. These conceptions will determine what gets done just as much as will the men, the buildings, the computers, the research designs and the methods of development and dissemination. Our conceptions of teaching will give direction to our choices of the kinds of variables that we study, measure and manipulate.

For the behaviour of teachers is one of the major avenues through which a society can influence what its children learn. Apart from the curriculum materials, the physical facilities and the administration of the schools, it is through teachers that a society implements its interest in having students learn certain things.

Concern with teaching in educational psychology

Although this kind of stress on teaching may seem banal to anyone outside educational psychology, within that field it has not been adequately honoured. The educational psychologist has not been

* Reprinted and abridged from N. L. Gage, 'Psychological Conceptions Teaching', *International Journal of Educational Science*, 1, 1967, pp. 151–61.

giving prospective teachers enough of the kind of training they need. Most of the first course in educational psychology is concerned primarily with the characteristics of learning and the learner, with the learner's adjustment, with the learner's growth and development and with measurement and evaluation of the learner. It is not sufficiently focused on methods of teaching or how teachers should behave. And yet, since it is largely through the process of teaching that our theories and principles of learning can be put to use, it is conceptions, theories and methods of teaching that educational psychologists should develop. Then the educational psychology course could help more with the problems of teaching.

This is not to say that a prior concern with learning is misplaced. It is to say that we should not stop with learning, but go on from there to develop what such knowledge means for how teachers should behave. The course in educational psychology ought, in its essentials, to be a course in the general methodology of teaching, general in the sense of transcending the special requirements of any given subject-matter or grade-level. This general methodology would then serve as the basis for deriving the special methods of teaching that would apply to any particular grade-level or subject-matter.

Can teaching be autonomous?

Let us now consider briefly a somewhat more extreme position than the one I am advocating. This is the position that teaching should be regarded as an autonomous, self-determined process coordinate with learning. This point of view would erect the study of teaching as a discipline in its own right, independent of the study of learning, just as learning can be studied independently of teaching. In this view, the teaching process would be regarded as the given, and the learning process would become something to be adapted to the teaching process. Thus, we would formulate the theory of teaching – of how teaching does go on – and then we would determine what such theory means for the learning process, for how learning should go on. In short, we would describe what teachers do and then see if we can derive from that description a formulation of what the learner should do.

The trouble with this idea – the idea of making teaching the autonomous process with learning the adaptive one – is that our schools, after all, have learning as their objective, with teaching only a means to that end. We cannot let teaching go on in whatever way seems to be convenient or necessary and then require learners to adapt to the kind of teaching they are provided with. Instead, if teaching procedures and learning procedures are not well suited to each other, then it is teaching that will have to change so that it brings about the kind of learning that the school is intended to produce.

Interdependence of teaching and learning

But even as we reject this notion of making teaching an autonomous discipline, we must perceive that, if teaching is not to have hegemony, neither must learning. The two processes must indeed be adapted to one another so as to make whatever combination of procedures pays off best. We need not consider learning to be an immutable, fixed, given process to which teaching must be adapted. Instead we should conceive of a teaching–learning process, both of whose parts can be changed to make learning more effective.

So we come to the position that any valid conception of teaching must be integrally related to a conception of learning. How human beings learn should provide much of the basis for our derivations of how teachers should teach. In the past, treatments of human learning have not often been followed through to the point of making such derivations. The analysis of the learning process has too often been the end of the matter, and not enough effort has been made to spell out what the learning process implies for the method of teaching. It is such implications for teaching that may be derived from various conceptions of learning that I now wish to consider.

TYPES OF LEARNING TASK AND PROCESS

One basic proposition that I want to offer at the outset is that learning does not go on in the same way for all behaviours learned. Some things are learned by one process, and some by another. Some fallacies die hard, and the notion of a single general theory of learning to account for all the kinds of learning that human beings can manifest seems to have more viability than most. We can still hear today the contiguity theorists, the reinforcement theorists, the identification theorists and the cognitive theorists claim that each of them has the formulation that is adequate to account for all the learning that takes place, in all species, and certainly in the human species.

But the idea has certainly had its critics. In 1942, Lewin asked, 'Have we any right to classify the learning to high-jump, to get along without alcohol, and to be friendly with other people under the same term, and to expect identical laws to hold for any of these processes ?' Lewin distinguished at least four types of changes within what is called learning: changes in cognitive structure; motivation; group belongingness or ideology; voluntary control of the body musculature. In 1949, Tolman suggested that 'our familiar theoretical disputes about learning may *perhaps* . . . be resolved, if we can agree that there are really a number of different kinds of learning. . . . The theory and laws appropriate to one kind may well be different from those appropriate to other kinds.' Tolman tentatively offered six types of learning, which he called cathexes, equivalence beliefs, field expectancies, field-cognition modes, drive discriminations and motor patterns; for each of these he saw the possibility of a different theory of learning.

In the volume edited by Arthur Melton we find six categories that were 'chosen because they seem to represent the categories most commonly employed by investigators in thinking about and doing research on human learning, and have become for this reason part of the tradition of descriptive language of the science of human learning'. The categories were conditioning; rote learning; probability learning; skill learning; concept learning and problem solving. But even these were regarded by Melton as having little usefulness in the scientific analysis of learning; he regarded as more useful the rather large and steadily increasing set of 'subcategories of these primitive major categories' whose dissimilarities in terms of process and phenomena were 'much more striking than the similarities'.

A further attempt at the delineation of types of learning was offered in 1965 by Gagné; he proposed eight kinds in the following order of increasing complexity: signal learning, stimulus-response learning, chaining, verbal-association learning, multiple discrimination learning, concept learning, principle learning and problem solving.

The basic distinction between one of these forms of learning and another, according to Gagné, lies in its prerequisites, or what the individual must previously have learned. He considers each of his types of learning to depend on certain outcomes from types earlier in his hierarchy.

Thus far, I have urged that teaching be made a central concern in educational psychology, that teaching and learning processes are interdependent and that a pluralistic view of the learning process must be adopted. Now I should like to offer a general conception of teaching, to examine some special conceptions of teaching that follow from the general one, and to consider some of the implications of such conceptions of teaching for research and practice.

TEACHING AS THE EXERTION OF PSYCHOLOGICAL FORCE

First, I propose that we conceive of teaching in general as the exertion of psychological force. Everyone agrees that learning should be defined as a change in capabilities or ways of behaving that may be attributed to experience. The experience must, however, be psychological in character rather than physiological or mechanical. That is, we rule out changes in behaviour due to drugs, fatigue, disease or sensory adaptation, and we also rule out the effects of being mechanically pushed or pulled by something. Psychological experience is hard to define, but surely it includes the effects of stimuli that get into us via sensation and perception and act upon the central nervous system in some way. Without going into these matters, let us merely characterize learning as a fairly stable change in behaviour due to psychological rather than other kinds of forces.

Three kinds of teaching force

How these forces operate to produce learning is one problem to which theories of learning are offered as solutions. Theories of learning, or families of such theories, fall into three broad categories: conditioning theories; imitation theories; cognitive theories. Let us accept these conceptions of the learning process as having some value for the organization of our ideas about learning. When we do so, it becomes possible to regard conceptions of teaching as dealing with the kinds of force that bring about learning. Hence, these are the kinds of force that teachers can exert. Thus, we can speak of teaching by conditioning the learner; teaching by modelling imitation on the part of the learner; and teaching by changing the cognitive structure of the learner.

Conditioning force

Teaching by conditioning consists in arranging stimuli so as to bring forth desired responses and then providing a reinforcement as quickly as possible. For example, we want a child to volunteer more often in class, and when he finally does make the desired response, we call on him and praise him as quickly as possible, so that this desired response will be more likely to occur the next time he is in this situation. For certain kinds of behaviour, the idea of teaching by exertion of conditioning force makes eminently good sense. Just what kinds of behaviour these are, is not yet altogether clear, but it may well be that affectively-toned behaviours, much involved with fears and hopes, and not much bound up with any logic, lend themselves well to being viewed as behaviours to be taught by conditioning.

Modelling force

Teaching by modelling consists in the teacher's behaving in ways that he wants the learner to acquire through imitation. As Bandura and Walters have formulated it, such exposure to a model can have three kinds of effects:

1. A modelling effect, whereby the learner acquires new kinds of response patterns.

2. An inhibitory or disinhibitory effect, whereby the learner decreases or increases the frequency, latency or intensity of previously acquired responses.

3. An eliciting effect, whereby the learner receives from the model merely a cue for releasing a response that is neither new nor inhibited.

The modelling effect occurs when a teacher shows a pupil how to hold a pencil or write a capital 'Q', and thus indicates a new behaviour. The inhibiting or disinhibiting effect occurs when he lets the pupil know, through modelling, that it is or is not permissible to look at pictures of nudes in an art book, and thus inhibits or disinhibits an old response. The eliciting effect occurs when, through modelling, he teaches a pupil to rise when a lady enters the room and thus provides a cue eliciting a response neither new nor inhibited.

It should be noted that I have chosen, as my examples of things learned by imitation, behaviours that have no intrinsic logic or rationale. The situations or stimuli calling forth these behaviours have no structure that makes one kind of response more logical or 'true' than another. Learning through imitation seems to be especially appropriate for tasks that have little cognitive structure.

Cognitive force

Teaching by changing cognitive structure consists in arranging for the student to understand facts, concepts and principles in such relationships that the desired kinds of learning will result. If we want a student to understand a strange phenomenon, we can force him to understand it by showing him how it is merely an instance of a general principle. We can force someone to understand why mercury rises in a thermometer when the temperature goes up, by referring to the more general principle that heat causes metals to expand. We can compel someone to understand why water doesn't fall out of a can when we swing the can around vertically, by showing that this phenomenon is an instance of centrifugal force. In doing so, we can exert perceptual and cognitive forces such as those of figure and ground; similarity and contrast; grouping; emphasis; analogy; context; logic. Properly used, these forces will make the student see the cues to a concept, a principle or the solution to a problem. These forces operate to bring about the change in cognitive structure that many kinds of learning consist in.

The distinguishing mark of learnings that can be produced by the use of cognitive forces is that they possess a cognitive structure. The tighter the logical or perceptual ties that hold a body of ideas or behaviours together, the better we can teach in this way. It makes little sense to employ conditioning or modelling forces to teach the multiplication table, for example, when the cognitive forces in those tables are so strong.

An ambiguous case: teaching forces in fostering creativity

Sometimes it is not easy to distinguish the kinds of forces that ought to be employed to bring about a given kind of learning. My examples have thus far been as pure as I could make them, in order to show as convincingly as possible the ways in which different kinds of teaching force make better sense for different kinds of things to be learned.

But what about such an outcome as creativity? This is a relatively new concern in education, and conceptions of what it consists in are understandably not as well formulated as those that call for convergent thinking. Perhaps this is why it is possible to find the teaching of creativity characterized by one writer as a matter of conditioning, by another as modelling and by a third as cognitive restructuring. One of my students, Rosemary Allen, recently furnished me with the following quotations from various writings on methods of training for originality or creativity:

First, a believer in modelling theory speaks as follows:

'It is, of course, necessary that the teacher himself be original, flexible and enthusiastic and that, in his teaching, he emphasize experimentation and discovery rather than routine.'

Another writer takes a similar position:

'If the students perceived the instructor as a model worthy of identification or imitation, a superordinated person . . . who held creative behavior as an important value – it could be learned, creative behavior was good – then they, too, could relax and become confident participants in the creative process. . . .'

Another writer, however, seems to be invoking conditioning theory:

'Creativity . . . is a way of life that involves constant error; hence it is interesting to study how a human being learns error as a way of life. Since reward is, even in human beings, a fundamental way of establishing learning, a reasonable hypothesis is that anyone who follows error as a way of life, must have had his errors reinforced by rewards, until error *as a response* was firmly established, while at the same time his correct responses were few in number or not as strongly reinforced as the incorrect.'

Finally, a cognitive theorist writes as follows:

'When we think creatively, we shake ourselves loose from our old assumptions, we see old instruments as capable of new functions – the rigid structure of the field has been broken down so as to permit new configurations. From this point of view, it is obvious that wherever restructuring takes place there is the possibility of creative thinking.'

My student concluded from these statements that 'all three of the theories of teaching could be utilized in the training of creative individuals'. I am inclined to agree, except that I should add that each of the different theories, or kinds of teaching force, seems to apply better to a different aspect of the teaching task. That is, the teacher's over-all role is a complex one and has many facets. Some aspects of the teacher's role can be understood best in terms of one kind of teaching force, and some in terms of another.

THE CONCEPT OF TEACHING FORCE AND TEACHER CHARACTERISTICS

The view that teaching is the exertion of a force clarifies these aspects as it throws light on some of the variables that have impressed research workers with their validity as characteristics of effective teachers. To make clear how this kind of clarification may be gained, I should like to deal with two characteristics of teachers: warmth and cognitive validity. Each of these is, of course, merely a label for something quite complex. For each of these characteristics, I shall first give an operational definition, then an example of the evidence that it is desirable, and finally a rationale as to how the characteristic follows from one or another of the conceptions of teaching.

Warmth

Warmth refers to the degree to which the teacher tends to be approving; to provide emotional support; to express sympathetic attitudes; to accept pupils' feelings; and so on. It has been studied more, perhaps, than any other characteristic of teachers. It can be measured with the Categories for Interaction Analysis developed by Flanders;

with the Minnesota Teacher Attitude Inventory; with the California F Scale; and parts of the Teacher Characteristic Schedule developed by Ryans.

Quite consistently, measures of warmth correlate positively with the evaluations of teachers by pupils, principals and observers. At the elementary school level especially, warmth seems to be important to many pupils, and it correlates with how well pupils like their teacher. Sometimes teacher-warmth is related to pupil-productivity; to achievement in subjects like mathematics and social studies; or to creativity.

Warmth may be understood in relation to conditioning theory as the teachers' over-all tendency to emit positive reinforcements. Hence, pupils who have warm teachers are less inhibited about making responses, because whatever they do is more likely to be met with positively reinforcing behaviour on the part of the teacher.

In another sense, however, the value of teacher warmth may be understood in terms of Heider's theory of cognitive balance, which predicts that we will tend to like someone whom we recognize as liking us. Warm teachers are perceived by pupils as liking them, and the pupils tend to reciprocate the affection. Heiderian theory also predicts that pupils who regard a teacher favourably, with high esteem, will tend to adopt that teacher's attitudes and orientations towards the objects and ideas in the environment. So we have a rationale for the importance of warmth in terms of modelling theory. Heiderian theory also predicts that pupils who perceive a teacher as liking them and liking their fellow pupils will tend themselves to like their fellow pupils; this is exactly what Sears found, namely that 'teachers who like pupils tend to have pupils who like each other'.

Cognitive validity

By cognitive validity I mean the degree to which the teacher possesses, and reflects in his behaviour, a valid, systematic cognitive structure of the concepts and principles of the discipline he is trying to teach. Here is where we would ordinarily put the teacher's 'knowledge of his subject', except that the latter term does not signify well enough the organization and sequence of ideas, at the concrete as well as the abstract levels, with which we are here concerned.

In recent years, some new ideas about cognitive validity and sub-ject-matter structure have been developed by students of programmed instruction and technical training. Gagné and his co-workers have provided illustrations of how a task performance set up as a goal can be analysed into prerequisite sub-tasks, ordered in successive steps that are true both to the logic of the subject and to the way in which it can be learned. Such planned sequence of instruction militates against skipping essential steps in the development of understanding of a problem, a principle or concept. This kind of meticulous analysis of what, cognitively speaking, amounts to walking before one runs – and to crawling before one walks – in any given content has often been done intuitively and artistically by skilful teachers. We are now beginning to have some principles to guide this kind of subject-matter analysis and any sequencing into learning structures.

The importance of cognitive validity, and of all that I am trying to connote with that term, is that the teacher must understand what he is to teach. B. O. Smith has called out attention to the miserable logic that can too often be found in classroom discussions of the definition of a concept, for example imperialism, or of the explanation of an event or a state of affairs such as the Boxer Rebellion. Smith and his co-workers find that such logical operations are poorly carried out by teachers and students. These research workers are proceeding on the hypothesis – which is altogether consistent with a conception of teaching as the exertion of cognitive force – that 'the quality of teach-ing will improve if the performance of the logical operations involved is improved'.

The same kind of conception of teaching seems to imbue the work of Hilda Taba, who has been formulating teaching strategies aimed at developing the ability of pupils to form concepts, make inferences, induce generalization and explain phenomena. Her explorations and analysis have led her to imply some rather severe demands on the teacher. She states for example that:

'Prolonged assimilation of facts without a corresponding re-shaping of the conceptual schemes with which to organize them is bound to retard the maturation of thought. On the other hand, a premature leap into a more complex or a higher level of thought is likely to immobilize mental activity and cause reversion to . . . a lower level of thought. . . . An appropriate transition from one [level of thought] to the other demands a proper match between the current level and that which is required. Determining the proper match is one of the most difficult tasks in teaching. . . .'

Thus Taba's teacher is required to make quick and subtle judgements about the cognitive processes of her pupils, about when the discussion has got to the point that an attempt at generalization is called for. But that is not the teacher's only burden; she also has the problem of individual differences. Even if she possesses the teaching strategies for implementing the principles of sequence, some of her pupils need more concrete instances than do others before they are ready for the leap to formal or abstract thought. Indeed, as Taba says:

'It is not beyond possibility that by far the most important individual differences may be found in the amount of concrete thinking an individual needs before formal thought can emerge.'

The demands of cognitive validity and individual differences

So our concern with cognitive processes and the cognitive validity of the teacher can lead us into what looks like an impasse. The task of teaching begins to seem too hard, if not impossible. I am not the first student of teaching to find himself facing this problem, even if my path may have been unique. Note that I have not followed B. F. Skinner's reasoning from the enormous need for reinforcement contingencies that led him in 1954 to throw up his hands in despair at a major part of the task of the classroom teacher. I have come to the problem by an acceptance of the need for cognitive validity in teaching, a need of the kind to which the analyses of research workers like Smith and Taba inexorably lead us, and by a confrontation with the unyielding facts of individual differences.

If good teaching makes demands for impossibly complex, subtle and rapid cognitive feats on the part of the teacher, and if the individual differences among pupils in both stable and momentary cognitive readinesses inevitably force the teacher to miss many of his targets, what can be done? According to this analysis, what we need, for some important kinds of teaching, is some kind of individualized, self-paced, prearranged yet flexible sequences of give-and-take between teacher and pupil. This kind of give-and-take is well known to all of us and occurs in most classrooms. It is likely, as Arno Bellack has reported in his meticulous study of fifteen classrooms, that:

> 'The basic verbal interchange in the classroom is the soliciting–responding pattern. Teachers often shape and frame this basic pattern with reacting moves and occasionally with structuring moves.'

This means that for most of the time teachers ask questions and pupils answer them, and then the teachers evaluate the answers; sometimes the teacher may also tell the pupils what to think about, or provides background information. But the trouble is that the teacher's side of the conversation cannot be as cognitively valid and carefully planned as Smith and Taba (and I) would like it to be. And, in any case, even when the teacher is saying the right thing for some of her pupils, she may very well be saying the wrong thing for the rest of them.

Programmed instruction

As you probably have guessed by now, I am leading the argument towards programmed instruction. The 'individualized, self-paced, prearranged yet flexible sequences of give-and-take between teacher and pupil' to which I referred a few moments ago, are exactly what programmed instruction tries to provide. It is little wonder that many thoughtful students of teaching are moving towards programmed instruction as a solution to *part* of the problem of teaching. For example, here is how Gagné took his stand, near the end of his book-length analysis of the conditions of learning:

> 'The major possibilities of predesigning instructional content to allow for individual differences have been exhibited, not in the classroom or in the textbook, but in *programmed instruction*.' Similarly, Harry Broudy, whom we may regard as non-partisan on this issue, holds that:

> '... there is less ground than is commonly assumed, to believe that there are kinds of instruction that only a live teacher can pro-

vide . . . any material that can be symbolized, that has some kind of logical and syntactical structure, can be adapted for machine instruction. . . . As to strategies of motivation, presentation, eliciting of a trial response, correction of trial responses, practice of correct responses, inducement of insight into relational patterns and evaluation of any and all responses, there is little doubt that properly programmed machines will not let us down, for this is their strong point. . . .'

So we see that analyses of teaching as the manipulation of cognitive forces lead to programmed instruction just as conditioning theories do. Just how will the issue be resolved between programmed and live instruction for many kinds of cognitive learnings? In some quarters, it is held that the programmed instruction bubble has already burst, and that schoolmen are now feeling somewhat embarrassed over their brief surrender to the fad. In other quarters, it is held that programmed instruction is steadily gaining; that better theory and practice are being developed; that further technological advances through computerization are being made; that programmed instruction's promise of giving teachers surcease from certain grave problems of live teaching will be realized.

THE OUTLOOK

However programmed instruction goes, there is little question that the role, the task, the behaviour and the education of the human teacher are going to be carefully studied in the years ahead. The national interest in such study has been expressed through firm support for research and development in teaching and learning. Scientific interest in teaching has brought learning-theorists and researchers out of the laboratory and into the school. Theory and research on teaching may hold the attention of psychologists in the next decade with the same intensity as learning-theory and research have in the past. Conceptions of teaching of the kind we have considered should then give way to the rigorous, productive and educationally relevant principles and laws that will deserve to be called theories of teaching.

3   Some theorems on instruction*

J. S. BRUNER

This paper by Bruner considers some specific areas of concern for a theory of teaching. In line with the views of several other authors he considers that such a theory should have general applicability across subjects and age ranges. Of particular interest are his arguments that the theory should be prescriptive, and his model of different methods of 'representation'.[1]

The original paper contains a lengthy section applying his theorems to a specific problem, the teaching of mathematics. Unfortunately this could not be included because of lack of space, but interested readers are referred to the original article for an interesting practical application of Bruner's theses.

NATURE OF A THEORY OF INSTRUCTION

A theory of instruction is *prescriptive* in the sense that it sets forth rules concerning the most effective way of achieving knowledge or skill. By the same token, such a theory provides a yardstick for criticizing or evaluating any particular way of teaching or learning.

A theory of instruction is a *normative* theory. It sets up criteria and states the conditions for meeting them. The criteria must have a high degree of generality: for example, a theory of instruction should not specify in an *ad hoc* fashion the conditions for efficient learning of third-grade arithmetic. Rather, such conditions should be derivable from a more general view of mathematics learning.

One might ask why a theory of instruction is needed, since psychology already contains theories of learning and of development. But theories of learning and of development are descriptive rather than prescriptive. They tell us what happened after the fact: for example, that most children of 6 do not yet possess the notion of

* Reprinted and abridged from J. S. Bruner, 'Some Theorems on Instruction Illustrated with Reference to Mathematics' in E. R. Hilgard (Ed.), *Theories of Learning and Instruction*, National Society for the Study of Education, Chicago, 1964, pp. 306–35. Mrs Blythe Clinchy assisted in the preparation of this paper.
[1] See also J. S. Bruner, 'The Course of Cognitive Growth', *American Psychologist*, 19, 1964, pp. 1–15.

reversibility. A theory of instruction, on the other hand, might attempt to set forth the best means of leading the child towards the notion of reversibility. A theory of instruction, in short, is concerned with how best to learn what one wishes to teach, with improving, rather than describing learning.

This is not to say that learning and developmental theories are irrelevant to a theory of instruction. In fact, a theory of instruction must be concerned with both learning and development, as well as with the nature of particular subject-matter; and there must be congruence among the various theories, all of which have a complementary relation to each other.

A theory of instruction has four major features:

(1) A theory of instruction should specify the experiences which most effectively implant in the individual a predisposition towards learning – learning in general or a particular type of learning. For example, what sorts of relationships towards people and things in the preschool environment will tend to make the child willing and able to learn when he enters school?

(2) Second, a theory of instruction must specify the ways in which a body of knowledge should be structured so that it can be most readily grasped by the learner. Optimal structure refers to the set of propositions from which a larger body of knowledge can be generated, and it is characteristic that the formulation of such structure depends upon the state of advance in a particular field of knowledge. In a later section, the nature of different optimal structures will be considered in more detail. Here it suffices to say that since the goodness of a structure depends upon its power for *simplifying information,* for *generating new propositions* and for *increasing the manipulability of a body of knowledge,* structure must always be related to the status and gifts of the learner. Viewed in this way, the optimal structure of a body of knowledge is not absolute but relative. The major requirement is that no two sets of generating structures for the same field of knowledge be in contradiction.

(3) Third, the theory of instruction should specify the most effective sequences in which to present the materials to be learned. Given, for example, that one wishes to teach the structure of

modern physical theory, how does one proceed? Does one present concrete materials first in such a way as to elicit questions about recurrent regularities? Or, does one begin with a formalized mathematical notation that makes it simpler to represent regularities later encountered? What results are in fact produced by the use of each? The question of sequence will be treated in more detail later.

(4) Finally, a theory of instruction should specify the *nature and pacing of rewards and punishments* in the process of learning and teaching. Intuitively, it seems quite clear that as learning progresses there is a point at which it is better to shift away from extrinsic rewards, such as teacher's praise, towards the intrinsic rewards inherent in solving a complex problem for one's self. So, too, there is a point at which immediate reward for performance should be replaced by deferred reward. The shift rates from extrinsic to intrinsic and from immediate to deferred reward are poorly understood and obviously important. Is it the case, for example, that wherever learning involves the integration of a long sequence of acts, the earliest shift should be made from immediate to deferred reward and from extrinsic to intrinsic reward?

It would be beyond the scope of any single paper to pursue in any detail all of the four aspects of a theory of instruction set forth above. What I shall attempt to do here is to explore a major theorem concerning each of the four. The object is not comprehensiveness but illustration.

PREDISPOSITIONS

It has been customary, in discussing predispositions to learn, to focus upon cultural, motivational and personal factors affecting the desire to learn and to undertake problem-solving. And indeed, such factors are of enormous importance. But we shall concentrate here on a more cognitive level: upon the predisposition to explore alternatives. For it is this predisposition that is often most affected by cultural and motivational factors.

Since learning and problem-solving depend upon the exploration of alternatives, instruction must facilitate and regulate the exploration of alternatives on the part of the learner.

There are three aspects to the exploration of alternatives, each of them related to the regulation of search behaviour. They can be described in shorthand terms as *activation, maintenance* and *direction*. To put it another way, exploration of alternatives requires something to get started, something to keep it going and something to keep it from being random.

The major condition for *activating exploration* of alternatives in a task is the presence of some optimal level of uncertainty. Curiosity, it has been persuasively argued,[1] is a response to uncertainty and ambiguity. A cut-and-dried routine task arouses little exploration; one that is too uncertain may arouse confusion and anxiety, with the effect of reducing exploration.

The *maintenance of exploration*, once it has been activated, requires that the benefits from exploring alternatives exceed the risks incurred. Learning something with the aid of an instructor should, if instruction is effective, be less dangerous or risky or painful than learning on one's own. That is to say, the consequences of error – exploring *wrong* alternatives – should be rendered less grave under a regimen of instruction, and the yield from the exploration of *correct* alternatives should be correspondingly greater.

The appropriate *direction of exploration* depends upon two interacting considerations: a sense of the goal of a task and a knowledge of the relevance of tested alternatives to the achievement of that goal. For exploration to have direction, in short, the goal of the task must be known in some approximate fashion, and the testing of alternatives must yield information as to where one is with respect to it.

STRUCTURE AND THE FORM OF KNOWLEDGE

Any idea or problem or body of knowledge can be presented in a form simple enough so that any particular learner can understand it.

The structure of any domain of knowledge may be characterized in three ways, each affecting the ability of any learner to master it: (*a*) *the mode of representation* in which it is put, (*b*) its *economy* and (*c*) its *effective power*. Mode, economy and power vary in appropriateness to different ages, to different 'styles' among learners and to the differences between subject-matters.

[1] D. E. Berlyne, *Conflict, Arousal, and Curiosity*, McGraw-Hill, 1960.

Any domain of knowledge (or any problem within that domain of knowledge) can be represented in three ways: (*a*) by a set of actions appropriate for achieving a certain result (*enactive representation*), (*b*) by a set of summary images or graphics that stand for a concept without defining it fully (*ikonic representation*) and (*c*) by a set of symbolic or logical propositions drawn from a symbolic system that is governed by rules or laws for forming and transforming propositions (*symbolic representation*). The distinction can most conveniently be made concretely in terms of a balance beam. A very young child can plainly act on the basis of the 'principles' of a balance beam, and indicates that he can do so by being able to handle himself on a see-saw. He knows that to get his side to go down farther he has to move out farther from the centre. A somewhat older child can represent the balance beam to himself either by drawing or by a model on which rings can be hung and balanced. The 'image' of the balance beam can be varyingly refined, with fewer and fewer irrelevant details present, as in the typical diagrams in an introductory textbook in physics. Finally, a balance beam can be described in ordinary English, without diagrammatic aids, or it can be even better described mathematically by reference to Newton's Law of Moments in inertial physics. Needless to say, actions, pictures and symbols are differentially difficult for people of different ages, different backgrounds, different styles. Moreover, a problem in the law would be hard to diagram, one in geography lends itself to imagery. Many subjects, such as mathematics, have alternative modes of representation.

Economy in representing a domain of knowledge refers to the amount of information that must be held in mind and processed to achieve comprehension. The larger the number of items of information that must be carried to understand something or deal with a problem, the greater the number of successive steps one must take in processing that information to achieve a conclusion; hence, the less the economy. For any domain of knowledge one can rank summaries of it in terms of their economy. It is more economical (though less powerful) to summarize the American Civil War as a 'battle over slavery' than as 'a struggle between an expanding industrial region and one built upon a class society for control of federal economic policy'. It is more economical to summarize the characteristics of free-falling bodies by the formula $S = \frac{1}{2}gt^2$ than to put a series of numbers into tabular form summarizing a vast set of observations made on different bodies dropped different distances in different gravitational fields. The matter is best epitomized by two ways of imparting information: one requiring carriage of much information, the other more a pay-as-you-go type of information-processing. A highly embedded sentence is an example of the former ('This is the rat that the cat that the dog that the boy chased, teased and killed'); the contrast case is more economical ('This is the boy that chased the dog that teased the cat that killed the rat'). Economy, as we shall see, varies with mode of representation. But economy is also a function of the sequence in which material is presented or the manner in which it is learned – over and beyond the optimum structure that can be achieved. The case can be exemplified as follows. Suppose the domain of knowledge consists of available plane service within a twelve-hour period between five cities in the northeast – Concord, New Hampshire; Albany, New York; Danbury, Connecticut; Elmira, New York; and Boston, Massachusetts. One of the ways in which the knowledge can be imparted is by asking the student to memorize the following list of connections:

Boston to Concord
Danbury to Concord
Albany to Boston
Concord to Elmira
Albany to Elmira
Concord to Danbury
Boston to Albany
Concord to Albany

Now we ask, 'What is the shortest way to make a round trip from Albany to Danbury?' The amount of information-processing required to answer this question under such conditions is considerable. We increase economy by 'simplifying terms' in certain characteristic ways. One is to introduce an arbitrary but learned order – in this case, an alphabetical one. We rewrite the list:

Albany to Boston
Albany to Elmira
Boston to Albany

Boston to Concord
Concord to Danbury
Concord to Elmira
Danbury to Concord

Search then becomes easier, but there is still a somewhat trying sequential property to the task. Economy is further increased by using a diagrammatic notation and again there are varying degrees of economy in such recourse to the ikonic mode. Compare the diagram on the left and the one on the right.

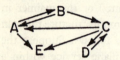 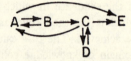

The *effective power* of any particular way of structuring a domain of knowledge refers to the generative value of a set of learned propositions. In the previous section, rote learning of a set of connections between cities results in a rather inert structure from which it is difficult to generate pathways through the set of cities. Or, to take an example from a recent report by Donaldson,[1] children who are told that 'Mary is taller than Jane, and Betty is shorter than Jane' are often unable to say whether Mary is taller than Betty. One can perfectly well remark that the answer is 'there' in the logic of transitivity. But to say this is to miss the psychological point. *Effective power* will, to be sure, never exceed the inherent logical generativeness of a domain – although this is an admittedly difficult statement from the point of view of epistemology. In common-sense terms, it amounts to the assertion that grasp of a field of knowledge will never be better than the best that can be done with that field of knowledge. The effective power within a particular learner's grasp is what one seeks to discover by close analysis of how in fact he is going about his task of learning. Much of Piaget's research seeks to discover just this property about children's learning and thinking. There is an interesting relationship between economy and power. Theoretically, the two are independent: indeed, it is clear that a structure may be economical but powerless. But it is rare for a powerful structuring

[1] Margaret Donaldson, *A Study of Children's Thinking*, Tavistock Publications, 1963.

technique in any field to be uneconomical. This is what leads to the canon of parsimony and the faith shared by many scientists that nature is simple: perhaps it is only when nature can be made reasonably simple that it can be understood. The power of a representation can also be described as its capacity, in the hands of a learner, to connect matters that, on the surface, seem quite separate.

SEQUENCE AND ITS USES

Instruction consists of leading the learner through a sequence of statements and restatements of a problem or body of knowledge that increase the learner's ability to grasp, transform and transfer what he is learning. In short, the sequence in which a learner encounters materials within a domain of knowledge affects the difficulty he will have in achieving mastery.

There are usually a variety of sequences that are equivalent in their ease and difficulty for learners. There is no unique sequence for all learners, and the optimum in any particular case will depend upon a variety of factors, including past learning, stage of development, nature of the material and individual differences.

If it is true that the usual course of intellectual development moves from enactive through ikonic to symbolic representation of the world, it is likely that an optimum sequence will progress in the same direction. Obviously, this is a conservative doctrine. For when the learner has a well-developed symbolic system, it may be possible to by-pass the first two stages. But one does so always with the risk that the learner may not possess the imagery to fall back on when his symbolic transformations fail to achieve a goal in problem-solving.

Sequencing must take into account the limited capacities of any organism to process information. In this sense, a sequence that begins economically will usually be advisable. This hypothesis is further premised on the assumption that more economically presented materials, learned first as a model, will serve to reduce the potential complexity of materials encountered later.

Exploration of alternatives will necessarily be affected by the sequence in which material to be learned becomes available to the learner. It is an empirical question as to when the learner should be encouraged to explore alternatives widely and when he should be encouraged to concentrate on the implications of a single alternative hypothesis. To this subject we return in the next section.

Reverting to the earlier discussion of activation and the maintenance of interest, it is necessary to specify in any sequence the level of uncertainty and tension that must be present to initiate problem-solving behaviour and what is necessary to keep active problem-solving going. This again is an empirical question.

Optimum sequences, as already stated, cannot be specified independent of the criterion in terms of which final learning is to be judged. A classification of such criteria will include at least the following: (a) speed of learning, (b) resistance to forgetting, (c) transferability of what has been learned to new instances, (d) form of representation in terms of which what has been learned is to be expressed, (e) economy of what has been learned in terms of cognitive strain imposed, (f) effective power of what has been learned in terms of its generativeness for new hypotheses and combinations. Achieving one of these goals does not necessarily bring one closer to others. Speed of learning is sometimes antithetical to transfer or to economy, and so forth.

THE FORM AND PACING OF REINFORCEMENT

Learning depends upon knowledge of results at a time when and at a place where the knowledge can be used for correction. Instruction increases the appropriate timing and placing of corrective knowledge.

'Knowledge of results' is useful or not depending upon (a) when and where the learner is able to put the corrective information to work, (b) under what conditions such corrective information can be used, even assuming appropriateness of time and place of receipt, and (c) the form in which the corrective information is received.

Learning and problem-solving are divisible into phases. These have been described in various ways, but all the descriptions agree on one essential feature: that there is a cycle involving the formulation of a testing procedure or trial, the operation of this testing procedure, and the comparison of the results of the test with some criterion. It has variously been called trial-and-error, means-end testing, trial-and-check, discrepancy reduction, test-operate-test-exit (TOTE),[1]

[1] See Further Reading, Miller et al., 1960.

hypothesis testing and the like. These 'units', moreover, can readily be characterized as hierarchically organized: we seek to cancel the unknowns in an equation in order to simplify the expression in order to solve the equation in order to get through the course in order to get our degree in order to get a decent job in order to lead the good life, and so on. Knowledge of results, it follows from this, should come at that point in a problem-solving episode when the person is comparing the results of his tryout with some criterion of what he seeks to achieve. Knowledge of results given before this point either cannot be understood or must be carried as extra freight in immediate memory. Knowledge given after this point may be too late to guide the choice of a next hypothesis or trial. But knowledge of results must, to be useful, provide information not only as to whether or not one's particular act produced success but also whether the act is in fact leading one through the hierarchy of goals one is seeking to achieve. This is not to say that when we cancel the term in that equation we need information as to whether it will all lead eventually to the good life. Yet there should at least be some 'lead notice' available as to whether or not cancellation is on the right general track. It is here that the tutor has a special role. For most learning starts off rather piecemeal without the integration of component acts or elements. Usually, the learner can tell whether a particular cycle of activity has worked – feedback from specific events is usually quite simple – but often he cannot tell whether this completed cycle is leading to the eventual goal. To sum up, then, instruction uniquely provides information to the learner about higher-order relevance of his efforts. In time, to be sure, the learner must develop techniques for obtaining such higher-order corrective information on his own, for instruction and its aids must eventually come to an end. And finally, if the problem-solver is to take over this function, it is necessary for him to learn to recognize when he does not comprehend and, as Roger Brown[1] has suggested, to signal incomprehension to the tutor so that he can be helped. In time, the signalling of incomprehension becomes a self-signalling and equivalent to a temporary stop-order.

The ability of problem-solvers to use information correctively is known to vary as a function of internal state. One state in which

[1] Roger W. Brown, 'From Codability to Coding Ability'. Unpublished manuscript, Harvard University, 1963.

information is least useful is when the learner is impelled by strong drive and anxiety. There is a sufficient body of research to establish this point beyond reasonable doubt. Another such state has been referred to in the literature as 'functional fixedness' – a problem-solver is, in effect, using corrective information exclusively for the evaluation of one single hypothesis that happens to be wrong. The usual example is treating an object in terms of its conventional significance when it must be treated in a new context – we fail to use a hammer as a bob for a pendulum because it is 'fixed' in our thinking as a hammer. The studies of Maier, Luchins, Duncker and others all point to the fact that during such a period there is a remarkable intractability or even incorrigibility to problem-solving. There is some evidence to indicate that high drive and anxiety lead organisms to be more prone to functional fixedness. It is obvious that corrective information of the usual type, i.e. straight feedback, is least useful during such states and that an adequate instructional strategy aims to terminate the interfering state by special means before continuing with the usual provision of correction. In such cases, instruction verges on a kind of therapy, and it is perhaps because of this therapeutic need that one often finds therapy-like advice in lists of aids for problem-solvers, e.g. Humphrey, who suggests that one turn away from the problem when it is proving too difficult.

If information is to be used effectively, it must be translated into the learner's way of attempting to solve a problem. If such translatability is not present, then the information is simply useless. Telling a neophyte skier to 'shift to his uphill edges' when he cannot distinguish on which edges he is travelling provides no help; simply telling him to lean into the hill may succeed. Or, to take a more cognitive sphere, there is by now an impressive body of evidence that indicates that 'negative information' – information about what something is *not* – is peculiarly unhelpful to a person seeking to master a concept. Translatability of corrective information can, in principle, also be applied to the form of representation and its economy. If learning or problem-solving is proceeding in one mode – enactive, ikonic or symbolic – corrective information must be provided either in the same mode or in one that translates into it. The point is obvious, to be sure, but so often violated as to be pedagogically interesting. In mathematics particularly, one finds that teachers often provide information for correction in a highly symbolized notation when, in fact, the student is proceeding either without knowledge of the symbolic language used or by the use of some sort of approximate imagery. The result is incomprehension or defeat. Again, the matter of economy is obvious but also frequently overlooked. Corrective information that exceeds the information-processing capacities of a learner is obviously wasteful.

Finally, it is necessary to reiterate one general point made above in passing. Instruction is a provisional state that has as its object to make the learner or problem-solver self-sufficient. Any regimen of correction carries the danger that the learner may become permanently dependent upon the tutor's correction. The tutor must correct the learner in a fashion that eventually makes it possible for the learner to take over the corrective function himself. Otherwise the result of instruction is to create a form of mastery that is contingent upon the perpetual presence of a teacher.

SOME CONCLUSIONS

A first and obvious conclusion is that one must take into account the issues of predisposition, structure, sequence and reinforcement in preparing curriculum materials – whether one is concerned with writing a textbook, a lesson plan, a unit of instruction or, indeed, a conversation with didactic ends in view. But there follow from this obvious conclusion some rather non-obvious implications.

The type of supporting research that permits one to assess how well one is succeeding in the management of relevant instructional variables requires a constant and close collaboration of teacher, subject-matter specialist and psychologist. A curriculum should be prepared jointly by the subject-matter expert, the teacher and psychologist with due regard for the inherent structure of the material, its sequencing and the psychological pacing of reinforcement and the building and maintaining of predispositions to problem-solving. As the curriculum is being built, it must be used as the material for testing in detail by close observational and experimental methods to assess not simply whether children are 'achieving' but, rather, what they are making of the material and how they are organizing it. It is on the basis of 'testing as you go' that revision is made. It is this procedure that puts the evaluation process at a time when and place where its results can be used for correction in the enterprise of making curricula.

Little save passing reference has been made to the issue of individual differences. Quite plainly, they exist in massive degree – in the extent to which children have problem-solving predispositions, in the degree of their interest, in the skills that they bring to any concrete task, in their preferred mode of representing things, in their ability to move easily through any particular sequence, and in the degree to which they are initially dependent upon extrinsic reinforcement from the teacher. The fact of individual differences argues for pluralism and for an enlightened opportunism in the materials and methods of instruction. Early in this paper it was asserted, rather offhandedly, that no single ideal sequence exists for any group of children. The conclusion to be drawn from that assertion is not that it is impossible to put together a curriculum that would satisfy a group of children or a cross-section of children. Rather, it is that if a curriculum is to be effective in the classroom it must contain different ways of activating children, different ways of presenting sequences, different opportunities for some children to 'skip' parts while others work their way through, different ways of putting things. A curriculum, in short, must contain many tracks leading to the same general goal.

Finally, a theory of instruction seeks to take account of the fact that a curriculum reflects not only the nature of knowledge itself but also the nature of the knower and the knowledge-getting process. It is the enterprise *par excellence* where the line between subject-matter and method grows necessarily indistinct. A body of knowledge, enshrined in a university faculty and embodied in a series of authoritative volumes, is the *result* of much prior intellectual activity. To instruct someone in these disciplines is not a matter of getting him to commit results to mind. Rather, it is to teach him to participate in the process that makes possible the establishment of knowledge. We teach a subject not to produce little living libraries on the subject but, rather, to get a student to think mathematically for himself, to consider matters as a historian does, to embody the process of knowledge-getting. Knowing is a process, not a product.

4 Methods of scientific research in the psychology of instruction*

Z. I. KALMYKOVA

Kalmykova, a leading Soviet psychologist, presents some interesting examples of approaches to research into teaching in the U.S.S.R. The 'natural experiment' described has been used for some years in Soviet pedagogical investigations and provides some pointers to work in the field of applied science research referred to by Hilgard (pp. 91 ff.). Also of interest is the stress on developing methods of analysing teaching problems to discover the logical structure of the study material and the psychological problems involved in helping pupils master the material. There is a close parallel between such concerns and the arguments of Gage (pp. 98 ff.). The problems are very similar; the approaches to their solution somewhat different. One important problem of common concern is the need to develop diagnostic tests which will enable teachers and researchers to pinpoint pupil competence in a given field of study. These tests would inform researchers in a fairly precise way of the results of their teaching experiments. To some extent the methods outlined resemble the micro-teaching experiments developed by Gage and associates, although the Soviet concern with creating 'conflict situations' between old and new learning is quite distinctive.

An increase in the effectiveness of instruction cannot be attained without discovering and taking into account the laws governing the assimilation of knowledge and the specific character of their manifestation in dependence on content, methods of instruction and individual peculiarities of students. The discovery of these laws is the task of the psychology of instruction.

Diverse methods of research are employed in the psychology of instruction. A description of several of them, the most important ones, will be given in this article.

The leading method in investigations into the psychology of instruction is the method of the natural experiment. First described

* Reprinted and abridged from Z. I. Kalmykova, 'Methods of Scientific Research in the Psychology of Instruction', *Soviet Education*, **VIII** (6), 1966, pp. 13–23. The author is associated with the Scientific Research Institute of Psychology of the R.S.F.S.R. Academy of Pedagogical Sciences.

in our country by A. F. Lazurskii, this method has received wide dissemination in Soviet educational psychology and has been developed and perfected. At the present time, new forms of it have been elaborated which differ significantly from the variation employed by A. F. Lazurskii.

The natural experiment arose as a result of attempts to overcome the negative aspects of the laboratory experiment while retaining the positive ones. A negative aspect of the laboratory experiment is the artificiality of the conditions in which it is carried out: a special place that is new to the students, an unfamiliar experimenter, unusual assignments that are constructed from non-academic material etc. This engenders serious doubts as to the possibility of direct utilization of the results of laboratory experiments for an understanding of the peculiarities of students' psychological activity during the assimilation of knowledge. How do unusual laboratory conditions influence the course of the psychological process being studied? What is the correlation between success in solving thinking problems from artificial and from academic material? Is it possible, and to what extent, on the basis of successes or failures in solving thinking problems from artificial material in a laboratory experiment, to predict the degree of success of analogous activity in school and to what degree is this activity analogous? These questions still demand an answer. However, there are already data testifying to the absence here of a direct correlation.

The natural experiment, as distinguished from the laboratory experiment, is accomplished in conditions of school work to which the students are accustomed and is usually based upon academic material. The experimenter becomes acquainted with his future subjects beforehand. The experiment itself is most often conducted as a lesson in the classroom or in the guise of supplementary and club studies. As a result, the influence of the novelty of the conditions on the course of the psychic processes being studied is reduced significantly.

At the same time, the researcher strives to approximate the natural experiment to the laboratory experiment as regards accuracy: he strives to assure identical conditions in the experiments during their repetition many times over, as well as the possibility of arbitrarily changing only those factors which he wishes to study while holding the rest of them constant. This is much easier to achieve under laboratory conditions. Thus, during study of memorization processes in the laboratory, material for visual memorization is exhibited on a screen and for auditory memorization it is given by tape-recorder, which assures equality of conditions during repeated reproduction of the material (time intervals, clearness, intonations etc.). Using artificial material, it is easier to maintain given distinctions: series of words for memorization, abstract and concrete, which are synonymous in magnitude; of words or nonsense syllables, depending on the research problem; it is also easier to assure the absence of distracting factors.

The degree of approximation of the natural experiment to the laboratory one in terms of accuracy of data obtained can be highly diverse. It depends not only on the skill of the creators of the experiment's methods, but also on the peculiarities of those psychological processes that are being subjected to investigation and on the material upon which the investigation is based. Thus, during study of the process of concept formation with the aid of the laboratory experiment based on the methods of Vygotskii–Sakharov, the influence of previous experience is removed in that the laboratory experiment is based on artificial material. Figures of various colours, shapes and sizes are placed before the subject in disorder; on the reverse side of each of them is written some word which is at first without meaning for the subjects ('gatsun', 'fal' and others). The experimenter takes one of the figures, shows the subject its name and suggests that the subject pick out the other figures having, in his opinion, the same name. The subject makes a choice, receives an indication as to its correctness and, taking into account this indication, takes the next figure, and continues in this manner until he understands the meaning of the term which was unknown to him earlier ('gatsun' – large and short figures; 'fal' – small and tall figures etc.).

During study of the process of formation of real concepts or of the effectiveness of one or another method of instruction in a natural experiment, the researcher cannot completely 'remove' the influence of previous experience on the process of assimilation of knowledge, as is done, for example, in the laboratory experiment described above. However, in order to obtain more comparable results the device of 'equalization' of knowledge is often resorted to. On the basis of careful analysis of the academic material from which the experiment is to be constructed, a minimum of preliminary knowledge which is necessary for successful assimilation manifests itself; the presence of this knowledge among the pupils designated for the experiments is checked; those who have not mastered this minimum finish learning it. In this way a more or less identical beginning stage – 'reading point' – is created; this removes the influence of the difference in mastery of the initial data on the further process of assimilation, which is determined by the conditions of the experiments.

With the same aim of levelling the differences in conditions of assimilation which do not depend on the experiment itself, study material is utilized that has not yet been studied by the pupils (the device of 'running ahead'). However, complete equalization of all conditions influencing the assimilation of knowledge is very complex (especially the influence of life and school experience). Often the relationship between the life experience of students and the knowledge being introduced serves as a special goal of research (for example, during study of the natural process of concept formation), and then the necessity for preliminary equalization of knowledge no longer arises.

During the elaboration of a natural experiment a considerable amount of attention is paid to ensure that the instructions given to the students are accurate and identical and to clear-cut variation of the conditions of the experiment, as well as to methods of establishing the experiment's results. With the aim of increasing the objectivity and accuracy of data from experiments, experimenters have begun, in recent years, to use tape-recorders and cameras; however, they make a great effort to avoid having these instruments influence the subjects (they are usually concealed).

At the present time, various kinds of the natural experiment are being employed, the best known of which are the ascertaining and teaching experiments.

The ascertaining experiment, as is shown by the name itself, is employed first of all with the aim of ascertaining, of determining, the peculiarities of assimilation and application of knowledge, of the formation of habits and of the modes of intellectual activity under given, already formed, conditions of learning. For this the experimenter, on the basis of comprehensive analysis of appropriate material and the results of preliminary experiments, carefully selects questions and problems and considers their sequence, the system of promptings which can be used during solution of the problems, those concrete indicators by which it will be possible to judge the results of the experiments, and methods of quantitative processing of the material. The accuracy of the experimental data depends on the thoroughness of this preliminary work.

The ascertaining experiment has found wide application in many investigations, in particular in the works of the Laboratory of the Psychology of Instruction directed by N. A. Menchinskaia, at the Institute of Psychology of the R.S.F.S.R. Academy of Pedagogical Sciences. Thus, studying the problem of the psychology of the application of knowledge in practice, the members of this laboratory placed before themselves first of all the task of elucidating how students apply knowledge under existing conditions of instruction that are typical for school. For this purpose individual ascertaining experiments were conducted with pupils from various grades. The assignments required that a definition of the concepts or regularities studied be given, and then that they be applied to the solution of problems similar to those which had been solved in class and to relatively new ones which required a certain independence in the utilization of knowledge. Correlation of the theoretical positions being formulated with the character of their application to the solution of practical problems yielded material for judgements about the peculiarities of knowledge application and about the difficulties which arise in this process, on the basis of which ways of overcoming the still existing discrepancy between theoretical knowledge and its application were outlined. The success of experiments is determined in significant measure by the system of varying the problems being set before the pupils, something to which the researchers have paid no little attention. In the psychology of instruction the device of creating conflict situations is widely utilized. The experimenter consciously creates in the assignment conditions under which there occurs a clash between the knowledge being assimilated and the pupil's previous experience, if the latter contradicts this new knowledge. The pupil's behaviour in such a situation and the method of solution which he chooses will provide evidence of the depth and firmness of the new knowledge and of the degree of its effectiveness.

In Z. I. Kalmykova's research, which is aimed at study of the peculiarities of assimilation and application of knowledge in physics, the subject was required to give definitions of concepts and regularities for a selected (in the capacity of material for research) topic of the physics course; it was also required that units of measurement of appropriate physical magnitudes and methods of their determination, both by formula and in practice, be named, and that the difference between concepts similar in their elements be indicated etc. The problems set before the subjects varied in terms of the place in them of computing operations (quantitative and qualitative problems were given), in terms of the character of the material (textual and practical) presented in them and in terms of the possibility of solving them by various methods – by a more elementary method, on the basis of solving a series of particular problems, and by a more generalized method requiring application of a new principle. The problems varied widely as to composition of data: essential and sufficient data; hidden, superfluous and insufficient data. In many problems conflict situations were specifically created. Thus, students still in the primary school were accustomed to the dividend being larger than the divisor. In experiments conducted with 6th-graders, who were already well acquainted with fractions, they were presented with two problems in immediate proximity to each other on the determination of area of support according to the magnitude of pressure for which, according to the principle being studied by them, they had to divide the magnitude of the force of the pressure by the pressure (this rule they knew). In one problem the force of the pressure was, in magnitude, more than the pressure, but in the other problem it was less; in the latter case the students had to act contrary to the habit which had been formed in primary school. As the experiments showed, individual pupils who solved the first problem quite correctly acted contrary to the rule in the second one, which testified to the incompleteness of assimilation and to the lack of firmness of the new knowledge.

Conflict between form and content is widely utilized in the construction of experimental assignments directed at study of the peculiarities of assimilation and application of knowledge in grammar. In A. M. Orlova's investigations, for example, during study of the peculiarities of assimilation of the concept of subject, in sentences for analysis the logical subject often did not coincide with the grammatical one ('With the girl from tiredness were stuck together the eyes'), and the direct object was moved into first place in sentences ('The fables of Krylov read everyone'). S. F. Zhuikov, during study of the peculiarities of assimilation of parts of speech by students of lower grades, included in a series of nouns such words as 'movement', 'running' and in a series of verbs, for example, the word '[he] sleeps' (verbs show action, but 'to sleep is to do nothing') etc.

Geometry is usually studied from abstract materials. V. I. Zykova presented students with problems on discovery of the geometric principle of operation of uncomplicated workers' tools, on geometric comprehension of a worker's actions during the marking-out of articles and on the measuring of the patterns of components having various geometrical forms. Such a selection of problems afforded her the possibility of revealing the difficulties in applying geometrical knowledge under actual conditions and of outlining several ways to overcome them.

The ascertaining experiment provides the possibility of judging the peculiarities of assimilation of knowledge under given conditions of instruction and the results, but not the very process of acquisition of knowledge, which is a defect of this kind of experiment. Researchers strive to overcome this defect, employing the method of sections. This method presupposes the conducting of a series of short-term ascertaining experiments: either with analogous content of assignments being carried out by students from various grades, or with the same pupils at various stages of instruction, with changes in content of the experimental assignments corresponding to these stages. This method affords the possibility not only of ascertaining the level of knowledge already reached, but also of catching in some measure the process of assimilation itself, its basic stages and steps, and of revealing the most characteristic individual and age peculiarities of the students.

Each of the indicated ways has its advantages and defects. The first makes it possible in a relatively short time to get a broad coverage of representatives of different ages and to trace the basic stages of formation of concepts, habits and modes of intellectual activity. However, only extremely sharp and significant changes are caught, the critical points of this process, as it were. Sections of this sort make it possible to trace the process of formation of physical concepts, beginning with children of preschool age and ending with graduates of the school, and the process of formation of grammatical, biological and historical concepts among children of all school ages. They also reveal the correlation of concrete and abstract components of thought and its alteration at various stages of instruction.

The second way requires far more time, due to which a shorter age period (from 1 to 4 years) is usually encompassed by the research. However, always working with the same pupils, the researcher can trace the whole process in more detail and catch its more subtle qualitative changes. This method affords especially rich material during research on individual differences and on the influence on them of various modes of instruction etc.

A highly original and effective variety of the method of sections was proposed by E. I. Ignat'ev, who has done research on the psychological peculiarities of the imitative activities of children. He would give the subjects six or seven sheets of thin paper fastened together at the top, a piece of carbon paper lying under the first of them. The subject, in accordance with the goal given to him, would begin drawing on the upper sheet. After a certain interval (two or three minutes) the experimenter would pull out the second sheet and lay the carbon under the next one, and thus it would continue until the whole assignment had been carried out. Comparison of the sections obtained in this way gave the researcher the possibility of tracing the entire process of creating the drawing. Methods of this sort can be used where a person is working with pencil and paper (drawing, sketching, solving problems on the construction of diagrams etc.).

For the purpose of overcoming the limitations of the ascertaining experiment and of obtaining the possibility of testing more effective principles and methods of instruction and of revealing more deeply the influence of instruction on students' development, a new kind of natural experiment – the teaching experiment – has been created and has received wide development in Soviet psychology. It was first used in the research of N. A. Menchinskaia. If in the ascertaining experiment the researcher registers the results of an already formed method of instruction, then in the teaching experiment he himself constructs these methods in accordance with a hypothesis, outlined on the basis of observation and preliminary experiments, about the influence of one or another fact on the process of instruction.

At the present time two varieties of the teaching experiment have been singled out: the testing (or searching) experiment and the verifying experiment (this division had already been outlined by P. P. Blonskii). The first one is resorted to at the beginning stage of research, when the experimenter, having outlined a hypothesis, does not yet conceive with sufficient clarity the organizational forms of its verification and is working them out in the process of the experiment itself, or when he is outlining a series of variants of the method and wants to determine the most effective of them. The verifying experiment appears at the second stage, when the researcher, having conclusively worked out a more effective, according to his data, method or principle of instruction and having made more precise the techniques of the experiments, sets himself the goal of obtaining sufficient grounds for proof of its effectiveness.

Let us cite an example of research whose basic method was the teaching experiment.

On the basis of analysis of the difficulties arising in the process of application of knowledge in practice, there was advanced a supposition about the effectiveness of realization in instruction of the principle of early comparison and contrasting of similar material. A series of investigations were conducted in order to verify this hypothesis. In particular, a teaching experiment, based on material from A. V. Poliakova's grammar, was conducted in which the effectiveness of three methods of working with similar material was compared: the isolated method of introducing this material, the method of simultaneous introduction and, finally, sequential comparison and contrasting of similar facts. The students were divided into three groups that were equal in preparation and development; each of the groups was taught with one of these methods. The remaining conditions of instruction were equalized to the maximum. After the instruction all the pupils were subjected to identical checks. Analysis of the peculiarities of assimilation of the material in the teaching process and its results confirmed the hypothesis which had been advanced.

In experiments of this sort the selection of groups equal in preparation and development, and the equalization of all other conditions of instruction, have great significance. However, no matter how groups of subjects are equalized, the individual peculiarities of students are so varied that the doubt always remains: are not the results obtained explained not so much by the influence of the teaching methods employed as by the peculiarities of the students themselves, and first of all by their capacities for study? That is why researchers often employ the device of 'crossing' for increasing the accuracy of data obtained: the same variations of the teaching methods are repeated, but in such a way that a group which had assimilated material by one method would, when working on a new topic, assimilate it by a second method; the group which had worked with the second method would assimilate the new material by the first method. If in both cases, irrespective of the group in which it had been employed, one and the same method gave the better result, this testified that the effect was determined precisely by the method of introducing the material, and not by extraneous factors.

In the case described above the teaching experiment was conducted with relatively small groups of pupils. In other cases it is carried on individually, with each of the experimental groups, which secures the possibility of more subtly and accurately catching the peculiarities of the psychological processes which are being accomplished during this. However, both the individual and the group experiments have a certain element of artificiality; besides that, they require a lot of time and are inevitably conducted with a relatively small number of students.

Experimental instruction, conducted under ordinary school conditions with the entire class, is acquiring ever wider dissemination in the psychology of instruction, especially in recent years. Depending on the goal set by the experimenter, such instruction may be of relatively short duration or it may stretch out over a long period, sometimes for a year or even for a number of years. In the latter case the experimental classes, as one of their creators, D. B. El'konin, put it, become a sort of clinic for the normal development of children.

The appearance of this actually new variety of the teaching experiment was tied to the necessity of solving the problem set before psychologists by modern life of the interrelationship of instruction and development. Psychologists believe that its solution will provide the basis for creating the possibility of meeting those demands which are made of the school: to secure mastery of modern knowledge and to cultivate the ability to apply it creatively under the rapidly changing conditions of our reality. Experimental instruction, directed at the resolution of this problem, already cannot be limited to verification of the effectiveness of individual principles or methods of instruction based on material from individual, isolated topics. It assumes critical analysis of the entire system of instruction for the given subject or of their aggregate, re-examination of the content of instruction and their reconstruction in accordance with the set goal – to increase to the maximum the influence of instruction on development, being guided by the growth, determined by the best teaching conditions, of the pupils' possibilities for assimilation of knowledge. Experimental programs are being created and a system for working with them is being elaborated, in accordance with which instruction in experimental classes is also being carried on. Researchers pay great attention not only to elaboration of the experimental lessons themselves and to their execution, but also to the system of observations and experiments that permits judgements about the influence of this sort of instruction on the pupils' development and on the formation of given qualities of mind and personality traits.

Such experimental instruction is usually accomplished on the basis of collaboration between psychologists and methodologists and teachers; it requires serious consultations with scholars in the appropriate specialties (linguists, physicists, mathematicians etc.). It is natural that, having turned to the problem of instruction and development, the psychologists first of all occupied themselves with the lower grades of the school. S. F. Zhuikov, together with a group of teachers, accomplished experimental teaching of an expanded course of grammar beginning with the 1st through 4th grades, paying special attention to the formation of correct modes of intellectual activity which assure advancement in linguistic development. D. B. El'konin and V. V. Davydov, together with a group of co-workers, have been carrying on, for a number of years, experimental instruction in grammar, mathematics and other subjects beginning with the 1st grade, special attention being paid in their investigations to the content of instruction and to the system of its presentation. The results of these investigations have not yet gone beyond the framework of experiments.

The results of investigations by L. V. Zankov and his co-workers, who earlier than others set out on the path of creating class-laboratories and who have already accumulated much positive experience, show the possibility of covering the primary school course in three years while achieving the best quality of knowledge and the general development of the pupils. Their experience is now being applied in many classes of the mass school. Experimental teaching of the elements of geometry and algebra in the primary school is being conducted in the Ukraine. Experimental teaching of the elements of physics in the primary school is being conducted by large collectives of scholars and teachers in Sverdlovsk, Cheliabinsk and a number of other cities. Their positive experience has found partial reflection in the practical proposals elaborated by the commission to determine the content of education (on the study of certain physical knowledge in the lower grades). After very extensive verification in the mass school of the effectiveness of the new method of teaching writing that was worked out by E. V. Gur'ianov, the question of its introduction in all schools was raised in the Ministry of Education of the R.S.F.S.R.

Thus occurs the transition from the first testing experiment to the realization of its positive results that were confirmed by wide verification.

Unfortunately, experimental teaching of this sort for the secondary school is still only developing. One may note, for example, the teaching of physics in the 8-year school which the methodologist–physicist S. I. Ivanov and the psychologist Z. I. Kalmykova are directing.

The problem of the interrelationship of instruction and development is closely linked with the question of the students' individual differences, the causes determining them and the conditions which permit the development of strong sides and the elimination or compensation of deficiencies. In order to solve these questions it became necessary to combine the natural experiment, conducted on the basis of various academic material, with the laboratory experiment, and not only with the psychological experiment but also with the physiological one, which is connected with determination of the typological peculiarities of higher nervous activity.

In connection with the wide dissemination of experimental teaching aimed at increasing the influence of the educational process on the students' development, the question has sharply arisen of creating special diagnostic methods that will permit judgements about the progress in intellectual development occurring under the influence of particular experimental methods of teaching. It should be noted that since the 1930s, when the endowments tests were justly condemned, the question of diagnostic methods has for a long time remained almost completely untreated in our country. At the present time, methods are beginning to be created that differ in principle from the tests, which were directed towards measurement of the 'pure intellect', the coefficient of intellectual giftedness, which was determined, as the creators of the test method thought, almost exclusively by innate factors. Soviet scholars proceed from the notion that conditions of life determine the attainable level of development; for students these are, first of all, the conditions of instruction. The efforts of Soviet scholars are directed towards discovery of the qualitative peculiarities of the various levels of intellectual development and of their criteria, towards revealing not only that which has already been attained by the child, but also his immediate possibilities, the 'zone of his immediate development', which does not exclude the use of quantitative indicators that are essential for comparison both of individual students and of experimental classes. Lengthy experiments with the elements of instruction meet these tasks in great measure.

As an example, I shall dwell on the characterization of the peculiarities of the diagnostic method created for the purpose of obtaining certain objective data about the influence of experimental teaching of an expanded physics course on the students' intellectual development. The author of this method, Z. I. Kalmykova, proceeded from the proposition that intellectual development manifests itself first of all in that which is characteristic of human thinking – on a unique plane, in the method of solving new problems relying on the formation of new generalizations. In accordance with this, the method is constructed in the form of a relatively short-term (one or two school hours) individual teaching experiment. A series of experiments are demonstrated to the pupils; in analysing the results, they must more or less independently discover a physical regularity that is new to them and apply it to the solving of problems. The presence of the initial minimum of knowledge is secured as a preliminary, and there is no time limitation; in order to lead all the students to a successful resolution of the problem, minimal help, necessary only as a push for continuation of the search for a solution, is rendered when there is difficulty. The help is graduated beforehand, on the basis of preliminary experiments, from minimal to more and more detailed help. The entire process of the solution, including the help, is fixed as far as is possible. (It should be noted that in the endowment tests non-academic material is used, the initial minimum of knowledge is not secured, the time allowed for the solution is limited, the process of solution is broken off when the time runs out, and help is not rendered.) The material obtained in this way affords sufficient data for qualitative analysis, for singling out of indicators of progress in development, and for the use on this basis of quantitative indicators. In our method the indicator 'economy of thought' was proposed. It reflects the substantial differences between students with high and low levels of development: the very short path, due to facility in the formation of generalizations, of solution of the problem among the first and the extremely long and multi-stage path among the latter, which manifests itself in the number of judgements or 'steps' on the basis of which the problem is solved. In the future it is intended to elaborate, on these same principles, methods constructed from the material of various school subjects, which will afford the possibility of revealing the general peculiarities of the formation of generalizations and their specifics, depending on the character of the material from which it is accomplished.

A number of authors of diagnostic methods, when introducing into them elements of instruction, construct them from non-academic material, which permits the inclusion of students of a greater age range, although it hampers transfer of the data being obtained to intellectual activity that is accomplished during work with academic material. Ia. A. Ponomarev, seeing the 'key condition for the development of man's intellectual forces' in the capacity to act in the mind, constructs accordingly a method directed towards revealing the stages of development of the 'inner plane of actions', using the game, well known to pupils, 'in classes'. The experimenter shows the pupils a page with nine squares (the centre is hatched), explains a chess move with a knight and suggests they determine in their heads (the page is taken away after the initial coaching) the ways of going from one indicated square to another. With the help of such a method the researcher traces the process of formation of this aspect of intellectual activity among students beginning with the 1st and ending with the 10th grade. G. P. Antonova, striving to obtain as much data as possible about the individual peculiarities of intellectual activity of younger pupils, along with other methodologists, employed the 'Game of 5s', a variant of the well-known 'Game of 15s' which was proposed by D. N. Zavalishina for purposes of diagnosis, in research on the peculiarities of spatial thought. (The player must rearrange numbered blocks in a definite sequence with the least possible number of moves; the blocks occupy five of six possible squares, the free square serving as a reserve for reshuffling.)

Recent years are characterized by the penetration of mathematical and cybernetic methods into many disciplines, and in particular into the psychology of instruction. Decreasing the influence of random factors on the results of experiments is achieved by increasing, in correspondence with the rules of large numbers, the number of experiments conducted, by a special, rigorously thought-out selection of their objects etc. Researchers are beginning to pay special attention to analysis, which precedes the experiments, of the objective logical structure of the study material and to disclosure of those demands with which intellectual activity is presented by this material, to revelation of this activity's structure, and to construction of models of the processes which must be formed in the students' consciousness. Under the influence of mathematics and cybernetics the experiment employed in the psychology of instruction is acquiring great scientific rigorousness.

The experimental research developed includes the following features:

(a) construction, guided by a preliminary search experiment, of a working hypothesis;

(b) logical analysis of the structure of that study material which is to be used in the experiment, and the creation on its basis of an ideal model, a standard, a norm, as the most rational and scientific means of carrying out the given activity with the correction which ensues from taking into account the requirements presented by psychology and pedagogy;

(c) disclosure of the real course of the process of knowledge assimilation under existing conditions of instruction and comparison of it with the model elaborated earlier;

(d) elaboration, on the basis of such comparison of the teaching experiment and methods of calculating its effectiveness;

(e) accomplishment of the experiment itself;

(f) quantitative and qualitative processing of its results in accordance with the criteria elaborated earlier.

As an example of research constructed in accordance with these requirements, I shall cite one of the works accomplished in the laboratory of the Psychology of Instruction at the Institute of Psychology of the R.S.F.S.R. Academy of Pedagogical Sciences. Investigating the problem of the interrelationship of instruction and development, this laboratory came to the conclusion that in order to make the process of instruction more controllable and to increase its influence on the students' intellectual development, it is essential to specifically form rational modes of intellectual activity. Mastery of these modes will secure the ability to employ knowledge in practice and the possibility of acquiring and perfecting this knowledge independently in the future. The necessity arises of revealing the structure of that knowledge and of those abilities which pupils must master and of finding rational modes of intellectual activity and concrete ways for their formation.

Logical analysis of the content of study material and construction of optimal models of learning activity increase the accuracy of the experiments. However, they must not overshadow that which is basic in experiments employed in the psychology of instruction – the qualitative analysis of the peculiarities of psychological activities accomplished in the process of assimilation and application of knowledge (and there is such a danger, as certain new investigations in this field show). Moreover, it should be taken into consideration that the choice of one or another method of research depends on the material and the degree to which the problem posed in it has been elaborated. In the psychology of instruction there are not a few problems whose resolution is still at a very beginning stage, and we are only searching for means of approaching them. When one is at the beginning stage of research or is working with very complex aspects of psychological activity, the experimental approaches to which are not yet elaborated, it is necessary to resort to other, less accurate methods, but ones which afford the necessary orientation in the problem – observation, questionnaires, conversations, analysis of written work. These methods are often combined with experimentation and afford the possibility of supplementing the material obtained experimentally and of verifying certain of its data on the basis of mass material.

Observation always precedes organization of the experiment and helps find the problems which are urgent for pedagogical practice. It accompanies the experimental instruction accomplished in the classroom and makes it possible to take into account the difficulties which arise, the students' attitude towards their studies, their interest in them etc. Thus, in the works of A. I. Lipkina and her associates, lengthy, systematic observation of the process of studying works of literature in class was used widely in research which reveals the dependence of the level of analysis of a work of literature on the conditions of its apprehension. Observation occupied a large place in the research on the peculiarities of the application of botanical knowledge to work on the experimental-training plot in the works of E. M. Kudriavtseva etc. In recent years, there has been a tendency in educational psychology to approximate the study of the peculiarities of cognitive activity, and first of all of thinking activity, to the study of the personal peculiarities of students, their interests, attitude towards study and their world view. Here observations, conversations and the questionnaire method, which is relatively little used in the psychology of instruction, will have to be employed more widely. Securing the possibility of obtaining mass material in a relatively short time, this method gives a good initial orientation in the problem and makes it possible to outline some beginning approaches to its solution. The method of analysis of the readers' diaries of students in schools for working youth has proven effective in studying their reading experience, which must be taken into account when making up literature lessons in a school for adults. Combined with other methods, the conversation method acquires a leading significance in a number of investigations.

In the present article the author was forced to limit herself merely to an enumeration of these methods, inasmuch as she considered it essential to give, above all, a fuller characterization of the leading method of educational psychology – the natural experiment. Acquaintance with the methods of research employed in the psychology of instruction will, the author hopes, help draw new cadres of teachers into fruitful scientific work, facilitating an increase in the effectiveness of instruction.

5 An experimental study in the formation of mental actions*

P. Ia. GAL'PERIN

P. Ia. Gal'perin is one of the most influential Soviet workers in the field of the psychology of learning and teaching. This paper is a detailed statement of his views on the nature of the teacher's influence on children's learning and thinking. These views have considerable following in the U.S.S.R. but so far have made little impact elsewhere. This is unfortunate in view of their obvious importance to teachers and theorists as examples of research at the 'applied level'.

Mental actions make up a considerable part of what children are taught in school. Mathematical reckoning, calculation of the ways physical bodies interact, learning how to write words and phrases correctly, the analysis and evaluation of historical events – all these are different aspects of mental action. Mental acts do not, of course, exist in isolation; they are always inseparably linked with knowledge and concepts of one thing or another. But such knowledge itself only acquires real significance, full value and effectiveness, in connection with particular mental actions. An understanding of the concrete structure of mental actions, of the laws governing their formation and

* Reprinted and abridged from P. Ia. Gal'perin, 'An Experimental Study in the Formation of Mental Actions' in B. Simon (Ed.), *Psychology in the Soviet Union*, Routledge & Kegan Paul, 1957, pp. 214–25.

the conditions for their effectiveness, of the different disturbances and methods of recovery – this is the prerequisite of successful teaching.

In our experimental investigation, we wanted to study mental actions which were simple and clear in content, and which could be kept completely under control during their formation, depending entirely on the instruction given. After preliminary discussion, we decided on the most elementary mental actions in arithmetic, and our subsequent researches were concerned with their formation and composition in pre-school children of varying ages, and children of the first class (7 to 8 years).

In general outline, the method of research consisted in setting the child an arithmetical task requiring a specific degree of knowledge and ability, and finding out whether he could carry out this task 'in his head', aloud, and with objects; how he did it by himself, and whether he could do it when methods were suggested to him; to what extent these methods were generalized; and how far they were mastered, i.e. how readily they were applied and could be interchanged.

Several investigations were carried out on these lines, isolating stages of particular importance in the chain of mental actions, and then systematically investigating their formation. The principal conclusion drawn from these researches was that, during learning, an action may change simultaneously in four relatively independent directions.

1. *Generalization.* An action may be generalized to a greater or lesser degree: one child could perform a particular action solely, or more easily, with particular apparatus, while another found it just as easy whatever the apparatus; one child found no difficulty in doing addition with numbers from 1 to 10 (e.g. $4 + 3$), but could not add numbers from 11 to 20 ($14 + 3$), while his classmate could add easily in any numerical range, and also do 'carrying'. There may obviously be a different measure of generalization.

2. *Completeness* (Abbreviation). An action may be performed not only with a differing degree of generalization, but also with differing completeness, with a complete or incomplete structure of operations. One child, for example, will carry out addition in the most extended form: he makes up each number separately, then joins them together

in one group, and finally counts this out afresh one by one from the first to the last. Another child works rather more briefly: taking the first number as a whole he counts the second on to it in ones. A third does addition in different groups, adding each one according to the table of additions. There can obviously be differences in the *measure of completeness* with which an action is performed – how extended (complete) or how abbreviated (incomplete) it is.

3. *Mastery* (Familiarity). Furthermore, forms of one and the same action, differing in degree of generalization and abbreviation, may be learned by the child to a differing degree. For example, a child may often, at his teacher's request, carry out an action by the best method, but he may not use this method when working on his own because he has not mastered it sufficiently. On the other hand, weak pupils often show a high level of mastery of simple action-forms, such as exceptionally quick addition (or even subtraction) by directly counting objects one by one, and they make these automatic; such premature automatization is a great obstacle to the learning of more advanced abbreviated and generalized forms of an action. Thus the *degree of mastery* (familiarity) of differing forms of an action is a special index of the action, and may stand in differing relations with the other indices.

4. *Assimilation* (Level of Mastery). But, in addition to this, a child may perform an action on differing planes: with the aid of objects, 'speaking aloud' but without using objects, or 'speaking to himself', 'in his head'. In the first case, the child can only perform the action with the help of objects; in the second, objects are no longer indispensable, but talking aloud still is; in the third, the child can dispense with both external objects and audible speech. This is a measure of his independence of various external aids. Here we have a new parameter – different degrees or *levels of assimilation* of an action.

There is a highly variable relationship between this latter parameter and others. The lowest level of assimilation (action with external objects) may be combined with quite a high degree of generalization and abbreviation; while on the other hand an action 'in the head' may be combined with the most extended form or with limitation to some particular apparatus, though this, of course, is only represented 'in the head'. But a given series of levels of assimilation are always related to each other in strict succession, since a higher level always assumes the presence of all the preceding ones. It is true that there appear, at first sight, to be frequent exceptions to this rule. A child may, for example, perform an action 'in his head' but be unable to do it aloud; or he may perform it aloud and be unable to do it with objects. But, in these cases, investigation always shows that the action is being performed 'formally', i.e. that the child is recalling some part or other of the action without understanding its real content. These, therefore, are only apparent exceptions to the rule of the succession of levels.

Levels of mastery (assimilation) are successive degrees on a separate parameter. But, since they signify not so much quantitative as qualitative changes of action, it is preferable to call them *levels* of mastery (assimilation), to distinguish them from measure or *degree* of mastery (familiarity).

The measures of generalization, abbreviation, familiarity and the levels of mastery of an action are, then, relatively independent parameters. For the formation of a fully effective mental action, each one must be worked through in a definite relation with the others. But, of all the parameters, it is the change of levels which leads in a direct line from action with external objects to action 'in the head', that constitutes the fundamental line of development of a mental action as such. It is, accordingly, with changes along this parameter – the level of mastery (assimilation) of an action – that this account is principally concerned.

There is an initial stage when the child cannot act himself, but follows the explanations and demonstrations of his teacher, so getting a preliminary idea of the action he is to learn; the learning of every mental action then passes through the following five basic stages:

(1) Creating a preliminary conception of the task.
(2) Mastering the action using objects.
(3) Mastering the action on the plane of audible speech.
(4) Transferring the action to the mental plane.
(5) Consolidating the mental action.

Within each stage an action follows a specific course of development, but the present account will be confined to the general characteristics of these stages.

(1) Creating a preliminary conception of the task

We became increasingly convinced of the special importance of this neglected and vaguely defined stage. Two methods of becoming familiar with a task have been discovered which differ profoundly in their effect on the subsequent formation of an action. First, after the teacher's initial explanations, the child immediately proceeds to make himself familiar with the material by his own efforts (though under the teacher's direction); second, the child does not himself perform any action for a long time, but takes an active part in the teacher's explanation by prompting his next operation or naming its result. We expected that the first method, which appears to be more active, would give the better results, but in fact the second proved rather more productive.[1]

How can we account for this ? We can only surmise that the second method frees the child from the task of performing the action physically and at the same time organizes his orienting activity, his attention; this results in a more thorough acquaintance with the object and a fuller and more correct conception of it, which in turn enables the child to master the task more quickly, easily and correctly.

Though the preliminary conception of an action is of great significance, its actual application by the child is limited in principle by the potentialities of previously acquired abilities. In other words, it does not include ability to perform the action, nor that knowledge of the properties of objects which is acquired through practical activity, but only knowledge of the external aspect of the new activity; it is not actual knowledge, therefore, but only the condition for its discovery.

(2) Mastering the action using objects

The child cannot learn a new action by means of a single observation, 'purely theoretically'; he first becomes familiar with a new action in the course of activity with external things – he learns to count, add and subtract with objects. Thus an action that must in due course become a mental action is not originally formed as such, but as an external and material action.

[1] An investigation by Zaporozhets, into the formation of motor skills, has shown analogous results.

This material action is, of course, built up in continuous verbal intercourse with the teacher, under the guiding influence of his instruction, explanations and corrections. But, at this stage, the role of speech, in the case of both teacher and pupil, is limited to indicating objective features of the goal, the objects available and the methods of dealing with them. These instructions, however important, do not take the place of action; the action can be completed only on the level of things, being based on them and determined by them, and remaining essentially an external, material action.

Psychological processes naturally have their part in this external action: in conceiving the goal, controlling the virtually fluid action, and regulating it in accordance with the task set. But this psychological activity constitutes only a part – an important one, but yet only a part – of the external action actually performed. This is because, at this stage, a child can carry out the reorganization which constitutes the content of every action only with external objects, and only by reconstructing them in a material way; he cannot do this in thought or imagination. Therefore, his action only exists at this stage in the form of an external action of this kind.

The kernel of the matter is that this material form of action is not only the inevitable initial form of a child's independent activity, but also the origin of the content and structure of the mental action subsequently elaborated. As has been noted, preliminary conception of the task includes only the external indications of what is to be achieved and how the initial material should be used. It does not include knowledge of the properties of things and the relations between them, still less does it include the necessary skills for dealing with them. The actual properties and relationships of objects and instruments (including the 'natural instrument' of the arm) are first manifested in practical activity with objects in efforts to reorganize these in the direction of the goal set. It is not surprising, therefore, that the child discovers the objective content of an action, in full measure and in the real world, not as a result of his preliminary conception of the task in the light of the teacher's explanations, but from his own action with things. Only in the collision between the material properties of object and instrument in the performance of a task, does a child perceive the objective logic of things and of his own action. This has been demonstrated by experiment, in a very simple, even naïve form. A child, counting buttons, takes them away singly with his fingers. A mitten is put on his hand, and, as the next 'unit', he takes at one go as many buttons as he can cover with the mitten. When the mitten is removed, the child at once returns to counting the buttons correctly, removing them with his fingers one by one.

An action with objects is strictly determined by the properties of the objects and, at the same time, is substantially supported by them: they seem to prompt and direct the action. Because of this, action with material things is exceptionally easy and has incomparable advantages over all other forms. The facts incline us more and more to the view that the basic reorganizations of an action as it evolves towards a fully effective mental action – generalization and abbreviation, testing, explanation and proof, correction and re-learning where required, and the actual formation of new conceptions – that all these should proceed, either directly at the level of activity with material things, or with a fresh approach to this level.

It would be incorrect, therefore, to attribute the advantages of activity with external objects only to its visual graphic nature. Such activity is significant, not because it illustrates a mental action, but because the child discovers the objective, concrete content of the action for himself, and achieves his first practical mastery of this content.

(3) Mastering the action on the plane of audible speech

When an action has been sufficiently mastered with objects, it is transferred to the plane of audible speech: the child learns to count aloud without the help of objects. This frees the action from the constant necessity of manipulating external things, but above all it represents a full advance to action with concepts.

Research has shown that, while an action remains on the plane of material things, words relating to it (in our case numerals) act mainly as indications of the objects. These signs may be well generalized and finely differentiated. A child may fetch any five objects, know by how much five is more than four and less than six, and readily continue counting from any number; but when he is given a problem, say $5 + 4$, he does not use '5' as a directly given number but begins counting it over again to recall it. To this end he turns to objects at hand, and counts them off or, if there are none, tries to imagine them. Only when he himself reaches the number given does he go on to add the second number to it. At this stage, the numeral represents for him only a sign for a specified aggregate of units and he returns to these units again and again in accordance with the sign. A numeral has not yet become a fully effective concept, which is itself a specific object of mental activity; it is not yet a meaningful sign for a certain quantity conceived as a simple whole.

It would appear that our belief in the child's ability to grasp the first item as a whole may be just as fallacious as our view of the child's other arithmetical actions. A child can be taught to add a second number directly to the first, given verbally or as a written figure, but if the number is simultaneously given in objects, he once more starts counting these out. In this case, the number or verbal sign serves only as a signal 'to count further', without denoting the nature of the first item as a simple whole, and the manipulation of numbers is 'formal'.

To turn a word-sign (in this case a numeral) into a real concept, it is necessary to enrich its meaning. This calls for a fresh return to objects and for additional work with them. If the addition of a second number is taught in this way, with actual objects, the action is immediately carried over to the spoken or written numeral. This shows that it has acquired full value in the sense indicated.

Arriving at a concept, therefore, requires a further return to objects; without this, words cannot acquire their proper meaning and provide an adequate foundation for a theoretical action 'in the head'. But the use of language in the course of action with objects, though it creates the essential conditions for a transition to the verbal-conceptual plane, does not of itself bring this about. When an action is performed only with objects, the failure to work out new concepts is clearly demonstrated by the child's inability to give an accurate account of his action. At first sight this picture seems strange: the child can act correctly, and with obvious understanding of objective relationships, yet he cannot give a comparable account of them and of his action. But this observed inability accounts for a familiar phenomenon: the delay between ability to perform an action and ability to give a verbal account of it, the 'retardation of the transition to the second signal system'.

(4) Transferring the action to the mental plane

When a full reflection of a material action has been achieved on the plane of audible speech, the stage of transference to the mental plane begins. The child is now taught to count in a whisper, then silently, to himself; he is advancing to action 'in the head'.

Of course, even 'in the head', he continues to use language and sense-images. The fundamental question is: How must the relation between concepts and sense-images be changed in order to ensure fully effective transfer to the 'mental plane' in different tasks and with different material (arithmetic and geometry, physiology and literature)? But from all the variations a rule gradually emerges: a perceived, and in this sense full-scale action 'in the head' – one which can be used accurately and confidently – forms only after the action has been thoroughly practised on the plane of audible speech.[1]

By virtue of its method of transfer, an action 'in the head' is initially an accurate reproduction of the final form to which the action evolved at the preceding level. But this action 'in the head' is now, of course, reproduced only in accordance with its own objective content and quickly proves to be a mere recollection of the former external action. The more habitual this recollection becomes, the more easily and automatically it takes its course, the more it becomes apparent that this is not really the action any longer, but rather a flow of concepts about it. However, that the process becomes automatic in its later stages should not blind us to the fundamental fact that at the right time, we learn to reproduce this recollection; to reproduce it in exact correspondence with the course of the objective process and then to carry it out just like any other action. In short, this is a real action, even though it occurs 'in the head' and has become automatic.

(5) Consolidating the mental action

Representing an action correctly 'in the head' (i.e. so that it corresponds with objective objects) is naturally more difficult than per-

[1] This appeared alike from our own investigations, from those of Slavina (carried out before our own and independently of them) and from those of E. I. Ignatiev (undertaken primarily for purposes other than investigating the development of mental actions). Ignatiev showed that practice on the plane of audible speech is indispensable if sense-perceptions are to be formed capable of providing a full-scale foundation for drawing objects.

forming it with things, or even with concepts spoken aloud. Things can be seen and can guide our action: words spoken aloud can be heard, as if they were those of another person, and their guiding power is even greater; whereas 'in the head' we have to imagine both the objects themselves and the actions to be performed with them, and also to check that both are correct. But, for the most part, it is not essential to reproduce all this fully. As a result, an action 'in the head', after becoming an accurate reflection of the final form of action reached at the preceding stage, is inevitably abbreviated or compressed and proceeds to the final stage, consolidation of the mental action.

Since an action recalled, or conceived 'to oneself', is one that has previously been carried out in reality, the correctness of the recall or conception can only be checked by returning to this external action; but it soon becomes evident that there is no point in following through the whole course of an action 'in the head'. We know the result in advance, and surveying the intermediate stages adds nothing. Equally, nothing obliges us to make such an inspection: omitting it evokes no negative reinforcement, nor does carrying it out evoke a positive one, so that the intermediate stages of the action gradually begin to drop out. At the conclusion of this process the course of an action runs as follows: having received instructions about initial data and what is to be done with them, we proceed immediately to the result, which is known as a result of frequent repetitions in past experience. Such an abbreviation fundamentally changes the character and 'external appearance' of a mental action. In 'external appearance' it loses the remnants of sense content, so that introspection cannot now reveal its actual course.

As for the character of the mental action, this is changed in so far as nothing is now produced beyond affirmation of what the end result would be if the corresponding external action had been carried out; whereas it formerly reorganized and performed, the action now anticipates and warns. As a result of this change, a mental action is placed in a new relation to its practical prototype. Having absorbed the experience of the latter, it now begins to orient this (not only, as previously, during the actual course of the action, but also up to and including its final results) and thereby discloses new possibilities for practical action. At the same time, the mental action shows a certain dependence on practical action and even rests upon it. As a result of this change in form and function, a mental action at last realizes its 'specifically psychic nature', or, as we are accustomed to put it, makes its appearance in 'direct experience'.

This, then, is the process of teaching a mental action: it begins with the task of learning something, a task usually set by other people; on the basis of demonstration and explanation, the child builds up a preliminary concept of the action as seen in the external action of another person. He then makes himself familiar with the action in its external material content, and gets to know it in practice, in its application to things. The first independent form of such activity in the child is, thus, inevitably the external material action.

Next, the action is separated from things and transferred to the plane of audible speech, where its material foundation is fundamentally changed: from being objective, it becomes linguistic, verbal. But the crux of this change is that, from being an action with things, it becomes an action with concepts, i.e. a genuinely theoretical action.

Finally, the action is transferred to the mental plane. Here, having undergone its final changes, it assumed that purely 'psychological appearance' revealed in introspection, which has so often been taken to be its real nature.

The first independent form of the child's new action is a material one; the final form is 'mental' ('conceptual'); the whole process of transition, from the first form to the last, consists in the formation of a series of qualitatively different reflections of this material action, with consequent abstraction of a particular aspect and the transformation of a material reorganization of things into a means of thinking about them; a material phenomenon is turned into a phenomenon of consciousness.

Another aspect of the matter may be briefly considered. The stages in which a mental action is formed are also stages at which a new theoretical ability is acquired. As we have seen, this process is by no means a simple reinforcement of such an ability in one and the same form; on the contrary it comprises a series of successive and qualitative changes in it.

But understanding – becoming mental – is only one parameter of the new ability. A mental action may be made up in different ways, both correct and incorrect, and in the end may not prove to be very effective. Whether it attains its full value depends not only on the level of understanding reached but also on other parameters – on the way it is generalized, abbreviated and duly mastered in the course of instruction. In general, the quality of the final mental action is determined by the following factors:

(1) Whether, at the first stage, there is formed a correct conception of the task, of the content of the action to be mastered;

(2) whether the material form of the action is fully developed and its objective content mastered at the outset;

(3) whether all the operations of the action, and the action as a whole, are generalized at the right time;

(4) whether proper and timely abbreviation also takes place;

(5) whether there is a careful and timely transfer of the action to the plane of audible speech;

(6) and the same careful and timely transfer to the 'mental plane';

(7) whether, in the course of all these changes, the intermediate forms of action are duly mastered. By 'duly' is meant, sufficiently to ensure the free application of the new forms of action, but not to such an extent as to interfere with the transition to higher forms; for, while it is important that each form of an action should be mastered at the right time, it is no less important that it should be given up at the right time for the following, more advanced, form;

(8) whether the final form of the action is consolidated, and whether this mastery is carried to the point of becoming fully automatic.

This system of requirements provided us with a scale for evaluating the mental actions mastered by children, and so for diagnosing success and failure in school and determining remedial measures.[1] When the latter are necessary, pupils should first be taken individually, with

[1] Davydov analysed the arithmetical knowledge and skills of retarded children in the first class; Slavina undertook an earlier analysis without making systematic use of the above criteria. Golomshtok extended this analysis to all levels of children's achievement at the end of their first school year; his data show that, for one and the same achievement (and all the more for a failure), the qualitative shortcomings in arithmetical mental actions are often extremely varied and so require various remedial measures.

the aim of raising their level of achievement. In practice, in the schools, attempts to remedy qualitative shortcomings in the mental actions of retarded children lead to a paradoxical situation: these pupils are given additional activities but these only mean additional practice and further reinforcement of precisely those defective methods of action from which they are in prime need of being freed.

Slavina's systematic experiments, and our separate but parallel attempts to make good the qualitative shortcomings in children's mental actions, have so far resulted in unsuccessful children becoming successful. There is nothing surprising about this, since we had a clear picture of the nature of these shortcomings. We obtained this picture on the basis of the scale of parameters and their indices given above; then, still using them, we systematically remedied the particular deficiency. To do this, we took the children back to the preceding stage in the formation of a given action – almost always to its material form, but sometimes even to the explanation of the task – and then systematically conducted them up the ladder of the requisite changes to the conscious 'action according to formula'. Thus the children mastered the full-scale mental action; and found that they were able to carry out corresponding tasks; the results drew approval and surprise from their elders and comrades, and it was worth seeing the change in their attitude to arithmetic, a subject towards which they had previously felt nothing but dislike!

Both this work and Slavina's were carried out with individuals, a modification of method is, of course, required when working with a class. But, whether instruction is individual or collective, formation in stages remains the essential content of the process of mastering new skills. Precisely the same scale of basic parameters can be used in the evaluation of a mastered action, whatever the factual content and other qualities of the instruction. It may be hoped that knowledge of the way in which mental actions are formed stage by stage will provide a firm theoretical foundation for the development of effective teaching.

6 The stage theory of the formation of mental operations*

N. TALYZINA

This paper develops a common Soviet thesis that the intervention of a teacher working with a systematic plan of instruction based on psychological principles fundamentally changes the mental activity of the child. What seem the 'natural' methods and sequences of acquiring new modes of thinking are largely the result of unsystematic non-psychological methods of learning. It is interesting to contrast this view with the arguments of the more extreme supporters of discovery learning. A key aspect of the argument is an approach to instruction which follows Gal'perin's stage theory (see page 142 ff.). Other aspects are similar to Western views on the enhancing of concept formation by presenting a variety of exemplars. Also of great interest is the emphasis on providing the learner with help in his orientation to the learning task and with guidance on learning strategies (algorithms).

The mental development of man is impossible without the influence of learning. The level and features both of general and of intellectual development are determined by the quality of learning – above all, by its content and by the nature of the direction given to the course of the process of assimilation.

The role of learning stands out with particular sharpness in the process whereby the principal forms of mental activity come into being.

In current learning practice, it is not normally considered necessary to employ special methods to learn general and special techniques of intellectual activity. Therefore these techniques take shape as knowledge is acquired with the learner giving completely inadequate direction to the learning process. Learning organized in this way both determines and corresponds to the process which shapes the principal forms of mental activity. Such learning takes a long time and there is a confused diversity of intermediate stages, while the results attained by different pupils show a high degree of scattering.

* Reprinted and abridged from N. Talyzina, 'The Stage Theory of the Formation of Mental Operations', *Soviet Education*, X (3), 1968, pp. 38–42. The author is associated with the M. V. Lomonosov Moscow State University.

In psychology, this poorly controlled course of assimilation of concepts and of the principal types of intellectual activity is actually equated with intellectual development. On the other hand the majority of contemporary psychological theories regard this course of the process of assimilation to be a manifestation of its necessary internal logic.

The line of research founded in Soviet psychology by the writings of L. S. Vigotsky, continued by the works of A. N. Leont'ev, and today formulated as P. Ia. Gal'perin's stage theory of formation of mental operations has resulted in the development of a different course for the process of assimilation and has posed the question of clear-cut delimitation of the criteria of mastery of various types of mental activity and the indices of intellectual development. According to this theory, the various forms of intellectual development, of necessity, require mastery in a special fashion in the process of learning. Moreover, new forms cannot be mastered immediately in the form of ideas. The initial form of intellectual activity is external, materialized activity. It becomes mental and ideational only after a number of qualitative changes occur.

Along with the transformation of the operational aspect of activity, changes in its objects occur: material entities are gradually replaced by ideational ones. In this case, cognitive activity appears simultaneously as a means of assimilating data about the world and as a distinct subject to be mastered. In accordance with this, the organization of the learning process should include new requirements that are not met in consistent and systematic form in the usual learning process. In the first place, operations (activity) on the part of the pupil adequate to the knowledge to be mastered should be identified as necessary means of assimilation. In the second place, these actions should be initially modelled in external, material (or materialized) form, which makes it possible not only to make their content clear to the pupil but to ensure that they will be mastered. In the third place, a program should be drawn up for step-by-step changes in these acts, and they should be modified at each stage in accordance with four independent characteristics. In the fourth place, at each of the steps in the modification of the operations, control over their performance should be provided, operation by operation. In the final stages of assimilation, this becomes self-monitoring. All this taken together permits planned direction of the shaping of mental actions and, through them, of the shaping of knowledge as their products. It becomes possible to shape in all pupils knowledge and abilities with properties determined beforehand, to reduce considerably the time required to assimilate this knowledge, to diminish considerably the scattering of grades received, and to cause the successes scored to approximate the upper possible limits. Moreover, the diversity of the intermediate stages disappears, as do the errors characteristic of each stage. It becomes possible to shape various types of intellectual activity at an earlier age than is generally regarded as possible.

Let us cite some experimental data. We employed the technique of stage formation of mental operations to follow the course of assimilation of elementary geometrical concepts by 184 schoolchildren who had previously not studied geometry. Moreover, pupils who had shown average and poor grades in the major school subjects (experiments of Talyzina, Butkin, Nikolaeva etc.) were deliberately selected. The act of recognition was employed as the means of forming concepts.[1]

From the very outset, the subjects were given not only a system of necessary and sufficient criteria of the respective concepts, but a rule for operating with them. The system of criteria and the rule for operating with them were initially employed by the subjects in external, material form, then spoken aloud, and only at the closing stage of assimilation were they employed in internalized, mental form. The fulfilment of the requirements specified above had the consequence that, in recognition of geometrical entities, all the subjects were guided from the very outset by a system of significant criteria and fulfilled all the assignments correctly. What errors there were, were random in nature, and they did not exceed 5 per cent of all the assignments carried out. Moreover, all errors were corrected by the subjects themselves. The criteria selected acted in the nature of a standard against which the subjects compared the objects presented to them. As a result of the application of a selected system of criteria to various types of objects, all subjects formed not only the

---

[1] In the usual forms of learning, even in secondary-school grades, the operation of recognition is found not to have become firmly established in the majority of pupils (research of M. B. Volovich).

corresponding concepts, but an act of recognition which, in the shaping of the subsequent concepts, served in some part as a finished technique of ideation. For example, in one of our researches (experiments of E. I. Kochurova), the subjects were offered biological objects for recognition after they had mastered a certain number of geometrical concepts.[1] They were given pictures indicating the distinguishing characteristics of various classes of animals and plants, and descriptions of all the objects presented for recognition. But no algorithm for recognition was offered. None the less, all the subjects not only coped successfully with the assignments but were able to validate the correctness of their replies.

Thus, the algorithm for recognition, reflecting the logical content of the act of recognition, served in the control series of experiments as a ready-made technique of thought. When we turn to the content of the criteria of recognition and the means of establishing their presence in concrete objects, we enter the realm of characteristics specific to thought. They can come into being only on the basis of a strictly defined content of entities. Transfer of this aspect of the act of recognition from geometrical to biological entities could not occur.

The technique of step-by-step shaping of mental operations was also employed by us in work with children 5 and 6 years of age. In forty children of that age group, the act of recognition was made the special subject of assimilation in the formation of artificial Vygotskii–Sakharov concepts (experiments by Kh. M. Teplen'kaia and G. P. Baraeva). It was found that, from the very outset, all the children also oriented themselves upon a system of properties called to their attention (the height and base area of figurines). The transition stages found in the experiments of L. S. Vigotsky did not appear.[2]

The algorithm for recognition after step-by-step mastery of an operation was successfully transferred to new concepts by all the children. It was thus found that the tendency on the part of pre-school children to orient themselves on the obvious properties of objects rather than on the significant ones is not at all an inherent characteristic of that age group, but merely the re-

[1] The subjects had had no previous study of biology.
[2] But transitional forms existed in the control group, in which shaping of concepts was conducted by the Vigotsky–Sakharov technique.

sult of assimilation of particular acts of cognition being poorly guided.

Entirely analogous results were obtained in the shaping of other mental actions.

The researches conducted also showed that the decisive component defining the course and quality of mastery is the orienting component of the cognitive activity of the pupils: the totality of those objective conditions upon which the pupil orients himself in performing various actions. In this connection it is particularly necessary to emphasize the importance of planned direction of the formation precisely of this portion of mental actions. Monitoring of the end product of the act and monitoring merely of its implementing portion are inadequate, inasmuch as the identical end result and the identical implementation may occur on the basis of significantly different bases of orientation.

We shall demonstrate the importance of the orienting basis of action in the formation of but one of the characteristics of ideational activity: generalization.

It has been experimentally established that generalization proceeds with respect to those properties – and only those – that became part of the orientational basis of the action. The other characteristics, even if they are present in all the objects being changed by the individual undergoing learning, are not perceived as essential to the action. Thus, in the shaping of geometrical concepts among schoolchildren who had not previously studied geometry (experiments of E. V. Konstantinova), the orienting basis of the act of recognition included the system of necessary and sufficient criteria of the corresponding concept. Moreover, an algorithm of recognition was provided, and objective operation-by-operation monitoring over the course of implementation of the action was provided. Thus, orientation upon the selected criteria was assured in all the assignments. In all the assignments with which the pupils worked, geometrical figures were presented in a single position in space. This characteristic was universally present in all the instances with which the subject dealt. In the control series of tasks, the pupils were shown figures in the most diverse positions in space. Classification of the control objects was conducted in proper fashion. Consequently, the common characteristic – the position in space of the objects to be analysed – was not reflected as significant, and generalization took place only with respect to the criteria that were included in the orienting basis of the act.

Analogous results were obtained in the studies with children of 5 and 6, to which we have referred. The dimensions of height and base area of figurines were included in the orientation basis for the act of recognition. The figurines with which the children worked differed from each other in form, colour and volume, but all were made of wood. This characteristic was possessed in common by all the figures. In the control series of experiments, the children were offered figurines made of other materials. They were asked whether these latter could be classified in the concepts they had been given. The children used the standards they possessed to check the height and base area of the figures and, on that basis, classified them in one of the four concepts known to them. It is characteristic that even mis-leading suggestions and questions by the experimenter did not pre-vent the subjects from acting correctly.

Thus, generalization does not proceed merely on the basis of per-ception of that which exists in common in objects. A property is reflected as significant only after it has become part of the orientation basis of the act of an individual directed to analysis of the correspond-ing objects. The numerous cases in which generalization is per-formed on the basis of common but non-significant characteristics are readily explained: in the best of cases, the pupil is merely given a set of characteristics by which he is to orient himself (via a definition), but he is not provided with a means of orientation with their aid in the course of his activity. As a consequence, these characteristics do not become part of the orienting basis of the action. The pupils build a working orienting foundation themselves, incorporating in it, above all, those criteria of the object that lie at its surface. As a conse-quence, generalization proceeds not on the basis of the criteria in the definition, but via random, non-significant characteristics.

Thus, in order to synthesize mental actions and knowledge on the basis of the properties comprising that which is specific to the region under study, it is necessary to organize learning in such a fashion that these specific features become part of the orienting basis of the acts of the pupils, and are not present merely in the material offered them to act upon.

The manner in which the features specific to the object are incorporated in the basis of orientation may differ. They may be presented in a concrete form suited to orientation only in a single, special case. In this case, other instances in the given region will appear to the pupils to be new and, for the transformation of these, the learned criteria of orientation will not be applicable. But the basis of orientation in the action may also be presented in generalized form. Mastery of an action on this basis of orientation makes it possible for the learner to apply it successfully and independently to other special cases as well. Thus, in a study – conducted jointly by us and Iu. V. Iakovlev – employing elementary chess skills, one group of subjects was shown the significant characteristics of the positions in chess in the concrete form characteristic of these figures in a particular arrangement. In the other group of subjects, the characteristics of the positions that had to be taken into consideration in choosing the next move were incorporated from the very outset in the basis of orientation in generalized form – in the form of general principles making it possible to evaluate any position. In the latter case, the positions on the board from which the principles were learned appeared to the subjects not in the light of concrete, special properties, but in terms of the general properties characteristic of all the other positions. In both groups, learning followed the technique of stage-by-stage shaping of mental actions, and was identical in other respects as well. In solving the initial tasks, if one judges by the implementing portion of the actions and their final product, there were no differences between the groups at the end of the learning period: the subjects in both groups solved the problems correctly. But in solving new problems (other figures, different arrangement) requiring a high content of concreteness in the basis of orientation, the difference between the groups proved enormous: the subjects in group I yielded 33 per cent correct answers, while those in the second group gave 93 per cent.

Finally, it is necessary that the basis of orientation of the action differentiate between the specific content and the content of formal logic. The first reflects features in the domain of things in which the subject is acting, while the second reflects the logical structure of the operations with things. The limits of generalization of the first part are determined by the specific features of the region on the materials

7 Learning by discovery: an interpretation of recent research*

B. Y. KERSH and M. C. WITTROCK

As the authors of this paper point out, learning by discovery is currently very fashionable in educational circles. A substantial amount of literature has been produced on the subject and many hundreds of teachers have attempted to use discovery methods in their classes. However, there are problems in deciding what discovery learning is and there is often a singular lack of supporting evidence for the views of some of the more ardent exponents of the method. This paper discusses these problems and presents some research findings which should help to bring the subject into a more useful perspective.

The teaching method frequently labelled the discovery method is not new but is very much in the forefront of attention in education today. This observation is supported by the substantial curriculum efforts in mathematics and science and by the programmatic research endeavours on cognition, not to mention the numerous independent efforts by researchers over the country. In the opinion of the authors of this review, present interest in learning by discovery more than rivals that which centres around the new technology of programmed instruction.

The literature on learning by discovery dates back many years but is limited in this present review to the research studies published or reported since 1955. There is a break of approximately six years prior to 1955 during which very little research activity is evident, and afterwards a rash of publications appear which bear directly on the topic. Also, many studies of problem solving, thinking and other complex processes related to discovery were ruled out because they were not conducted in the context of learning.

As is the case with defining programmed instruction, it is difficult to find a clear definition of discovery. In the research literature, the

* Reprinted and abridged from B. Y. Kersh and M. C. Wittrock, 'Learning by Discovery: An Interpretation of Recent Research', *Journal of Teacher Education*, **13**, 1962, pp. 461–8.

term 'discovery' frequently describes a learner's goal-directed behaviour when he is forced to complete a learning task without help from the teacher. Hereafter, in this article, discovery is described in the same way. If the learner completes the task with little or no help, he is said to have learned by discovery. The most significant teaching variable is the amount of guidance or direction provided by the teacher during the discovery process. In practice, considerable help from the teacher may be provided and still the learner may be said to have learned by discovery, but in such instances the process is usually qualified and called guided discovery. As the amount of help from the teacher increases, it is said that opportunities for discovery decrease and the learner may rely more on rote processes.

Actually, the terms 'discovery' and 'rote' are probably not polar terms at all. It may be more correct to confine the one term, discovery, to that phase in learning which precedes the learner's making the response desired by the teacher for the first time (the problem-solving stage) and the other, rote learning, to the phase which follows when the learner is memorizing or acquiring increasing skill.

It should be noted that the above definition is stated in operational terms, i.e. it states how the teacher operates with the learner or the conditions under which the learner operates during discovery. The definition does *not* infer anything about the learner's sensations or perceptions during or at the point of discovery.[1] When the learner first makes the required response with little or no help from the teacher he may or may not have experienced 'insight', and he may or may not understand. Also, he may have been acquiring some other skills quite incidentally in the discovery process. Similarly, even after first making the required response, when the learner is memorizing it or practising it, he may still ascertain something new (to him) about that which he is practising.

---

[1] This is not to say that the term 'discovery' refers to something other than covert behaviour. The authors prefer to think that discovery is a type of covert behaviour which is most likely to *occur* prior to the learner's first acceptable response, but which may actually occur at any time during the learning process. Although the term defies rigorous definition, even in operational terms, it should not be used to characterize stimuli presented to the learner, as in the 'discovery method'. Also, 'discovery phase' should not be construed to refer to an interval of time, *per se*.

COMPARISON OF LEARNING TASKS

It is becoming increasingly more evident that the somewhat inconsistent findings by researchers in recent years may actually reflect different learning outcomes resulting from two or three quite different processes of learning by discovery. We can no longer speak of the discovery method in general terms and make all-encompassing claims about it any more than we can speak of the auto-instructional method now as if it were one technique.

In this article, an attempt is made to look at the learner's task – what he was required to discover and under what circumstances – in each of the recent research studies and to infer what the learner might have learned in addition to the measured outcome. From this perspective it can be shown that the apparently different findings of some of the more recent studies are actually highly consistent and that it is possible to make some new interpretations of the research findings.

Formal phases in the learning process

In the diagram in Fig. 1, the line represents the learning process from start to finish. For convenience, the letter symbols are used to designate formal steps in the sequence. Formal steps in learning are determined by the teacher. Between A and B there is what might be called the discovery phase. Point B marks the point at which the

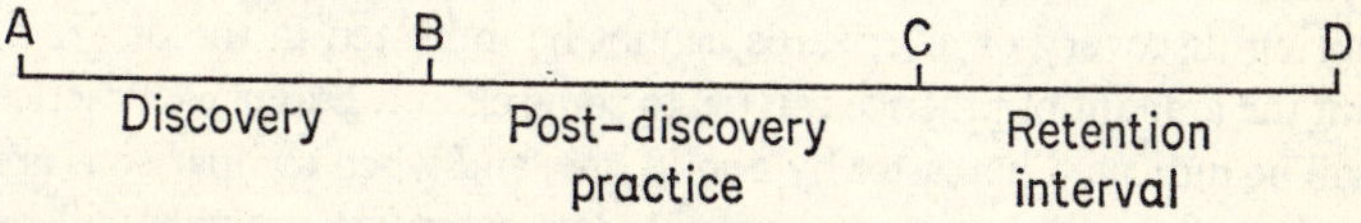

Figure 1. Formal phases in the learning process

learner first makes the required response, with or without help from the teacher.

Starting at B in the learning process, the learner is memorizing or acquiring increasing skill in using whatever was ascertained at B. He could be learning to transfer to new situations, to make discriminations, or to increase the rate of his responses.

Point C designates the end of formal practice, after which the teacher no longer has direct control over the learning process. Formal testing may begin at C. If the first test is at C, it would be called a test of immediate recall or a learning test. If another test is given after some designated time interval, the test would occur at D in the learning process.

Not all learning involves the entire sequence A through C. In typing, for instance, the student typically is started at B, as if there is very little to discover in learning to typewrite. The teaching of typewriting assumes that the student already has acquired certain fundamental skills and can begin by practising the use of these skills in a new context. In teaching mathematics, however, it is often assumed that the student may have to work for some time on a problem before he learns the principle involved, or, we might say, 'discovers' the solution. In this case the learning process may be said to start at A.

In the previous discussion it may have been suggested that the learner does not practise during the discovery phase. Actually, it is not a matter of practice or no practice, but rather what is practised and reinforced, how and to what extent. During the problem-solving or trial-and-error process which characterizes discovery learning, the learner may try to apply a principle to examples in order to verify his solution. This may constitute 'practice' of the sort that may be restricted formally to the post-discovery phase. Even more likely, during discovery the learner may be practising other behaviours called 'employing search models', 'seeking relationships' and 'shifting approaches'.

Exactly what is practised and how the reinforcement is scheduled during discovery or afterwards cannot be indicated in the diagram, but the amount of practice can be, to some extent. Extensive practice will be indicated hereafter by a solid line, and when comparisons are made between experimental groups, less extensive practice will be indicated by a dotted line.

Typically, in experiments on discovery, learning tasks are used which may either be started at A or at B. In other words, the learner may be required to discover the answer for himself or he may be told the answer and then be given practice in using it. Requiring the student to begin at A is described as learning by discovery, and starting at B is described as directed learning or learning by reception. As implied earlier, typically there is an intermediate type of learning described as guided discovery which starts the learner at A but provides some guidance from the teacher during the discovery phase.

Kersh's experiment

Consider now some of the more recent studies in terms of the diagram. B. Y. Kersh employed an arithmetic task in an experiment which compared groups of college students taught by the three methods described above. The procedure may be diagrammed as in Fig. 2.

This diagram shows that one group, the Discovery Group, was required to discover the arithmetic rules for itself without help from the experimenter. This extensive discovery experience is indicated by the solid line from A to B. No formal practice was required after

Discovery: A————B		C (Post-experimental practice)	D (Test for B)
Guided D: A — — — — B		C	D (Test for B)
Directed:	B————C		D (Test for B)

Figure 2. Kersh's experiment (1958)

the rules were discovered at B. Instead, the formal learning period was terminated at C with a test of immediate recall. However, subjects in the discovery group tended to continue practising the rules or to continue their efforts to discover the rules after the formal learning period had terminated.

The Guided Discovery Group was also required to discover the rules but was given some help in the form of clues in its efforts to discover them. The fact that help was given during the discovery process is indicated by the dotted line from A to B in the diagram. In every other respect, this group was treated as the Discovery Group was, but there was no evidence of post-experimental practice with the Guided Discovery Group.

The third group, the Directed Group, was told the rules outright and given some examples for practice. Learning started at B and terminated at C.

All three groups were retested approximately one month later (D) for their ability to remember the rules and apply them in the solution of appropriate examples. In other words, they were tested on whatever was acquired at B.

From the diagram, it would be predicted that at the end of the learning period (C) the Directed Group would be superior to the other two groups in ability to apply the rules to solve specific addition problems because of the practice in this activity during learning. This is what Kersh found. In fact, some of the individuals in the Discovery Group failed completely to discover the rules during the time allowed.

However, after one month, the tables were turned. On the test given at D, the Discovery Group was superior to both of the other groups. Presumably, the superior performance of the Discovery Group reflected the post-experimental practice. Individuals in the Discovery Group probably were motivated to continue their efforts to learn the rules and to practise the rules after the formal learning period. In another experiment, Kersh substantiated this interpretation.

Kittell's experiment

By way of contrast, J. E. Kittell reported an experiment which employed a word task with sixth-grade subjects. The various treatments are shown in the diagram in Fig. 3. The Discovery Group

```
Discovery: A _____ B _ _ _ _ C      D (Test for B and A–B
                                              Transfer)

Guided D: A _ _ _ _ B _____ C      D (Test for B and A–B
                                              Transfer)

Directed:              B _ _ _ _ C      D (Test for B and A–B
                                              Transfer)
```

Figure 3. Kittell's experiment (1957)

(Kittell's Minimum Direction Group) was given examples of the principles involved in the word task with directions indicating only that there was a principle involved. If the principle was discovered early enough, some practice in applying it was possible. The Guided Discovery Group (Intermediate Direction) was given the same directions and a statement of the general rule so that actually it had only a limited discovery experience, if any. Finally, the Directed Group (Maximum Direction) was told not only the principle but also the answer to each of the examples. The Directed Group had a relatively restricted practice opportunity, consequently.

The diagram of Kittell's experiment indicates that the Discovery Group actually had little opportunity to practise the application of the general principles because the task proved to be very difficult for the sixth-grade youngsters. They discovered, on the average, less than three principles out of fifteen in addition to those measured on a pre-test. The dotted line from B to C indicates this lack of practice. In the case of the Guided Discovery Group the dotted line from A to B indicates little practice in discovery of the principles, and the solid line from B to C suggests extensive formal practice in applying them. The Directed Group had no discovery experience and limited formal practice in applying the general principles involved.

The post-test measured the learners' ability to apply the principles and to discover new principles from new examples. In effect they were tested on what was acquired at B and on their ability to transfer discovery skills learned during discovery (A–B) or elsewhere.

In view of the formal practice provided the Guided Discovery Group, it may be expected that this group would be superior to the other groups in applying the principles. Kittell's findings do indicate this. From the solid line between A and B, it may be predicted that the Discovery Group would be superior to the other groups in discovering new principles from new examples. Instead, Kittell's findings indicate that the Guided Discovery Group was also superior in this respect. However, when one recalls that the Discovery Group learned less than three of the fifteen principles, it is not difficult to understand Kittell's findings. In effect, their discovery behaviour may have been extinguished rather than reinforced.

The Gagné and Brown experiment

The last experiment to be discussed is diagrammed in Fig. 4. Using an arithmetic task similar to that used in the Kersh experiment, R. M. Gagné and L. T. Brown constructed three self-instructional programs designed to teach in the three modes discussed previously. Each group was instructed in the basic mathematical concepts and notations involved. The Discovery Group was then required to discover the rules for several different problem series. The Discovery

Group had no formal practice in the application of the rules. In the Guided Discovery Group, the learner was carried rather systematically through a series of steps leading to his own formulation of the general rule. Again, no formal practice on specific examples of the rules was provided. The Directed Group (Rule and Example) was told the rules and then was given formal practice in the application of each rule to a series of examples.

The test in the Gagné and Brown experiment came almost immediately after the end of the formal learning period. The test measured only the learner's ability to discover new rules from different problem series. As such, it was a transfer test of discovery

Discovery: A_____B   C (Test for A–B Transfer

Guided D: A_ _ _ _ _ _B   C (Test for A–B Transfer

Directed: B_____C (Test for A–B Transfer

Figure 4. Gagné and Brown's experiment (1961)

skill, *not* a test of recall or application of rules. The average time and the number of hints required to discover the new rules were used to compare the teaching treatments.

From the diagram of the Gagné and Brown experiment, it may be predicted that the Discovery Group would be superior on the transfer test, followed, in turn, by the Guided Discovery Group and the Directed Group. The findings indicate that the Guided Discovery Group was slightly superior to the Discovery Group but both discovery groups were definitely superior to the Directed Group.

Although the Gagné and Brown experiment does not provide data on retention of rules learned, it may be predicted that on a retention test the Directed Group would perform most effectively, since this group had had the most practice in the application of the rules.

A comparison of the diagrams of the three experiments will reveal one finding which is not easily explained in terms of the relative amount of practice. In Kersh's experiment the Discovery Group engaged in post-experimental practice, and this finding was not reported by either of the other two researchers. Gagné and Brown did not allow much time for such practice, but there were approximately twenty-four hours during which their subjects could have engaged in post-experimental practice. Presumably the findings of both Gagné and Brown and Kittell would have been influenced by the extra practice, had it occurred.

One explanation for the unique finding in Kersh's study becomes evident when one examines the learning process in each case and infers what was learned in addition to the particular rules or principles involved.

In the Kersh experiment, reinforcement was provided intermittently for discovering, *per se*. The experimenter gave support and encouragement regardless of the learner's success or failure. In the Kittell experiment, reinforcement was provided regularly for providing answers to specific examples, and Gagné and Brown similarly reinforced only the correct response. The fact that Kersh's treatment fostered a kind of searching behaviour explains the 'motivating effects' of the discovery experience. The findings of the three experiments may actually be reflecting different learning outcomes resulting from two quite different processes of learning by discovery.

In general these studies, along with a number of other recent experiments, suggest that learning by discovery is indeed many faceted. Answers to problems, general rules for solving problems and even the motivation to continue learning may be acquired separately or in combination. Moreover, it is often possible to predict, from a careful analysis of the practice and reinforcement schedules involved in discovery learning, which facets will be acquired. Also, it is probable that more facets may be acquired simultaneously under conditions of discovery (guided or not) than when learning is highly directed.

COMPARISON OF TEACHING TECHNIQUES

What do these findings mean to the teacher? It is evident that one can learn different things by the process labelled 'discovery'. Therefore, to talk intelligently about discovery methods of teaching or learning, one must state one's desired outcome or teaching objective.

The comments which follow bear only upon those tasks which can be either discovered or memorized. Also, it is presumed that whatever the objective, it is desirable to achieve the goal as rapidly as possible, all other things being equal.

Even within the context of such tasks the teacher's goal may be more or less specific. The teacher may be satisfied to have the learners memorize rules and learn to apply them for purposes of a particular project or activity. At the other extreme, a teacher may use a particular exercise as a means of teaching the children techniques for discovering new rules from different examples or as a means of stimulating their interest in a particular area of study.

For the goal of teaching specific aspects of subject-matter – aspects which could be either memorized or discovered – it is clear that the process which was described as 'directed learning' is the most efficient. Generally speaking, a teacher should not employ highly directed techniques if she wishes to develop long-term retention and transfer effects. However, the directed procedure does not necessarily produce learning outcomes which are short-lived. Retention and transfer effects primarily reflect the practice and reinforcement schedules.

With organized bodies of information, very often the teacher is most interested in teaching the organizational framework itself. Usually this framework is in the form of principles, rules, generalizations and conceptual schemes. If so, the research evidence suggests the intermediate direction or guided discovery techniques. It makes little difference, apparently, whether the rule or principle is discovered or is taught directly, provided the learner is reinforced for effective practice in using the rule or principle. Organizational schemes, however, often need to be understood through the establishment of relationships between new and previous learning. When the learner lacks the necessary background of information and is not motivated, generally it is more effective to establish such relationships by using techniques of guided discovery rather than more or less directed techniques. The important thing is that the new learnings are established in relationship to previous learning. Provided the learner has the related knowledge and willingness to assimilate the material, the directed technique may be equally effective and more efficient than guided discovery.

Very often the teacher has as his objective techniques of discovery, *per se*. The actual subject-matter involved may be of secondary importance. The purpose of the learning experience is to exercise and to reinforce the learner in what may be called 'searching behaviour' – strategies of problem solving, divergent as opposed to convergent thinking, flexibility in thinking – in essence, the characteristics of what is often labelled 'the creative person'. With such objectives, discovery or guided discovery techniques are most appropriate. However, if the task is so difficult that the learner does not succeed in discovering the relationships which he is supposed to discover, there will be little opportunity for reinforcement of that very process which is being taught. It is most important that the learner have success experiences when learning by discovery.

It has become increasingly apparent that the learners' attitudes towards a subject-matter area may be as important as what he learns in the cognitive sense. If a student is highly interested in a subject, he is likely to continue to learn. Under appropriate conditions of practice and reinforcement, the discovery technique will foster favourable attitudes and interests. It is interesting and challenging for students to discover, particularly if their efforts are successful, or at least occasionally so. The opposite effect may result when their efforts never or almost never meet with success. Also, there is reason to believe that an intermittent or irregular pattern of success may be more effective than a regular pattern in maintaining interest.

SUMMARY

Consistent throughout the recent research, as interpreted above, is evidence that the discovery method is effective for what it requires the learner to do and for what is reinforced during learning. The learner may acquire more effective ways of problem solving through the discovery process than through another process simply because he has an opportunity to practise different techniques and because his more effective techniques are reinforced. Similarly, the learner may become more proficient in applying rules through the directed process of teaching simply because, through formal practice, he has more opportunity for effective practice and reinforcement than otherwise. Guided discovery seems to offer a happy medium between independent discovery and highly directed learning. Some of the efficiency of directed learning is maintained along with the benefits of the discovery process, specifically, motivation and problem-solving skill.

Learning is a complex process. It cannot be explained solely in terms of practice and reinforcement. However, these two concepts are powerful and do enable us to understand much of what a student learns by discovery.

8 Words, meanings and concepts*

J. B. CARROLL

The particular interest of this paper lies in the way in which the author takes some of the more commonly held views on the nature of concepts and concept formation and shows how they may be related to school learning. By taking an example of a concept which will probably be unfamiliar to the reader he places him in similar situation to a child in school when the teacher moves on to a new subject. The reader is thus able to gain an insight into the problems of concept learning and teaching which we take up with more specific reference to school subjects later.

I suspect that anyone who has examined the concept formation literature with the hope of finding something of value for the teaching of concepts in school has had cause for some puzzlement and disappointment, because however fascinating this literature may be, as it wends its way through the detailed problems posed by the methodology itself, its relevance to the learning of concepts in the various school subjects is a bit obscure.

Let us look at the major differences between concept learning in school and in the laboratory.

1. One of the major differences is in the nature of the concepts themselves. A new concept learned in school is usually a genuinely 'new' concept rather than an artificial combination of familiar attributes (like the concept 'three blue squares' such as might be taught in a psychological experiment).

2. New concepts learned in school depend on attributes which

* Reprinted and abridged from J. B. Carroll, 'Words, Meanings and Concepts', *Harvard Educational Review*, **34** (2), 1964, pp. 191–202.

themselves represent difficult concepts. In more general terms, concepts learned in school often depend upon a network of related or prerequisite concepts. One cannot very well learn the concept of derivative, in the calculus, until one has mastered a rather elaborate structure of prerequisite concepts (e.g. slope, change of slope, algebraic function etc.). Further, the attributes on which school-learned concepts depend are frequently verbal, depending on elements of meaning that cannot easily be represented in terms of simple sensory qualities as used in concept formation experiments.

3. Many of the more difficult concepts of school learning are of a relational rather than a conjunctive character; they deal with the relations among attributes rather than their combined presence or absence. Concept formation experiments have thus far revealed little about the acquisition of relational concepts.

4. An important element in school learning is the memory problem involved in the proper matching of words and concepts. Thus, the problems of paired-associate memory are added to those of concept learning itself. For example, a student in biology or social studies has to learn not only a large number of new concepts, but also a large number of unfamiliar, strange-looking words to be attached to these concepts. The rate at which new concepts can be introduced is probably limited, just as the rate at which foreign language words can be acquired is limited.

5. The most critical difference between school concept learning and concept learning in psychological experiments is that the former is for the most part deductive and the latter is generally inductive. It would be relatively rare to find a concept taught in school by the procedure of showing a student a series of positive and negative instances, labelled as such, and asking him to induce the nature of the concept with no further aid. Such instances could be found, of course, perhaps they would exemplify a pure 'discovery method', and perhaps there should be more use of this method than is the case. The fact is that a pure discovery method is seldom used, because it is rather slow and inefficient. Even if a teaching procedure incorporates 'discovery' elements, it is likely to be combined with deductive elements. The concept to be taught is described verbally – perhaps by a rule or definition – and the student is expected to attain the concept by learning to make correct identification of positive and negative

instances. For example, he is told what an 'indirect object' is and then is given practice in identifying the indirect objects (positive instances) among other words (negative instances). Many simple concepts can be taught by a wholly deductive procedure. For most students, the dictionary definition of *tarn* will be a sufficient stimulus for attainment of the concept. On the other hand, it is well known that purely deductive verbal procedures are frequently insufficient to help learners attain concepts. Concept formation experimentation would be more relevant to school learning problems if it could give more attention to examining the role of verbalization and other deductive procedures in concept attainment.

Nevertheless, there are certain similarities between concept attainment in school and concept formation in psychological experiments. These arise chiefly from the fact that not every concept is learned *solely* in a formalized, prearranged school setting. The school environment is in many ways continuous with the out-of-school environment; concepts are learned partly in school, partly out of school. The process whereby the elementary concepts of a language are learned closely parallels that of the psychological concept formation experiment. A child learns the concept 'dog' not by having the concept described to him but by learning to restrict his usage of the word *dog* to instances regarded as positive by the speech community. In this process there are many false responses – either false positives (calling a non-dog a dog) or false negatives (believing a dog to be a non-instance), before an appropriate series of reinforcements produces correct concept attainment. Similar phenomena occur with concepts in the school curriculum. A child who has been told that his cousins visiting him from Peoria are 'tourists' may not realize that tourists do not need to be relatives, and when he is told that the Germans who have settled in his town are 'immigrants', he may believe that all foreigners visiting his town are immigrants. Concept formation experiments yield information as to the range and variety of instances that have to be furnished for efficient and correct concept formation in the absence of formal instruction.

But if the foregoing statement is true, concept formation studies should also yield insights as to what information has to be furnished for *deductive* concept formation, e.g. from a formal definition. Obviously, a formal definition is successful only to the extent that it correctly identifies and describes all the criterial attributes that are likely to be relevant for a concept, and to the extent that it communicates the proper values and relationships of these to the learner. The burden is both on the definition itself and on the learner. A student may fail to learn the concept *tarn* from the definition previously cited either because it omits some essential criterial attribute (e.g. that a tarn must contain *water* rather than, say, *oil* or *lava*), or because the student fails to comprehend the meaning of its elements (for example, how small is 'small'?).

What is actually going on in most school learning of concepts is a process that combines in some way deductive and inductive features.

Descriptions and definitions provide the deductive elements of the process. The several parts of a description or definition specify the attributes and relationships that are criterial for the concept. The order in which these specifications are arranged in the description and presented to the student may have something to do with the ease of concept attainment, particularly in the case of complex concepts with many attributes and complex interrelationships (like the case of *tort* discussed below). As yet we have no well-founded generalizations about the order in which the criterial attributes for a concept should be presented.

At the same time, inductive procedures entail the citing of positive and negative instances of the concept. We know from concept attainment research that learning is facilitated more by positive than by negative instances, even though the 'information' conveyed by these instances is the same in a given experimental context. But in real-life concept learning, the number of dimensions that may possibly be relevant is less limited; the function of positive instances is as much to show *which* dimensions are relevant as it is to show what values of them are critical. We may speculate that the real value of what we are calling inductive procedures in concept learning is to afford the learner an opportunity to test his understanding of and memory for the elements of verbal descriptions and definitions. This testing may even involve the construction and testing of alternative hypotheses.

For example, consider the following verbal statement of what a 'paradigm' (for research on teaching) is:

Paradigms are models, patterns, or schemata. Paradigms are not theories, they are rather ways of thinking or patterns for research that, when carried out, can lead to the development of theory.[1]

As a verbal statement, this is hardly adequate; fortunately, Gage proceeds to exhibit a number of positive instances of 'paradigms' by which his readers can test out their notions of what this concept might be. Many readers will still have difficulty, however, because he fails to exhibit *negative* instances of paradigms.

What is needed, eventually, is a scientific 'rhetoric' for the teaching of concepts – assembled not only from the traditional rhetoric of exposition but also from whatever scientific experiments on concept teaching can tell us. We will be better off, however, if concept-attainment studies begin to give attention to the manner in which real-life, non-artificial concepts can be taught most efficiently – presumably by combination of both deductive and inductive procedures.

ILLUSTRATIONS OF CONCEPT TEACHING PROBLEMS

To suggest the kinds of problems that arise in the teaching of concepts or that might be investigated through formal research, I propose to analyse a small number of concepts of various types, at several levels of difficulty.

Tourist versus immigrant

A fourth-grade teacher reported difficulty in getting her pupils to understand and contrast the meanings of the words *tourist* and *immigrant*. To an adult, the differentiation between the concepts designated by *tourist* and *immigrant* looks almost trivially simple. Aside from the sheer memory problem in learning and differentiating the words themselves, what are the sources of confusion for the child? In specific cases, a tourist and an immigrant might have many common characteristics: both might be from a foreign country, or at least from some distance away from the local community; both might be of obviously non-native culture because of dress, complexion, speech and behaviour; both might be doing what would appear to be 'sight-

[1] N. L. Gage, 'Paradigms for Research on Teaching', *Handbook of Research on Teaching*, ed. N. L. Gage (Chicago: Rand McNally, 1963), pp. 94–141.

seeing', though possibly for different purposes. The differences between a tourist and an immigrant might not be very apparent, being primarily differences of motivation. Indeed, a tourist might become an immigrant overnight, just by deciding to be one.

As we have seen, there is a sense in which the concept-attainment experimental literature is relevant to the child's problem in learning the meanings of the words *tourist* and *immigrant*. If the child is presented with various instances of people who are either tourists or immigrants, properly labelled as such, but with no further explanation, it will be the child's task to figure out what attributes or characteristics are relevant to the differentiation of these concepts. This might occur either in school or outside of school. Most likely the instances of tourists and immigrants will be relatively sporadic over time, and the instances may not vary in such a way as to show what attributes are truly relevant. For example, all the tourists may be obviously American whereas all the immigrants may be obviously Mexican, let us say. The tourists may all be well dressed, the immigrants poorly dressed, and so on. If the natural environment is like a grand concept-formation experiment, it may take the child a long time to attain the concepts *tourist* and *immigrant*; indeed, the environment may not be as informative as the usual experimenter, since the child may not always be informed, or reliably informed, as to the correctness of his guesses. No wonder a child might form the concept that a tourist is any well-dressed person who drives a station-wagon with an out-of-state licence plate!

The purpose of teaching is to short-cut this capricious process of concept attainment within the natural environment. Through the use of language, there should be relatively little difficulty in explaining to a child that an immigrant is one who moves from one country or region to another in order to change his permanent residence, while a tourist is one who travels around for pleasure without changing his permanent residence. One can use simple explanations like: 'He's going to stay here, have his home here...' or 'He's just travelling around for the fun of it while he's on vacation, and some day he'll get back home'. There should be no difficulty, at any rate, if the child has already mastered certain prerequisite concepts. Among these prerequisite concepts would be: the concept of home or permanent residence and all that it implies; the concept of the division of world territory into different countries and those in turn into regions; and the concept of travelling for pleasure or curiosity. It is very likely that the child who is having trouble understanding the concept of tourist *v.* the concept of immigrant has not got clearly in mind these prerequisite notions that constitute, in fact, the criterial attributes upon which the distinction hangs.

Alternatively, a child might be having trouble because he has not dispensed with the irrelevant aspects of these concepts: he might think that a tourist has to be always an American, whereas an immigrant must be a foreigner, because he has seen *American* tourists and *foreign* immigrants, no *American* immigrants nor *foreign* tourists. The ingenious teacher will think of the possible misunderstandings that could arise through the influence of irrelevant attributes of tourists and immigrants.

Time

K. C. Friedman[1] pointed out that elementary school children have much trouble with various time concepts. A child sees no incongruity, for example, in saying, 'My older brother was born a long time ago'. According to Friedman, it was not until Grade VI that all children in his school could state the date or list the months in perfect order. They had difficulty, he reports, in forming a concept of the 'time line' and then in recognizing the placement of various historical events on such a time line. It is easy to see why the child would have these difficulties; even as adults it is difficult for us to appreciate the significance of the fantastically long periods implied by geological time. It should be noted that our concept of a time line is essentially a *spatial* concept whereby we translate temporal succession in terms of spatial order and distances. For a child time does not flow in a straight line nor in any other particular direction, unless it is around the clock, in a circular or spiral dimension! How can the child form a concept of time and its units? Is time a class of experiences? Does it have criterial attributes? The paradigms of concept-formation experiments do not seem to apply here readily. But let us examine the situation more closely. How can the child have experiences of time

[1] Kopple C. Friedman, 'Time Concepts of Elementary-school Children', *Elem. Sch. J.*, **XLIV**, (1944), pp. 337–42.

and generate the concept of a time line? Certainly there can be experiences of intervals of time – watching a second hand of a clock move through the second-markings, or experiencing the succession of night and day, noticing the change of seasons or waiting for the end of the school year. Moving from one time period to another could be likened to moving from one square of a sidewalk to the next. It should be an easy transition to thinking of the time line as a sidewalk of infinite extent in both directions – towards the past and towards the future. Marking off the days on the calendar and naming the days and months should help to reinforce this cognitive structure. Extrapolation of the time line is like generalizing these time experiences to all possible such experiences.

One of the difficulties comes, presumably, from the fact that the far reaches of the past and the future cannot be immediately experienced, and one immediately has trouble if one attempts to show a time line that includes historical events in the distant past along with a representation of the relationship between today, yesterday and the day before yesterday. Time lines of different scales must be used, and the concept of scale will itself be hard for children to understand unless it is carefully explained – perhaps by showing maps of the immediate environment in different scales. Only after such ideas have been mastered will it be possible for the child to have any appreciation of such concepts as *year*, *century*, *1492* (as a date), *B.C.*, *generation*. *Generation* and *eon*, by the way, would have to be introduced as somewhat flexible, arbitrary units of time, as contrasted with fixed, measureable units such as *year* and *century*.

Quantitative expressions like 'many', 'few', 'average'

Ernest Horn[1] pointed out that certain quantitative concepts like *many*, *few* and *average* are often so difficult that children do not give reasonable interpretations of them. It is very likely that the source of the difficulty is that children tend not to be able to think in relative terms. Children (and perhaps their teachers) would like to be able to assign definite ranges of numbers for such words as *many*, *few*, *average*, *a sizeable amount* etc., when actually they are all relative

[1] Ernest Horn, *Methods of Instruction in Social Studies* (New York: Scribner, 1937).

terms. There has even been a psychological experiment to demonstrate this: Helson, Dworkin and Michels[1] showed that adult subjects will consistently give different meanings to a word like 'few' when it is put in different contexts. For example, 'few' meant about 12 per cent on the average, in relation to 100 people, whereas it meant 4 per cent, on the average, in relation to 1,728,583 people.

In teaching a child these relational concepts the problem would be to exhibit or describe numerous instances in which the absolute base varies but in which the actual numbers of quantities meant would at the same time vary sufficiently to give the impression that these words do not indicate anything like exact amounts. It should be pointed out that 100 things might be 'many' in some situations and 'few' in others. The use of 'average' in such a context as 'There was an average number of people in church today' can be taught by drawing attention to its relation to the probable extremes of the numbers of people that might be in church, generalizing the concept to other situations like 'I caught an average number of fish today'. This might lead to the introduction of the average as a statistic or number that gives information about the 'central tendency' of some frequency distribution. It may help to use an unfamiliar or unusual context to bring out this concept in sharp relief. For example, I like to illustrate the utility of the statistical mean or arithmetic average by asking students to imagine that the first space men to reach Mars discover human-like creatures there whose average height is – and this is where the mean becomes really informative – 3 inches!

The basic concept of the mean arises in the context of experiences in which there is a plurality of objects measured in some common way. As a first approximation, as far as a child is concerned, the average is a number that is roughly halfway between the highest and lowest measurements encountered, and in some way 'typical' of these measurements. Only at some later stage does the child need to learn that the mean is a number that can be computed by a formula and that it has certain properties.

[1] Harry Helson, Robert S. Dworkin and Walter C. Michels, 'Quantitative Denotations of Common Terms as a Function of Background', *Amer. J. Psychol.*, **LXIX**, (1956), pp. 194–208.

Longitude

It is difficult to understand why E. B. Wesley[1] says that concepts related to the sphericity of the earth, like latitude and longitude, are not easily taught to the average child before Grades VI and VII. Wesley was writing before the advent of the space age when every child knows about space capsules travelling around the globe. Though it may still be difficult to get a child to see how the flatness of his immediate environment is only apparent and that the immediate environment corresponds to just a small area on the globe, it can certainly be done, well before Grade VI, through suitable demonstrational techniques. Having established the sphericity of the earth, one should be able to teach latitude and longitude as concepts involved in specifying locations on the globe. Their introduction should properly be preceded by simpler cases in which one uses a system of coordinates to specify location – e.g. equally spaced and numbered horizontal and vertical lines drawn on a blackboard with a game to locate letters placed at intersection of lines, a map of one's town or city in which marginal coordinates are given to help locate given streets or places of interest and finally a Mercator projection map of the world with coordinates of latitude and longitude. Children exposed to the 'new maths' with its number lines and coordinates should have no trouble with this. Then let us show children by easy stages how a Mercator projection corresponds to the surface of the earth (certainly an actual globe marked off with latitude and longitude should be used), then how it is necessary to select a particular line (that passes through the Greenwich Observatory) as the vertical coordinate from which to measure, and how the circumference of the earth is marked off in degrees – 180° West and 180° East from the Greenwich meridian.

The object is to build for the child a vivid experience of the framework or cognitive structure within which the concept of longitude is defined. The further complications introduced by the use of other kinds of world projections or by the use of regional or even local maps could then be explored. Easily-obtained U.S. Geological Survey maps of one's locality would concretize the meanings of further

[1] E. B. Wesley and Mary A. Adams, *Teaching Social Studies in Elementary Schools* (Rev. ed.: Boston: D. C. Heath, 1952), p. 307.

concepts, e.g. the division of degrees into minutes and seconds, and the fact that a degree of longitude will gradually shrink in length as one moves northward from the equator.

Tort

The concept of *tort* is very likely to be unfamiliar or at least vague to the average reader. Even a dictionary definition[1] may not help much in deciding whether arson, breach of contract, malicious prosecution or libel are positive instances of torts. The case method used in many law schools, whereby students examine many positive and negative instances of torts in order to learn what they are, is somewhat analogous to a concept formation experiment of the purely inductive variety.

A study of the various laws and decisions relating to torts yields the following approximate and tentative characterization of the concept as having both conjunctive and disjunctive aspects:

$$\text{TORT} = (A + B + C + D + E + F + G + H)$$
$$(I + J)(K)(-L)(-M)(-N)(-O)$$

where

A = battery
B = false imprisonment
C = malicious prosecution
D = trespass to land
E = interference to chattels
F = interference with advantageous relations
G = misrepresentation
H = defamation
I = malicious intent
J = negligence
K = causal nexus
L = consent
M = privilege
N = reasonable risk by plaintiff
O = breach of contract

[1] The *American College Dictionary* defines *tort* as 'a civil wrong (other than a breach of contract or trust) such as the law requires compensation for in damages; typically, a willful or negligent injury to a plaintiff's person, property, or reputation'.

Within a parenthesis, terms joined by the sign + are mutually dis-junctive attributes; a minus sign (−) within a parenthesis signifies 'absence of'; the full content of each parenthesis is conjunctive with the content of every other parenthesis. Thus, we can read the for-mula as follows:

> 'A tort is a battery, a false imprisonment, a malicious pros-ecution, a trespass to land, . . ., or a defamatory act which is done either with malicious intent or negligently which exhibits a causal nexus with the injury claimed by the plaintiff, *and* which is done without the plaintiff's consent, *or* without privilege on the part of the defendant, *or* without a reasonable risk by the plaintiff, *or* which is not a breach of contract.'

Thus, *tort* turns out to be a concept very much on the same order as *tourist* – a collocation of criterial attributes with both conjunctive and disjunctive features. Deciding whether an act is a tort requires that one check each feature of a situation against what can be put in the form of a formula (as done above). Presumably, a person pre-sented with a properly organized series of positive and negative instances of torts could induce the concept, provided he also under-stood such prerequisite concepts as *battery*, *misrepresentation* etc.

Mass versus weight

One of the more difficult concepts to teach in elementary physics is that of *mass*. What kind of concept is it and how can one learn it and experience it? How can it be distinguished from the concept of weight? Actually, if we ignore certain subtle questions about mass, such as that of whether inertial and gravitational mass are demon-strably identical, the concept of mass is not as difficult as it might seem; the real difficulty is to teach the sense in which it is different from weight. In fact, weight is perhaps the more difficult concept, because the weight of an object can vary to the point that it can become 'weightless'.

The concept of mass, one would think, ought to develop for the learner (be he a child or an adult) in much the same way that con-cepts of other properties of the physical world develop – analogously, that is, to concepts of colour, number and volume. For mass is a property of objects that differentiates them in our experience: there are objects with great mass (like the earth, or a large boulder) and there are objects with small mass (like a feather or a pin or the air in a small bottle), and our experiences of objects with respect to mass can differ enormously, particularly in our proprioceptive senses. Further, mass is a property of objects that is *conserved* regardless of whether the object is in motion or at rest: conservation of mass is learned through experience just as conservation of other properties is learned. Even the physical definition of mass as that property of things which accounts for the relative amount of force which has to be applied to produce a certain amount of acceleration is perceived in common-sense terms as the property of objects that determines the amount of force or effort that one would have to exert to move or lift it. The well-known 'size–weight' illusion (in which, for example, we exert an undue amount of effort to lift or push some large but relatively light object) illustrates the fact that our perceptions of an object typically include some impression of its mass. The physical operation of measuring mass by determining the ratio of force to acceleration is an operational extension of the kind of behaviour we exhibit when we see how much force it will take to move a heavy trunk.

The real trouble comes in the fact that we are too prone to equate mass with weight, mainly because equal masses also have equal weights when compared by means of a balance, or when measured with a spring balance at the same point on the earth's surface (at least, at the same distance from the earth's centre). If we were more easily able to experience the fact that the weight of an object of given mass changes as acceleration due to gravity changes – for example, by going to the moon and observing the 'weight' of objects there, or by experiencing 'weightlessness' in an orbital flight around the earth, weight and mass might be just as easy to distinguish as size and mass. Since such experiences would be rather hard to come by, to put it mildly, we have to be content with the imaginal representation of weight as a *variable* property of objects that really depends upon a relation between the gravitational force exerted on an object and its mass (actually, the product of these two). A child might be made to understand how objects of different masses could have equal 'weight' – a relatively large object on the moon and a relatively small one on the earth, for example, as measured by a spring balance which is sensitive to the pull of gravity; or how an object of constant mass would have different weights at different distances from the earth (the pull of gravity thus varying). We would have to conclude that weight, properly speaking, is a relational concept that can only be understood when the total framework in which weight can be defined is described. Mass, on the other hand, is a concept that corresponds much more directly to immediate perceptions of reality.

It will be noted that the teaching of mass and weight concepts involves several prerequisite concepts – e.g. the pull of gravity, the relation between the mass of an object like the earth or the moon and the gravitational force it exerts, and the concept of acceleration. The pull exerted by a magnet could be used for illustrating certain aspects of gravitational force; a large magnet and a small magnet could represent the respective gravitational pulls of earth and moon; the concept of acceleration can be introduced verbally as 'how fast something gets started' and later as an accelerating curve of velocity.

Without really meaning to do so, this discussion of mass and weight has turned out to be a consideration of how such concepts might be taught at relatively early stages – say, somewhere in the elementary school. Nevertheless, some of the same teaching techniques might not be amiss even at high school or college levels. At these levels the chief problem is to give meaning to mathematical formulas such as

$$\text{mass} = \frac{\text{force}}{\text{acceleration}}$$

The implication of this formula, that mass is constant for a given object, can be illustrated by showing with actual physical materials that as force is increased, acceleration is increased proportionately. The effect of increasing mass could be shown by demonstrating that acceleration (roughly indicated by distance travelled against friction) under a constant force diminishes. To a large extent, such experiments can be considered as yielding in precise mathematical terms the relationships that are perceived in every-day experience and that lead to our intuitive understanding of such a concept as mass.

Above all, it should be noted that *mass* is a relational concept, a constant property of objects that reveals itself through the relation between the forces applied to the object and the resultant acceleration.

Negative instances can only be properties of objects like weight, size etc., that are not revealed in this way.

SUMMARY

The basic concern of this paper has been with the teaching of concepts and the relevance of psychological and psycholinguistic theory and experimentation in guiding such teaching.

It has been necessary, first, to point out that concepts are essentially non-linguistic (or perhaps better, *a*linguistic) because they are classes of experience which the individual comes to recognize as such, whether or not he is prompted or directed by symbolic language phenomena. Because the experiences of individuals tend to be in many respects similar, their concepts are also similar, and through various processes of learning and socialization these concepts come to be associated with words. The 'meanings' of words are the socially-standardized concepts with which they are associated. One of the problems in teaching concepts is that of teaching the associations between words and concepts, and this is analogous to a paired-associate learning task.

At the same time, new concepts can be taught. One procedure can be called inductive: it consists of presenting an individual with an appropriate series of positive and negative instances of a concept, labelled as such, and allowing him to infer the nature of the concept by noticing invariant features or attributes. This is the procedure followed in the usual concept formation experiment: although our present knowledge allows us to specify several *necessary* conditions for the formation of a concept, we still do not know what conditions are *sufficient*.

Another procedure for concept teaching may be called deductive, and it tends to be the favoured procedure in school learning (and, in fact, in all expository prose). It is the technique of presenting concepts by verbal definition or description. This technique has received relatively little attention in psychological experimentation, but it seems to parallel inductive concept attainment in the sense that verbal descriptions are specifications of criterial attributes that can enable the individual to shortcut the process of hypothesis, discovery and testing that typically occurs in the inductive concept-attainment procedure. Nevertheless, it is not known how relevant our knowledge of critical factors in inductive concept formation is for the guidance of deductive teaching procedures.

It is pointed out, however, that the efficient learning of concepts in school probably involves both inductive and deductive procedures. An analysis of typical concepts of the sort taught in school shows that they do indeed follow the models studied in psychological experimentation, but that they are more likely to involve complex relationships among prerequisite concepts. The difficulties that learners have in attaining a concept are likely to be due to their inadequate mastery of prerequisite concepts and to errors made by the teacher in presenting in proper sequence the information intrinsic to the definition of the concept.

9 The psychology of learning*

D. N. BOGOIAVLENSKI and N. A. MENCHINSKAIA

There is a growing interest in the way in which the learner stores and retrieves information. This paper presents a Soviet view which has much in common with that of other psychologists, notably D. P. Ausubel and R. Gagné (see pp. 79 ff. and 205 f.). A common feature of the ideas of these writers is the belief in the importance of the systematization of knowledge in the learning process. In particular the notion of a type of hierarchical structure of concepts of different levels of generality is being accorded considerable prominence.

Knowledge consists chiefly in systems of concepts the mastery of which establishes certain connections and relations between concepts. Research into the process of acquiring knowledge cannot therefore, be limited to study of ways of differentiating concepts; no

* Reprinted and abridged from D. N. Bogoiavlenski and N. A. Menchinskaia, 'The Psychology of Learning' in B. Simon and J. Simon (Eds.), *Educational Psychology in the U.S.S.R.*, Routledge and Kegan Paul, 1963, pp. 130–3.

less important is an explanation as to how pupils form associations between concepts, form *systems of connections* reflecting the relations between objects and phenomena of the real world.

The mastery of systems of concepts is of first importance to the development of thinking. Vigotsky noted that concepts mastered by pupils can only be fully understood in their relations with other concepts and that the formation of hierarchies of concepts, established on the basis of relations of generality, the relations of *coordinated concepts*, is of universal significance in the development of thought.

Recent research has produced facts upholding this position. Thus Zykova has shown that separate concepts about angles in geometry (adjacent, vertical etc.) are mastered with more understanding when they are included in the wider concept 'angles with a common apex'. Redko has shown that concepts about the constitution of different classes ('slave', 'slave-owner') only achieve full development when the higher concept of a 'slave-owning system' has been formed, based in its turn on existing knowledge about the constitution of different classes.

But there is more to the systematization of knowledge than logical systematization. Corresponding to the many-sided character of relationships in the real world are many-sided relations between concepts which joint these into systems (spatial, temporary, causal etc.).

The research of V. V. Bogoslovski and M. N. Shardakov concerned with pupils' understanding of causally consequent connections distinguishes elementary and logical levels of causal explanation. It is characteristic of the elementary level that pupils designate only one cause of the given phenomenon or one consequence of the given cause, and that the cause and consequence indicated are often external and secondary. In mastering historical laws the children confuse cause and effect. At a higher level pupils begin to designate a number of causes. However, these causes are taken together; either partial causes are not distinguished from the general causes which unite them, or the pupils point out partial and general causes without connecting them with each other. Later pupils begin to understand the interconnection between partial causes, but do not, however, differentiate general from partial causes. Separate partial phenomena now find a correct explanation but the pupil's thought does not reach to generalization and the formulation of general laws or rules. According to the degree of accumulation of knowledge and development of thought the pupil begins to abstract essential causal connections in different phenomena and proceeds by induction to establish general laws or rules.

Research into pupils' understanding of the relations between living plants and environmental conditions, undertaken by E. M. Kudriavtseva permits the noting of some additional characteristics of the process of systematization. The author distinguishes different types of causal explanation in dependence upon stages of concretization.

In primary classes studying botany causal explanations of the necessity of each component of the environment (soil, water, sun) for the life of plants are common and rest on differentiation in everyday observation. ('Earth is needed because without it the plants wither, dry up'; 'Because I have seen flowers planted in soil'.) More differentiated explanations are observed in pupils of Classes III and IV. They are usually given in the form of general opinions without reference to particular observations. ('Because plants can't grow without soil anywhere'; 'Because plants always live in soil'.) Here there is wider generalization but genuine causal explanation is lacking. According to Shardakov's material causal explanation begins with the establishment of particular relations between plants and the environment. ('Soil is needed because it has moisture.') A correct indication of the conditions for the growth of plants is here given but this dependence is understood in an undifferentiated and simplified way. With the systematic study of botany in Classes V and VI the pupils' causal explanations begin to include generalized elements of knowledge and their differentiation from concrete knowledge. ('Because plants take nourishment from the soil – water and mineral salts.') The content of causal explanations is therefore changed from a general undifferentiated enumeration of a one-sided character into an explanation of the generalized causes of plant life each of which is specifically singled out. The establishment of causally-consequent relations between concepts leads to the formation of systematic knowledge.

Attempts have been made to classify systems of associations by Iu. A. Samarin. He separates associations into 'local', or 'single line', connections between different phenomena which do not belong to a system of these phenomena; limited system associations within the bounds of a given theme or chapter of a textbook; intra-system connections consisting of a systematized series of associations according to some principle (for instance, relations between historical events according to time); inter-subject or inter-system associations, establishing relations between different branches of knowledge. The author notes that the order of this classification corresponds to basic stages of difficulty in systematizing knowledge. The difficulties in forming inter-subject connections have a particular relevance to the formation of a general outlook. Without special exercise in the comparison of knowledge from different branches inter-system associations are not formed. Though in research of this kind the psychological aspect of the process of systematization has not been fully revealed, the classification of systems of connections undoubtedly constitutes a step in this direction.

The methodological aspect of the formation of systems of connections has been dealt with by research workers of the Leningrad Institute of Education. Their work emphasizes the importance of the principle of ordering the knowledge mastered by pupils in the syllabus of a given class and particular aspects of the transition from one class to another. In the light of this an analysis has been undertaken of school programmes and textbooks to establish the most rational succession of concepts in the school course and the possibilities of comparing and bringing together knowledge from different school disciplines.

The psychology of the formation of systems of connected concepts has been less fully dealt with than that of the formation of concepts. The data we have, however, show that in the general process of mastering knowledge two kinds of problem may be singled out. One of these is connected with the process of differentiating separate concepts, with avoiding the confusion of concepts similar in inessential features; the other problem, on the contrary, relates to the bringing together of separate concepts in a strictly scientific system – a process involving the development of traits of dialectical thinking permitting the pupil to see objects and phenomena in their different connections and relations. At a higher stage of development a similar synthesis of thinking activity results in the formation of a general outlook. This last requires special investigation.

10 Reception learning and the rote-meaningful dimension*

D. P. AUSUBEL

The author of this paper has been extremely influential in bringing about a reconsideration of the role of reception learning and expository teaching. He has also proposed a view of meaningful learning which provides a very useful model for looking at school learning. An important aspect of his general thesis is that rote and meaningful learning on the one hand, and reception and discovery learning on the other hand, are two distinct dimensions of learning and that the equating of reception learning with rote learning is profoundly mistaken.

THE NATURE OF RECEPTION LEARNING

Few pedagogic devices in our time have been repudiated more unequivocally by educational theorists than the method of expository verbal instruction. It is fashionable in many quarters to characterize verbal learning as parrot-like recitation and rote memorization of isolated facts, and to dismiss it disdainfully as an archaic remnant of discredited educational tradition. In fact, quite apart from whatever intrinsic value they may possess, many educational innovations and movements of the past three decades – activity programmes, project and discussion methods, various ways of maximizing non-verbal and manipulative experience in the classroom, emphasis on 'self-discovery', and on learning for and by *problem-solving* – owe their origins and popularity to widespread dissatisfaction with the techniques of verbal instruction. It is commonly accepted today, for example (at least in the realm of educational theory), (*a*) that meaningful generalizations cannot be presented or 'given' to the learner, but can only be acquired as a product of problem-solving activity, and (*b*) that all attempts to master verbal concepts and propositions are forms of empty verbalism unless the learner has recent prior experience with the realities to which these verbal constructs refer.

Excellent reasons, of course, exist for the general disrepute into

* Reprinted and abridged from D. P. Ausubel, *The Psychology of Meaningful Verbal Learning*, Grune and Stratton, 1963, pp. 15–24.

which expository teaching and verbal learning have fallen. The most obvious of these is that notwithstanding repeated policy declarations of educational organizations to the contrary, meaningful subject-matter is still presented to pupils in preponderantly rote fashion. Another less obvious but equally important reason why meaningful-ness is perceived as an exclusive product of problem-solving and discovery techniques of learning, stems from two serious short-comings of modern learning theory. First, psychologists have tended to subsume many *qualitatively* different kinds of learning processes under a single explanatory model. As a result, widespread confusion exists regarding basic distinctions between reception and discovery learning, and between rote and meaningful learning. It has not always been sufficiently clear, for example, that such categorically different types of learning as problem-solving and the understanding of presented verbal material have different objectives, and that condi-tions and instructional techniques facilitating one of these learning processes are not necessarily relevant or maximally efficient for the other. Second, in the absence of an appropriate theory of meaningful verbal learning, many educational psychologists have tended to interpret long-term subject-matter learning in terms of the same concepts (e.g. retroactive inhibition, stimulus generalization, re-sponse competition) used to explain instrumental conditioning, paired-associate learning, rote serial learning, maze learning and simple discrimination learning.

An attempt will therefore be made in this paper to distinguish between reception and discovery learning, to sharpen the existing distinction between rote and meaningful learning, and to consider the distinctive role of each of these types of learning in the total educational enterprise. It should then be clear that verbal reception learning can be genuinely meaningful without prior discovery experi-ence or problem-solving activity, and that the weaknesses attributed to the method of expository verbal instruction do not inhere in the method itself but are derived from various misapplications.

Reception versus discovery learning

From the standpoint of enhancing intellectual development, no theoretical concern is more relevant or pressing in the present state of our knowledge than the need for distinguishing clearly among the principal kinds of cognitive learning (i.e. rote and meaningful verbal learning, concept formation and verbal and non-verbal problem-solving) that take place in the classroom. One significant way of differentiating among the latter types of classroom learning is to make two crucial process distinctions that cut across all of them – distinctions between reception and discovery learning and between rote and meaningful learning. The first distinction is especially important because most of the understandings that learners acquire both in and out of school are presented rather than discovered. And since most learning material is presented verbally, it is equally important to appreciate that verbal reception learning is not necessarily rote in character and can be meaningful without prior non-verbal and problem-solving experience.

In reception learning (rote or meaningful) the entire content of what is to be learned is presented to the learner in final form. The learning task does not involve any independent discovery on his part. He is only required to internalize the material (e.g. a list of nonsense syllables or paired associates; a poem or geometrical theorem) that is presented to him so that it is available and reproducible at some future date. The essential feature of discovery learning (e.g. concept formation, rote or meaningful problem-solving), on the other hand, is that the principal content of what is to be learned is not given but must be independently discovered by the learner before he can internalize it. The distinctive and prior learning task, in other words, is to discover something – which of two maze alleys leads to the goal, the precise nature of a relationship between two variables, the common attributes of a number of diverse instances etc. The first phase of discovery learning, therefore, involves a process quite different from that of reception learning. The learner must rearrange a given array of information, integrate it with existing cognitive structure,[1] and reorganize or transform the integrated combination in such a way as to create a desired end-product or discover a missing means-end relationship. After this phase is completed, the discovered content is internalized just as in reception learning.

It should be clear up to this point, therefore, that reception and discovery learning are two quite different kinds of processes, and

[1] i.e. the learner's system of concepts in that field. [E.S.]

that most classroom instruction is organized along the lines of reception learning. In the next section it will be shown that verbal reception learning is not necessarily rote in character, that much ideational material (e.g. concepts, generalizations) can be meaningfully internalized and made available without prior discovery experience, and that at no stage does the learner have to discover principles independently in order to be able to understand and use them meaningfully.

Reception and discovery learning are not only basically different in essential nature and process, but also differ with respect to their principal roles in intellectual development and cognitive functioning. Essentially, large bodies of subject matter are acquired through reception learning, and the everyday problems of living are solved through discovery learning. Some overlap of function, however, does exist: the knowledge acquired through reception learning is also used in everyday problem-solving, and discovery learning is commonly used in the classroom to apply, extend, integrate and evaluate subject-matter knowledge and to test its comprehension. In laboratory situations discovery learning also leads to the contrived rediscovery of known propositions and, when employed by gifted persons, to significant new knowledge. Typically, however, the propositions discovered through problem-solving methods are rarely significant and worth incorporating into the learner's subject-matter knowledge. In any case, discovery techniques hardly constitute an efficient primary means of transmitting the content of an academic discipline.

Discovery learning is a psychologically more involved process than reception learning because it presupposes a problem-solving stage that precedes the emergence of meaning and the interiorization of information. But reception learning, on the whole, appears later developmentally and, in most instances, implies a greater degree of cognitive maturity. The young child learns most new concepts and propositions inductively through autonomous discovery, although self-discovery is not essential if concrete-empirical props are available. Reception learning, however, although occurring earlier, is not really prominent until the child is both capable of internal mental operations and can comprehend verbally presented propositions in the absence of current concrete-empirical experience. The typical contrast here is between inductive concept formation with the aid of concrete-empirical props, on the one hand, and direct concept acquisition through verbal exposition, on the other.

Is reception learning meaningful?

It is frequently maintained, as already pointed out, that abstract concepts and generalizations are forms of empty, meaningless verbalism unless the learner discovers them autonomously out of his own concrete, empirical, problem-solving experience. Careful analysis of this proposition reveals, in my opinion, that it rests on three serious logical fallacies: (a) a straw-man representation of the method of verbal learning; (b) the prevailing tendency to confuse the reception–discovery dimension of the learning process with the rote–meaningful dimension; and (c) unwarranted generalization of the distinctive developmental conditions of learning and thinking in childhood to adolescence and adult life.

The use of the straw-man technique was, of course, the simplest and most effective way of discrediting the method of verbal exposition. Instead of describing this procedure in terms of its essential characteristics, it became fashionable to picture it in terms of its worst abuses. Examples of such abuses were naturally not very difficult to find, since an appreciable number of teachers still rely on rote verbal learning in teaching meaningful subject matter. Some of the more flagrantly inept practices include premature use of verbal techniques with cognitively immature pupils; arbitrary presentation of unrelated facts without any organizing or explanatory principles; failure to integrate new learning tasks with previously presented materials; and the use of evaluation procedures that merely measure ability to recognize discrete facts or to reproduce ideas in the same words or in the identical context as originally encountered.

Although it is entirely proper to caution teachers against these frequent misuses of verbal learning, it is not legitimate to represent them as inherent in the method itself. An approach to instruction which on logical and psychological grounds appears appropriate and efficient should not be discarded as unworkable simply because, like all pedagogic techniques in the hands of incompetent or unintelligent teachers, it is subject to misuse. It would seem more reasonable to guard against the more common misapplications, and to relate the method to relevant theoretical principles and research findings that actually deal with the long-term learning and retention of large bodies of meaningful, verbally-presented materials.

The distinction between rote and meaningful learning is frequently confused with the reception–discovery, distinction discussed above. This confusion is partly responsible for the widespread but unwarranted twin beliefs that reception learning is invariably rote and that discovery learning is inherently and necessarily meaningful. Both assumptions, of course, are related to the long-standing doctrine that the only knowledge one *really* possesses and understands is knowledge that one discovers by oneself. Actually, each distinction constitutes an entirely independent dimension of learning. Hence a much more defensible proposition is that *both* expository and problem-solving techniques can be either rote *or* meaningful depending on the conditions under which learning occurs. In both instances meaningful learning takes place if the task can be related in non-arbitrary, substantive fashion to what the learner already knows, and if the learner adopts a corresponding learning set to do so.

It is true that by these criteria much potentially meaningful knowledge taught by verbal exposition results in rotely learned verbalisms. This rote outcome, however, is not inherent in the expository method *per se*, but rather in such abuses of this method as fail to satisfy the criteria of meaningfulness. There is much greater reluctance, on the other hand, to acknowledge that the aforementioned preconditions for meaningfulness also apply to problem-solving and laboratory methods. It should seem rather self-evident that performing laboratory experiments in cookbook fashion, without understanding the underlying substantive and methodological principles involved, confers precious little meaningful understanding, and that many students studying mathematics and science find it relatively simple to discover correct answers to problems without really understanding what they are doing. They accomplish the latter feat merely by rotely memorizing 'type problems' and procedures for manipulating symbols. Nevertheless it is still not generally appreciated that laboratory work and problem-solving are not genuinely meaningful experiences unless they are built on a foundation of clearly understood concepts and principles, and unless the constituent operations are themselves meaningful.

The art and science of presenting ideas and information meaningfully and effectively – so that clear, stable and unambiguous meanings emerge and are retained over a long period of time as an organized body of knowledge – is really the principal function of pedagogy. This is a demanding and creative rather than a routine or mechanical task. The job of selecting, organizing, presenting and translating subject-matter content in a developmentally appropriate manner requires more than a rote listing of facts. If it is done properly it is the work of a master teacher and is hardly a task to be disdained.

Finally, it is important to appreciate the relationship between reception learning and various developmental considerations that affect its meaningfulness. Learners who have not yet developed beyond the concrete stage of cognitive developments are unable meaningfully to incorporate within their cognitive structures a relationship between two or more abstractions unless they have the benefit of current or recently prior concrete-empirical experience. During the concrete stage, roughly covering the elementary-school period, children are restricted by their dependence on concrete-empirical experience to a semi-abstract, intuitive understanding of abstract propositions. Such learners therefore cannot meaningfully comprehend verbally or symbolically expressed propositions without the aid of these concrete-empirical props, although they by no means have to discover these propositions autonomously in order to understand them meaningfully. Even during the elementary-school years the act of discovery is not indispensable for intuitive understanding and need not constitute a routine part of pedagogic technique. As every elementary-school teacher knows, meaningful verbal reception learning – without any problem solving or discovery experience whatsoever – is perhaps the commonest form of classroom learning, provided that the necessary props are available.

During the abstract stage of cognitive development, however, beginning in the junior-high-school period, students acquire most new concepts and learn most new propositions by *directly* grasping higher-order relationships between abstractions. To do so meaningfully, they need no longer depend on current or recently prior concrete-empirical experience, and hence are able to by-pass completely the intuitive type of understanding reflective of such dependence. Through proper expository teaching they can proceed directly to a level of abstract understanding that is qualitatively superior to the intuitive level in terms of generality, clarity, precision and explicitness. At this stage of development, therefore, it seems pointless to enhance intuitive understanding by using discovery techniques.

This is the point at which some of the more zealous proponents of Progressive Education took a disastrously false turn. John Dewey had correctly recognized that meaningful understanding of abstract concepts and principles in childhood must be built on a foundation of direct, empirical experience, and for this reason advocated the use of project and activity methods in the elementary school. But he also appreciated that once a firmly grounded first-storey of abstract understandings was established, it was possible to organize secondary and higher education along more abstract and verbal lines. Unfortunately, however, although Dewey himself never elaborated or implemented this latter conception, some of his disciples blindly generalized childhood limiting conditions, with respect to meaningful verbal reception learning, broadly enough to encompass learning over the entire life span. And this unwarranted extrapolation, frequently but erroneously attributed to Dewey himself, provided a pseudonaturalistic rationale for, and thus helped perpetuate, the seemingly indestructible myth that, under any and all circumstances, abstractions cannot possibly be meaningful unless preceded by direct, empirical experience.

Is reception learning passive?

The emergence of meaning, as new concepts and ideas are incorporated into cognitive structure, is far from being a passive phenomenon. In view of the complex and variable nature of learners' intellectual backgrounds, much activity is obviously involved, but not the kind of activity characterizing discovery. Activity and discovery are not synonymous in the realm of cognitive functioning. Merely because potential meanings are presented, we cannot assume that they are necessarily acquired and that all subsequent loss is reflective of forgetting. Before meanings can be retained they must be acquired, and the process of acquisition is exceedingly active.

Meaningful reception learning involves more than the simple cataloguing of ready-made concepts within existing cognitive structure. In the first place, an implicit judgement of relevance is usually required in deciding under which proposition to catalogue new knowledge. Second, some degree of reconciliation with existing knowledge is necessary, particularly if there are discrepancies or conflicts. Third, new propositions are customarily translated into a personal frame of reference consonant with the learner's experiential background, vocabulary and structure of ideas. Lastly, some degree of reorganization under different, more inclusive concepts is sometimes required if a basis for reconciliation cannot be found.

All of this activity, however, stops short of actual discovery or problem-solving. Since the substance of the learning task is presented rather than discovered, the activity involved is limited to that required in understanding new meanings and integrating them into existing cognitive structure. This is naturally of a qualitatively different order than that involved in independently discovering solutions to new problems, i.e. the task of integrating and reorganizing new information and existing knowledge to satisfy the requirements of a given problem situation.

The extent of activity involved in meaningful reception learning obviously depends on the learner's general readiness and level of cognitive sophistication and on the availability within his cognitive structure of relevant subsuming concepts. Hence the degree of activity necessary would be substantially reduced if the presented material were appropriately programmed to fit his experiential background and level of readiness. The extent to which meaningful reception learning is active is also a function of the learner's drive for integrative meaning and of his self-critical faculty. He may either attempt to integrate a new proposition with all of his existing relevant knowledge or remain content with establishing its relatedness to a single concept. Similarly, he may endeavour to translate the new proposition into terminology consistent with his own vocabulary and ideational background, or remain satisfied with incorporating it as presented. Finally, he may strive for the acquisition of precise, unambiguous meanings or be completely satisfied with vague, diffuse notions.

The main danger in meaningful reception learning is not so much that the learner will frankly adopt a rote approach, but that he will delude himself into believing that he has really grasped precise intended meanings when he has only grasped a vague and confused set of generalities and no real meaning whatsoever. It is not so much that he does not want to understand but that he lacks the necessary self-critical ability and is unwilling to put forth the necessary active effort involved in struggling with the material, looking at it from different angles, reconciling it with related and contradictory knowledge and translating it into his own frame of reference. He finds it easy enough to manipulate words so as to create an appearance of knowledge and thereby to delude himself and others that he really understands.

A central task of pedagogy, therefore, is to develop ways of facilitating an active variety of reception learning supplemented by an independent and critical approach to the understanding of subject-matter. This involves, in part, the encouragement of motivations for and of self-critical attitudes towards acquiring precise and integrated meanings, as well as the use of other techniques directed towards the same end. Precise and integrated understandings are, presumably, more likely to develop if the central, unifying ideas of a discipline are learned before more peripheral concepts and information are introduced; if the limiting conditions of general developmental readiness are observed; if precise and accurate definition is stressed, and emphasis is placed on delineating similarities and differences between related concepts; and if learners are required to reformulate new propositions in their own words. All of these latter devices come under the heading of pedagogic techniques that promote an active type of meaningful reception learning. Teachers can help foster the related objective of critical thinking with regard to subject-matter content by encouraging students to recognize and challenge the assumptions underlying new propositions and to distinguish between facts and hypotheses and between warranted and unwarranted inferences. Much good use can also be made of Socratic questioning in exposing pseudo-understanding, in transmitting precise meanings, in reconciling contradictions and in encouraging a critical attitude towards knowledge.

MEANINGFUL VERSUS ROTE LEARNING

By 'meaningful learning' we also refer primarily to a distinctive kind of learning process, and only secondarily to a meaningful learning outcome – attainment of meaning – that necessarily reflects the completion of such a process. Meaningful learning as a process presupposes, in turn, *both* that the learner employs a meaningful learning set and that the material he learns is potentially meaningful to him. Thus, regardless of how much potential meaning may inhere in a given proposition, if the learner's intention is to memorize it verbatim, i.e. as a series of arbitrarily related words, both the learning process and the learning outcome must necessarily be rote and meaningless. And conversely, no matter how meaningful the learner's set may be, neither the process nor outcome of learning can possibly be meaningful if the learning task itself consists of purely arbitrary associations as in paried-associate or rote serial learning.

Meaningful learning set

In meaningful learning the learner has a set to relate substantive (as opposed to verbatim) aspects of new concepts, information or situations to relevant components of existing cognitive structure in various ways that make possible the incorporation of derivative, elaborative, correlative, supportive, qualifying or representational relationships. Depending on the nature of the learning task (i.e. reception or discovery) the set may be either to discover or merely to apprehend and incorporate such relationships. In rote learning, on the other hand, the learner's set is to discover a solution to a problem, or to internalize material verbatim, as a discrete and isolated end in itself. Such learning obviously does not occur in a cognitive vacuum. The material is related to cognitive structure, but not in a substantive, non-arbitrary fashion permitting incorporation of one of the relationships specified above. Where discovery learning is involved, the distinction between rote and meaningful learning corresponds to that between 'trial and error' and insightful problem solving.

Potentially meaningful material

A meaningful set or approach to learning, as already pointed out, only eventuates in a meaningful learning process and outcome provided that the learning material (task) itself is *potentially* meaningful. Insistence on the qualifying adjective 'potential' in this instance is more than mere academic hair-splitting. If the learning material were simply considered meaningful, the learning process (apprehending the meaning and making it functionally more available) would be completely superfluous; the object of learning would obviously be already accomplished, by definition, before any learning was ever attempted and irrespective of the type of learning set employed. It is true that certain component elements of a current learning task as, for example, the individual words of a new geometrical theorem, may already be meaningful to the learner; but it is the meaning of the relational proposition as a whole which is the object of learning in this situation – not the individual meanings of its component elements. Thus, although the term 'meaningful learning' necessarily implies the use of potentially meaningful learning tasks, it does not imply that the learning of meaningful as opposed to rote material is the distinctive feature of meaningful learning. Meaningful material may be perceived and reacted to meaningfully, but cannot possibly constitute a learning task in as much as the very term 'meaningful' connotes that the object of learning was previously consummated.

Two important criteria determine whether new learning is potentially meaningful. The first criterion – non-arbitrary relatability to relevant concepts in cognitive structure, in the various ways specified above – is a property of the material itself. New material is not potentially meaningful if either the total learning task (e.g. a particular order of nonsense syllables, a list of paired adjectives, a scrambled sentence) or the basic unit of the learning task (a particular pair of adjectives) is only relatable to such concepts on a purely arbitrary basis. This criterion of potential meaningfulness applies solely to the current learning task itself – not to any of its structural elements which may already be meaningful, such as the component letters of a nonsense syllable, each member of an adjective pair, or the component words, for example, no more detracts from the lack of potential meaningfulness in the task of learning the correct sequence of jumbled words in a scrambled sentence, than it adds to potential meaningfulness in the task of learning the meaning of a geometrical theorem. In both instances the meaningful components, although structurally part of the learning material, do not constitute part of the learning task in a functional sense.

The second important criterion determining whether learning material is potentially meaningful – its relatability to the *particular* cognitive structure of a particular learner – is more properly a characteristic of the learner than of the material *per se*. Phenomenologically, meaningfulness is an individual matter. Hence for meaningful learning to occur in fact, it is not sufficient that the new material simply be relatable to relevant ideas in the abstract sense of the term. The cognitive structure of the particular learner must include the requisite intellectual capacities, ideational content and experiential background. It is on this basis that the potential meaningfulness of learning material varies with such factors as age, intelligence, occupation, cultural membership etc. In other words, it is subsumability within or incorporability by a particular cognitive structure which converts potential into actual meaning, and which (given non-arbitrarily relatable material and a meaningful learning set) differentiates meaningful from rote learning.

As long as the set and content conditions of meaningful learning are satisfied, the outcome should be meaningful and the advantages of meaningful learning (economy of learning effort, more stable retention and greater transferability) should accrue irrespective of whether the content to be internalized is presented or discovered, verbal or non-verbal.

Process differences between rote and meaningful reception learning

In view of the foregoing, plausible reasons exist for believing that rotely and meaningfully learned materials are organized quite differently in cognitive structure and hence conform to quite different principles of learning and forgetting. First, meaningfully learned materials are related to existing concepts in cognitive structure in ways making possible the understanding of various kinds of significant (e.g. derivative, qualifying, correlative) relationships. Most new ideational materials that pupils encounter in a school setting are non-arbitrarily and substantively relatable to a previously learned background of meaningful ideas and information. In fact, the curriculum is deliberately organized in this fashion to provide for the untraumatic introduction of new facts and concepts. Rotely learned materials, on the other hand, are discrete and relatively isolated entities which are only relatable to cognitive structure in an arbitrary, verbatim fashion, not permitting the establishment of the above-mentioned relationships. Second, because they are not anchored to existing ideational systems, rotely learned materials (unless greatly overlearned or endowed with unusual vividness) are much more vulnerable to forgetting, i.e. have a much shorter retention span.

These differences between rote and meaningful learning categories have important implications for the underlying kinds of learning and retention processes involved in each category. Rotely learned materials are essentially isolated from existing conceptual systems within cognitive structure, and hence are primarily influenced by the interfering effects of *similar* rote materials learned *immediately* before or after the learning task. Thus it is not unreasonable to explain the learning and retention of discrete rote units in such stimulus-response terms as intra-task and inter-task similarity, response competition and stimulus or response generalization. With regard to meaningful learning and retention, however, it seems reasonable to suppose that learning materials are primarily influenced by the attributes of relevant and cumulatively established ideational systems in cognitive structure with which they interact. Compared to this type of extended interaction, concurrent interfering effects have relatively little influence and explanatory value.

11 Interaction analysis as a feedback system in teacher preparation*

E. J. AMIDON and E. POWELL

One of the problems many student teachers have is that they are prone to talk too much. To some extent this reflects the influence of the

* Reprinted and abridged from E. J. Amidon and E. Powell, 'Interaction Analysis as a Feedback System in Teacher Preparation' in R. Raths and R. R. Leeper (Eds.), *The Supervisor: Agent for Change in Teaching*, Washington, D.C., A.S.C.D. Publications, 1966.

traditional view of the teacher as the dispenser of information. However, even when a student is convinced that he should be less oracular, it is not always easy for him to get a realistic picture of the extent to which he is involving the children in classroom discourse. It is even more difficult for him to appreciate the *nature* of their involvement.

In this paper the authors describe the application to teacher preparation of interaction analysis, a technique which offers a means whereby students can be made objectively aware of the relative contributions to classroom discourse of teacher and children. Interaction analysis enables a teacher to record classroom events and analyse them later.

One of the great benefits of this technique is that it provides objective feedback about a very important aspect of a teacher's work. As the authors point out, a student could record his own lessons, analyse them afterwards and use his analysis as feedback to help him improve his teaching. Apart from this, the awareness of different categories of classroom discourse in itself provides useful insights for the teacher. It might well be worth while asking students to do such an analysis as an exercise linked to their school practice.

Many educators and social scientists have pointed out that supervision is primarily a social process which involves interaction between two or more people. The most important elements of the supervisory relationship appear to be concerned with the ability of supervisors to communicate effectively with teachers. Educators have spoken these words for many years and yet little systematic research has been focused on the study of the supervisory process.

Any study of the improvement of teaching through supervision seems to necessitate a focus on three problem areas:

(1) The interaction of the teacher and supervisor as they attempt to discuss what the teacher is doing and how he can improve.

(2) The description of interaction between teacher and class which serves as the basis of the supervisory conference.

(3) The social skills involved in any group situation, whether it is in a conference, a classroom or a faculty meeting.

PRINCIPLES

In order to work on all three of these problems simultaneously, several principles have been examined and used as guideposts in the development of the study reported in this paper.

1. The supervisor must be given a *tool* for assessing the effects of his own behaviour on the teacher or student teacher.

This tool was provided by training a group of cooperating teachers in the use of Flanders' System of Interaction Analysis. The teachers were asked to think about the way they interacted with their student teacher while they were having a conference following a classroom observation.

The cooperating teachers were also exposed to role-playing situations which allowed them to receive feedback about the extent to which they were producing defensiveness in the student teacher. For these purposes, some of the categories proposed by Blumberg were used.

2. The supervisor must have a *tool* available for objectively describing what the teacher or student teacher does in the classroom.

In order to satisfy this need, each cooperating teacher was given about twenty hours of training in the use of Interaction Analysis. The cooperating teachers were asked to have five conferences during the semester with their student teacher. At this time they would present the student teacher with an interaction matrix.

3. Feedback is essential to the improvement of both teaching and supervisory skills.

This principle was made operational through the use of the interaction matrix. This matrix summarized the data collected through the use of the ten-category system of Interaction Analysis. This matrix enables a teacher to determine how much he talks, how he responds to student talk and what happens after he asks a question. In one sense the matrix helps a teacher to determine whether or not his teaching intentions are met.

4. Both teachers and supervisors must be free to experiment with those skills which they wish to improve.

This can only be done through providing the appropriate environment in the school and classroom. This is the reason for the training of cooperating teachers. Still, structured role playing enables teachers and supervisors to try out those behaviours which seem to be important to the improvement of their teaching and supervisory skills.

5. The direction of improvement must be arrived at by the teacher with the help of his supervisor.

Implementation of procedures in accordance with this principle resulted in a rather structured approach to the supervisory conference. All cooperating teachers were asked to present the interaction matrix to their student teacher and then let the student teacher decide in which ways he would like to change.

INTERACTION ANALYSIS

Interaction Analysis has been mentioned here several times, yet not everyone is familiar with it. The Flanders System of Interaction Analysis is an observational procedure which can be used to classify the verbal behaviour of teachers and pupils. Using this system, verbal behaviour in the classroom is classified into ten category designations. There are seven categories for teacher behaviour, four of which are classified as indirect influence. They are: (1) accepting pupil feeling, (2) praising or encouraging, (3) accepting pupil ideas, (4) asking questions. There are three categories of direct teacher influence, which are: (5) giving information or opinion, (6) giving directions and (7) criticizing. Two categories of pupil talk are used in the system: (8) pupil response to the teacher, and (9) pupil initiated talk. Category 10 is used to indicate silence or confusion. These categories are summarized in Fig. 1.

A trained observer notes every verbal behaviour as it occurs, and if it persists, puts down the same number every three seconds until there is a change. After a lesson has been categorized, the data collected by the observer must be summarized so that it can be interpreted. This is done by entering the category numbers in the form of tallies into a ten-row by ten-column table called a matrix. The completed matrix gives the observer a picture not only of the percentage of interactions falling in each category but also of the general sequence of responses. Although an exact representation of the sequential time element of the entire lesson is not shown, recording the numbers in the matrix in an overlapping fashion preserves the sequential time element of adjacent numbers. Thus, the researcher might note that praise followed student response about 10 per cent of the total lesson time and yet be unable to extract from the matrix whether the praise occurred during the first or last fifteen minutes of the particular lesson. For specific information

		1.* *Accepts feeling:* accepts and clarifies the feeling tone of the students in a non-threatening manner. Feelings may be positive or negative. Predicting and re-calling feelings are included.
	Indirect Influence	2.* *Praises or encourages:* praises or encourages student action or behaviour. Jokes that release tension, not at the expense of another individual, nodding head or saying 'uhhuh?' or 'go on' are included.
Teacher Talk		3.* *Accepts or uses ideas of student:* clarifying, building or developing ideas or suggestions by a student. As teacher brings more of his own ideas into play, shift to category five.
		4.* *Asks questions:* asking a question about content or procedure with the intent that a student answer.
		5.* *Lecturing:* giving facts or opinions about content or procedure; expressing his own ideas; asking rhetorical questions.
	Direct Influence	6.* *Giving directions:* directions, commands or orders with which a student is expected to comply.
		7.* *Criticizing or justifying authority:* statements intended to change student behaviour from non-acceptable to acceptable pattern; bawling someone out; stating why the teacher is doing what he is doing; extreme self-reference.
Student Talk		8.* *Student talk-response:* talk by students in response to teacher. Teacher initiates the contact or solicits student statement.
		9.* *Student talk-initiation:* talk by students, which they initiate. If 'calling on' student is only to indicate who may talk next, observer must decide whether student wanted to talk. If he did, use this category.
		10.* *Silence or confusion:* pauses, short periods of silence and periods of confusion in which communication cannot be understood by the observer.

Figure 1. Categories for Interaction Analysis[1] (Minnesota, 1959)

* There is *no* scale implied by these numbers. Each number is classificatory; it designates a particular kind of communication event. To write

about sequence the observer relies on his raw data which was initially recorded in a column. The following example is offered to help clarify the use of the matrix.

Suppose that after the observer enters the classroom the following sequence of events takes place. The teacher starts by saying, 'Boys and girls, sit down in your seats and take out your workbooks' (category 6). Bill, one of the brighter children, responds to this by saying, 'But, Mrs Adams, I thought you said we were going to have a story this morning' (category 9). The teacher then reacts to Bill by saying, 'Bill, you know that you were so noisy today that I decided to punish you by making you work in your workbooks. I don't like it when you forget these things, Bill' (category 7).

(The observer records two 7's in a row because of the length of the statement.) Then the teacher continues, 'Now I think we can forget about the story and get to work in the workbooks. If we do a good job then we will have the story tomorrow.' (The first part of the teacher's statement is a 6 and the last part, a 5.) The observer has recorded the following column of numbers, pairing them as shown below:

$$\begin{bmatrix} 6 \\ 9 \end{bmatrix} \\ \begin{bmatrix} 7 \\ 7 \\ 6 \end{bmatrix} \\ \begin{bmatrix} 5 \end{bmatrix}$$

These numbers are then entered into a matrix in sequence pairs in such a way that each number is entered twice, once as the first and once as the second number in each pair. The rows of the matrix represent the first number in the pair and the columns, the second. For example, the first sequence pair, 6–9, would be tallied in the cell that is located at the intersection of row 6 and column 9. The next

---

these numbers down during observation is to enumerate, not to judge a position on a scale.

[1] Edmund J. Amidon and Ned A. Flanders, *The Role of the Teacher in the Classroom: A Manual for Understanding and Improving Teachers' Classroom Behaviour*, Minneapolis, Minnesota: Paul S. Amidon & Associates, Inc., 1963, p. 12.

pair is entered in cell 9-7, the third pair 7-7, into the cell located at the intersection of row 7 and column 7 etc. Figure 2 shows the actual location of these five tallies in the matrix.

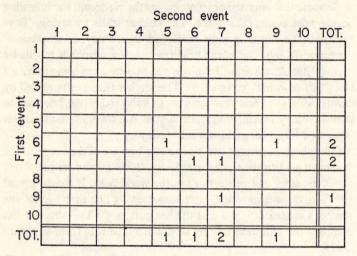

Figure 2. Sample matrix

Objectives

Of course any program, if it is to be replicated, must be part of a research design and have the appropriate controls built into it. The present study is designed as a $2\frac{1}{2}$-year study to test the relationships between the training of cooperating teachers and certain course content, and the behaviour and attitudes of student teachers.

The study tests the following hypotheses:

(1) Student teachers taught Interaction Analysis are more indirect at the end of their student teaching experience than student teachers not so taught.

(2) Student teachers who are taught Interaction Analysis and are supervised by cooperating teachers trained in Interaction Analysis are more indirect at the end of student teaching than student teachers not receiving such training and supervision.

Procedures

General Design. There are two important variables: student teaching course content and the training of the cooperating teacher. The course content for student teachers consists of either traditional learning theory or Interaction Analysis. The cooperating teacher is trained in the use of Interaction Analysis as an observational technique, or receives training in learning theory.

This design makes it possible to treat the influence of two independent variables: the training of cooperating teachers and student teaching course content, upon the dependent variables: ratings of student teachers' teaching effectiveness, attitudes of student teachers, pupil perception of student teacher change and student teachers' teaching patterns. The four groups are compared with one another to determine whether student teaching course content or the training of the cooperating teacher or a combination of the two has the most significant influence on the dependent variables. The study will be carried on for five successive semesters in order to provide for replication of the experiment.

Group I. Student teachers in this group are taught Interaction Analysis in a 2 hour a week lecture and a 2 hour a week laboratory. In addition, they have a 2 hour a week seminar with their college supervisor in which they can discuss problems they are having in their teaching. The cooperating teacher, using Interaction Analysis, observes the student teacher formally once a week for 30 to 40 minutes, and spends 1 hour a week discussing the observation with the student.

Group II. Student teachers in this group are taught Interaction Analysis in a 2 hour a week lecture and a 2 hour a week laboratory. In addition, they have a 2 hour a week seminar with their college supervisor in which they can discuss problems they are having in their teaching. The cooperating teacher observes the student teacher formally once a week for 30 to 40 minutes, and spends 1 hour a week discussing the observation with the student.

Group III. Student teachers in this group are taught learning theory in a 2 hour a week lecture and a 2 hour a week laboratory. In addition, they have a 2 hour a week seminar with their college supervisor in which they can discuss problems they are having in their teaching. They are also observed formally for 30 to 40 minutes once a week by their cooperating teacher, who spends 1 hour a week discussing the observation with them. Although the cooperating teacher may use Interaction Analysis in his observation, he is clearly instructed not to discuss this tool or any of its terminology with the student teacher under any circumstances.

Cooperating Teacher

		Supervision is done by a cooperating teacher trained in Interaction Analysis	Supervision is done by a cooperating teacher trained in learning theory
Course Content	Interaction Analysis and Seminar	15 Students Group I	15 Students Group II
	Learning Theory and Seminar	15 Students Group III	15 Students Group IV

Figure 3. The four experimental groups

Group IV. Student teachers are taught learning theory in a 2 hour a week lecture and a 2 hour a week laboratory period. In addition, they have a 2 hour a week seminar with their college supervisor in which they can discuss problems they are having in their teaching. The cooperating teacher observes the student teacher formally once a week for 30 to 40 minutes, and spends 1 hour a week discussing this observation.

Research by Hough and Amidon, Zahn and Kirk indicates that 12 to 30 hours of training in Interaction Analysis affects the behaviour and/or attitudes of student teachers. The present design which includes 105 hours of training in and application of Interaction Analysis therefore appears to be adequate.

Data and instrumentation

Student teacher rating. Student teachers are rated at both the beginning and end of their student teaching experience by the same measuring instrument which the Department of Secondary Education normally uses to rate student teachers. Student teachers are rated by both their college supervisors and by impartial observers not involved in supervision. The impartial observers do not know which student teachers are in which of the four experimental groups.

Student teaching behaviour. The Flanders System of Interaction Analysis is not only taught to student teachers, it is also used to assess changes in behaviour that may take place over the semester. Each student teacher is observed for 2 hours at the beginning of the semester and for 2 hours at the end of the semester by a trained observer using the Flanders system. These observers are not the college supervisors and do not know which student teachers are in which of the four experimental groups.

Student teaching rating by pupils. The Student Perception of Teacher Influence Scale is used to assess the perception that the children have of their student teacher's behaviour. The data are gathered on a nine point scale, and are analysed statistically. This instrument was used initially by Amidon and Anderson with secondary school pupils, and has been adapted for use in the elementary school by Kirk. Both Amidon and Anderson report high reliability for this instrument.

Student teacher attitude. The Teaching Situation Reaction Test is used to assess student teacher attitudes. In general this test measures the student teacher's reaction to a classroom situation in terms of the direct–indirect dichotomy. A student teacher with a low score sees himself reacting fairly indirectly to a classroom situation, while a high score indicated a more direct reaction. This test is given both at the beginning and end of the student teaching experience.

Student teacher personality. Rokeach's Dogmatism Scale is used to measure personality. The aspect of personality measured by the test is the openness or closedness of a person's belief system.

RESULTS AND CONCLUSIONS

The results of the present study must be interpreted in the light of the early work which was done by Flanders and his associates.

Interaction Analysis was developed and refined by Flanders in the early 1950s. The early research on Interaction Analysis was designed to relate children's attitudes to patterns of teacher behaviour. Flanders found that pupils of teachers who were observed to be indirect had more positive attitudes than pupils of teachers who were perceived by observers as being direct. These findings indicated that pupils of indirect teachers were more interested in subject-matter and liked the methods used by their teachers better than did students of direct teachers.

The results of this early research support the validity of Interaction Analysis as a procedure for predicting the general attitudes of children in a particular classroom.

The next research effort undertaken by Flanders and his associates was designed to determine the relationship between teacher behaviour and student achievement. Several large studies were conducted both in a controlled laboratory setting and in normal classroom situations. All of these studies were carried out at the junior high school level and involved the teaching of social studies and mathematics.

In the first of these studies, Amidon and Flanders found that dependent-prone eighth-grade students who were taught geometry by indirect teaching methods learned more than dependent-prone children taught by direct methods.

In a large-scale study, Flanders isolated, for purposes of analysis, junior high school teachers whose pupils learned the most and the least after a two week experimental program in social studies or mathematics. Teachers of the higher achieving classes were found to differ from teachers of the lower achieving classes in the following ways: (a) they used five to six times as much acceptance of student ideas and encouragement of student ideas, (b) they used five to six times less direction and criticism of student behaviour, (c) they talked 10 per cent less and (d) they encouraged two to three times as much student-initiated talk.

Similar results to those found by Flanders between teachers of high achieving pupils and those of low achieving pupils were found by Amidon and Giammatteo when they compared 30 superior teachers with 150 randomly selected teachers in elementary schools. The 30 superior teachers were nominated by their supervisors and administrators.

Since all of this research appeared to have implications for teacher education, Flanders instituted an in-service program in which Interaction Analysis was taught as an observational tool. The in-service program was able to effect observable changes in teacher patterns of verbal behaviour. In general, at the end of the experimental in-service program, these teachers evidenced more encouraging and accepting behaviour and were less critical and more indirect than they had been at the beginning of the experiment.

Kirk conducted a study with student teachers in elementary education in which he taught Interaction Analysis to an experimental group and compared this group with student teachers who had no Interaction Analysis. He found that the experimental group talked less, had more pupil-initiated talk and more often accepted pupil ideas than did student teachers in the control group. Zahn found that student teachers who learned Interaction Analysis developed more positive attitudes towards student teaching than did a control group of student teachers who were not taught Interaction Analysis.

Little, if any, systematic research has been done on the training of cooperating teachers to supervise student teachers. However, the recent work of Medley and Mitzel and Zahn does suggest that there is a relationship between the behaviour and attitudes of cooperating teachers and growth in student teaching. While they found that the effect of the college supervisor on the student teacher was slight, the influence of the cooperating teacher and the classroom situation appeared to be great.

Much of the data from the present study is still not analysed. However, the direction indicated by the early analysis is significant because of the consistency of the findings. When comparisons were made at the end of the semester between the student teachers who learned Interaction Analysis and those who did not, the following results were obtained:

(1) Student teachers who knew Interaction Analysis talked less in the classroom than those who were trained in learning theory.

(2) Student teachers who learned Interaction Analysis were more indirect in their use of motivating and controlling behaviours than those who were trained in learning theory.

(3) Student teachers who were taught Interaction Analysis were more indirect in their over-all interaction patterns than student teachers who were trained in learning theory.

(4) Student teachers who were taught Interaction Analysis used more extended indirect influence than student teachers who were trained in learning theory.

(5) Student teachers whose cooperating teachers learned Interaction Analysis used less extended direct influence than student teachers who were trained in learning theory.

(6) Student teachers who were taught Interaction Analysis used less extended direct influence than student teachers who were trained in learning theory.

(7) Student teachers who were taught Interaction Analysis used more extended acceptance of student ideas than student teachers who were trained in learning theory.

Perhaps the most significant implications of the early results of the continuing study are that they are consistent with, and support the previous work which has been done on the effect of Interaction Analysis on student teachers, as well as the earlier studies on the relationship between Interaction Analysis patterns and student attitudes and achievement.

In general, when student teachers are trained in Interaction Analysis they become more indirect, accept more student ideas and criticize less than student teachers not so trained. Since Flanders found that teachers of children who had high achievement and positive attitudes were more indirect, accepted more student ideas and used less criticism than teachers of children with low achievement and negative attitudes, there appears to be substantial evidence that the Interaction Analysis training is helping to produce teachers with appropriate teaching skills.

Implications

Perhaps the best estimate of the role of Interaction Analysis in the supervisory process is that it provides a basis for what might be termed the 'self-directed supervisor'. With Interaction Analysis the supervisor does not need to point to the teacher and give him directions for changing his behaviour; the teacher can see this in the matrix. The teacher can observe himself, using a tape-recorder, and thus provide his own feedback without the presence of another person. While many teachers find the use of Interaction Analysis threatening at first, many also find it refreshing to be able to have objective data that they can study and thus make their own decisions about how they would like to change.

FURTHER READING

E. Amidon and E. Hunter, *Improving teaching: the analysis of classroom verbal interaction*, Holt, Rinehart and Winston, 1967.

E. J. Amidon and M. A. Flanders, *The role of the teacher in the classroom*, Minneapolis, Minnesota, Paul S. Amidon and Associates, 1963.

D. P. Ausubel, *Educational psychology, a cognitive view*, Holt, Rinehart and Winston, 1968.

D. P. Ausubel, *The psychology of meaningful verbal learning*, Grune and Stratton, 1963.

B. S. Bloom *et al.*, *Taxonomy of educational objectives 1: cognitive domain*, Longmans, 1956.

J. S. Bruner, *Toward a theory of instruction*, Belknap, 1966.

J. P. De Cecco, *The psychology of learning and instruction*, Prentice-Hall, 1968.

J. P. De Cecco (Ed.), *The psychology of language thought and instruction*, Holt, Rinehart and Winston, 1967.

N. L. Gage (Ed.), *Handbook of Research on Teaching*, Rand McNally, 1963.

N. L. Gage, *Three pressing concerns of educational research*, School of Education, Stanford University, March 1967.

R. M. Gagné and N. E. Paradise, 'Abilities and learning sets in knowledge acquisition', *Psychological monographs*, **75** (14), 1961.

R. M. Gagné and E. C. Smith, Jnr, 'A study of the effects of verbalisation on problem solving', *Journal of Experimental Psychology*, **63**, 1962, pp. 12–16.

R. M. Gagné, *The conditions of learning*, Holt, Rinehart and Winston, 1965.

N. I. Gez, 'Interrelationships between oral and written forms of communication', *Soviet Education*, **13** (8), 1966, pp. 24–32.

E. R. Hilgard, *Theories of learning and instruction*, N.S.S.E. Yearbook, University of Chicago, 1964.

B. Y. Kersh, 'The motivating effect of learning by directed discovery', *Journal of Educational Psychology*, **53** (2), 1962, pp. 65–71.

E. A. Lunzer, 'Psychology and the teacher' in E. A. Lunzer and J. F. Morris, *Development in human learning*, Staples, 1968, pp. 439–64.

A. W. Melton (Ed.), *Categories of human learning*, Academic Press, 1964.

E. Stones, *Learning and teaching, a programmed introduction*, Wiley, 1968.

H. Taba and F. E. Freeman, 'Teaching strategies and thought processes', *Teachers College Record*, **65**, 1964, pp. 524–34.

R. M. W. Travers, 'A study of the relationship of psychological research to educational practice' in R. Glaser, *Training Research and Education*, Wiley, 1965, pp. 525–58.

J. R. Verduin, *Conceptual models in teacher education*, American Association of Colleges for Teacher Education, 1967.

Some aspects of subject teaching

As might be surmised from Hilgard's remarks concerning the gap between psychological research and classroom practice, the literature on the psychology of teaching specific school subjects is extremely limited. The literature on the general problem of the psychology of school learning is expanding rapidly and most subject specialists are reappraising teaching methods and content in their own fields. What is sorely needed is cooperation between psychologists and subject specialists to expand knowledge in the areas of common concern.

The papers which follow cover most of the key subjects but lack of space and suitable material preclude more extensive coverage. There is, in most papers, which are drawn from a wide range of sources, an interesting common thread already mentioned in earlier chapters. Almost all the papers have a central concern in ensuring that children learn the concepts in a subject and not just the words which stand for the concepts. We might say, in other words, that the emphasis is on meaningful learning. Many of the papers also make clear the ways in which children's learning differs markedly from the conception teachers have of their learning. The experiments of Piaget are widely known as illustrations of the way in which teachers can hold erroneous views on the nature of children's thinking. The paper by Beard in this section outlines Piaget-type experiments which explore the way in which certain important mathematical concepts develop in young children. Skemp deals with the teaching of mathematics at secondary level and takes a critical look at some aspects of 'modern' mathematics.

One of the most difficult problems in teaching for concept development, especially with younger children, is that the inessential visual aspects of phenomena dominate the child's perception and interfere with accurate conceptualizing. This is a common finding in Piagetian experiments. In the paper by Natadze we see how he found this sort of problem when he investigated the learning of scientific concepts in young children.

Peel and Fleshner, discussing the teaching of history and physics respectively, show how the everyday notions of the nature of phenomena can interfere seriously with the learning of scientific and historical concepts.

The papers by Reid and Merritt raise some of the most important questions in the teaching of reading. They provide further examples of the unsuspected difficulties which children have in learning.

The paper by Brocklehurst raises matters on which educational psychology has little to say. The teaching of music involves thinking about aesthetics and the psychology of aesthetics is virtually virgin territory. However, Brocklehurst raises many points which impinge on our general line and are of undoubted value to anyone involved in the field of musical education.

---

1 Educational research and the learning of mathematics*

R. M. BEARD

Piaget's investigations into the acquisition of mathematical concepts have brought to light fundamental misconceptions in children's thinking, of which teachers are often unaware. In this paper the author describes Piaget-type experiments which explore the grasp which young children have of certain mathematical concepts. Similar findings to those of Piaget are observed but, in addition, the way in which experience can affect children's concept formation is interestingly brought out.

* Reprinted from R. M. Beard, 'Educational research and the learning of mathematics' in F. Land (Ed.), *Aspects of Education: The New Look in Mathematics Teaching*, University of Hull Institute of Education, 1965.

1. INTRODUCTION

In general, educational research has little influence on *what* should be taught. The kind of mathematics included in school syllabuses alters chiefly under pressure of the changing needs of society. At the present time the advent of calculating machines and computers makes skill in mechanical arithmetic practically unnecessary in offices and shops; but the enormously increasing uses of mathematics in the physical sciences, technology, biological sciences, sociology and psychology, the study of communication etc., and the need to understand mathematics in making programs for computers, to make sense of statistical information provided in newspapers, on hoardings, or on television etc., makes it imperative to teach more mathematics to more people in such a way that mathematical concepts and under- lying principles are understood. Since it is generally believed that mathematics is a difficult subject, that many children dislike it, and appear unable to understand it, research which casts light on their misconceptions and suggests means to eradicate them has a special value at the present time.

2. CHILDREN'S MISCONCEPTION

Piaget's investigations have brought to light fundamental miscon- ceptions in children's thinking of which teachers are often unaware. These appear in failure to understand that numbers and quantities are conserved in amount when arrangement or shape is altered, by inability to classify objects logically, from difficulty in making or relating sequences or series of different kinds (whether of numbers, times, lengths, areas or volumes), in failure to see relationships between a class and sub-classes or a whole with its parts and by inability to comprehend even simple spatial relationships. It is instructive to look at a few of these experiments to see that they were neither difficult nor confusing but that nevertheless concepts which are basic to understanding were lacking in many children at the top of the junior school or even in the secondary grammar school.

The experiments described below were made with children in England but are very similar to experiments made originally by Piaget and his collaborators. The first four require understanding of conservation of different kinds, the remaining two of simple spatial concepts.

Experiment *1*. Conservation of substance

Between two and three hundred children from primary schools in five different areas of England were tested; not more than five children being taken from any one school. The children were shown equal quantities of water in two exactly similar glasses and three empty small glasses. They agreed that there would be the same to drink from the two large glasses. The experimenter then said 'I'm going to pour yours into three small glasses. Now I have this one to drink and you have all those three glasses of water to drink. Will you have more to drink, or shall we still both have the same, or shall I have more to drink? . . . How do you know? . . .' If he answered correctly the child was asked in addition 'Suppose I poured yours into ten small glasses. Would you still have the same amount to drink then?'

The results were as follows:

Age	4·10–5·9	5·10–6·9	6·10–7·9	7·10–8·9	8·10–10+
% conserving	10·2	20·9	40·5	58·5	63·0
Number of children	(49)	(72)	(42)	(53)	(27)

Nearly all children who supposed that the quantity changed gave as the reason that more glasses must hold more water. This is instructive, for the children must have known relationships such as 1 quart = 2 pints and 1 gallon = 8 pints etc., and would have used them countless times in sums applying the four rules to weights and measures. But these had remained specific pieces of information which many children, even at 10 years, could not generalize to the situations likely to be met in everyday life or in problems relating to quantities in arithmetic or in science.

Experiment *2*. Conservation of weight

The same sample of children were shown two balls of plasticene in the pans of a balance. The experimenter said 'These two balls of plasticene weigh the same. They just balance.' She then removed one, handed it to the child and added 'Flatten this one like a biscuit. . . . Do you think it still weighs the same as the ball ? . . . Why (not) ? . . . If you flattened it still more until it looked like a pancake would it still weigh the same ?'

Percentages who believed that the weight would be conserved in both cases were as follows:

Age	4·10–5·9	5·10–6·9	6·10–7·9	7·10–8·9	8·10–10+
% conserving	33·3	45·0	48·9	29·2	58·3
Number of children	48	60	63	109	58

By the numbers of infants who understand conservation in this item it appears to be an easy question; but the number of 10-year-olds able to understand it is still appreciably less than two-thirds of the total. It is clear that work done with weights in the junior schools has aided understanding even less than that done with capacities. Subsequently, when the children were asked to compare the weights of objects many were unable to use a balance.

Experiment 3. Conservation of volume

Two equal sized objects of different weight were shown and handled by the children. The lighter one was dropped into a glass of water and the effect on the water level observed. The children were then asked 'If I take this one out and put in the heavier one instead will the water rise higher still, to the same height or not rise so high ?'

Among a number in the same primary school sample, percentages of correct answers were as follows:

Age	4·10–6·9	6·10–7·9	7·10–8·9	8·10–10+
% correct	8·6	19·1	3·2	9·4
Number tested	(35)	(47)	(31)	(32)

In an older sample of children tested in a similar experiment in which one tin was three times as heavy as another, numbers giving different kinds of answers and percentages correct were:

Age in years	7 and 8	9 and 10	11 and 12	13 and 14	15 and 16
Don't know	2	1	9	6	0
Higher (if heavier)	6	10	0	0	3
Three times higher	0	0	2	1	1
Correct – the same height	1	3	3	12	10
% correct	11·1	21·4	21·4	63·2	71·4

The sample of older children was biased since it included unduly large proportions of grammar-school and selective secondary-school pupils and some younger children from a private preparatory school.

Since volume is not usually taught in school until children are about 10 or 11 the small amount of success among the first sample is not surprising except that juniors did rather worse than infants. In the secondary schools there was a substantial improvement, but some 15-year-olds who were studying rural science or physics still believed that weight influenced the level of the liquid although a single demonstration would have sufficed to show otherwise.

Experiment 4. Conservation of area, with fractions

This experiment was used by the writer with 235 Ghanaian and 100 English primary school children aged approximately 8 years and 10 years (though some of the Ghanaian children were older, and a few did not know their ages). Three equal squares of coloured card were shown. Two were then cut in halves, one parallel with a side, the other diagonally. The children were asked what fraction each piece was and what they knew about two halves. This they all found easy. A triangular half and a rectangular half were then combined to make a 'house', and the children were asked to write down whether they thought there was more paper in the 'house', more in the whole square or the same amount of paper in each. Percentages who believed that the amounts of paper were the same were as follows:

Age	About 8	About 10	Number tested
Ghana	32·5	56·0	235
England	32	62	100

Again, roughly 40 per cent have failed to understand conservation of area, in this instance, at about 10 years (at the end of the third year in the junior school). In discussion with one-fifth of the sample they could be led to say that each part of the 'house' was a half, that two halves made one whole and that, consequently, the areas of the 'house' and the square were equal; a few children spontaneously laughed at their error, but the majority still looked doubtful and appeared unconvinced.

Experiment 5. Some spatial concepts

In a series of questions relating to spatial concepts with the Ghanaian and English primary school children they were required to imagine a picture from a different point of view and to select the correct view from three provided. One of the pictures showed a long table across a room, a chair under it to the left and a schoolgirl entering the room on the far side of the table. The children were required to select her view of the table and chair. Three solutions were possible: children could select their own view of the picture, they could choose a picture with the chair on the other side of the table but still to the left, or they could choose the correct view appreciating that both relations before/behind and right/left would be reversed. Percentages choosing each picture were as follows:

Age	About 8		About 10	
	Ghana	England	Ghana	England
Own view chosen	62·2	32	59·5	14
Chair still at left	19·7	32	18·1	26
Correct view	18·1	36	22·4	60

The results are of interest since they highlight the differences of experience in the two environments. Ghanaian children do comparatively poorly in this item, but many of them have simple homes, spend much time out of doors and have few or no constructional toys from which these relationships could be learned. But in an item where children were required to select the view seen from an upside-down position the older Ghanaian children did as well as their

English counterparts. In selecting a bird's-eye-view, however, they did very badly whereas the English sample did astonishingly well. English children see such views from the tops of high buildings, in looking down at constructional toys, in aerial pictures in books or on television, and in illustrations of space travel in comics; Ghanaian children almost entirely lack these experiences. Ten years ago, however, the writer found that few English 6- and 7-year-olds could draw a bird's-eye-view. It seems probable that the quite astonishing improvement is due chiefly to aerial pictures on television, for teachers confirm that infants in the nursery class now draw bird's-eye-views spontaneously.

Although simple spatial concepts are not taught in school their understanding is needed to follow directions in P.E., to predict the movements of traffic, to visualize relationships shown in maps and how they change with point of view, and to comprehend both two- and three-dimensional problems in geometry. The English sample are better prepared than the Ghanaians for all of these tasks; but there is still a substantial number of 10-year-olds who need to be given more experiences and to be led to see the spatial relations. Opportunity for observation alone is not sufficient to teach concepts. Unless interest is aroused in a relationship as a result of some activity, or in discussion following a demonstration, even daily opportunities for observation may be ignored as we shall see in the next experiment.

Experiment 6. The concept of horizontal in relation to liquids

As it is unlikely that children will be able to give a definition of 'horizontal' we can only ask for their observations in specific situations. Piaget found that Swiss children realized the importance of the horizontal in buildings and in the surfaces of lakes, or liquid in a bottle, by about the age of 9. At this age he found that there was immediate prediction of horizontal and vertical as part of an over-all frame of reference. Other experiments showed that this did not hold good of English children even by the age of 11 +. We supposed that school children in this country had most opportunity to notice the horizontal in relation to the surface of liquid in bottles for they have a daily bottle of milk, or they might see it in playing with water, in pouring from jugs etc.

The experiment consisted in showing a bottle half full of orange-ade standing upright, while a similar empty bottle was shown tilted in two positions – near vertical and near horizontal. The children were asked to draw, in blanks provided, the position of the liquid in the half full bottle if it was tilted in each of these positions. The results were unexpected: twenty-eight of the 172 juniors drew liquid suspended in space, greatly expanded and with a nearly vertical curved surface, or still parallel with the base of the bottle, a further sixty-four children drew the surface of the liquid almost parallel with the side of the bottle regardless of its position, nearly vertical in both cases, or nearly parallel with the base in both cases. Only nine children drew the liquid horizontal in both blanks; of these seven were boys and all were rated 'bright'. The remaining children drew lines somewhere between the horizontal and parallel with the base of the bottle, usually succeeding better in the nearly horizontal bottle. Scores assigned to their drawings showed marked improvement with age and a substantial difference between the sexes in the boys' favour; but out of a possible five the mean score of boys aged 10·5–11·4 was less than three.

These few experiments suffice to show that, however efficient teaching may be in inculcating speed and accuracy in performing operations with figures, it all too often leaves basic concepts uncomprehended. Many more examples could be given of misconceptions about numbers, time and ages, areas, volumes and other spatial concepts or measures. In short it appears that mathematical teaching builds, in many cases, on insecure foundations, giving too little practical work, and too little opportunity for thought or discussion for teachers to realize that the gaps exist or to see how to fill them. It is easy to account for the many children who 'can't do mathematics' or who hate the subject; the learning of tables about numbers and quantities has left them with specific pieces of information which are inadequate when they face practical problems in daily life or when they attempt to do problems from textbooks. Since a concept is not learned unless general properties are observed, at least two illustrations are needed, preferably in quick succession. For example, to develop the concept of conservation of weight children might be asked to balance two balls of plasticene on scales, to deform one, weigh them again, to record what they observe and to repeat the exercise with other materials or different deformations. Some children would at once deduce the general result that weight was conserved if only shape was altered; others would need to be led to the generalization by questions and, possibly, through further experiments.

It may be objected, however, that failure to understand concepts is at least as much a function of age as of teaching or of daily experiences, so that although a concept may be beyond a child at 10 years he will understand it at 14. There is certainly truth in this where more complex or difficult concepts are concerned; concepts such as proportionality, for example, appear to be beyond the capacity of nearly all younger children. But in the experiments described so far infants showed a fair measure of understanding. Even allowing for individual differences of ability and interest the reasons for failure of a large number of children as old as 10 years can only be sought in experience and teaching. Whereas infants are on the whole well catered for by the kind of teaching they receive it appears that the majority of juniors are given instruction in arithmetic or mathematics which is not well suited to their needs.

2 Concept formation and its significance in mathematics teaching and syllabus reform*

R. SKEMP

The concern which has been shown in other papers with teaching for a thorough grasp of concepts is nowhere more important than in mathematics. The higher order concepts in this subject are particularly abstract and there is a corresponding danger that the children will learn the words without the underlying concepts. In this paper the author tackles this basic problem and also gives critical considera-

* Reprinted from R. Skemp, 'Concept Formation and its Significance in Mathematics Teaching and Syllabus Reform' in F. Land (Ed.), *Aspects of Education: The New Look in Mathematics Teaching*, Hull University, Department of Education, 1965, pp. 59–70.

tion to some of the topics of modern mathematics. He suggests that they are sometimes taught more because they are fashionable than because they enhance a child's grasp of mathematical concepts. The important question of the relationship between techniques (learning tables etc.) and conceptual understanding is also discussed and recommendations made.

The importance of this topic, for a study of the teaching of mathematics, is that while some areas of knowledge deal mainly or largely with facts, mathematics is concerned entirely with concepts.

To justify such a statement, it will first be necessary to try to explain what I mean by this distinction. First, here are a few examples of facts.

The capital of Zambia is Lusaka.

The following words have their plural in x: bijou, caillou, chou, genou, joujou, hibou, pou.

The train for London leaves Stockport at 08.10.

This iron bar sinks if I drop it in the river.

(To call these facts is really an over-simplification – whenever one looks closely at a 'fact', it usually turns out to be a low-order concept. Nevertheless, the distinction is a useful one while establishing our basic ideas in this field.) In contrast, let us look at a statement which is certainly about a concept.

The density of iron is greater than that of water.

Density is a *concept* by which we *relate* the weight of many different lumps of iron, their volumes and the weights and volumes of many different samples of water from pools, rivers, lakes, seas or reservoirs. Provisionally, we could describe it as a mental awareness of something in common between a number of experiences.

We can tell someone a fact and they can then use it without necessarily understanding it. I do not know why the train leaves at 08.10 – it just does (usually), and I can use this fact to plan my getting-up and breakfast times. The plural of bijou is bijoux – it just is. Iron bars sink, so you do not use them to build a raft.

But if I simply say 'The density of iron is greater than that of water', my hearer will not necessarily be able to use it, or to understand it. Being able to use *depends* on being able to understand it: given which, the concept is often much more powerful – we can make iron ships which do not sink.

So the next question is, what do we mean by this much-used word, 'understand'? And how can we arrange for someone to understand a concept, if we cannot do so by telling them?

Let us imagine a man blind from birth, who by a surgical operation is given his sight in adult life. He is thus entering a new field of experience for the first time, so offers a useful parallel to a pupil starting in a new field of knowledge. He asks, 'What does "red" mean?'

It would be useless to say, 'Red is the colour we experience from light of wavelength in the region of 6,500 Ångstrom units.' This is an accurate definition, which he could learn by heart and use for an answer to an examination question. He might even get full marks! But would this indicate that he really knew what was meant by 'red'? Of course not: they would be, for him, just words, empty of meaning.

In such a case there would be no way of *telling* him the meaning of red so that he understood. The only effective method would be to point to a number of real objects, saying 'This is a red tie, that is a red tulip, that is a red book . . .'. In this way, though we could not tell him, we could arrange for him to find out for himself the meaning of 'red'.

To give him only a single example would not be enough. If we just said 'That is a red tie', he would not know whether 'red' meant 'red', or 'tie', or 'red tie'. We must vary the examples, so that the irrelevant parts cancel out, while that which they have in common sums.

Nor have we any guarantee that our 'pupil' will form the concept. (He might, for example, be colour-blind.) We can only arrange for him to have a series of experiences from which we hope that he will do so. This kind of uncertainty could be hard to accept if we wanted to be quite sure that he would learn the meaning of red, and a quest for certainty could (and does) all too easily lead to the giving and memorization of standard definitions. But all that this would guarantee (in the absence of the kind of experience described above) is an appearance of knowledge without the reality.

How could this be verified? Easily enough, in this case, by showing him various objects and asking whether they were red or not. The test of whether someone has a concept is whether or not he can use it correctly, not whether he can give a verbal definition. (In mathematics, verbalization can even be a hindrance. Most mathematical statements are easier to understand in mathematical symbolism than in words.)

Not all concepts can be communicated in this way. Suppose that our subject now asks, 'What is "colour"?'. We cannot convey this by pointing to various coloured objects. Instead, we would say 'Red, blue, green, yellow . . ., – these are all colours'. For the examples from which the concept of colour is formed are themselves concepts. So before the subject could form the new concept, he would need to have available at least some of these other concepts (red, blue, green, yellow . . .).

This introduces a 'distinction' between the kind of concepts formed from sensory experiences of the outside world (such as 'red'), which I call primary concepts; and those formed from other concepts (such as 'colour'), which I call secondary concepts. We can also think of the concept of colour as being of a higher order than its contributory concepts, red, blue, green, yellow. . . . Similarly, we can form another secondary concept of higher order still, say that of a visual sensation, examples of this being colour, brightness, shape. . . . We now have the beginning of a hierarchy of concepts, some of higher order than others, some of lower order and some (e.g. red, blue . . .) of the same order. And within such a hierarchy, concepts of a higher order than those which the subject already has can only be communicated to him by the indirect method already described.

If words cannot be used for 'telling', of what use are they at all?

Once we are in the field of secondary concepts, we cannot do without them. We can call our subject's attention to a red tie nonverbally if necessary, by waving it at him or pointing to it. But how can we call his attention to the concepts red, green . . .? Only by using these names, which we have linked in his mind with the concepts themselves at the time of their formation. (Recall the repetition of the concept-name, and the variation of the words naming its various embodiments.) When we say one of these words, we hope to call to his consciousness the corresponding concepts; and by our grouping of the words together, we hope that he will group the concepts together in his mind to form a new, higher order, concept.

And if definitions are of no use for conveying a new concept, then of what use are these?

Firstly, I did not say that they were never of use for conveying a new concept: only, that this is so when the new concept is of a higher order than the others which are available to the person concerned. Concepts of the same or lower order often can be conveyed by definition. For example, if someone has the concepts of green and brown, one can explain to him that 'autumn green' means green with some brown in it, and he can then show that he has the concept by pointing correctly to objects of this colour. New concepts can be formed as the intersection of existing classes: e.g. 'blue rose' is meaningful to anyone who has the concepts of blue and of rose, even if he has never seen an example. Used in this way, a definition also shows how a given concept is related to the others which are referred to in the definition.

But the main function of a definition is, as the word implies, to make clear the limits of the concept – where it starts and finishes. It is a tidying up process, which cannot be done until after the concept is formed. 'Shall we call this red ? Or this ?' Borderline cases must be settled by agreement – 'We will only call it "red" if the wavelength comes between 6,500 and 7,700 A.U.' This agreement about a criterion, for distinguishing between examples and non-examples of a concept, is what is embodied in a definition.

Apart from its practical value in settling possible disputes, the production of a definition also forces us to become more explicitly aware of just what we do mean by a particular concept. It crystallizes it in our minds, making the outline sharper and the structure more visible. But it is the process of thinking about the concept in order to reach a definition which has this effect, and perhaps even more, the interplay of minds and ideas which may also be involved. Since the exercise is as important as the end product, being given a ready-made definition is still no substitute for doing it oneself.

To conclude this section, let us look at one mathematical concept, say sin θ, to see what are some of the subordinate concepts in this particular hierarchy.

Since we are talking about sin θ and not, for example, sin $24°$, there is the concept of a *variable*, which is what θ stands for. If sine is taught in the traditional way (which I still prefer) as the ratio of the lengths of a certain two sides of a right-angled triangle, there are the concepts of ratio, triangle, angles of various sizes, right angle. These ratios are each of two lengths, so there are the related concepts of length and measurement. The sine of an angle does not depend on the size of the right-angled triangle used, so there are the concepts of similar triangles and corresponding sides.

This mathematically elementary example gives a clue to the power of concepts, ince it combines and relates many different experiences and ideas. It also indicates why mathematics is of such practical mportance in science, engineering and other fields. 'There is nothing so practical as a good theory.' Mathematics is the most theoretical of all theories, which is why nearly all theories find their eventual expression in terms of mathematical ideas.

SIGNIFICANCE FOR MATHEMATICAL TEACHING

Since mathematics is a complex hierarchy of concepts, it follows from the argument of the first section that it has to be communicated in a different way from facts if it is to be understood. Failure on the part of their teachers to appreciate this difference is, I believe, one of the main reasons why so many intelligent children – and adults – 'cannot understand mathematics'.

The method of teaching for concept formation has, I think, been intuitively used for many years by some teachers, some of the time. But anyone who cares to look through the school mathematical texts in general use, both traditional and contemporary, can see for himself how widespread the opposite method, of definitions followed by examples for practice, still is.

To apply the former method deliberately, two principles must be made explicit.

(i) New concepts are to be formed in the mind of the pupil by carefully chosen collections of examples.

(ii) We must make quite sure that all the contributory lower order concepts are available.

The first of these principles means, among other things, that one collection of examples must be concerned with communicating one concept only. This concept has to be very clear in the mind of the teacher (by which I include also anyone who is compiling such a collection for use by others), in order that truly appropriate examples may be chosen. This includes being aware what it does *not* include, without which irrelevant attributes may unconsciously influence the choice of examples, and thereby unintentionally be taught as if they were part of the concept. To take a simple example it is rather easy, when teaching trigonometrical ratios, to show the right-angled triangles all in this position. This then becomes part of the pupils' concepts of sine, cosine and tangent, with the result that they afterwards have difficulty in using them for triangles which are differently oriented, except by rotating either the paper, or themselves! Teachers who use the term 'base' for the side marked 'a' in the figure

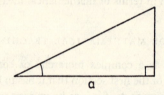

thereby suggest that this orientation may unconsciously be part of their own concepts. With reflection, they would discard this, as not being really part of the concepts of sine, cosine, tangent: and with understanding of principle (i), they would then vary the position of the triangles so that the concept were formed without this irrelevancy.

The second principle means that we must, before trying to teach any new idea in this way, 'take it to pieces' in order to see what concepts must be available for the pupil. The pieces themselves must be taken to pieces, and so on till we have reached primary concepts. Mathematically we can then go no farther – we have reached what the mathematician calls 'undefined ideas', such as point, line, add. But these ideas must themselves come from somewhere, namely from concrete sensory experience of objects in the outside world, and as teachers we have to make sure that the experience is available. Hence, at the lower end, the importance not only of 'structured material' – objects which physically embody certain mathematical ideas – but of other mathematically significant experience such as weighing and measuring, one-to-one correspondence (one milk bottle to each child), real and play shopping and the like.

The results of the teacher's analysis will usually need to be given to the pupils in the reverse order to those in which they were found when taking to pieces the concept. The teacher analyses, the pupil re-synthesizes. It is sometimes necessary to remind oneself of this, for I have on occasion caught myself beginning to explain something to pupils in the same sequence as I have first succeeded in making it clear to myself.

I have also found that if they did not understand what I was trying to convey, this was often because what had seemed to me a single concept was really a combination of several. My own conceptual analysis had not gone far enough, and I was therefore not keeping to principles (i), first corollary (one set of examples, one concept).

The results of carrying out a thorough analysis of this kind, even of quite elementary mathematics, can be both surprising and far-reaching. Topics which were once encountered for the first time in a university mathematics course are now successfully taught to 11-year-olds. Others, which were once thought to be elementary, turn out when carefully analysed to be unexpectedly complex. Examples of both categories will be given in the third section, where we shall explore more fully this point which has now come to light: namely, that a need for certain changes in the content and order of mathematical syllabuses arises directly from applying these psychological principles of teaching for concept formation.

Another result of re-structuring their mathematics in this way has been a marked increase of the pupils' enjoyment of the work. This again has surprised some who have read the text based on the foregoing ideas without seeing the work in operation in classrooms where it is being used. The greater degree of mathematical accuracy which arises out of a careful conceptual analysis has seemed to these readers to have been taken too far, at the risk of losing the pupils' interest.

Experience, however, has proved exactly the opposite. Of all the comments made by teachers who are trying out this approach, that made most frequently is 'The children certainly seem to enjoy it'. This is sometimes said with surprise, and even apparent misgiving! This result was, of course, hoped for: that by making mathematics more understandable, it would also become more enjoyable. And it was believed that greater accuracy makes for greater ease of understanding, not less.

Related to this is the pleasure which we all experience on gaining insight into a problem: the Eureka effect, in miniature. This pleasure is short-circuited if one is told the answer beforehand – no one wants to hear the answer to a puzzle before having had a chance to try it themselves. The aim should therefore be to give pupils the satisfaction of gaining as many insights as possible for themselves. At the beginning, at least, this will be possible only if the work progresses by sufficiently small stages: 'one new concept, one collection of examples'.

This principle is already partly understood by the advocates of what is usually called the 'discovery method'. But this surely means guided discovery? Simply to leave children to find out for themselves all that they need to know would be to deprive them of the privilege of 'standing on our shoulders', by which each generation is able to see a little farther than its predecessors. Our task as teachers is not to abdicate our authority, but to exercise it without being authoritarian. This means that we must plan to provide for our pupils the experiences from which they can form, in years, concepts which have taken the human race many centuries. And by leaving them free, within these limits, to make these discoveries for themselves and in their own way, we shall be giving them the kinds of activity and enjoyment which are most likely to lead to true originality in the future.

SYLLABUS REFORM

At present, many of the reformers of school mathematics seem to be more concerned with changing its content than with helping the children to think more mathematically. Without a set of valid criteria, this may lead to the inclusion of topics for reasons of fashion or personal preference: both transitory influences.

I suggest that the principles discussed in the two earlier sections, conceptual analysis by the teachers combined with concept formation by the pupils, give two lasting criteria. (These are not the only ones – others arise from other aspects of the psychological basis of learning mathematics, which there has not been space to deal with here.) The two suggested are whether a topic is either (1) fundamental, or (2) polyvalent.

By a fundamental concept, I mean one which contributes to many higher order concepts; for example sets (but not necessarily the algebra of sets); mapping; function; triangulation. And by poly-valent, I mean that it is a high-order concept with many particular applications; for example matrices, vectors. These ideas are comple-mentary: the first looks at the conceptual structure from below up-wards, and the second from above downwards. Both mean that the topic is an important part of the mathematical structure which we are trying to build in the pupil's mind – or rather, help him to build in his own mind.

This criterion enables us to choose selectively from the ideas of 'modern mathematics'. Some topics, at present popular, need per-haps a closer examination on this score. The idea of a set is certainly fundamental. On it, together with that of one-to-one correspondence, depend the elementary concepts of number, counting, addition, multiplication. The rather subtle idea of a variable can best be explained as 'an un-named element of a set'. By using letters to stand for variables, we can begin to state general properties of known sets, and we are then into algebra.

This is not how the idea of a set is always used, however. The children learn about unions and intersections, and apply these to artificially constructed examples. ('Ten of those who passed in Geography also passed in English, but of the seventeen who passed in English, only three also passed in Latin...') After which, the whole affair is left aside and never used again. This kind of treatment suggests that sets may have been included because they are fashion-able, and not for genuinely mathematical reasons.

Another topic which is fashionable today is the binary system of numeration (often called 'binary numbers' by those who do not distinguish between numbers and numerals). This is alleged to be necessary knowledge in this computer age. But I am told by a com-puter expert that the input to computers is still in denary, conversion to binary being done by the machine. So why teach children to do the mechanical task of converting denary to binary, or adding in binary? As an example of numeration to bases other than ten it might deserve inclusion, but we ought then also to include other bases, especially those in everyday use, such as dozens and grosses. A much stronger case could, however, be made in relation to the mathematics of two-state systems, for children are already aware that most electrical switches have to be either 'on' or 'off'. So – depending on the way it is treated – binary numeration may also be an example of fashionable mathematics, or the result of some careful thinking by the teacher.

What *is* needed for those who are going to work with computers is a very thorough understanding of the various operations of mathematics. A computer only does what it is told, and you can only tell it what to do if you know yourself with complete precision and detail.

This criterion also tells us to change our emphasis away from techniques, towards fundamental principles. For example, away from *doing* strings of long multiplications to seeing why they can be done that way. Consider

$$
\begin{array}{r}
417 \\
\times \quad 35 \\
\hline
12,510 \\
2,085 \\
\hline
14,595
\end{array}
$$

The correctness of this method depends on the distributive property, in this instance that

$$35 \times 417 = 30 \times 417 + 5 \times 417$$

But we did not in fact work out 30×417, in line 3: we calculated 3×417 and added a zero. This assumes that $10 \times (3 \times 417) = (10 \times 3) \times 47$, the associative property for multiplication. Had we multiplied by factors, $7 \times 5 \times 417$, we should also have assumed the associative property. So we do not need to look for new topics to find examples of 'modern mathematics', or what I prefer to call the structure of mathematics. For the pupil, it is these properties of number systems which save him from having to learn his 35 times table, and which make the desk calculator (working on the same principles) give the right answers. And for the teacher, the process of conceptual analysis made necessary on the psychological grounds described earlier turns out to bear a close relationship to the study of the structure of mathematical ideas which is one of the chief interests of contemporary mathematics. This, and not fashion, I regard as the reason for introducing 'modern mathematics' into school syllabuses.

Though techniques come second to basic principles, they must not be regarded as without any importance at all. Far from it: I spoke of a shift of emphasis, not a complete abandonment of technical skills. We want to produce children who know that $7 \times 9 = 9 \times 7$, and also that both equal 63.

Moreover, one cannot form the more advanced concepts unless one can handle the basic techniques effortlessly. For example, I came across an 11-year-old child who was having difficulty with an exercise, which was intended to lead her to discover that the result of expressing a given number in prime factors was unique, whatever the order of factorization. Her stumbling block was that she could not divide, quickly and accurately, by 2, 3, 5 . . .!

Similarly more advanced pupils will be greatly impeded in their learning of calculus or analytical geometry, unless they can remove brackets, collect like terms, expand a binomial, without having to stop and think. If they cannot, so much of their effort is taken up with these elementary processes, and progress is so slow, that they cannot pay proper attention to what is the purpose of these manipulations, nor see yet an over-all view of what is going on. So the new concepts are never formed. (I sometimes find myself in a comparable position when trying to decipher a particularly illegible examination script. After reading a page word by word, I have lost track of what the writer was trying to say.)

In a proper synthesis of conceptual learning and technical proficiency, the basic techniques should be automatic, but not mechanical A machine does not know what it is doing; but a mathematician, having run through a routine algebraic manipulation automatically – that is, without stopping to think about it – could nevertheless at any time explain, justify or in some other way demonstrate that he understood what he had been doing. Given prior conceptual learning, practice will lead to this kind of technical proficiency. If, however, we begin the other way about, with rote-learning of rules followed by practice in unintelligently following them, it will be more difficult retrospectively to incorporate understanding. And if the process is continued for any length of time, the concepts necessary for understanding will never be learnt. So again, understanding must come first: techniques second, but that does not mean nowhere.

3   The mastery of scientific concepts in school*

R. G. NATADZE

One of the problems which faces the primary school teacher is making sure that children are not misled by the external appearance of phenomena when he is trying to teach them the essential conceptual features. In the paper which follows, Natadze describes investigations with young children which provide interesting insights into the persistence with which they cling to the visual aspects of phenomena in classification tasks.

Many years of experimental study of the development of thinking in concepts at school age has convinced us that what presents the greatest difficulty for the child is distinguishing the essential features of a concept and understanding their significance.

The child can easily grasp the visual properties common to a certain group of objects and abstract these, and masters concrete concepts in practice considerably earlier, i.e. at a younger age, than he can master the essential features of a concept as such. Of all the moments in the mastery of a concept the last is the grasping of its essential features and their significance, the establishment from this point of view of the essential (not simply the common) features. Our experiments have shown that the child finds it particularly difficult to master the essential features (of a concept) when the visual aspects of specific objects do not coincide with, or perhaps contradict, the essential non-visual features of the concept. He finds it much easier to master the essential non-visual features of a concept when they coincide with the visual aspects of the exemplar of the concept.

We undertook an experiment with pupils from Classes I to VIII (inclusive). The aim was to observe and study the process of mastery of essential features of a concept at different ages.

* Reprinted from R. G. Natadze, 'The Mastery of Scientific Concepts in School' in B. and J. Simon, *Educational Psychology in the U.S.S.R.*, Routledge and Kegan Paul, 1963, pp. 192–7.

Four concepts were used in the experiment – 'mammal', 'fish', 'bird' and 'insect'. These concepts are among those with which children are familiar long before they are specially 'studied' in science lessons.

At the first stage of the experiment we found out the child's knowledge in relation to each of the concepts named. Later, in conversations, we gradually gave the child a simplified definition of each concept and the concepts were 'illustrated' by some pictures of corresponding (typical) animals. The pictures were distributed among the four groups.

In defining a mammal we emphasized the following features: this animal is viviparous, rears its young with milk and (by contrast with fish) breathes air through the lungs. In defining fish we emphasized that they do not give birth to young, do not rear them with milk and 'breathe water' through gills. In relation to birds we emphasized only the feature of feathers (the body covered with down) showing pictures of non-flying birds such as the ostrich. In relation to the insect we emphasized only one feature – this is an animal which has six legs.

To the features named we added repeated comparisons between the concepts, particularly mammal and fish, but also mammal and bird (in relation to birds the method of breathing was not emphasized). We went on to the second stage of the experiment only when the child had a precise and stable recall of the features named, could himself easily give a definition based on these features and in comparing the concepts could indicate these features. It should be noted that this was easily achieved even with our youngest subjects and even with 6-year-olds in the kindergarten with whom the experiment was also conducted.

At the second stage the child was given a series of pictures representing mammals, fish, birds and insects, and was asked to say what sort of animal each represented and to place the picture in a corresponding group. The subject had to substantiate each answer and placing of a picture in accordance with the corresponding concept. We put questions such as: 'Why do you think this is a fish?', 'Can this be a mammal?', 'Why can't it be?' etc. The conversation continued until the child, in relation to each animal belonging to a specific concept, indicated the corresponding essential features.

At the close of the second stage of the experiment the child was given unusual pictures of uncommon species of animal unknown to most young children which were attributed to the four concepts by these features. The expected mistakes were corrected by the experimenter.

At the third stage, the critical stage of the experiment, the subjects were given pictures portraying animals, which according to external aspect (as it were by phenotype) belonged to one concept but in essence (according to essential features) to another; for instance, belonged by external aspect among fish and in essence among mammals. The subjects were given pictures portraying a dolphin, a whale, a sea unicorn (narwhal) and other animals, the external aspect of which is typical of fish but which from the point of view of essential features mastered by the subjects at preceding stages of the experiment are mammals and not fish.

They were also given pictures portraying a bat and a series of cheiroptera; most of these portrayed winged animals, some of which were shown in flight. They were also given pictures of flying butterflies, the six legs being separately shown in the picture.

Thus, the task of this 'critical' stage was counterposition of the content of concepts known to the subjects in the aspect of definition of essential features and the external visual form of the object. The aim of this experiment was to clarify whether the child could analyse essential features of the concept when confronted with the visual form and how easy it was for him.

In the course of the experiment help was gradually extended to the child in the form of more and more leading questions and explanations assisting him to perform the task. When giving the child the 'critical object' the experimenter first asked him what he must know about this animal in order correctly to say what it was – a mammal, fish or something else. If this question proved insufficient, the experimenter himself informed the child about the essential features of the animal, for instance, giving a picture of a dolphin, he told the child that dolphins rear their young on milk and breathe air through lungs and therefore leap out of the water every minute etc. Or, when giving a picture of a bat, the experimenter stressed that its wings are not feathered but covered with skin, that it does not have down on the body, that it gives birth to young and feeds them with milk etc. If this assistance was also insufficient, the experimenter directly explained to the child what sort of animal the given animal is and why.

At the fourth stage of the experiment conversations were held, with the aim of clarifying how the child used these four concepts in the *context of intellectual operations which were not immediately directed to distinguishing essential features of the concept, which did not require direct determining of the concept and the understanding of its essential features*. For instance, after the child had been told about the colossal strength and large size of the whale, he was told which mammals are the largest and strongest and which fish are the strongest and largest. Or, for example, he was told about fish (and then mammals) which have a sharp and long nose. Meanwhile, shortly before this, the subject had seen pictures of a sea unicorn with an exceptionally long and sharp nose ('horn') which could not fail to draw attention. Therefore, in the process of these conversations, it became clear whether our subjects really judged from the point of view of essential features after receiving the 'lesson' or slid back anew to the 'phenotypic' point of view, that is to say to practical operation with our concepts.

The experimental data collected showed that in time all the children easily overcame the 'phenotypic' point of view. Each age stage gives some step in this direction. We can give only a few basic results at basic stages of the experiment.

(1) Our younger subjects – children of 7 who had only just entered school – mastered well the concepts given to them at the first stage of the experiment, to the extent that, first, on the basis of correctly determining all four concepts they indicated the corresponding essential features (i.e. 'This one feeds its young with milk', 'They breathe air', 'They have lungs') and, second, they related to these concepts, almost without mistake, pictures portraying animals of a usual (typical) species. The few mistakes made were easily corrected as a result of leading questions from the experimenter.

However, the 7-year-olds usually could not *substantiate* this attribution of a particular animal to the corresponding concept by referring to the relevant essential features; when they tried to explain such an attribution in answer to the experimenter's questions children of this age usually did not refer to the relevant features. Clearly, in their understanding of the concept taught to them, the essential features were not represented.

Presentation to the subjects of the 'critical' pictures showed that all the 7-year-olds without exception and without any hesitation related particular animals to one or another concept *exclusively* according to external aspect – the visual image of the animal (e.g. dolphin, whale etc. to fish, bat to bird etc.). Leading questions and direct explanations with references to the definitions mastered by the subjects could not make the child change this point of view. Perceiving the dolphin (in the picture) we may say he 'sees with his own eyes' a fish before him and he is not a bit interested how this in fact breathes or propagates. The external aspect, i.e. the perceived visual image of the animal, 'eclipses' to such an extent in the child's consciousness the counterposed essential 'non-visual' features that he does not sense the contradiction between them, does not *take note of the collision.*

Despite the fact that the subject correctly repeated the definitions of mammal, fish etc. that he had mastered, and listened with interest to the explanation that the dolphin rears its young and breathes air, he was always steadfastly confident that there was before him a *fish*. To the question, what animals rear their young on milk and breathe air, the child answered mammals but none the less considered the dolphin to be a fish and assigned it to the group fish, though he already knew from the experimenter that the dolphin rears its young and breathes air. The child also firmly recalls that all birds have the body covered with down but none the less considers the bat to be a bird although fully aware that its wings are covered with skin.

Thus, at this first stage, the child, in the conditions of our experiment, does not take his stand from the point of view of the essential features even when these are specially taught to him.

(2) At a somewhat higher level of development which is characteristic of Class II (age 8) the child, at the second stage of the experiment when putting pictures portraying common animals to the corresponding concept, *argues* this attribution, referring to the essential features of these concepts.

At this stage the critical objects are put to the concept according to essential features only after exhaustive explanations on the part of the experimenter (leading questions do not help). But this achievement is unstable enough, for at the succeeding stage of the experiment, i.e. in the process of using these concepts in the context of an intellectual operation, the child *anew 'slid back'* to the *'phenotypic' point of view* (e.g. considered as a mammal an elephant but not a whale, and the sea unicorn as the most long-nosed and sharp-nosed of fish).

(3) At the stage of Class III (9–10) there is a new change: though here also the attribution of critical objects takes place without a shadow of doubt according to external form, with the need *to substantiate* such an attribution ('Why do you think the dolphin is a fish?') the child now argues this attribution by referring to essential features characteristic for the given concept, i.e. 'arbitrarily' ascribes to the 'critical animal features belonging to the given concept (attributing, for instance, the dolphin to fish, the subjects argued that the dolphin 'breathes water' with the aid of gills, spawns etc.).

Therefore, in classifying 'critical' objects and attributing them to a concept the child in fact was wholly guided by their external aspect (the visual image). When the possibility arose of substantiating this attribution, i.e. understanding its basis and making it understandable for others, then he considered it necessary to refer to essential features but features belonging to the concrete object again *in its external aspect*, i.e. *the determining moment was again the visual image*.

Further indications of development of the phenomena with which we are concerned are illustrated in the following stages:

(1) Adequate correction of mistakes made by the children with corresponding explanations on the part of the experimenter, so that the subjects 'pricked up their ears' in relation to the remaining critical objects and, before attributing them to one or other concept, referred to the relevant corresponding essential properties of the relevant animal. For instance, after an explanation that the dolphin is a mammal the child does not attribute the sea unicorn and other mammals to this or that concept without demanding beforehand how they reproduce and breathe, and after the explanation of this question, attributes them to a concept according to essential features despite the external aspect of the animal.

(2) Occasionally there is a special solution of the question: the child senses the contradiction and not ignoring on the one hand essential features, on the other the external aspect, seeks a way out in 'reconciling' both moments. Knowing the essential characteristics of the dolphin or sea unicorn he considers it a 'mammal fish'.

(3) After systematic help from the experimenter the child takes such a firm stand from the point of view of essential features that he does not 'slide back' from this point of view at the succeeding stage of the experiment. For instance, considers the whale and not the elephant as the most powerful mammal etc.

It is not without interest to note that at the level of Class IV (10–11) there is a sudden change in the mastery of the concepts 'mammal', 'fish', 'bird' in which, of course, a great part is played by acquisition of the relevant knowledge in school at the beginning of the year. At this stage, however, there are quite a number of children who attribute species of sea mammals unknown to them (i.e. sea unicorns) to fish according to their external aspect, not putting questions about how these animals reproduce, breathe etc.

There were some subjects (it is true only a few) who, though they remembered that the whale is a mammal, in the last analysis considered it to be a fish, which rears its young with milk and has lungs, and classified the picture standing for the whale in the group they considered as fish and not with mammals. No such cases were, however, observed above Class IV.

4 The mastery by children of some concepts in physics*

E. A. FLESHNER

One of the problems involved in learning and teaching is the way in which previous learning may interfere with current learning. This problem obtains in the conceptual field as well as in the field of motor skills and affective learning. In the learning of scientific concepts it sometimes happens that our everyday notions about phenomena are

*Reprinted and abridged from E. A. Fleshner, 'The Mastery by Children of Some Concepts in Physics' in B. and J. Simon, *Educational Psychology in the U.S.S.R.*, Routledge and Kegan Paul, 1963, pp. 202–12.

at odds with the scientific viewpoint. Since children usually become familiar with the non-scientific ideas first, these ideas tend to interfere with the learning of scientific concepts in the same field. When the concepts are in an entirely novel field the problem does not arise.

In this paper Fleshner reports on investigations into the learning by children between 11 and 13 of concepts in physics. He found that a pre-scientific concept of weight so much interfered with some children's learning that they made no progress in acquiring the scientific concept. In an attempt to solve this problem he used the technique of 'counterposition' which receives a good deal of attention in Soviet pedagogy. This technique involves bringing the two views together and deliberately pointing out the points of conflict and similarity. Fleshner's use of the technique, together with his findings, are interesting pointers to methods of coping with the problems of forming scientific concepts.

The importance of previous experience, above all everyday experience, in forming scientific concepts is particularly great in the learning of such subjects as physics which involves many concepts in everyday use. When they begin the study of physics, schoolchildren naturally already possess whole systems of knowledge formed in their personal life. Among these are concepts of 'volume' and 'weight' which are studied in the section of the physics course 'Simple Measurement'.

Knowledge and skills connected with the concept 'volume' are enriched and deepened in study of this term in physics lessons – the system of associations connected with this concept is extended. New knowledge is not thereby brought up against the old, does not meet with 'resistance' from it. It is, however, otherwise with the concept 'weight'.[1] A preliminary interrogation of children who had completed Class V (11–12) made it clear that the content of this concept formed in everyday experience does not coincide with the content of the physical concept 'weight'.

The physical essence of weight is the force with which a body is drawn to the ground. It follows from this that there is a series of

[1] With the aim of getting a general picture of the pupils' understanding of the terms 'weight' and 'volume' before studying these in physics we conducted a preliminary inquiry with pupils of Class V at the end of the scholastic year. This was undertaken in School No. 379 in Moscow and thirty-nine subjects took part. Analogous conversations were held with pupils in Class VI after they had studied the theme 'Density'.

elements which are important for the formation of a correct concept of 'weight'. We may enumerate those which must be mastered by pupils of Class VI (12–13) studying the 'Weight of Bodies'.

First, it must be understood that weight is a property of all bodies. In the interrogation we found that pupils described weight as a property only of those bodies which they had weighed on the scales. The question therefore arose as to whether they knew that weight is inherent in all bodies. They were, therefore, asked: 'Do all bodies have weight?' Those who answered in the negative were asked how, in their view, a body could lack weight and how they explained this.

The second essential element in forming a correct scientific concept of weight is knowledge of the connection between the earth's pull and the free fall of a body. We therefore asked pupils: 'Why do all bodies fall?' – and consolidated their answers with a second question: 'Is this connected with their weight?'

The third element, of essential importance, is the concept of force which is studied later. Therefore we asked pupils: 'What is force? What is there in common between weight and force?'

Finally, having noted in the preliminary questioning a discrepancy in understanding of the words 'weight' and 'gravity' we asked the pupils a question about gravity and explained the interrelation between the meaning of the words 'weight' and 'gravity'.[1]

We may quote the record of one of the preliminary conversations, the subject of which was Zhenia A., a pupil of Class VI, School No. 650.

Experimenter: What is weight? Tell me all you know about it.

Subject: Weight is, how shall I say? It is how much a body weighs if it is put on the scales. We put it on the scales and weigh it, how much it weighs. . . .

Experimenter: What more can you say?

Subject: That all bodies have a different weight. Some have a big weight, they are heavy, for instance that house (points to a large

[1] This does not, of course, exhaust the physical category 'weight'. However, pupils of Class VI cannot master it fully since they do not yet know the universal law of gravity, nor grasp the concept of force as degree of change of motion etc. For this reason we concentrated mainly on those aspects of the concept 'weight' of which the children's understanding, as was shown by conversations with those of Class V, differed from a scientific understanding.

building on the corner and laughs) it couldn't even be weighed. . . .

Experimenter: You said that weight is how much a body weighs, but then you said that that house can't even be weighed. Do you think the house has a weight or not?

Subject: If it can't be weighed then how can it have a weight?

Experimenter: It is heavy but we cannot weigh it?

Subject: We know it's heavier than, for instance (looks round for an object to compare; catches sight of a machine for clearing snow in the street). It is heavier than ten of those machines.

Experimenter: You said that all bodies have weight. How do you mean?

Subject: They have weight only this is something else.

Experimenter: Explain how all bodies have weight?

Subject: They have some kind of weight . . . how shall I say (shows effort). Well, they weigh . . . they have gravity. All things have gravity.

Experimenter: And what is gravity?

Subject: Gravity is what we feel when we hold a body in our hand. It is in all bodies. Even a balloon has gravity, only not much. The air in it doesn't weigh anything but the rubber weighs. Everything has its own gravity.

Experimenter: What makes gravity different from weight?

Subject: Gravity is in all bodies. We know there is gravity in them. But weight is when we know exactly how much they weigh. We get to know weight when we weigh bodies.

Experimenter: Good. Now tell me something else: do you know what force is?

Subject: Force is what is needed, for instance, to move aside that cupboard. Force is needed for that.

Experimenter: Has weight got anything in common with force?

Subject (after a pause): Yes. For instance to weigh a body you have to pick it up and put it on the scales. Force is needed for this.

Experimenter: Can you give another example?

Subject: I can't think of any more.

Experimenter: Tell me, have you thought of any reason why a body falls?

Subject (very surprised): They have gravity and can't stay in the air, they drop down.

Experimenter: Where do they drop?
Subject: They drop down, to the ground. Everything always drops down. If we throw up a ball, for instance, then after, it falls to the ground and rolls. If there is any hole it rolls down the hole.

This conversation is typical enough for the pupils of Class VI we examined. The majority gave a definition of weight of this type: 'Weight is how much a body weighs.' The concept 'weight' was connected with the act of weighing by 40 per cent of the children. ('Weight is how much a body weighs. It must be weighed and we get the weight.') Another 30 per cent connected the concept 'weight' not with the action of measuring but with its result. For them weight is the figure making known the result of weighing. ('Weight is how much a body weighs, how many kilograms or tons.') Finally, and this is very important, 80 per cent of subjects were convinced that bodies which they had not measured had no weight.

These data uphold the proposition that before studying 'weight' in physics the children attribute weight only to those bodies they have weighed, it is for them the numerical result of the action of weighing.

It is interesting to note that, having denied that bodies have weight if it is impossible to weigh them, the children answered the more abstract question – do all bodies have weight – positively but preferred to use in this case the word 'gravity' (as did Zhenia A.). From the expressions used by the subjects it is clear that weight and gravity are, for children who have not mastered physics, synonymous concepts. There is also a basis for thinking that the content of the everyday concept 'gravity' is closer in meaning to the physical content of this concept than the content of the everyday concept of 'weight'.

To the question, whether weight has anything in common with force, several children gave a positive answer, illustrating this by the following examples: 'When a body is very heavy you must use a lot of force to lift it on to the scale and weigh it' (Boris Y.). 'The more a man weighs the more force he has' (Valia S.). In neither of these two expressions (nor in other analogous ones) did we find anything to correspond to the physical meaning, an understanding of the connection between these concepts. The understanding of 'weight' as 'force' is lacking in schoolchildren according to the present teaching of physics. It must be brought out and reinforced in lessons.

However the concept 'force' itself, as also 'weight', is familiar to children long before studying it in the physics course. Consequently this concept has a specific content, formed in everyday life.

The pupils' answers to those questions which were directed to clarifying the everyday content of the term 'force' showed that their images of force (before studying it) are connected mainly with muscular effort; 'force is when we strain our muscles', 'force is needed when it is necessary to do (move, carry etc.) something'. These were the most characteristic definitions of force we heard. From these expressions it followed that the children narrowed the content of this concept, limiting it only to muscular effort, having place mainly in the actions of men or animals on any other body.

Attention should be drawn to the fact that with such an understanding of 'force' it was difficult for the children to explain the free dropping of a body drawn to the ground, since the earth, according to their image, can never be the source of force. The direction of the body in its free fall they explained not by movement to the centre of the earth but by movement down. 'Everything heavy goes down. When there is water and oil in a glass the water goes down. When a body is in the air it falls down and the air rises up' – reasoned one of the subjects. It was obvious from the expressions used by the children that the freely falling body is directed to earth not because it is drawn there but because that direction coincides with the downward direction. If it were not for the earth, which is a barrier in the way, the body, in the children's view, would fall farther. Such expressions as the following bore witness to this: 'Bodies fall down, to the earth, then they are stopped because this is the lowest place.'

Therefore the scientific content of the concept 'weight' does not correspond with knowledge about weight formed in the children's personal life. It is necessary to reorganize this knowledge. It should be noted that this is not adequately taken into account in advice on method.[1] On the contrary advice is given to approach the study of the concept 'weight' as a fact, drawn from experience, depending in this way on the children's sensations received from lifting and supporting weight, observation of the free fall of a body etc. This point of view is most clearly expressed in the methodological advice of E. N. Goriachkin who in his book *Methods of Teaching Physics in the*

[1] In Soviet pedagogy and textbooks (E.S.).

Seven-Year School (1948) recommends: 'No definition of weight need be given in study of the given theme but we can utilize those ideas which the pupils have about it from their own living practice.'

Following this advice the teachers in both schools in which research was taking place did not extend the physical meaning of the term 'weight' beyond the knowledge the children already had about it. No steps were taken to ensure that the pupils knew the difference between the understanding of force which had developed in their personal experience and the physical meaning of this term. In addition, the term 'force' was not only repeatedly used in lessons on the theme 'The weight of bodies' but even figured in the form of this concept: 'The force with which a body is drawn to the earth is called the weight of the body.'

As was found in the earlier research, the pupils had difficulty in mastering the new content of the concept 'weight'. They distorted the definition in lessons and made mistakes in doing work. Despite the fact that problems in which 'weight' is an unknown quantity were more often correctly solved than those determining density or volume, the pupils (as the class work showed) made more mistakes in problems 'on weight'.

When 8–10 weeks had elapsed after study of the given theme in Class VI we conducted individual experiments. The aim was to study the specific characteristics of applying a concept, formed according to the given organization of interaction between newly mastered knowledge and that acquired earlier. Each of the twenty pupils investigated performed three tasks. Two of these were analogous to those done during lessons. These were textbook problems on finding the weight of a body according to its volume and density. The third task involved determining the weight of a glass stopper of irregular form without being able to weigh it. The pupils had at their disposal beakers and tables of density. They could therefore measure the volume of the given body, find from the table the density of glass and on the basis of this data find the weight of the object, utilizing the same knowledge included in solution of the textbook problems.

The experiments showed that in a considerable number of pupils the skill of applying knowledge about weight to the solution of problems was diminished. Only thirteen pupils (65 per cent) solved the first two problems correctly whereas, in the original class work, exercises had been correctly done by seventeen out of the twenty pupils. There were still worse results with the third problem, ten pupils (50 per cent) being unsuccessful. These pupils tried hard, though without success, to weigh the body when they had every possibility of determining its weight through density.

Postulating that the diminished success in solving problems is connected with changes in the pupils' knowledge about weight, we held a conversation with each with the aim of discovering what content this concept had for them at the moment of the experiment. Analysis of the material collected permitted a division of the children into four groups.

Group I (five of the most proficient pupils). For these the term 'weight' was connected only with the new physical meaning. They indicated everything new without any of the everyday content of the concept (e.g. weight is force, all bodies have weight etc.). They also correctly understood the phenomenon of falling and explained it in their own words. Comparison of the expressions used with answers given during the preliminary conversations testified to the fact that the old content of the concept 'weight' had been completely reorganized in these children.

Group II (four very weak pupils). It was characteristic of these pupils that the expressions they used about weight almost exactly coincided with those used in teaching about the concept. A comparison may be made between answers to the question – what is the weight of a body – given by one of these pupils at both conversations. (Anatoli G., pupil of School No. 368, weak in mastery of physics.)

Preliminary conversation

Weight is when we weigh something and choose the weights, in order to get the finger of the scale level (shows with his hands the position of balance of scales). When we find the weights then we know how much the object weighs.

Following conversation

We take something and weigh it on the scales. We choose the weight so that it balances.

The units of weight are grammes, kilograms, tons. However many grammes, kilograms or tons a body weighs this is the weight.

The juxtaposition of these two conversations clearly indicates that the content of the concept 'weight' has not changed for Anatoli G. After the lesson he used the term 'balances', also naming the degree of weight, but for the rest even the incorrect formulation of the definition remains as before.

Such is an example of what may be found in the backward pupils of the given group. Weight, before it has been studied, is described by the pupils as the result of measurement and, consequently, as a property belonging only to those bodies which are weighed. As formerly, pupils of Group II saw no connection between the phenomenon of free falling of bodies and the earth's pull, since they preferred to consider that bodies fall as a consequence of a property of their nature, gravity. The pre-scientific content of the concept of weight was fully stabilized.

Group III (eight, mainly average, pupils). These had mastered the physical content of the concept 'weight' but there could often be observed a merging in the definition of weight of elements of the old 'pre-scientific' idea. Characteristic in this connection is the answer of Kolia A.

Weight is the force with which a body is pulled to the earth, pressing on the part of the scales. We see what weight it is necessary to put on the other pan and see the weight of the body. When we hold any body in the hand, then we feel it pressing on our hand because it is heavy.

In conversations with other pupils of this group it was easy to find an analogous merging of old and new knowledge. Elements of the new and the old, as in the case of Kolia A., are actualized simultaneously and independently of each other. As a consequence the content of the concept 'weight' revealed represented a conglomeration of propositions some of which were contradictory. Thus, for instance, one of the pupils, after correctly saying that a body falls because the earth pulls it, then added: 'Bodies fall because all heavy things fall down: they are stopped by the earth because they can't get through it.'[1]

[1] An analogous kind of statement in relation to botanical concepts is described by I. M. Kudriavtseva.

Thus, knowledge about weight acquired by the pupils of Group III in physics lessons showed significant changes expressed in the 'concurrence' of two different systems of knowledge, old and new. As a consequence of this concurrence newly mastered knowledge was partly ousting that acquired earlier. Characteristic of this group was the actualization of both systems which leads to the merging of two contents of the concept 'weight' – the everyday and the physical.

Group IV (three pupils, one proficient and two average). With pupils of this group another variety of the merging of two systems of knowledge is observed; new knowledge is partly ousted by the old but the process of actualizing proceeds otherwise – there is not such an interlacing of the elements of both systems as there is in the case of pupils of Group III. The pupils belonging to this group do not distort the specific concept learned in lessons but, in giving its content, draw on old propositions about weight. But there is an essential difference between the two groups. The pupils of Group IV, stating any incorrect proposition, are brought to a stop and refuse to give a further answer. We may quote the record of a conversation with one of the subjects of the group (Tamara E., proficient pupil).

Experimenter: What is the weight of a body?

Subject: The weight of a body is the force with which the earth pulls it . . . I don't know any more.

Experimenter: Tell me in your own words all you know about weight.

Subject: We know that every body has a definite weight. We see this when we put it on the scales. *When we put a body on the pan it presses it down, we put a weight on the other. . . .*

Experimenter: Go on, why did you stop?

Subject: I think I'm saying it wrong. We learned it a long time ago and I've forgotten it.

Experimenter: Tell me what else you remember.

Subject: I only remember that when we do problems we have to multiply density by volume then we get weight. I remember too that it was shown to us that every body has gravity and *this gravity pulls them down. . . .*

Experimenter: Why do you break off?

Subject: No, it's wrong, I won't say it.

We see that in Tamara E., by contrast with pupils of Group III, the old and new knowledge are not actualized independently of each other. In the course of conversation the pupil twice turned to everyday knowledge about weight (these sentences are italicized in the above record) and then came to a stop and in the end refused to answer. The two other pupils in this group behaved in a similar way. ('I don't remember and I don't want to talk nonsense', and 'I forget about what we learned. Why say it wrong?') Obviously in pupils of Group IV there took place a confrontation of both systems of knowledge and some of their differentiations. The old knowledge was inhibited as not corresponding to reality but the newly mastered knowledge was hardly consolidated and not always reproduced.

Thus the data of conversations showed that in a significant proportion of pupils (eleven subjects – 55 per cent) there took place under the action of time essential changes in knowledge about weight acquired in lessons. These changes took place in all the average pupils and one proficient pupil and resulted in the supplanting of the newly acquired knowledge by the old knowledge.

The results of our investigation upheld facts established by many psychological researches as to the supplanting in the course of time of newly acquired knowledge by old knowledge. In particular these have been advanced in work dealing with changes in imagery.

The circumstance that the characteristics of the interaction between old and new knowledge, shown in material from different subjects and at different stages of learning, fully coincide, testifies to the fact that we have to do here with a general regularity. Its scientific basis is to be found in the proposition that 'the old does not vanish, the new is only deposited upon it', advanced by Pavlov in his theory about the dynamic stereotype.

A question deserving particular attention is how knowledge of 'weight' is applied in the solution of problems by the pupils of the different groups. The number of correct solutions in each group taking part in the original class work and in the experiment which lasted 8–9 weeks is illustrated in the following table.

As may be seen from the table the success of pupils of Group I in applying newly acquired knowledge was not diminished. In conversations we satisfied ourselves that the old knowledge was fully inhibited and the newly acquired easily actualized, extending to effective application to the solution of problems. No change had taken place in pupils of Group II who, as was noted, had mastered nothing new about weight.

The results of the two remaining groups are of the greatest interest. In both groups there took place a diminution of success in applying knowledge. This, without doubt, is the result of those changes which, as revealed in conversations, took place in the course

Number of correct solutions in class work and experimental tasks

Groups	No. of pupils in group	Correct solutions in class work		Correct solutions in experimental work			
				Two textbook problems		One visual-active	
		No.	%	No.	%	No.	%
I	5	5	100	10	100	5	100
IV	3	3	100	5	83·3	2	66·6
III	8	6	77·7	10	62·5	3	37·5
II	4	1	25	2	25	0	0

of time in the newly acquired knowledge. It is interesting that in the solution of visual-active problems the result achieved is worse than in the solution of textbook problems. It was precisely the visual-active problems that were not coped with in the experiment by one-third of those belonging to Group IV and more than half of those belonging to Group III (all of which had shown skill in applying newly acquired knowledge at the time of the original exercises).

The data collected shows that success in applying newly acquired knowledge, mastered in interrelation with old, everyday knowledge, is diminished not only under the influence of time (as has been shown by a number of experiments) but also under the action of a visual-active situation. The closer the situation to everyday experience the greater the readiness to actualize old, everyday knowledge, as a consequence of which the new which was mastered by the children in lessons is forgotten though at the same time it is successfully used by them in textbook tasks. Our data indicated that in teaching physics it is necessary to direct particular attention to the application in visual-active conditions of those physical concepts the meaning of which is subject to reorganization in lessons.

What kind of work in organizing the content of physical concepts is needed to ensure stable mastery of the given knowledge and success in applying it to the solution of problems?

According to the data of earlier experiments the most effective way of differentiating the new from similar old knowledge is that of systematic counterposition of the two in class work. Underlying the effectiveness of this procedure is the fact established by psychological research that the chief means of forming differentiation is the repeated admixture of counterpositions.

On the basis of our results we postulated that the negative influence of old knowledge on the process of applying the newly acquired physical concept of 'weight' results from a general law and may be eliminated by clear-cut differentiation of the two meanings of the given term.

A further experiment was undertaken in School No. 368 when some changes were introduced in the process of studying the theme 'Weight of bodies'.

At the lesson pupils taking part in the experiment were convinced visually that force is not only muscular effort, that in addition to this kind of force there exist others – force of pressure, the force created by a stream of water moving through the air etc. In addition, through verbal explanation a range of different aspects of force was described. All these aspects of force were counterposed to the old understanding of the term as muscular effort. Therefore all that had hitherto constituted the essence of the concept 'force' was differentiated from the wide physical understanding of it as any action of any body on another body.

On the basis of experiments and verbal explanations it was possible to establish that if, by pushing, an object is set in motion it is necessary to talk about the action upon it of force. This approach provided a basic physical characterization of the concept 'force'. The children learned that to bring a body into motion it is necessary to exercise force on it, that without the application of force there is no change in movement.

Thus there was achieved in the lesson the basic aim of differentiating those features of the everyday concept of 'force' which could exercise a negative action on the formation of the concept 'weight'.

Further the teacher counterposed to the everyday understanding of weight and gravity as two different concepts, their physical meaning as two different terms signifying one and the same physical magnitude. Only after this was it possible to demonstrate such phenomena of weight as pressure of a solid on a support or the stretching of a spring. Formerly the pupils, when this was shown to them, considered these as phenomena of the force of gravity and not weight so that the demonstration did not achieve its aim. Now, after counterposition of the everyday understanding of 'weight' and 'force' to their physical meaning, the children could perceive the phenomena as manifestations of force which acts on a solid drawing it to earth, i.e. were in a position to recognize the physical essence of the observed phenomenon. Familiarization with instruments for measuring weight, with units and ways of measurement, was introduced only when it was possible to reckon with a basically correct understanding of weight already stabilized. Up to this moment there were no weights on the demonstration table in order not to fix the children's attention on the instruments and actions of weighing.[1]

A check of results showed that in the new conditions the majority of pupils (nine out of ten subjects), even the weaker ones, preserved the new knowledge about weight after a protracted interval and easily applied it in the solution of problems.

The effectiveness of the method indicated in raising the level of mastery and application of knowledge in physics was also upheld by analysis of the work of the experienced teacher V. E. Zotikov whose pupils correctly and easily operated with the concept of 'weight'. Zotikov did not only discriminate between the everyday and scientific meaning of the term 'weight' in teaching but also attempted to use all the pupils' images (for instance, about gravity) which might serve as a support for the formation of the scientific concept.

The results of the pedagogical experiment and analysis of the work of an experienced teacher fully upheld the possibility of significantly increasing success in the application of those physical concepts which are mastered in interrelation with corresponding everyday know-

[1] With the aim of bringing together the theme 'Weight' with preparatory work in creating a general conception of force there were, as in the year before, four lessons, one of which was devoted to laboratory work on weighing bodies.

ledge. In addition they convincingly demonstrated the necessity of special work by the teacher to differentiate new and old knowledge in class and strongly emphasized the effectiveness of methods of counterposition.

5 Some problems in the psychology of history teaching: historical ideas and concepts*

E. A. PEEL

History is a subject particularly difficult to teach with understanding. One of the problems is the difficulty of conveying an adequate notion of time scale. Another problem is the interference between the historical concept and everyday ideas which have the same name. (This problem is of the same type as Fleshner encountered in the teaching of physics.) In addition, since language plays such an important part in history teaching, there is a particular danger of rote learning. The learning of strings of dates or names of kings and queens is a prime example of rote learning when one examines the nature of children's concepts of time and royalty.

The author of this paper scrutinizes these important aspects of the teaching of history, shows how young children's historical concepts are vastly different from those of adults and makes suggestions to enhance the formation of historical concepts.

(i) Historical institutions and ideas and their names

Historical ideas and institutions such as nobility, government, peasantry, kingship, mercantilism and free trade have the qualities of concepts. Each implies some general property or definition as, say, to what conditions a person had to fulfil in order to qualify as a member of the nobility. This property or definition forms the intensive aspect

* Reprinted and abridged from E. A. Peel, 'Some Problems in the Psychology of History Teaching: Historical Ideas and Concepts' in W. H. Burston and D. Thompson (Eds.), *Studies in the nature and teaching of history*, Routledge and Kegan Paul, 1967, pp. 159-71.

of the concept. The extensive aspect of the concept, on the other hand, is seen in the set of individuals who make up the nobility, that is the actual princes, dukes, viscounts etc., referred to at any time when the term nobility is used. Lastly the concept has its name – the nobility.

All three parts: the extensive and intensive aspects and the name of the concept, play important roles in all school history teaching. Even if we were to hold the view that very little generalization is possible in history – in the sense of predicting from the past what will happen in the future – we recognize that history entails much conceptual material if only from its heavy dependence on language.

This dependence upon conceptual thought gives rise to three sources of difficulty in understanding history. There is first the tendency to over-generalize and to see similarities which do not exist. Secondly, since many of the names of historical ideas are words which carry existing, personal and concrete meanings, such as church, law etc., there is a tendency for these meanings to be carried over erroneously. Lastly, much of school history is taught through texts and new words are often introduced for fresh ideas and institutions merely through contextual passages without a precise definition being given. This makes for erroneous concepts.

The tendency to over-generalize, to see common causes and features between different events which are not warranted could be exaggerated by the *topic method* of learning history. However, the tendency would not be so evident in the methods of those who believe that each historical event is *unique* and that it is not the business of the historian to do more than fully describe its uniqueness.

Whether one is prepared to generalize in historical causation or not, there is the second source of erroneous extension common to unique event and topic methods which arises from the names of abstract ideas, statutes, movements and institutions in history. Many of the concept names used in history are words or groups of words with contemporary general meaning or meanings in other fields. As Burston observes about such words

because they are in very common use, they have varying connotations, and a class may be familiar with some but not all, or may attach the wrong one of several meanings.

The confusion is even greater when one realizes that it is an individual rather than a class who extends meaning. Words like *church*, *state*, *government*, *land*, *party*, *middle class*, *revolution* and *democracy* are well-known sinners in this respect and might well be avoided until their exact connotations in different parts of history have been made clear.

Beales also wrote, 'My illustrations are all of the one great difficulty: viz. that a history teacher is prone to use jargon terms without realizing that the words are already known to the class though his meanings are not, and hence a risk of erroneous images and quite unnecessary misunderstanding.' Here are some of the terms he recommends young teachers to avoid, or define carefully, *constitution*, *policy*, *executive*, *the economy*, *the church*, *French* and *Agrarian*.

The above difficulty arises from the use of words with an established and often concrete and more specific meaning. But there is the last source of confusion arising when new concepts with new unfamiliar names are introduced into connected texts and are not well defined in the process.

Thus we have such terms as *continental system*, *entente*, *mercantilism*, *indulgence*, *dispensation* and *franchise*. These are words which by themselves either convey no meaning at all to the younger school pupil or may carry a misleading existing meaning. Unless they are carefully supported by instances of the concept they symbolize or are precisely defined by the rule or intensive property they represent, they are likely to give rise to frequent misunderstanding. Even when they are established, it is not a bad plan to keep reminding a pupil of what it is they mean.

(ii) The concept of historical time

Even in adult years we judge time by various criteria: astronomical, physiological, social, epochal and geographical. Most significant of all we read time by changes occurring in our own life span. This can be disturbing, just because we have studied history, as, when we hear of man's profligate use of the world's stored energy in oil, coal, timber in the last half century and of the predicted doubling of the population of the world within the next half century, we come to think of sinister changes possible in the future within so short a span as a couple of generations. This colours our impression of past history, making us ask questions we should not ask if the tempo during our own lifetime was slower. Thus it comes almost as a shock to non-professional historians to read of the slow changes in life in England between the fifth-century coming of the Anglo-Saxons and the tenth-century arrival of the Danes. Did so little happen in those 500 years as appears from what we know of them? Five centuries of humanity's present rate of change will lead to un-imaginable consequences not excluding the possibility of its own self-elimination.

From numerous studies of children's awareness of time and history we have a broad picture of how the concept of historical time develops.

The total experienced time, including past, present and future, all of which are present in mind and affect action, changes from a span only of yesterday, today and tomorrow with 5- to 6-year-olds, to a span of three seasons in the case of 10- to 11-year-olds, a span of three years in the case of the pre-adolescent and finally to spans of five years in the past and future in the case of the adolescent.

Cohen and his co-workers showed that within the bounds of realized time the subject's estimates are such that 'as the actual intervals increase logarithmically, his estimates increase in approximately linear fashion'. Beyond the bounds of remembered time, the estimates are linear, that is, equal intervals of time are estimated and represented by equal units of scale. There thus appear to be two bases for the estimation of long-term time. Those outside the bounds of realization need the prop of dates and a spatially represented time scale. Jahoda criticizes the use of time charts with young children as being wholly unrealistic and suggests that it would be better to begin history with the present within the bounds of the child's awareness of his own time and work backwards. However, in view of Cohen's findings that there are two bases of understanding time, it would seem that for more remote history, the dates and time chart are not difficult to place, even with young children, but before this method is used discussion of events within the child's realized time should be undertaken, starting from the child's present.

Corresponding notions of history have been noted. Mythology revealed in tales and stories marks the 5- to 6-year-old child's awareness of history. At 9–10 history is that which can be verified by talking to older people. Only in pre-adolescence does a clear awareness of historical continuity appear and this grows in the order of biological continuity first, plants growing from seed to fruit; then by technical continuity, seen in inventions and machines, and lastly in cultural continuity, as in the Bronze Age etc. The continuity, however, is still patchy, 'The red patch rather than the continuous red line'. In adolescence the pupil is more aware of historical progress, seen in the continuous development of a person or period, and there are the beginnings of historical interpretation.

These findings, summarized by Jahoda, are confirmed by the results of a German inquiry conducted by Küppers on a large number of 10- to 18-year-old pupils drawn from several kinds of school. She showed that the historical understanding of the pupils developed from egocentric and personal judgements during the first few years of schooling to concrete judgements by pupils in the middle (7th–8th) grades. Only in the upper grades (9th–12th) was understanding marked by an awareness of historical time and structure.

(iii) The growth of historical concepts

Concepts grow by becoming more precise and relevant. Coltham studied the development of six common concepts used in history by asking junior school pupils to say verbally what the following were: *king, early man, invasion, ruler, trade, subject*. They were also asked to draw them. In the case of the concept of *king*, she demonstrated a clear progression by age from king with pomp, through king with power, to king with power and change. Only in the last stage is there a reference to the important time dimension in kingship and there were only a few mature answers, such as 'kings used to have power but not now'. The children's ideas of *trade* showed a similarly significant growth from giving a specific occupation (greengrocer etc.), through ideas of retail and transport, on to the principle of exchange, to exchange and commerce. The last two stages have the essence of the mature concept of trade and the last one has generalized the idea.

Another research worker investigated pupils' concepts of social relations which have historical significance by asking a group of 9- to 19-year-old pupils to define the twelve concepts of: *wages, rent, taxes, parliament, committee, king, prime minister, laws, trial, freedom.*

He was able to identify four categories of answers in ascending order of maturity. Thus for *king* he had such answers as:

(i) the king lives in a castle far away;

(ii) a king is somebody very important and a king is very rich, a famous man out of the royal family;

(iii) a king is a ruler of the country;

(iv) a person who may rule his country by himself, may rule it in coordination with advisers or a government, may simply be a figurehead.

Or for *committee:*

(i) a place like the Town Hall could be a committee;

(ii) a committee is a group of people at a meeting place, is a thing that helps the school;

(iii) a committee is a party of men who talk and decide things;

(iv) the committee is the organizing body of a society or similar institution, elected from the members of the same by the members.

Wood also found a clearly defined progression by age.

These four categories embody recognizable differences in the conceptual insights of the pupils, beginning with irrelevancies and non-essentials, going on to concrete aspects, then on to partial recognition of the essential formal qualities and finally at the last most mature level, showing a complete awareness of the two-directional reciprocal relation between a person and his society involved in most social concepts.

(iv) The importance of the pupils' mode of thinking

Since historical understanding depends heavily on the comprehension of language, it is not difficult to see why so many errors of concept enter from contextual ambiguity. Much could be done to make such errors less frequent by more adequate definition and exemplification. This recommendation would apply with equal force both to those entities and concepts bearing new names and also to those having familiar names which have established meanings for the pupils from other contexts.

But there are other barriers to understanding caused by more involved factors. Any historical happening is a complex human interaction and whenever we ask questions beginning: 'Why did . . . ? such as Why did Henry VIII dissolve the monasteries ? or Why did the American Revolution come about ? we expect pupils to analyse, interpret, judge and evaluate this complex human situation of the past and its consequences, in terms of their own limited perception, thinking and power of assembly.

In order to make sense of the situation, the pupil falls back on comparison and analogy with his own experience and the concepts which regulate it. But he does not seem to do this effectively until his thinking has reached some maturity. It takes some years to reach such maturity and the years of early and mid-adolescence are very formative in this respect.

6   Reading skills re-examined*

J. MERRITT

Since most teachers are extremely competent readers, they do not always appreciate the nature of the problems facing a young child first learning the skill. The author of this paper discusses some of the processes involved in learning to read and successfully brings home to the reader some of the difficulties a child might have.

THE PRIMARY SKILLS

Let us take a brief look, first, at the orthography and then at the sounds of the language which it is required to symbolize.

* Reprinted and abridged from J. Merritt, 'Reading Skills Re-examined', in *Special Education*, 58 (1), March 1969, pp. 18–21.

(a) The orthography

For an adult, or even for an experienced teacher, it is sometimes rather hard to see why learning to discriminate between different letters should be difficult. After all, even very young children can learn to make fine visual discriminations quite easily. Many pre-school children can name large numbers of toy car miniatures which an adult can often scarcely distinguish one from another. Again, even the least able child can often learn to distinguish quite small changes in facial expression and attribute meaning to them. Why, then, so much difficulty with letters?

'Ah,' we may say, 'motivation is vastly different in playing with toys and responding to human beings. Letters are far less important in the child's experience.'

Now, while there is much truth in this, it is also true that many children are desperately keen to learn to read but still have difficulty in recognizing letters – so motivation cannot be taken as the only problem. Let us therefore look more closely to see if we can distinguish some of the difficulties.

(i) Letter shape

In the following sets of letters, each letter differs slightly from the others in shape:

Set A: a–o–c–e: b–h–k: f–t: l–i–j: u–v

Now examine the sets:

Set B: A–a–*a*: G–g–g: Q–q–q,: Y–y–y–y–ɥ: T–t–t–t–t

Within each of these sets there are differences in shape at least as great as those in the first example – yet these letters must be learned as being 'the same'.

In order to get some idea of the effect on the young child of attempting to make these discriminations, imagine trying to learn the following sets of symbols which have been arranged in similar groups to provide an analogy with the child's task:

$$\text{ᚥ} - \text{◸} - \text{◹} - \text{◺}; \ \text{ᚦ} - \text{ᚧ} - \text{ᚨ}; \ \text{ᚦ-ᚱ}; \ \text{⌐-⌐.-⌐.:}$$
$$\text{◺} - \text{ᚥ} - \text{ᚨ}; \ \text{◁-ᚱ-ᚱ}; \ \text{Ψ-ᚦ-ᚦ-ψ-ψ} \ .$$

Imagine mixing the symbols up and trying to remember which were 'the same letter' and which were different. For how many children with some slight learning difficulty is this a minor but significant addition to an already difficult task?

(ii) Letter orientation

b–d–p–q: n–u: h–ɥ: t–f

Here we have a rather different problem; within each of the above sets of letters, the shapes are all identical and the letters can only be recognized by attending to the orientation of the letters on the page.

Almost all children have some difficulty with 'reversals' in beginning reading and this is usually ascribed to inadequate perceptual development. Yet even very young children respond correctly to orientation quite habitually. They put cups on the tops of tables – not on the underside; they climb on to chairs when necessary – not under them; they even draw objects the right way up, usually, and not upside down. Wohlwill *et al.* have shown that pre-school children have no difficulty in handling learning situations which entail a response to orientation. Why, then, does the 'reversal' problem exist?

The answer is quite simple. The truly surprising thing is the extent to which it has been neglected.

In the pre-school years a child learns that objects retain their unique identity regardless of their orientation. His toy bus remains a bus whether it is upside down, sideways or the right way up. He learns that 'a bus is a bus is a bus'. He learns, in fact, the orientation is not a recognition variable – that it tells him not what an object is, merely how to handle it. When faced with b, d, p and q, therefore, his first response must be that they are identical items. To learn to use orientation as a means of recognizing letters entails learning a response that is in absolute conflict with habits laid down during the early years. The problem, therefore, concerns the effect of early learning on perception, not the effect of immature perception on learning. Waiting for perception to mature, consequently, means allowing habits of rejecting orientation as a recognition variable to strengthen. Failure to emphasize orientation from the outset means that the early errors are simply over-learned and so become more difficult to eradicate.

(*iii*) Letter sequence

It might be argued that too much stress is being placed on letters. Many teachers of reading would insist that children do, and should, merely respond to the 'whole word'. This belief owes much to an experiment carried out by Cattell in 1885. In this experiment subjects were required to identify groups of single letters and short words exposed for very brief periods. He found that as many as three short words could be recognized in exposure conditions which permitted recognition of only four or five random letters. The conclusion was drawn that words are perceived 'as a whole', and are as unitary in perception as single letters.

In recent experiments it has been shown that subjects recognized pronounceable nonsense words more easily than unpronounceable combinations of the same letters. Readers might care to note for themselves the different times taken to learn by rote the words in the following lists:

List 1: DINK, BESKS, FUNTS, GLURK, QUEESK
List 2: NSUV, LPEBR, NDASL, LHTSI, CKURGL

If ability to recognize pronounceable sequences below the level of the whole word is so marked, even in adults, it seems a little implausible to argue that this skill plays an unimportant part in fluent reading.

(*b*) Phonemic variables

For the hearing child, speech comes before reading and speech presupposes an ability to attend to the significant acoustic differences between speech sounds (or phonemes) in the language. This ability tends to be taken for granted. It is not generally recognized, however, just how complex is the problem of distinguishing the speech sounds of the language. But just as there are many variant forms of the 'same' letter (such as A–a–*a*) so there are many variant forms (or allophones) of the 'same' speech sound (or 'phoneme'). And, as with letters, there are differences between variant forms of the same item which are as great as the differences between different items.

Take for example the words 'pin' and 'spin'. Pronounce these words with your hand held in front of your mouth and note the marked expulsion of air in pronouncing 'pin'. The 'p' in 'spin' is scarcely aspirated at all. In some languages a difference in aspiration may provide a phonemic difference, i.e. it could be used to distinguish different words.

There are also many languages in which other types of phonemic variable play an important role in distinguishing between words. In Chinese, completely different meanings can be conveyed by varying pitch.

In English, stress may alter meaning. For example, in 'What is the cóntênt?' and 'I am còntént' the word 'content' changes its meaning completely when the stress is shifted from the first syllable to the second.

Juncture, i.e. pauses in speech, is also an important variable. Thus an œ ſhan may be either 'an ocean' or 'a notion' according to the position of the juncture phoneme.

(An i.t.a. spelling has been adopted here as a reasonably familiar, if phonetically slightly inaccurate, representation of the sounds.)

This discussion cannot begin to indicate the extent and complexity of phonological analysis, that is, the analysis of the way in which the speech sounds in a language are organized. The intention here is merely to demonstrate that there are highly complex conceptual classifications formed in acquiring speech even at the phonological level, that is, below the level of grammar and of meaning. Even at this level there are numerous possibilities of misclassification which can cause serious difficulties in hearing speech, in spoken utterance and, subsequently, in reading. We begin to see that the training required for the reading specialist is rather more than that provided by the short part-time course!

THE INTERMEDIATE SKILLS

Most books on reading pay some attention to the use of context cues in reading. Only in the last decade, however, has there been any serious experimental work on the nature of the linguistic skills which underpin the use of context cues. No systematic effort has yet been made to relate this particular area of investigation to the teaching of reading. The linguistic skills concerned are those of anticipating sequences in language–speech sound sequences, grammatical sequences, word sequences and semantic sequences. In reading, the ability to relate these sequences to the printed sequences is of the essence of fluency. If the skills of recognizing letters and discriminating sounds may be regarded as 'Primary Skills' it seems reasonable to describe these skills of sequential anticipation as 'Intermediate Skills', for they lie between the primary skills and the higher order skills of reading for meaning. A few impressionistic illustrations may suffice to give some indication of how these intermediate skills assist the reading process.

(i) Phonemic sequences

A little experiment may be helpful in demonstrating how we can anticipate phonemic sequences. Say to someone that you are going to pronounce the first part of an English word which he has probably not heard before and ask him to guess what the complete word will be. You should then pronounce a short 'nonsense' word such as 'sondig . . .' or 'megdom . . .' Note how restricted are the endings which your subjects produce, e.g. sondiguous, sondiguity. The reason is that even below the level of the word there are expectations concerning the phonemic sequences which are likely to occur in our language. If real words are used and the first parts are pronounced in this way the possible endings are even more restricted. Try the following part-words on your subjects:

'acce' (as in 'accent'); 'acci' (as in accident); 'acciden'.

In reading, a child who is linguistically competent will automatically use this 'built-in' knowledge of phonemic sequences in tackling unfamiliar words. Given a few letters – and knowing the sounds they represent – he can make an informed guess as to what the word will be. By the same token, the child whose language development is poor is at a serious disadvantage. Given such a handicap, the irregularities of the alphabet can make a difficult job impossible.

To gain some idea of the difficulties, try to decipher the following word which has been spelled in a rather bizarre way – various values which the letters quite often take are listed below each letter to make the solution easier.

a	f	o	ḍ	a	n	ḍ
æ	f	o	t	æ	n	t
aʊ		ω		aʊ		
a	v	aʊ	ḍ	a		ḍ
ɑ (r)		œ		a (r)		
e		u		e		
o		i		o		

Note how much easier the problem becomes if only a few of the letters take on familiar values:

e	v	i	ḍ	ɑ	n	ḍ
				æ	n	ḍ
				aʊ		t
				a		
				a (r)		
				e		
				o		

The word is, of course, 'evident'. For the beginning reader, we must remember, none of the 'regular' values are established.

If we cannot do anything about the irregularities of our spelling, or if we are not prepared to adopt an initial teaching alphabet, then attention to linguistic competence becomes doubly important.

(ii) Grammatical sequences

It is perfectly possible to write sequences of words which are grammatically acceptable but which are incomprehensible or downright nonsense. A now well-known example is: 'Colourless green ideas sleep furiously.' If we delete any particular word in this sequence we note that we cannot substitute just any word in our vocabulary – it must be an appropriate part of speech.

In the case of the last word, in this example, the substituted word must be an adverb. Thus because we are familiar, through usage, with probable sentence constructions, we may – as we read a sentence – anticipate these grammatical sequences and predict the sort of word which may occur in a given context.

There is some evidence which suggests that children's response to grammatical sequences is particularly important. Carroll cites an experiment by Russell and Jenkins, who carried out word-association tests with children and with adults. Adults tended to produce paradigmatic responses, that is, responses that were of the same part of speech as the stimulus word, such as FAST – 'quick'. Children, on the other hand, tended to give syntagmatic responses, that is, responses that might naturally follow the stimulus word in a sentence, such as BRIGHT – 'sun'.

The importance of syntactic structure can be demonstrated by denuding the utterance of meaning completely:

The yigs wur vumly rixing hum in jegest miv.

Epstein found that this syntactically structured nonsense sequence was learned more easily than were the same 'words' presented in a random order. He found, in fact, that it was learned as readily as a similar number of real words presented in random order. As further evidence one may note that the ability to reproduce appropriate grammatical sequences is retained in certain abnormal mental states when the ability to produce the correct words is severely impaired.

The importance of grammatical sequences in reading was demonstrated in an interesting study of Ruddell. He found that comprehension scores were higher when children read passages in which the written patterns of language structure resembled their own oral language patterns. He also found that children's comprehension scores were higher on material that utilized the more common patterns of oral language structure than on materials that utilized patterns of language structure which are less common.

It is always easier to handle material which fits readily into a familiar framework and it is clear that syntax provides structures of this kind. When the structures are unusual the reader cannot take advantage of his existing language patterns. He must struggle to master the structure before he can perceive the message.

Struggling to master unfamiliar grammatical constructions may be an important aspect of learning to read but if fluent reading is to be promoted the rate of increase of difficulty must be carefully controlled. The case for controlling the introduction of unfamiliar grammatical structures is at least as strong as the case for controlling the introduction of new words into the sight vocabulary. Unfortunately, this feature is largely ignored in many popular reading primers. 'Look, Tom, look', 'see the flying object' and 'up, up, up'

are not patterns common in the speech of 5-year-olds of my acquaintance. 'Can Dan fan Nan; Nan can fan Dan' is equally unfamiliar.
Even higher up the reading age scale the sequences seem to bear too
little relation either to the speech patterns of children or to speech
patterns they will encounter later.

It is not that sentence structure has been ignored. On the contrary.
Great care has been taken to avoid excessive complexity. However,
greater knowledge of the ways in which language patterns should be
varied in order maximally to help the child is only now becoming
available as a result of the growing amount of research into linguistic
science. The time is overdue for some of this research to be related
directly to problems in teaching reading.

(iii) Word sequences

The frequency of association of words in a language is known as
'collocation'. Thus 'stop', 'station', 'conductor', 'conductress' and so
on are collocates of the word 'bus'. 'Axle', 'sign', 'panels' may also be
collocates but probably occur much less frequently in the experience
of most people.

In the text quoted earlier, 'Colourless green ideas sleep furiously',
the words are not collocates. In the sentence, 'He took a front seat
at the back' each successive word does collocate with the previous
word but the sentence is nonsense. Thus collocation is a factor which
may determine sequential expectancies above the level of syntax
but below the level of meaning.

The concept of collocation may be taken a stage further by considering longer sequences. For many single words the collocates are
so numerous that they would restrict lexical anticipations scarcely at
all. The word 'new', for example, leaves choice open to almost all the
possibilities not otherwise limited by syntax. Consider, however, the
following lexical contexts:

> She was wearing a new . . .
> Was she wearing a new . . .
> Did she wear a new . . .
> Will she wear a new . . .

The possibilities are now limited to words such as hat, dress,
anorak, ear-muff, pince-nez, with a clear probability that some words

are more likely to occur than others. The meaning of the sentence does nothing to limit choice within the set of syntactically acceptable responses.

Morton, in formulating this extension of the notion of collocation, proposed that the term 'thought units' should be used to refer to such contexts. This is perhaps the highest level of organization that can be conceived below the level of meaning.

In considering the implications for teaching reading we must recognize that an unexpected word can provide a stimulus to enjoyment. At the same time, a thoughtful use of collocation can provide cues to help the independent reader to tackle words which are in his spoken vocabulary but not in his sight vocabulary.

Interaction effects

The skills so far referred to do not simply act independently, as the following sentences clearly show:

(i) I went from Manchester to Birmingham by tr . . .
(ii) I went home by tz
(iii) I drove home in my . . .

Here we see how the context limits the number of possibilities, while a letter or two, outline or length may be sufficient to determine the final word.

Pollack has shown that the effect of multiple cues such as context and number of letters is greater than the sum of their individual contribution. Robinson, however, has shown that in a group of able fourth grade children (C.A.: 10–11 years), the ability to use context cues was extremely limited.

The problem is: can we expect children to develop their ability to use context cues efficiently if the language structures in their readers are unsatisfactory and if we give little or no systematic instruction? Can we improve either if no serious effort is made to apply the findings of basic research in linguistics and psycholinguistics to direct research on teaching reading?

I think, perhaps, the teacher can do something. It is surprising how often the sensitive teacher, having seen the problem clearly, can anticipate in his methods the findings of subsequent experimental investigation. At the same time, we cannot expect too much unless we provide adequate training for the teachers so that they can, at least, recognize the problems.

7 Learning to think about reading*

J. F. REID

When a child learns to ride a bicycle he knows what he is about. He knows what riding a bicycle is for. When children begin to learn to read they are in an entirely different situation. They have only the vaguest notions as to what it's all about.

This paper complements the one by Merritt by exploring the conceptions children have about the nature of reading, exposing further problems inherent in learning to read. The suggestions she puts forward for making children more aware of the nature of reading are of great interest.

This paper reports an attempt to study by means of structured interviewing the notions about reading with which a group of 5-year-old children came to the task of learning to read and write, and how these notions developed in the course of their first year at school.

In concentrating on these notions, and even more, as such a study must of necessity do, in concentrating on the language which the children used in order to talk about the process and about their experiences as learners, the investigation explores an area about which so far very little is known. It is true that the extent of children's vocabulary is now commonly taken into account in considering their 'reading readiness'. It has also been recognized that children from more literate homes start, other things being equal (and even sometimes when they are not), with a better chance. Many writers, notable in America, have also stressed that the teacher's conception of the place of reading in education, and hence the way she talks

* Reprinted and abridged from J. F. Reid, 'Learning to Think about Reading', *Educational Research*, **9** (1), November 1966, pp. 56–62.

about it to the children, is a major influence in developing children's conceptions of it. In a slightly different area, psychologists have of late given increasing prominence to the role of language as a mediating process in learning and in concept formation. But little has so far been done in the way of special observation of that part of children's linguistic equipment which might be called their 'technical vocabulary' – the language available to them for talking and thinking about the activity of reading itself.

The present study made use of questioning to explore the general level of concept formation with regard to reading and writing as embodied in the 'technical vocabulary', to follow the growth of these concepts and form some idea of the role they may play in the actual learning of the skills.

SUBJECTS AND PROCEDURE

Twelve children, seven boys and five girls, were selected at random from a class of over forty children in an Edinburgh school. The pupils in this school come from families of varied socio-economic status.

Each child was seen three times in the course of the first year at school. The first interview took place after the children had been attending school for approximately two months, the second three months later and the third after a further four months. The ages of the children at the time of the first interview ranged from 5 years 1 month to 5 years 5 months.

The interviews were loosely structured: that is to say a 'kernel' set of questions was chosen in advance, and each of these questions was put to the child in a standardized form; but the order varied with the course of the particular conversation and the answer obtained determined to some extent the subsequent questioning.

The questions were as far as possible worded in ways which left the children free to use, or not to use, terms like 'word', 'letter', 'sentence' and so one, and free to mention such things as the features of standard orthography. The way in which this worked in practice will become clear from the ensuing account. The questions were, of course, only a small selection from all those which might have been used, but it must be emphasized that their purpose was to get the children to talk and not, in any narrow sense, to obtain information on specific points.

RESULTS OF THE FIRST INTERVIEWS[1]

(a) Can you read yet?

None of the children could in fact read, and all but one knew it. This last child asserted that she was 'past reading'. The basis for this remark proved later to be that the class had just reached the end of the Reading Readiness book!

(b) Have you any books at home/in school? What is in them?

Only one child began by saying that books contained words. Ten referred to pictures, or named characters (Peter, Penny etc.). Some of these replies (for instance, 'about Peter and Penny and Susan, learning to read') suggested that the children giving them had print in mind and not just pictures. Further questioning, about things other than pictures, produced references to 'numbers' (five instances), 'Tip's name', 'letters' and 'writing'. The use of the term 'numbers' deserves special notice, because it became obvious from the children's comments and from what they later wrote that the term was being used to mean 'letters and numerals' or even just 'letters' alone. Some of the children, on the other hand, had achieved much greater differentiation in terminology and in thought: one, for instance, knew that words were 'made of letters', but that numbers showed you 'how many counters to put'.

(c) Can your mummy and daddy read? How does mummy know what bus to take?

Two of the twelve did not know whether or not their parents could read. Trying to describe how they read, only one child mentioned symbols ('names'). Some were obviously trying to express the notion of silent reading ('they read it in their head'). Some knew that the part their parents read was black, but others were very vague.

All but one of the children knew that a bus was identifiable 'by the number'. No child mentioned the name of the destination. In some cases it was not clear whether they really knew that the number was

[1] Questions grouped together here were not, of course, asked together though they frequently followed one on the other. Square brackets indicate parentheses in the report. Round brackets indicate words spoken by the interviewer.

visible, or whether they just thought of it as something the bus was called by ('the twenty-four').

(d) *Can you write something for me ?*
    Tell me about what you have written.

All the children but one understood by 'write' the producing of symbols – isolated letters or words or numerals. One child inter-preted it as 'draw' and replied: 'I'll write a house.' There was, however, great variation in what was produced and in the under-standing of what the symbols 'stood for'. Some could write only the first five numerals, while others wrote up to or beyond 20, but one child who wrote the numerals to 20 could not name any beyond 12. Those who chose to write letters or words ranged from the child who produced 'b' and 'o' but could make no comment, through those who wrote letters and said they were '"h" for "horse"' or '"o" for "orange"', to those who knew that letters could be 'for' many dif-ferent words, or who could write words or even a sentence. Except where indicated, the children referred to letters by their sounds, not by their names: 'b', for example, was 'buh', not 'bee'.

Carol, for instance, wrote 'Tip', and said it was 'Tip's name'. She also wrote several other letters, including 'b'. Asked what they were for, she replied: 'Well, for things. . . . Well, "b" for "bed".' ('For anything else ?') 'Yes.' ('What else ?') No reply. ('For "bat" ?') 'Yes.' She denied, however, that a lower-case 't' was for 'Tip'.

Tommy wrote: 'Here is Tip', saying as he did so: 'It says he's coming along here', thereby showing awareness that what he had written conveyed meaning. This awareness was notably lacking, however, in the response of some of the children.

Only three children used the term 'letter' in giving an account of what they had written and there were further instances of the use of the term 'number' instead.[1] It was also obvious that some of

---

[1] It may be argued, of course, that the fact that a child does not, when given opportunities to do so, use a certain term, is not proof that it is un-known to him. This is true. He may, for instance, understand it when some-one else uses it. And one must make allowance for sampling error. No interview is completely reliable: he might have produced the term on another occasion. But the absence of it in a child's protocol can be taken at least to indicate that it is not readily available to him as a classifying tool – that it is not one of the terms he habitually thinks with.

those who called 'h', '"h" for "horse"', did not know what this meant.

Ability to write their own names was very diverse. Five could write their first name, and of these two could also write their surname correctly. All used capitals. A third child reproduced her surname as 'BAꓺLR'.[1] She said she 'learned it on her door' and that it 'began with three'. She was one of those who called all symbols 'numbers' and was in fact the child who thought she was 'past reading'.

What emerged as important at this point, then, was the general lack of any specific expectancies of what reading was going to be like, of what the activity consisted in, of the purpose and the use of it, of the relationship between reading and writing; and a great poverty of linguistic equipment to deal with the new experiences, calling letters 'numbers' and words 'names' and print 'the reading', and individual letters '"h" for "horse"'. It was also found that the children did not mention that books contained stories, but when asked about 'stories' some said these were not anything to do with reading – these were 'for rods'. This stems from the use of Cuisenaire Arithmetic material, and from the habit of saying: 'What story do these make?'

RESULTS OF THE SECOND INTERVIEWS

(a) *Show me your reading book. Is it hard? Is it harder than the first one? What is hard about it?*

Answers to these questions fell into three groups: those giving no information about why the new book was 'harder'; those which were vague (e.g. 'The bits you forget' with no example given); and those which consisted of statements about and examples of phonic difficulties arising from irregularities in the orthography. Here, for instance, is Andrew:

'Because they [some words] are unusual. They're funnier than others – not the same letters as you say them in [*sic*]. "Play" – you shouldn't have the "y". It makes the "ā" say "a". Like "corn flakes" – you shouldn't have the "e", you should have a "x" in

[1] The name was 'BALFOUR'.

its place. . . . Mrs E. [the teacher] wondered how I knew "me". It was one we haven't had before. . . . It's a wonder they don't put "ē" instead of "e".' ('How could they do that?') 'Write mE, or they could put two e's.'

And here is Tommy:

'"t" and "h" together is hard. And "this" with a small "t". You'd think it's a different sort of word.'

[Tommy is referring here to finding 'this' in the middle of a sentence instead of at the beginning.]

('Is there anything funny about "have"?') 'It's got an "e" on the end. It should only have three words instead of four words being there. You go to sound it and you hardly know what to say. It's like a different word.'

There were other references also to 'thinking it was a different word'.

(b) *Show me today's page. Can you read it to me?*
How do you know what it says?
What do you do if you don't know?

Six children responded to the question about knowing what the book said by demonstrating, that is, by beginning to read again. The rest tried to state in some way how meaning is conveyed by print. For instance:

'It's the name at the top and big words at the bottom that tell you the story.' . . . 'They write words like "No, no, Tip come here".' . . . 'Writing – a lot of letters.' . . . 'All the words like "g" and "o".'

Asked about methods of discovering what new words were, all but three described (or demonstrated) some sort of independent action, usually 'sounding out'. The attempts to describe this are again important.

Joan: 'You say one word and then the next. . . . You say "m–a–t". Some people know them.'
Andrew: 'You spell it. You say the letters that make the words.'
[Demonstrated by sounding "come" and "here" letter by letter and pronouncing them correctly.]

Billy said he would 'copy the words', meaning he would sound the letters [his demonstration made this clear], and Tommy said he would 'spell' them, meaning also 'sound'.

Questioned about whether this process always helped, some said it did not always help, and gave examples like ' "t" and "h" together'.

(e) *Can you write something from your book? Show me.*
   [If this failed]
   Can you write 'pig' (or 'cat', 'dog' etc.)?
   How do you know what to put?
   What is 'b' for besides 'bed'?

Ten children wrote readily one or more words from their reading book, mostly from memory. But only two could say how they knew what to put. Most said: 'I just know', 'I learned it', 'I seen it'. Tommy, however, said: 'I hear myself saying the word', and Billy talked of 'copying' again, meaning sounding. Some children whispered sounds as they wrote, but could not comment on it.

Seven children could find further examples for a given initial letter, the rest could not.

There were some spontaneous references to capitals. Billy explained his spelling of 'cow' as 'Kow' by saying a 'big letter for a big animal'. Jane said that sometimes 'they' put 'mitten with a big "M"'. Asked why, she replied: 'to see if you know it'!

Tommy, in the course of writing letters, was asked if these were words and replied that they were not, but that 'come' was. He then wrote 'og', said it wasn't a word, but that he would 'make it into one'. He then added 'y', tried to sound it and said: 'It's not a word in my reading book, but it's a word I know.' Asked what words are made of, he said, very doubtfully, 'words . . .'

The important points here seemed to be two in number: (1) There was the development of terminology. The tendency to call letters 'numbers' had almost gone, but had been replaced by a tendency to call them 'words' instead. 'Sounding' was being called 'spelling' or 'copying' or 'saying' by some children.

(2) There was what might be called the beginning of the search for regularity and rule, and of awareness of the nature of an alphabetic system of writing. This was manifested in the comments on the

'letters which shouldn't be there', on these you 'don't say', on those which do not have the so-called basic values so that it is 'like a different word'. It was also apparent in the degree to which, in reading and writing, the children showed that they were with varying degrees of success using phonic analysis, and were prepared to try to reconstruct, from the sounds, a word that they had for the moment 'forgotten' how to spell. A further instance of the search for regularity was found also in the comments on capitals, which indicated that the children were looking for rational explanations. It is interesting but perhaps not surprising that no child invoked the concept of a convention – of something arbitrarily chosen as a signal.

RESULTS OF THE THIRD INTERVIEWS

(a) *Show me your reading book. What do you do if you don't know a word?*

There was a noticeable change in the response to this question since the second interview. Some children even anticipated it, and the rest were mostly eager to talk about difficulties and ways of dealing with them. There were comments on 'new words' or 'bigger words', for instance:

> 'You have to sound them hundreds and hundreds of times.'
> 'Some words are too big to spell.'

In all, nine of the eleven had now something articulate to say about this topic. The words 'spell', 'sound', 'copy', all appeared again, all referring to sounding. One child, verbalizing this for the first time, said: 'You say one word at a time.' ('Show me.') 'm–u–s–t. "m" is a word, "u" is a word.' Angus, who had said something like this last time, now talked of 'spelling'. Tommy described in detail how sounding could be confusing. Talking of the word 'kitten' he said:

> 'When I get half the other half goes half off. I get "n" in the first half when it's supposed to be last. I get it jumbled up. I say "kit-nen". The day after I got it like anything, 'cos' I seen the "i" and the "n".'

Several children volunteered to write, and more wrote sentences this time. Some of them wrote to illustrate sounding difficulties, like Tommy, who wrote 'mittin' and said:

'The "i" shouldn't be there but you spell it that way. It should just be "mittn".'

There were more comments on capitals: 'The beginning of a word', 'for an adult's book'.

(b) *What are these spaces for?* [pointing to spaces between words].
Are all these [on the page] *words?* Are there any that are not words?
[If the child said 'yes']
Show me one that is not a word. What is it?

All but three could give some explanation of the separation of words: 'They'd be all stuck together.' . . . 'You'd think it was all one word.' . . . 'So as you'll know it's a different word.' Asked whether 'everything on the page was words', two children mentioned pictures and punctuation as being 'not words'; one picked out isolated letters in a phonic drill exercise, and two mentioned numbers, saying: 'They're numbers. They're stories – the kind you get with rods'!

But some others selected certain words ['be', 'I' and 'where', for instance] and said these were 'not words'. The most interesting remarks here came from Joan.

Joan: ('Is that ["Penny"] a word?') 'No, it's a name.' ("Me?") 'No, it's "*me*".'("Will?") 'Yes.' ("Mother?") 'No. "Mother" is a name and "Penny" is a name.' ('Is "where" a name?') 'No.' ('What is it?') [Pause.] 'If you've lost anything you say "where?".'

Alan is interesting for his explicit statement that meaning is crucial in deciding if something is a word:

('Is "a" a word?') 'Yes, if you say "I have *a* ball".' ('Is "m" a word?') 'By itself? No! Just . . . just silly! "I m" – it doesn't mean anything – not just a letter like that. It must *say* something.'

It was now possible to detect something in the way of developmental sequences, in that some children could be seen arriving at a stage in the articulation of what they were doing that had been reached earlier by others; while the latter progressed, in whatever vocabulary was available to them, to more refined or sophisticated notions. Some children had moved from saying 'spelling' (presumably a form picked up from older siblings or parents) to saying 'sounding'. Others had begun to say 'spell' instead of giving an involved and unwieldy description of the process. One more child had arrived at the notion that some words were 'wrongly spelt' [cf. Andrew, in reply to question (a), p. 282], and two more children were speculating about a rule governing the use of capitals. Tommy got closest to the idea of a convention ('the beginning of a word') but he over-generalized. Andrew thought there was a correlation with the age of the reader!

Awareness of phonic structure was developing, too, in both reading and writing, and several children were now prepared to write 'new' words. But a new classificatory confusion appeared – in the assertions that some words were not words but 'names', or were 'what you say when you've lost something'. And a new criterion began to emerge. A word had to mean something – it was not just any group of letters.

DISCUSSION OF FINDINGS

The foregoing records appear to point to several important features of the process of learning to read.

Firstly, they show that this group of children, though almost all were aware that they could not read, had very little precise notion of what the activity consisted in, and this fact points to a difference between learning to read and, say, learning to ride a bicycle. In some senses of the word 'know', children do know, in advance, what riding a bicycle is going to consist in. But reading, prior to the experience, is a mysterious activity, to which they come with only the vaguest of expectancies. In some cases, owing to their total lack of reflection on the nature of the spoken language they had already mastered in its essentials, the children in this study were not even clear whether one 'read' the pictures or the other 'marks' on the paper.

Even less were they aware that written words were composed of letters which stood for sounds. The earliest encounter with Reading Readiness training, phonic practice (initial letters with pictures) and writing had made all of them aware, however, of a set of shapes (with, perhaps, mysterious names like '"h" for "horse"'); and several of them, not knowing the term 'letter' or 'sound', were nevertheless attempting to find a general name for these and had used the only term applicable to a single written symbol which they knew – namely, 'number'. Some children appeared not to be distinguishing one sort of symbol from another; but it may well have been that they did have some dim notion of the difference, yet were being hindered in clarifying this by having to use, inappropriately, the only term which their vocabulary could supply. Some of the others, who showed that they knew that the written symbols in their books somehow conveyed meaning, were limited to saying that 'numbers' told one about the story.

In contrast to the vagueness about the nature of reading, there was, even at this early period, some recognition that to 'write' was to produce these symbolic forms, as distinct from drawing. To most of the children, however, writing was the reproduction of isolated numerals, or single letters (perhaps a mixture of the two), or at most one or two disconnected simple words, and there was little explicit recognition of the connection between writing and reading.

These children can be seen, therefore, as exhibiting certain linguistic and conceptual uncertainties about the nature of the material which they had to organize. The resolution of these uncertainties lay in learning the difference between pictures and written symbols, as two modes of conveying information; and then learning to discriminate between two classes of symbol, the alphabetic and the numerical. They had to discover what 'words' are, and that almost all language, written or spoken, is composed of these, though written language also contains marks of other kinds. They had to learn, furthermore, to think of a 'sound', and to realize that written words are spatially ordered groups of letters bearing a systematic relation to the temporally ordered sounds of speech. To achieve effective understanding at this level, it is probably necessary to be able to use correctly the terms 'letter' and 'number' (or, better, 'numeral') and to associate these with reading and counting respectively; also to use the term 'word' in some sense which will distinguish it from 'letter' in writing and from 'sound' in speech.[1]

[1] It should perhaps be stressed that the teaching of the letter names is not being advocated as a part of early teaching of reading. Some do advocate it, for instance Durrell and Fries, but the danger of confusion with the basic

These distinctions involve immediately an understanding of hierarchical structure in its simplest form (that of the notion of a class with two or more sub-classes). In short, the children had to come to see that language and pictures are two kinds of symbol, that letters and numerals are sub-classes in the class of written symbols, that 'names' form a sub-class in the class of words and that capitals form a sub-class in the class of 'letters'.

The results of the second and third interviews showed that these steps were not easily or swiftly taken, but that the children groped towards the necessary ordering elements at varying speeds and with varying degrees of success. Part of the success seemed to depend (as one would expect) on whether or not a child had at his disposal the vocabulary which would help him to grasp the various schemata which even elementary discussion of language involves. On numerous occasions children were observed on the one hand to be confusing themselves by what they said (e.g. by the statement that 'words are made up of words')[1] and the other hand to be arriving at sudden new discoveries about how they did in fact make progress in reading as when the same child realized – and was able to say in some way – that he had avoided an error by seeing the relative position of the letters in a word.

Part of the success seemed to depend on whether or not a child was able to entertain not only the notion of one-to-one correspondence (in this case between the elements of spoken and those of written speech) but also, side by side with that notion, awareness of the possibility of exceptions and deviations. For instance, children who did not realize that a word did not always have 'the same letters as you say it in' were in a state of deeper confusion than those who did.

---

sounds is considerable. All that is being stressed here is the importance of a term with which to make a necessary distinction. The term 'sound' can, of course, be used at first for the written symbol, but as soon as the basic values have to be departed from one runs into the difficulty that a sound has then to be described as having, or making, 'a different sound' – exactly the sort of statement which, it is argued here, should be avoided. There is also no advocacy of the practising of sounds in isolation. Daniels and Diack state an important principle when they stress the need always to teach sound in words.

[1] That the prevalence and persistence of these difficulties is not, however, to be explained – or explained away – as merely a matter of vocabulary is evident from the studies of classification made by Piaget and Inhelder.

Just how much difference it might make to a child's learning in this area to be helped, consciously and carefully, to develop the kinds of awareness and the terminology to express them that have been the concern of this study is at present a matter of conjecture. But it might well be that it would make a difference not only to his learning of reading but to his general logical thinking and the more sophisticated thinking about language he will later be required to do. It seems that here is an area where fostering of the understanding of classification, order and regularity could be undertaken in the course of what is at the same time classroom work of prime importance. Systematic investigation of the effect of attempting to do this should certainly be undertaken.

8 Musical communication*

J. B. BROCKLEHURST

This paper differs from the others in this section in that it deals with aesthetics. Undoubtedly conceptual learning plays an important part in the aesthetic appreciation of music but affective factors also operate. The author explores the relationships between affective and cognitive factors in musical appreciation and discusses the place of other skills.

Compared with the volume of research and report in the psychology of cognition, the amount of work in the psychology of aesthetics is virtually nil. As a musicologist, Brocklehurst raises some of the important issues that such work would be concerned with and in addition makes some valuable suggestions for teachers.

I. MUSICAL COGNITION

There have been several investigations involving the measurement of listeners' responses to rudimentary auditory stimuli; some are more

* Reprinted and abridged from J. B. Brocklehurst, 'Musical Communication', in *Educational Review*, 19 (3), June 1967, pp. 173–82.

applicable to the psychology of hearing than that of music. Moreover, widely differing views on the complex nature of musical ability are revealed in the various studies which have been made of measurement and evaluation: some investigators argue that musical ability is essentially a unity while others subscribe to the atomistic or mosaic multifactor view that musical ability comprises several relatively independent variables. Furthermore, since most tests of musical ability are of a cognitive nature, they reveal little of the listener's aesthetic capacity. Musicality involves sympathetic emotional responsiveness to music as well as mere physical receptivity to sound and cognitive tests are thus no more an infallible guide to musical sensitivity than are tests of vocal or instrumental ability.

A few of the people working in the field of experimental aesthetics have studied the emotional response to music and attempted to devise tests of appreciative capacity and taste. Wing's tests of aesthetic judgement take the form of judging rhythmic accent, harmony, intensity and phrasing by means of paired comparisons. Most of the other tests, however, tend to measure achievement rather than innate capacity and consequently have poor validity and reliability. It is possible to argue that, because of the intangibility of music and the essentially subjective nature of the response to musical stimulus, aesthetic sensitivity and artistic sensibility do not lend themselves in the same way to scientific scrutiny as do cognitive and perceptual factors, especially since they are largely unconscious processes and are influenced by such factors as intelligence, musical knowledge and skill, musicality, personality and emotional maturity as well as by social and environmental considerations. However, because of the complex problems of musical taste posed by the impact of mass media and the fact that the majority of our pupils will be consumers rather than performers of music, it is essential that more research be carried out into the nature of aesthetic perception and its development in schools.

2. LISTENERS' REACTION PATTERNS

A number of investigators have attempted to classify listeners according to their response to music. The four reactions which have most frequently emerged are the sensory, emotional, associative-imaginal and objective. The sensory response is explained by the closely connected psychological and physiological effects of music. Motor imagery plays an important part in the response to music since there is a clear association between musical and bodily rhythms: the apparently irresistible urge of young people to respond physically to the convulsive, relentless beat of 'pop' music and the popularity the virtuoso performer has always enjoyed are instances of this. In the case of the emotional response, the listener tends to project his feelings into the music which he may associate with particular human characteristics. The tendency for auditory and visual imagery to be aroused by music is responsible for a great deal of associative-imaginal listening and helps to explain the popularity of music with a programmatic or descriptive basis. The fourth classification, objective, applies to the listener who describes his response in intellectual rather than subjective, emotional terms: thus he may comment on such features of a work as its craftsmanship, form, proportion and fitness, style and originality.

This type of investigation is open to several objections: the application of statistical methods to a random choice of subjects offers little guidance to the nature of aesthetic appreciation. The choice of music has occasionally been unfortunate and too little account has sometimes been taken of the duration of the quotations, the listener's span of attention, his prevailing mood and the changes in his response to a piece of music which may accompany increasing familiarity. Moreover, since the emotional response to music is largely an unconscious process, many adults find words inadequate to describe their aesthetic experience and have recourse to stereotyped responses. It is therefore inadvisable to expect young children to describe accurately or adequately their response to a piece of music: indeed, they may be able to give expression to their response much more easily and naturally through such creative outlets as art, movement and mime.

3. THE SUBJECTIVE RESPONSE TO MUSIC

In spite of their limitations, however, these investigations clearly reveal the remarkably wide diversity of listeners' reactions to music and confirm the fact that music is essentially a subjective mental phenomenon. Even in the case of music with a definite program-matic basis, investigations suggest that the majority of listeners are unable to identify with any degree of precision the events or moods the composers intended to portray or convey, and draw attention to the strictly limited imitative and descriptive capacities of what is essentially a non-articulate language.

The subjective nature of the response to a musical stimulus may reasonably lead one to assume that music is an emotionally flexible, indeed ambiguous, art form and that musical beauty is in the ear of the beholder rather than inherent in the music itself. Even if one is not prepared to subscribe to the view that there can be no objective musical values, one must acknowledge that the changing attitude towards dissonance clearly illustrates the importance of the in-dividual listener's response to an art form which is utterly dependent on re-creation and which has so many links in its complex chain of communication.

It can thus be argued that many of the characteristics applied to music would be more accurately ascribed to the response of listeners. Certain anti-romantic composers such as Stravinsky go much farther by maintaining that music is neither a language nor a communication of emotions since it is incapable of expressing anything; 'gebrauchs-musik', on the other hand, may be regarded as an expression of the belief in music as a means of communication, and of the concern at the alleged breakdown in communication between many twentieth-century composers and their audiences.

Several writers who take the view that music is a language of the emotions have attempted to isolate its principal emotive factors. Others regard tempo as the chief factor, while Henkin, as a result of his investigations into the affective response to music, emphasizes the importance of melody, rhythm and timbre. Cooke asserts that music is a much more precise language of the emotions than is generally realized and that all composers whose music has a tonal basis have used the same basic musical vocabulary to express and evoke particular emotions. His views have something in common with the doctrine of the affections which so dominated musical thought in the seventeenth and eighteenth centuries, his attempts to pin-point the inherent emotive effects of the various notes of the scale resemble those of Curwen and his methods of investigation are similar to those adopted by Sorantin. Cooke concludes that musical expression is achieved by a composer's colouring the vitalizing agents of volume, time and intervallic tensions (which function also in speech) by the characterizing agents of tone-colour and texture.

4. THE TEACHER'S ROLE

It is clear that, whatever one's attitude towards musical aesthetics, the teacher can play a vital role in strengthening important links in the chain of musical communication by developing his pupils' listening skills and receptive powers, providing them with creative and executive experiences and influencing their musical attitudes and tastes.

5. LISTENING SKILLS

Music is essentially an aural art, existing only in time; the art of listening thus demands sustained and concentrated attention and has to be acquired in the same way as creative and executive skills. The insufficient attention given in the past to the development of listening habits applies not only to musical education: in English teaching, also, listening comprehension has been neglected and little research has been conducted into listening as a communication skill. In music, the situation is seriously aggravated by the current habit of treating music simply as a background to other activities: music has become an almost inescapable phenomenon and this is largely responsible for the tendency to regard all music as 'musique d'ameublement' or as a mere auditory aerosol spray. Thus it is important that musical educationists evolve special listening (or auding) techniques in order to promote listening efficiency, especially since it is likely that music can contribute to the promotion of general auditory development.

Any course in musical aural training must take account of the importance of tonal memory and the listener's span of attention. All investigations into the nature of musical ability confirm that tonal memory is the most significant factor in such ability and that it forms the basis of all musical activities, whether they be of a creative, executive or appreciative nature. Musical literacy, instrumental experience and skilful use of audio-visual aids are of especial importance because of the part played by auditory, visual and kinaesthetic imagery in tonal memory. Literacy in this context implies not simply a knowledge of the rudiments of music but an ability to grasp the aural significance of musical notation. The span of attention of even the most sophisticated listener is limited because of the considerable physical and mental demands made by attentive listening. This implies the need for the teacher, not only to give careful consideration to the duration of the musical illustrations selected, but also to direct the pupils' listening and develop their powers of musical observation by focusing their attention on particular features of the music and making judicious use of well-planned and purposeful repetition.

6. APPRECIATION, CREATIVITY AND PERFORMANCE

If strengthening the links in the chain of musical communication is regarded as one of the principal objectives of teaching musical appreciation, this can provide an effective guide to both lesson content and method of presentation; moreover it enables the teacher to view all branches of the music curriculum as having the same ultimate objective, namely the development of the pupils' aural awareness, perception and receptivity.

Macpherson, Scholes and other early musical appreciationists tended to concentrate their attention on three aspects: orchestral instruments, musical history and form. The orchestra remains a popular subject in schools and there is available a considerable amount of audio-visual equipment relating to the subject. Musical history in schools was formerly restricted almost exclusively to biographical anecdote; the present tendency is to regard it as relevant only if it adds to the listener's understanding and enjoyment of music. In order to emphasize the fact that music reflects the spirit of the age in which it is written, attention is given to artistic and environmental influences: the social, political and economic background against which a musical work was composed is studied, as are the musical conventions, vocabulary, idioms, forms and styles of the period in which the composer lived. The evolutionary approach is eschewed and an attempt is made to develop historical listening. The conventional approach towards musical form is open to a number of objections. With so intangible an art as music, a study of musical form is of value only if it enables the listener to regard a work as a unity and a growing organism: a pedantic preoccupation with dissection, syntax and formulae can all too easily prevent this. The expressive function of form is frequently ignored and an unrealistic attempt is made to divorce form from content; the latter can best be approached by means of orchestral and diagrammatic scores and recently-developed functional analysis techniques.

In recent years an increasing emphasis has been placed on the value of providing children with varied executive and creative experiences. Singing remains the core of the musical curriculum, but instrumental playing, too, has many educative values: it encourages active musical participation and complements vocal experience; it is an aid to the study of musicianship and can develop kinaesthetic imagery and sensory motor skills and strengthen the executive links in the chain of musical communication. On the other hand, it would be wrong to assume that the process of acquiring instrumental skills is necessarily accompanied by the development of aesthetic perception.

Frequent reference has been made to the remarkable inventiveness of young children, and the apparent decline in the quality of their expressional work as they grow older has often been attributed to the failure to provide them with varied opportunities for creative self-expression or to recognize that creativity is largely intuitive. It is now generally recognized that creativity must be approached as an individual and spontaneous means of expression, that it involves guidance rather than formal instruction and that questions of technique should be introduced not as restrictions but as aids to spontaneous expression. Much thought is now being given to methods of stimulating and developing musical creativity in children. Creative work in music can provide valuable opportunities for artistic self-expression (especially for the less able child who does not wish to be reminded of his verbal inadequacies), it can enable each child to develop musically at his own pace, to explore and experiment with the basic raw materials of music and thus to gain some insight into the creative processes of musical composition. Group improvisatory activities, such as those devised by Carl Orff, make it possible for each child to contribute at his own level, according to his ability, interest and confidence. Moreover, such activities can be used as a means of introducing children to contemporary musical idioms since several 'avant-garde' techniques of composition can be effectively adapted for group improvisatory work.

7. ATTITUDE AND TASTE

The result of researches conducted into attitudes towards music and the relationship between musical taste and socio-economic status indicate that tastes are not absolute, but are culturally and environmentally determined. It follows that, since tastes are habits of thought and the product of conditioning, standards of taste cannot be arbitrarily imposed: children can be enticed but not wrenched away from mediocrity.

It is frequently asserted that young people's obsessive interest in 'pop' music is generally accompanied by a distaste for serious music. There can be little doubt that musical responses are conditioned by such factors as prejudice, fashion, experience and environment. Familiarity and habituation are perhaps the most important factors in determining taste: even the 'pop' music industry relies heavily upon 'plugging' and 'exposure'. It follows that it is the responsibility of schools to provide children with as wide a range of musical experiences as possible, in order to provide them with touchstones of taste and to counter-balance the enormous quantity of 'pop' music heard outside school. The importance of familiarity and habituation also points to the need for controlled, systematic repetition. It is unreasonable to expect a piece of music to be assimilated and enjoyed at a first hearing: the large number of inquiries made about musical items used regularly as signature tunes in broadcasts illustrates the considerable change in response and enjoyment which can accompany repetition and increasing familiarity.

Because of the problems of apathy and prejudice, some teachers argue that 'pop' music should be used as a starting-point in order to make use of young people's frenzied enthusiasm for such music, to illustrate the basic principles underlying all music and to remove harmful barriers between 'pop' and 'non-pop'. Although it would certainly be unwise to ignore the existence of 'pop' music or to adopt a disparaging attitude towards it, there is a danger that pandering to existing tastes would result simply in reinforcing them instead of widening them.

8. UNIFIED AESTHETIC RESPONSE

The implication to be drawn from some articles dealing with listeners' reaction patterns is that a person's response to a piece of music tends to be of a predominantly emotional or intellectual nature. Moreover, some writers have tended to overestimate the value and validity of the intellectual at the expense of the emotional response. Thus Hanslick denied the relevance of emotion in 'pure listening' and Révész has declared that 'not emotion, enthusiasm, love of music, a warm interest in it, but the mental conquest of music as an art characterizes the musical person'. For Wagner, on the other hand, musicality demands above all 'an uncorrupted sensibility and a feeling heart'.

The total effect of any work of art is much more than the sum of the effects of its constituent elements, for they interact and merge into a formal unity. The most satisfying aesthetic reaction to music is probably that which occurs when a listener's emotional response is enhanced and enriched by his apprehension of the music's intellectual qualities.

FURTHER READING

B. S. Bloom *et al.*, *Taxonomy of educational objectives 1: cognitive domain*, Longmans, 1956.

R. Brown, *Words and things*, The Free Press of Glencoe, 1963.

J. S. Bruner, *Toward a theory of instruction*, Belknap, 1966.

J. C. Daniels and H. Diack, *Progress in reading*, University of Nottingham Institute of Education, 1956.

J. C. Daniels and H. Diack, *The standard reading tests*, Chatto and Windus, 1958.

N. L. Gage (Ed.), *Handbook of research on teaching*, Rand McNally, 1963.

R. M. Gagné, *The conditions of learning*, Holt, Rinehart and Winston, 1965.

N. I. Gez, 'Interrelationships between oral and written forms of communication', *Soviet Education*, **13** (8), 1966, pp. 24–32.

B. Inhelder and J. Piaget, *The growth of logical thinking*, London, Routledge, 1958.

G. Jahoda, 'Children's concept of time and history', *Educational Review*, 15 (2), 1963, pp. 87–104.

W. D. King, 'The development of scientific concepts in children (2)', *British Journal of Educational Psychology*, 33 (3), 1963, pp. 240–52.

R. F. Mager, *Preparing objectives for programmed instruction*, Fearon, 1962.

J. M. Morris, *Standards and progress in reading*, London, Newnes with NFER, 1966.

J. Piaget, 'How children form mathematical concepts', *Scientific American*, November 1953, Offprint no. 420.

G. R. Roberts and E. A. Lunzer, 'Reading and learning to read' in E. A. Lunzer and J. F. Morris (Eds.), *Development in human learning*, Staples, 1968, pp. 192–220.

R. R. Skemp, 'Learning and development – schematic learning in mathematics' in E. A. Lunzer and J. F. Morris, *Development in human learning*, Staples, 1968, pp. 415–36.

H. Werner and E. Kaplan, 'Development of word meaning through verbal context: an experimental study', *Journal of Psychology*, 29, 1950, pp. 251–7.

Programming teaching

Since the early work of Skinner in the field of programmed instruction and teaching machines we witnessed in Britain an early high rise of interest in the subject, with machines attracting a great deal of attention. In the early days we saw the development of two inchoate, but nevertheless real, schools of thought. One school saw programmed instruction as a panacea for our educational problems, the other saw it as a dehumanizing influence with machines processing children into production line robots. As it turned out, children have not walked off into a shining future hand in hand with their teaching machines, nor have they been hurled into Skinnerian darkness. The early vogue for programs based on the operant conditioning of verbal behaviour and emphasis on hardware is giving way to an open questioning approach which emphasizes the precise statement of objectives and the analysis of the teaching task from the logical and the psychological point of view. This approach de-emphasizes hardware and calls on machines only when essential to a specific teaching task. Most important of all, the rigorous methods used in good program construction – precise specification of objectives, task analysis, test construction and empirical validation – are slowly permeating teaching practices.

In the papers which follow, problems of programming are considered from a variety of viewpoints. A paper by Skinner from his early writings on programming describes the background to his original work on teaching machines and the rationale behind his approach to programming. Leont'ev and Gal'perin put forward a view which is critical of the Skinnerian position and lays great emphasis on the need to focus on cognitive processes. Tobin reviews the literature on the place of machines in programmed instruction.

Stones discusses a flexible approach to programming which can be applied to relatively unstructured material. The paper by Gryde discusses the application of programming to educational television and in the process considers the key characteristics of programming and instructional television. The contribution by Stolurow considers developments in computer-assisted instruction. (This subject may seem to have little relevance to teachers in British schools but developments in computer technology are likely to make possible the use of computers or computer terminals in schools in the not too distant future.)

Finally, a note on the title chosen for this section: I hope that it more truly reflects developments in the field of the applied science of education than the term *educational technology* which is often used, somewhat pretentiously, in referring to the use of audio-visual aids. The emphasis I wish to give is on the analysis, planning and structuring of the total instructional system, rather than the modes of operation of the 'new media'.

1 The science of learning and the art of teaching*

B. F. SKINNER

This paper is a classic statement on the application of reinforcement theory to human learning. It has been seminal in its influence on the development of programmed learning and even though Skinner's views on programming have been severely attacked in many quarters, to him must go the credit for inspiring work in this field in many parts of the world.

The present contribution may be somewhat dated in its view of programming but it does discuss many of its salient features.

The reader will probably find it interesting to compare Skinner's

* Reprinted and abridged from B. F. Skinner, 'The Science of Learning and the Art of Teaching', *Harvard Educational Review*, 24, 1954, pp. 86–97.

view with its great emphasis on the efficacy of reinforcement, with the views of Leont'ev and Gal'perin who emphasize cognitive phenomena while Tobin's comments on teaching machines also set in perspective Skinner's use of the term and its relation to programming.

Some promising advances have recently been made in the field of learning. Special techniques have been designed to arrange what are called 'contingencies of reinforcement' – the relations which prevail between behaviour on the one hand and the consequences of that behaviour on the other – with the result that a much more effective control of behaviour has been achieved. It has long been argued that an organism learns mainly by producing changes in its environment, but it is only recently that these changes have been carefully manipulated.

Recent improvements in the conditions which control behaviour in the field of learning are of two principal sorts. The Law of Effect has been taken seriously; we have made sure that effects *do* occur and that they occur under conditions which are optimal for producing the changes called learning. Once we have arranged the particular type of consequence called a reinforcement, our techniques permit us to shape up the behaviour of an organism almost at will. It has become a routine exercise to demonstrate this in classes in elementary psychology by conditioning such an organism as a pigeon. Simply by presenting food to a hungry pigeon at the right time, it is possible to shape up three or four well-defined responses in a single demonstration period – such responses as turning around, pacing the floor in the pattern of a figure-8, standing still in a corner of the demonstration apparatus, stretching the neck or stamping the foot. Extremely complex performances may be reached through successive stages in the shaping process, the contingencies of reinforcement being changed progressively in the direction of the required behaviour. The results are often quite dramatic. In such a demonstration once can *see* learning take place. A significant change in behaviour is often obvious as the result of a single reinforcement.

A second important advance in technique permits us to maintain behaviour in given states of strength for long periods of time. Reinforcements continue to be important, of course, long after an organism has learned *how* to do something, long after it has acquired behaviour. They are necessary to maintain the behaviour in strength.

Of special interest is the effect of various schedules of intermittent reinforcement. Charles B. Ferster and the author are currently preparing an extensive report of a 5-year research program, sponsored by the Office of Naval Research, in which most of the important types of schedules have been investigated and in which the effects of schedules in general have been reduced to a few principles. On the theoretical side we now have a fairly good idea of why a given schedule produces its appropriate performance. On the practical side we have learned how to maintain any given level of activity for daily periods limited only by the physical exhaustion of the organism and from day to day without substantial change throughout its life. Many of these effects would be traditionally assigned to the field of motivation, although the principal operation is simply the arrangement of contingencies of reinforcement.

These new methods of shaping behaviour and of maintaining it in strength are a great improvement over the traditional practices of professional animal trainers, and it is not surprising that our laboratory results are already being applied to the production of performing animals for commercial purposes. In a more academic environment they have been used for demonstration purposes which extend far beyond an interest in learning as such. For example, it is not too difficult to arrange the complex contingencies which produce many types of social behaviour. Competition is exemplified by two pigeons playing a modified game of ping-pong. The pigeons drive the ball back and forth across a small table by pecking at it. When the ball gets by one pigeon, the other is reinforced. The task of constructing such a 'social relation' is probably completely out of reach of the traditional animal trainer. It requires a carefully designed program of gradually changing contingencies and the skilful use of schedules to maintain the behaviour in strength. Each pigeon is separately prepared for its part in the total performance, and the 'social relation' is then arbitrarily constructed. The sequence of events leading up to this stable state are excellent material for the study of the factors important in non-synthetic social behaviour. It is instructive to consider how a similar series of contingencies could arise in the case of the human organism through the evolution of cultural patterns. Cooperation can also be set up, perhaps more easily than competition. We have trained two pigeons to coordinate their behaviour in a cooperative endeavour with a precision which equals that of the most skilful human dancers.

From this exciting prospect of an advancing science of learning, it is a great shock to turn to that branch of technology which is most directly concerned with the learning process – education. Let us consider, for example, the teaching of arithmetic in the lower grades. The school is concerned with imparting to the child a large number of responses of a special sort. The responses are all verbal. They consist of speaking and writing certain words, figures and signs which, to put it roughly, refer to numbers and to arithmetic operations. The first task is to shape up these responses – to get the child to pronounce and to write responses correctly, but the principal task is to bring this behaviour under many sorts of stimulus control. This is what happens when the child learns to count, to recite tables, to count while ticking off the items in an assemblage of objects, to respond to spoken or written numbers by saying 'odd', 'even', 'prime' and so on. Over and above this elaborate repertoire of numerical behaviour, most of which is often dismissed as the product of rote learning, the teaching of arithmetic looks forward to those complex serial arrangements of responses involved in original mathematical thinking. The child must acquire responses of transposing, clearing fractions and so on, which modify the order or pattern of the original material so that the response called a solution is eventually made possible.

Now, how is this extremely complicated verbal repertoire set up? In the first place, what reinforcements are used? Fifty years ago the answer would have been clear. At that time educational control was still frankly aversive. The child read numbers, copied numbers, memorized tables and performed operations upon numbers to escape the threat of the birch rod or cane. Some positive reinforcements were perhaps eventually derived from the increased efficiency of the child in the field of arithmetic and in rare cases some automatic reinforcement may have resulted from the sheer manipulation of the medium – from the solution of problems or the discovery of the intricacies of the number system. But for the immediate purposes of education the child acted to avoid or escape punishment. It was part of the reform movement known as progressive education to make the positive consequences more immediately effective, but any one who visits the lower grades of the average school today will observe that a change has been made, not from aversive to positive control, but from one form of aversive stimulation to another. The child at his desk, filling in his workbook, is behaving primarily to escape from the threat of a series of minor aversive events – the teacher's displeasure, the criticism or ridicule of his classmates, an ignominious showing in a competition, low marks, a trip to the office 'to be talked to' by the principal, or a word to the parent who may still resort to the birch rod. In this welter of aversive consequences, getting the right answer is in itself an insignificant event, any effect of which is lost amid the anxieties, the boredom and the aggressions which are the inevitable by-products of aversive control.

Secondly, we have to ask how the contingencies of reinforcement are arranged. When is a numerical operation reinforced as 'right'? Eventually, of course, the pupil may be able to check his own answers and achieve some sort of automatic reinforcement, but in the early stages the reinforcement of being right is usually accorded by the teacher. The contingencies she provides are far from optimal. It can easily be demonstrated that, unless explicit mediating behaviour has been set up, the lapse of only a few seconds between response and reinforcement destroys most of the effect. In a typical classroom, nevertheless, long periods of time customarily elapse. The teacher may walk up and down the aisle, for example, while the class is working on a sheet of problems, pausing here and there to say right or wrong. Many seconds or minutes intervene between the child's response and the teacher's reinforcement. In many cases – for example, when papers are taken home to be corrected – as much as 24 hours may intervene. It is surprising that this system has any effect whatsoever.

A third notable shortcoming is the lack of a skilful program which moves forward through a series of progressive approximations to the final complex behaviour desired. A long series of contingencies is necessary to bring the organism into the possession of mathematical behaviour most efficiently. But the teacher is seldom able to reinforce at each step in such a series because she cannot deal with the pupil's responses one at a time. It is usually necessary to reinforce the behaviour in blocks of responses – as in correcting a work sheet or page from a workbook. The responses within such a block must not be interrelated. The answer to one problem must not depend upon the answer to another. The number of stages through which one may progressively approach a complex pattern of behaviour is therefore small, and the task so much the more difficult. Even the most modern workbook in beginning arithmetic is far from exemplifying an efficient program for shaping up mathematical behaviour.

Perhaps the most serious criticism of the current classroom is the relative infrequency of reinforcement. Since the pupil is usually dependent upon the teacher for being right, and since many pupils are usually dependent upon the same teacher, the total number of contingencies which may be arranged during, say, the first four years, is of the order of only a few thousand. But a very rough estimate suggests that efficient mathematical behaviour at this level requires something of the order of 25,000 contingencies. We may suppose that even in the brighter student a given contingency must be arranged several times to place the behaviour well in hand. The responses to be set up are not simply the various items in tables of addition, subtraction, multiplication and division; we have also to consider the alternative forms in which each item may be stated. To the learning of such material we should add hundreds of responses concerned with factoring, identifying primes, memorizing series, using short-cut techniques for calculation, constructing and using geometric representations or number forms and so on. Over and above all this, the whole mathematical repertoire must be brought under the control of concrete problems of considerable variety. Perhaps 50,000 contingencies is a more conservative estimate. In this frame of reference the daily assignment in arithmetic seems pitifully meagre.

The result of all this is, of course, well known. Even our best schools are under criticism for their inefficiency in the teaching of drill subjects such as arithmetic. The condition in the average school is a matter of widespread national concern. Modern children simply do not learn arithmetic quickly or well. Nor is the result simply incompetence. The very subjects in which modern techniques are weakest are those in which failure is most conspicuous, and in the wake of an ever-growing incompetence come the anxieties, uncertainties and aggressions which in their turn present other problems to the school. Most pupils soon claim the asylum of not being 'ready' for arithmetic at a given level or, eventually, of not having a mathematical mind. Such explanations are readily seized upon by defensive teachers and parents. Few pupils ever reach the stage at which automatic reinforcements follow as the natural consequences of mathematical behaviour. On the contrary, the figures and symbols of mathematics have become standard emotional stimuli. The glimpse of a column of figures, not to say an algebraic symbol or an integral sign, is likely to set off – not mathematical behaviour – but a reaction of anxiety, guilt or fear.

The teacher is usually no happier about this than the pupil. Denied the opportunity to control via the birch rod, quite at sea as to the mode of operation of the few techniques at her disposal, she spends as little time as possible on drill subjects and eagerly subscribes to philosophies of education which emphasize material of greater inherent interest. A confession of weakness is her extraordinary concern lest the child be taught something unnecessary. The repertoire to be imparted is carefully reduced to an essential minimum. In the field of spelling, for example, a great deal of time and energy has gone into discovering just those words which the young child is going to use, as if it were a crime to waste one's educational power in teaching an unnecessary word. Eventually, weakness of technique emerges in the disguise of a reformulation of the aims of education. Skills are minimized in favour of vague achievements – educating for democracy, educating the whole child, educating for life and so on. And there the matter ends; for, unfortunately, these philosophies do not in turn suggest improvements in techniques. They offer little or no help in the design of better classroom practices.

There would be no point in urging these objections if improvement were impossible. But the advances which have recently been made in our control of the learning process suggest a thorough revision of classroom practices and, fortunately, they tell us how the revision can be brought about. This is not, of course, the first time that the results of an experimental science have been brought to bear upon the practical problems of education. The modern classroom does not, however, offer much evidence that research in the field of learning has been respected or used. This condition is no doubt partly due to the limitations of earlier research. But it has been encouraged by a too hasty conclusion that the laboratory study of learning is inherently limited because it cannot take into account the realities of the classroom. In the light of our increasing knowledge of the learning process we should, instead, insist upon dealing with those realities and forcing a substantial change in them. Education is perhaps the most important branch of scientific technology. It deeply affects the lives of all of us. We can no longer allow the exigencies of a practical situation to suppress the tremendous improvements which are within reach. The practical situation must be changed.

There are certain questions which have to be answered in turning to the study of any new organism. What behaviour is to be set up? What reinforcers are at hand? What responses are available in embarking upon a program of progressive approximation which will lead to the final form of the behaviour? How can reinforcements be most efficiently scheduled to maintain the behaviour in strength? These questions are all relevant in considering the problem of the child in the lower grades.

In the first place, what reinforcements are available? What does the school have in its possession which will reinforce a child? We may look first to the material to be learned, for it is possible that this will provide considerable automatic reinforcement. Children play for hours with mechanical toys, paints, scissors and paper, noise-makers, puzzles – in short, with almost anything which feeds back significant changes in the environment and is reasonably free of aversive properties. The sheer control of nature is itself reinforcing. This effect is not evident in the modern school because it is masked by the emotional responses generated by aversive control. It is true that automatic reinforcement from the manipulation of the environment is probably only a mild reinforcer and may need to be carefully husbanded, but one of the most striking principles to emerge from recent research is that the *net* amount of reinforcement is of little significance. A very slight reinforcement may be tremendously effective in controlling behaviour if it is wisely used.

If the natural reinforcement inherent in the subject matter is not enough, other reinforcers must be employed. Even in school the child is occasionally permitted to do 'what he wants to do', and access to reinforcements of many sorts may be made contingent upon the more immediate consequences of the behaviour to be established. Those who advocate competition as a useful social motive may wish to use the reinforcements which follow from excelling others, although there is the difficulty that in this case the reinforcement of one child is necessarily aversive to another. Next in order we might place the good will and affection of the teacher, and only when that has failed need we turn to the use of aversive stimulation.

In the second place, how are these reinforcements to be made contingent upon the desired behaviour? There are two considerations here – the gradual elaboration of extremely complex patterns of behaviour and the maintenance of the behaviour in strength at each stage. The whole process of becoming competent in any field must be divided into a very large number of very small steps, and reinforcement must be contingent upon the accomplishment of each step. This solution to the problem of creating a complex repertoire of behaviour also solves the problem of maintaining the behaviour in strength. We could, of course, resort to the techniques of scheduling already developed in the study of other organisms but in the present state of our knowledge of educational practices, scheduling appears to be most effectively arranged through the design of the material to be learned. By making each successive step as small as possible, the frequency of reinforcement can be raised to a maximum, while the possibly aversive consequences of being wrong are reduced to a minimum. Other ways of designing material would yield other programs of reinforcement. Any supplementary reinforcement would probably have to be scheduled in the more traditional way.

These requirements are not excessive, but they are probably incompatible with the current realities of the classroom. In the experimental study of learning it has been found that the contingencies of reinforcement which are most efficient in controlling the organism cannot be arranged through the personal mediation of the experimenter. An organism is affected by subtle details of contingencies which are beyond the capacity of the human organism to arrange. Mechanical and electrical devices must be used. Mechanical help is also demanded by the sheer number of contingencies which may be used efficiently in a single experimental session. We have recorded many millions of responses from a single organism during thousands of experimental hours. Personal arrangement of the contingencies and personal observation of the results are quite unthinkable. Now, the human organism is, if anything, more sensitive to precise contingencies than the other organisms we have studied. We have every reason to expect, therefore, that the most effective control of human learning will require instrumental aid. The simple fact is that, as a mere reinforcing mechanism, the teacher is out of date. This would be true even if a single teacher devoted all her time to a single child, but her inadequacy is multiplied many-fold when she must serve as a reinforcing device to many children at once. If the teacher is to take advantage of recent advances in the study of learning, she must have the help of mechanical devices.

The technical problem of providing the necessary instrumental aid is not particularly difficult. There are many ways in which the necessary contingencies may be arranged, either mechanically or electrically. An inexpensive device which solves most of the principal problems has already been constructed. It is still in the experimental stage, but a description will suggest the kind of instrument which seems to be required. The device consists of a small box about the size of a small record player. On the top surface is a window through which a question or problem printed on a paper tape may be seen. The child answers the question by moving one or more sliders upon which the digits 0 to 9 are printed. The answer appears in square holes punched in the paper upon which the question is printed. When the answer has been set, the child turns a knob. The operation is as simple as adjusting a television set. If the answer is right, the knob turns freely and can be made to ring a bell or provide some other conditioned reinforcement. If the answer is wrong, the knob will not turn. A counter may be added to tally wrong answers. The knob must then be reversed slightly and a second attempt at a right answer made. (Unlike the flash-card, the device reports a wrong answer without giving the right answer.) When the answer is right, a further turn of the knob engages a clutch which moves the next problem into place in the window. This movement cannot be completed, however, until the sliders have been returned to zero.

The important features of the device are these: Reinforcement for the right answer is immediate. The mere manipulation of the device will probably be reinforcing enough to keep the average pupil at work for a suitable period each day, provided traces of earlier aversive control can be wiped out. A teacher may supervise an entire class at work on such devices at the same time, yet each child may progress at his own rate, completing as many problems as possible within the class period. If forced to be away from school, he may return to pick up where he left off. The gifted child will advance rapidly, but can be kept from getting too far ahead either by being excused from arithmetic for a time or by being given special sets of problems which take him into some of the interesting bypaths of mathematics.

The device makes it possible to present carefully designed material in which one problem can depend upon the answer to the preceding and where, therefore, the most efficient progress to an eventually complex repertoire can be made. Provision has been made for recording the commonest mistakes so that the tapes can be modified as experience dictates. Additional steps can be inserted where pupils tend to have trouble, and ultimately the material will reach a point at which the answers of the average child will almost always be right.

If the material itself proves not to be sufficiently reinforcing, other reinforcers in the possession of the teacher or school may be made contingent upon the operation of the device or upon progress through a series of problems. Supplemental reinforcement would not sacrifice the advantages gained from immediate reinforcement and from the possibility of constructing an optimal series of steps which approach the complex repertoire of mathematical behaviour most efficiently.

A similar device in which the sliders carry the letters of the alphabet has been designed to teach spelling. In addition to the advantages which can be gained from precise reinforcement and careful programming, the device will teach reading at the same time. It can also be used to establish the large and important repertoire of verbal relationships encountered in logic and science. In short, it can teach verbal thinking. As to content instruction, the device can be operated as a multiple-choice self-rater.

Some objections to the use of such devices in the classroom can easily be foreseen. The cry will be raised that the child is being treated as a mere animal and that an essentially human intellectual achievement is being analysed in unduly mechanistic terms. Mathematical behaviour is usually regarded, not as a repertoire of responses involving numbers and numerical operations but as evidences of mathematical ability or the exercise of the power of reason. It is true that the techniques which are emerging from the experimental study of learning are not designed to 'develop the mind' or to further some vague 'understanding' of mathematical relationships. They are designed, on the contrary, to establish the very behaviours which are taken to be the evidences of such mental states or processes. This is only a special case of the general change which is under way in the interpretation of human affairs. An advancing science continues to offer more and more convincing alternatives to traditional formulations. The behaviour in terms of which human thinking must eventually be defined is worth treating in its own right as the substantial goal of education.

Of course the teacher has a more important function than to say right or wrong. The changes proposed would free her for the effective exercise of that function. Marking a set of papers in arithmetic – 'Yes, nine and six *are* fifteen; no, nine and seven *are not* eighteen' – is beneath the dignity of any intelligent individual. There is more important work to be done – in which the teacher's relations to the pupil cannot be duplicated by a mechanical device. Instrumental help would merely improve these relations. One might say that the main trouble with education in the lower grades today is that the child is obviously not competent and *knows it* and that the teacher is unable to do anything about it and *knows that too*. If the advances which have recently been made in our control of behaviour can give the child a genuine competence in reading, writing, spelling and arithmetic, then the teacher may begin to function, not in lieu of a cheap machine, but through intellectual, cultural and emotional contacts of that distinctive sort which testify to her status as a human being.

2 Learning theory and programmed instruction*

A. N. LEONT'EV and P. Ia. GAL'PERIN

This paper develops a critique of the extreme behaviourist view of programmed learning. The crux of the argument is that the stimulus–response–reinforcement paradigm is inappropriate to human learning. The authors point out that such a view, by concentrating exclusively on the output in a given learning task, ignores the internal cognitive processes which lead to the output.

Much of their criticism is shared by psychologists in the West, many of whom have written in similar vein. However, they also advance an alternative approach to programming which owes much to Gal'perin's theory of the stages in the acquisition of mental skills, referred to by Gal'perin as 'actions'.

Analysing the traits characteristic of programmed instruction in its American interpretation, one is easily convinced that these traits are in complete agreement with a behaviourist conception of teaching and, more than that, flow directly from it.

The essence of this conception in its most general form is that any act of teaching is considered a process which proceeds according to the scheme: stimulus → reaction → reinforcement, and which is subject to the action of three laws: the 'law of preparedness', the 'law of effect' and the 'law of practice'. Although modern behaviourism introduced into this scheme a series of complications that outwardly bring it close to the schemes of processes with control, actually it continues to remain a scheme with direct determination of the end effect by means of direct influences operating together with past influences which have been stored up in experience.

Left out of the given scheme is the most essential and interesting, although indeed not the most striking, process on which the result of teaching directly depends, namely, the process of learning.

Learning represents the formation of a system of consecutively

* Reprinted and abridged from A. N. Leont'ev and P. Ia. Gal'perin, 'Learning Theory and Programmed Instruction' in *Soviet Education*, VII (10) 1965, pp. 7–15.

developed processes governing the fulfilment of the demanded actions and operations. In the process, the fulfilment of such actions and operations gradually becomes more and more independent of external material conditions and means and seemingly becomes the internal property of the student. Only the complete formation of internal actions and operations can lead the student to a genuine mastery of knowledge, skills and habits. Surely, even simple intelligent memorizing demands, as is known, the fulfilment of certain internal 'mnemonic actions' with the material. Its simple reiteration, accompanied by reinforcement or lack of reinforcement, appears to have little effect even for memorizing. All the more evident is the necessity for adequate activity by the student while he is mastering the concepts and skills to solve tasks, to prove theorems and so forth.

In overlooking the process of learning, programmed instruction, following the scheme of stimulus → reaction → reinforcement, leaves this determining link ungoverned. More precisely, it proceeds from the assumption that learning is simply determined by available influences, mediated by past experience and the action of reinforcement. But this is not so. As with any purposeful activity of the student, the activities which constitute the process of learning demand control in the very course of their fulfilment, i.e. their continuous monitoring on the basis of comparison with the given program and reference points determined earlier by the program. Precisely as a result of the exclusion from the examined scheme of the processes themselves, control proper of them actually turns out to be only at second hand, and they are selected, not on their intrinsic merits but on the results of their operation. Then, no matter how few are the various successive parts of the educational material, it is not the student's activity with the material that is corrected or reinforced, but only the result of the activity. Corresponding to this, only a system of influences on the student, a system demanding definite answers is directly programmed, and not his activity directed towards securing this answer and, even less, the process of mastering this activity.

Let us clarify this with a simple example taken from the teaching of manual work operations. In accord with the stated simplified general scheme of teaching the students, separate tasks to be fulfilled are given in a known sequence. It is understood that no matter in what detail or however thoroughly these tasks are worked out, the students in fulfilling them should effect a new coordination of movements which are not determined by the direct instructions they receive, and, on principle, cannot be determined by these instructions. In the system of teaching, the coordination is worked out as if by itself, according to the method of 'trial and error' – on the basis of positive or negative reinforcement of the partial results achieved. Here there is no control at all of the elaboration of the processes of coordination along the very path of their formation.

It is possible, however, to use a different method, namely: to introduce a visual sign, easily perceived by the student, which acts as a cue guiding his activity at appropriate points. In this case, the main process that should be formed – the process of new coordination of movement – is not shaped by the influence of 'trial and error', i.e. not by itself, but is governed by means of an unbroken visual signalling. Then this external, visually perceived signal given by a special mechanism is removed and replaced by proprioceptive stimuli, on the basis of which this whole process is later made automatic.

The data obtained by N. N. Sachko clearly indicate how much more effective this second method is. Comparative results of instruction according to the usual method and according to the method with complete control (other conditions being equal) are expressed in the following figures. In teaching longitudinal sawing without the preliminary introduction of the control signals, all the correctly fulfilled operations in the test, on the average for the school group, were 35 per cent; the incorrectly fulfilled operations – 43 per cent; those not fulfilled at all – 22 per cent. In teaching with the preliminary introduction of control signals, all the correctly fulfilled operations, on the average for the group, were 96 per cent; the incorrectly fulfilled operations – 4 per cent; the unfulfilled operations – 0. Thus, the introduction of control of the very process of formation of new motor coordination increased the effectiveness of instruction almost threefold. Along with this, a sharp decrease occurred in the dispersal of indices of success in the school group. This fact is very important from the general psychological and general pedagogical points of view.

Sachko's data have bearing on a very special area – the instruction of hand-motor operations. We used them only for an illustration of the difference between the scheme with determination and reinforcement and the scheme with control of the process of fulfilment. This example, however, does not express a number of other very important aspects of the problem of programmed instruction; we shall dwell on some of them below.

Contrary to a naïvely sensualistic view of the nature of learning, in reality, the basis of this process is not perception, which is its source, but action – external, practical or internal, intellectual. Along with this, the action should be strictly adequate to the knowledge being assimilated. But this fundamental theoretical position did not find any consistent realization either in traditional pedagogy or in the elaboration of methods of programmed instruction by American authors.

Of course, the point is not that the students are inactive when these methods are being applied, that they do not produce certain of the actions and operations – this cannot possibly be. The point being made is that the concrete content of the necessary actions and the very process of mastery through them remain unclear and un-programmed.

The proper mastery of knowledge presupposes in the first place, the mastery of corresponding actions and operations, the products of which are themselves knowledge. Therefore, the further and genuine optimizing of teaching methods requires that the formation of this 'operational' side of knowledge should not proceed spontaneously but by a governed – programmed and controlled – process.

To begin with, in order to do this it is necessary that this aspect be clearly marked out. Thus, the mastery of concepts proceeds as a result of actions with the essential signs of an object; such actions are the supplying of concepts, comparisons and so forth. These actions should also be actively formed by the student. At first glance, it may seem that to do this it is sufficient to give the student corresponding algorithms. However, the formation of actions represents a process of distinctive functional development which, like any other development, proceeds through definite stages. And this means that the final composition and structure of the action performed by the student differ from its original composition and structure, while transfer to the action in the assigned, i.e. the final, form can proceed only as a result of a series of transformations.

Moreover, the processes constituting the 'operational' basis of a concept are intellectual; their essential links proceed in the form of internal thought processes. But the internal thought processes represent 'hidden' processes so to speak, i.e. processes such that it is impossible directly to observe their course and even less possible to control their fulfilment. In order to have the student form these processes, he must master them beforehand in the form of detailed external actions, based on external distinctly marked reference points. In this external form, they are also originally structured by the students, and are worked out in this form according to the parameters of generalization, reduction and appropriate assimilation. Only then are the conditions introduced which secure the transformation of these external actions into internal ones that are conducted only 'in the mind'. For this, the actions proceeding on the plane of external motor behaviour are transferred to the plane of speech, i.e. they are fulfilled by the students in oral form, which thus permits them to be controlled and corrected in the very process of fulfilment. Only at the next stage do the students carry out these actions on the plane of speech to themselves; here the actions are subjected to their final transformations, and the traits are acquired that are specifically characteristic of the internal thought processes with the curtailed structure peculiar to them. Later, they sometimes give the impression of instantaneous acts, as if a direct grasp of relations and judgements of solutions is achieved. Therefore, neither the data of introspection nor the data of objective logical analysis of these 'prepared' processes can reveal either their genuine structure or the path of their gradual, step-by-step formation; a special investigation is required for this.

In order to show how one achieves instruction that answers the demands of direct control of the students' formation of actions which, in their originally detailed and external form, are the means of mastering concepts and, being transformed then into their internal form, are the means of its movement in the process of cognition, we shall cite an example of the primary mastery of elementary geometrical concepts.

The students are given a card printed with cues or signs of the concept to be mastered. For example, for the concept 'perpendicular', the following sign will be given: (1) two straight lines and (2) a right angle. In addition, the rule for discerning the perpendicular is also printed on the card.

Then a group of external objects, subject to recognition (supplying the concept), are presented to the student, and the external means which model the chosen signs are given; in the present example they are the line and the angle.

When the task has been explained to him, he uses his card to decide which of the objects exemplify the concept of perpendicular. At the given stage, the student's actions are characterized by the fact that they are manifested in external form, are completely detailed, and are fulfilled in strict accord with the necessary and sufficient signs of the concept and the rule for discernment of the concept, which have been written down for the student. Under these conditions, all the activities are fulfilled without mistakes. Experience has shown that, in this way, the students quickly memorize both the signs of the concept and the rule for their application.

In the next stage, the cards containing the designations of signs and the rule for supplying the concepts which were used by the students are removed, and instead of visually perceived objects, verbal descriptions of them are presented. Now the students only name the signs and apply the rule in verbal form. Thus, the process now proceeds on the plane of speech. What is essentially new in this is that the activity is freed from material supports and is wholly transferred to the plane of speech, which later can be systematically transferred on to a fully internal, intellectual plane.

As soon as the actions on the external plane of speech begin to be fulfilled with complete confidence, they proceed to the next stage: to the fulfilment of actions on the internal, intellectual plane. Here the process is effected in a form that is inaccessible to external observation; nevertheless, a certain control over the fulfilment of the action is maintained. It is true that it is limited by the results of separate operations, but in order to secure correct fulfilment of the internal forms of activity, after working through the two previous stages, this is sufficient for practical purposes. As we have already said, in the given stage, the action is sharply curtailed in its structure and becomes automatic, and as a result gives the effect of 'direct' discernment of the object.

The path of instruction just described may seem extremely laborious. But it should be noted that this type of careful elaboration is necessary only when an examination reveals shortcomings in the corresponding activities of the student, and that even in these cases it is required only for some of the primary concepts of a given class. Since the students master the corresponding operations of thought while they are mastering these concepts, in the future these operations are applied at once in the shortened intellectual form, and the whole process is sharply curtailed. Therefore, if one takes the instruction in some school subject (or a part of it), then, on the whole, in comparison with the usual instruction, a substantial saving of time is achieved. The main thing is that under this method a sharp improvement of the quality of knowledge is observed.

Let us introduce some data obtained as a result of instruction according to the method described above. The students of a 6th-grade class in which the formation of concepts was carried out according to the given methods, and the students of 6th- and 7th-grade classes that were taught by the usual school methods, were given new tasks that required the supplying of geometrical concepts. The given conditions of the tasks differed from the data of the sketch (according to the condition, for example, a line was curved, but on the sketch it was depicted straight). Other tasks demanded that a comparison of concepts be carried out (for example, can perpendicular angles be called adjacent?).

In the experimental class, the correctly solved tasks of this nature constituted 88 per cent of the total number of tasks presented, whereas in the 6th-grade control class they were only 9 per cent, and in the 7th-grade control class – 11 per cent.

In order to show the concrete difference between the program-governed instruction described above and programmed instruction with the linear programming of material, let us introduce an example from E. Curties' programmed course of plane geometry. Let us take the same concepts: perpendicular, right (angle).

The definition (sequence 355) is introduced at the outset, and during the course it is repeated with the absence of individual words. Thus, in the following 1,700 sequences, the definition is repeated more than 20 times in its general form and more than 10 times in concrete examples. In almost all the cases, either the word 'perpendicular' or the word 'right' (angle) is missing; the words 'line' and 'angle' are absent only in some cases. In this way, the actions fulfilled by the students while mastering the indicated concepts are activities of perception and the naming of perpendicular lines on a sketch. The operations of thought required for independent application of the concept are not assigned, and mastery of them is not programmed. If all of them are mastered, this occurs as a result of processes which remain unexpressed, unprogrammed and ungoverned.

A study of the process of learning by a person reveals its tremendous complexity, by far surpassing the complexity of processes in teaching machines. This is a corollary of the fundamental fact that learning has, as a necessary aspect the formation of adequate cognitive processes, i.e. it realizes the intellectual development of man. This also distinguishes the mastery of knowledge accumulated by preceding generations of people from learning in animals. In animals, learning represents a process of formation of individual experience, produced on the basis of their species' experience as recorded in their hereditary make-up (in their 'construction'). The function of such learning is to adapt the species experience of the animals to the changing conditions of the environment. Of course, such learning also takes place with man. However, the characteristic, specific process for man is not this, but that which we call assimilation. Its function is the acquisition by an individual in his lifetime of those achievements of the historical development of the cognitive activity of humanity which are crystallized in the form of socially produced knowledge, ideas and concepts. This specifically human process not only does not coincide wholly with learning in animals, but it also cannot be broken down into separate acts of instruction, i.e. it is not reducible to their simple sum.

The main trait that characterizes the process of assimilation of knowledge is the accompanying functional change of the structure ('structural plan', according to Wiener) of the cognitive apparatus ('system') itself. Therefore, the communication to the student, and the fixation in his memory, of the objective algorithm of 'prepared' activity, corresponding to the given aim, lead to success only in that case when he has already formed an adequate 'structural plan'. In the opposite case, we will receive only the effect of 'mechanical', as it is sometimes conventionally called, learning, with all the traits inherent in it: slowness in working things out, unavoidable extinction of knowledge, inadequate transfer and the impossibility for the subject to make this effect the object of his own relation, the object of his own analysis.

In practical pedagogy all this is well known. It is known, for example, that although it is possible, of course, to compel a child simply to learn the multiplication table by heart, i.e. to form and strengthen the corresponding associative ties, nevertheless he will not master the operation of multiplication. Therefore, before giving the child the multiplication table you must always first teach him how to carry out the operation of multiplication itself, and then lead him to this operation in its reduced, curtailed form – the multiplication table. In other words, the formation of relations of the type: $2 \times 3 = 6$, $2 \times 4 = 8$, should be the result, the end product, of reduction and automatization of the corresponding arithmetic operations, but it cannot serve as a means, a mechanism, for the mastery of these operations.

The situation is the same when what is involved is training in a definite skill. It is possible, let us say, to give the student a full algorithm of the operation of multiplication of quantities with the help of a slide rule and to achieve the result that he correctly fulfills this operation. If, however, he has not mastered beforehand the necessary concepts of elementary algebra, then the ability he has acquired to operate the slide rule would only 'simulate' the actual ability to use the method of addition of their logarithms in the multiplication of quantities. To put it bluntly, the student will not understand the mathematical meaning of the operations he has performed.

As a matter of fact, of course, instruction never proceeds in such a way. It is always aimed at securing the fullest possible understanding by the students of the educational material and the maximum conscious mastery of the acquired knowledge, and in normal cases this is actually achieved. However, the problem is not to achieve this result in one way or another, but to ensure it with the method that is most effective and, if one can express it thus, most guarantees success. But for this it is not enough in the process of instruction to give the student the fundamentals that are objectively necessary and sufficient for adequate understanding of the educational material. The task consists of actively governing the processes leading to understanding. And this is achieved by programming the educational operations, their successive, step-by-step and controlled fulfilment, i.e. by the programming of assimilation.

Just how is the programming of educational operations accomplished? As we have already said, it is necessary, in the first place, to transform the assigned 'final' operation and its objective algorithm. This transformation proceeds on the basis of a genetic analysis, permitting one to find its detailed and external (exteriorized) form, the only one in which it can be initially constructed. Correspondingly, of course, the algorithm of the operation is changed. Now, it also becomes much more detailed. We call such algorithms educational, as distinguished from logical mathematical ones.

In the second place, the correct fulfilment of the action must be secured. To do this, after the action is broken down in correspondence with the educational algorithm into separate partial operations – steps – the student is given a system of reference points that reflect the logic of the action. The function of this system of reference points (a guiding basis for the action) is that it secures the inverse connections regulating the action along the very path of its fulfilment. It fulfills, in this way, the role of a channel through which the action moves.

The introduction of reference points also makes the fulfilment of the activity conscious. Surely, under the conditions the student must be aware of these assigned programmed reference points; but 'to be aware of' also means 'to realize'. In so far as the system of reference points reflects the objective connections and relations that should be subordinate to the given activity, i.e. reflects its objective foundation, the realization of this system also creates what is called 'understanding'. The fuller the guiding basis of the activity, the fuller also is the understanding of the activity.

On the contrary, if the activity is fulfilled without the possibility of realizing its objective foundations, then this is an activity 'without understanding', an activity simply 'learned by rote' through training.

Finally, in the third place, the programming of educational material should be carried out. It is realized in connection with the fulfilment of the main demand to ensure, i.e. to make controlled, the process of mastery of material. Therefore, it depends on a dual foundation – objective (logical) and psychological (genetic). The first finds its expression in the objective algorithms of those processes which constitute the operational side of the knowledge to be mastered. This is a necessary condition and, therefore, emphasis on the significance of creating algorithms represents one of the most important progressive tendencies in the modern work on programmed instruction. The second, the psychological and genetic basis, is given by an analysis of educational material in terms of the criterion of optimal successive formation by the students of the cognitive processes – the intellectual activities and operations. As a result, there arises a seemingly two-pronged system of the preliminary arrangement of material within the limits of the school subject or a section of it. In order to transform this preliminary system into a working one, it is necessary, having transformed the discovered algorithms into educational ones, to construct a 'program of assimilation' by the method described above. In this, the full development of activities in their external form and their step-by-step mastery are provided for, but, as was already said, only for the new (in terms of their operational structure) knowledge and skills; owing to this the educational material as a whole is greatly compressed. However, in individual cases there is always the possibility of developing in the student those activities and operations which, for some reason or other, remain unsatisfactorily formed by him, i.e. to introduce a procedure reminiscent of one which is practiced on a completely different basis during instruction according to the so-called ramification system.

In conclusion, let us dwell briefly on the problem of the use of technical means (teaching machines) under the conditions of programmed instruction with controlled learning. First of all, the question of teaching machines of the 'examiner' type should be singled out. These machines, like other means functionally equivalent to them, retain their significance completely; only the programs realized by them are changed. More complicated is the question of teaching machines proper. In the experience of programmed instruction with control of learning, up to the present time only the simplest means have been used – cards used in the form of distributing material, and the so-called 'study cards', the system of which represents an original analogue of the programmed textbook.

This was warranted because, at the given stage, the main task consisted of the furthest development of the principles of programmed instruction, and not its technical means. The existing types of electronic teaching machines, which satisfy a quite different general scheme of the process of instruction, cannot be used, of course. But this does not at all mean that the question of the application of machines under the conditions of instruction with controlled learning is completely eliminated. The point being made is that, under these conditions, machines with 'programs of learning' are needed. Naturally, it is difficult to foresee how fully such machines can instruct. Only one thing is certain: in every case the method of instruction should not be subordinate to the scheme provided by the structure of the machine, but the structure of the machine should satisfy the demands of the method.

3 Teaching machines in programmed instruction*

M. J. TOBIN

To an unfortunately large number of teachers and members of the lay public the term 'programmed learning' is synonymous with 'teaching machine', and 'teaching machine' usually connotes some type of mechanical contrivance. Although gadgetry has its place in programmed learning the bulk of present generation teaching machines are nothing more than elaborate page turners which achieve nothing that a book programme can't achieve.

In this paper the author carries out an exhaustive review of experiments which have investigated the contribution of machines to programmed learning. He considers the problems raised by the mechanical image which programming has acquired, the evidence for and against using machines, and discusses the areas in which some types of machine might be valuable.

* Reprinted and abridged from M. J. Tobin, *Teaching Machines in Programmed Instruction,* a contribution to the UNESCO seminar on Programmed Instruction, Varna, Bulgaria, August 1968.

1. In much of the early writing about programmed learning there was a tendency for commentators to use the terms 'teaching machines' and 'programmed learning' as though they were synonyms. Skinner himself slips easily from one term to the other, as in 'There is a constant interchange between program and student . . . the machine induces sustained activity . . . the machine insists that a given point be thoroughly understood . . . the machine helps the student to come up with the right answer'. What he in fact is doing in the paper from which this quotation is drawn amounts to a description of some of the most common features of the concept we now generally refer to as programmed learning or programmed instruction. Most of the early programs were presented in some kind of mechanical device and it is, of course, common practice in language for the name of a part, or an attribute, of a thing to be used to refer to the thing itself. Stolurow takes this a stage further and argues that the teaching machine is properly a concept and not hardware and that the word 'mechanism' is used 'in the abstract and general sense referring to a set of specific functions' and that 'No physical machine should be confused with the general teaching machine concept'.

2. This perfectly valid use of language has, however, had some unfortunate consequences. In some countries, these new developments in education have had their introduction heralded by the mass media in terms that lay undue stress on their 'mechanical', 'mechanized' and 'automated' characteristics. The public, both lay and professional, have fastened on these 'hardware' aspects, aspects which they feel may rob the teaching–learning process of its important human element. The very terminology of this new movement has, it can be argued, served in some cases to interfere with its acceptance. In a survey of teachers' attitudes towards programmed instructional terms in 1963, Tobias found that teachers had the most favourable feelings to terms descriptive of traditional techniques, and went on to infer 'that mechanical terminology may well bias the teacher against programmed instruction'. Leith obtained findings very much in keeping with these.

3. One implication for research workers, teachers and others concerned with education is that we must have more information about the precise circumstances in which mechanical devices will make a positive contribution in the teaching–learning situation, since this

antipathy may delay the implementation of techniques that have been proved successful. The onus of proof lies with the innovators, however, when they recommend hardware in areas where book presentation may seem to be sufficient. In certain quite specific areas, which are discussed later, we already have some evidence to justify on educational grounds the use of various kinds of mechanical devices whose function may entitle them to be called teaching machines. These devices, often characterized by the possession of an 'audio' element, have much in common with special-purpose teaching machines such as simulators. In most learning situations where programmed learning is currently being used, the argument centres upon the relative merits of programmed textbooks and general-purpose teaching machines (designed, as Levine and Knight put it 'for multiple subject matter. The displays and types of student responses are universal in nature and applicable to an infinite number of related or unrelated subjects').

4. Goldstein and Gotkin reviewed eight studies which compared machine and book presentation of self-instructional materials and the major findings were 'no significant differences in mastery between the machine and the programmed-text forms of presentation'. Those studies were of linear programs. In a review of the current position the author examined twenty-three studies, nineteen linear and four branching. The subjects of the studies ranged from fourth-graders to university students, with about half the subject-matter being in the field of mathematics. In twenty cases no significant differences could be found in subject matter mastery between the presentation modes. Learning time was shorter for the book groups in a few instances.

5. While some tentative inferences may be drawn from those three studies in which there were significant differences between the treatments, the main bulk of the evidence must be considered as unhelpful. It would seem that the motivational and 'anti-cheat' qualities of the machines have been unable to produce any demonstrable effects on that conventional measure of learning, the test mastery of subject-matter. The would-be user of programmed materials is therefore forced to make his choice on what are, generally speaking, non-educational grounds. He must choose between books and machines on the basis of (i) availability in large numbers of programs suitable

for his students and curriculum, (ii) relative costs, (iii) storage facilities, (iv) durability of materials (machines and their programs probably having a longer life than books), (v) safety of machines, (vi) availability of power-points for the electro-mechanical devices and (vii) interchangeability of programs among the different makes and types of machines. This last point is of considerable importance since the purchase of the machine will largely determine which programs can be used. (A cheap, manually-operated linear designed to take foolscap sheets will, of course, be incapable of presenting programs made on 35-mm film or spools. An initial purchase of a piece of hardware will limit the user to programs made specifically for that device; the purchase of a programmed book, on the other hand, will not place any constraints on future purchases. In the U.K., the British Standards Institute has been collaborating with all those concerned to draw up machine specifications so that, for example, programs printed on quarto sheets can be used on any make of sheet-presenting device. The advantages to the teacher of this kind of standardization are obvious.) Useful data on the other points are hard to come by and probably only of relevance in the country in which collected. With regard to (i), even the 1,800 commercially-produced programs available in the U.K. in 1967 cover only a small part of the whole range of the curriculum, and the choice of the individual teacher is even further restricted since over 50 per cent of this material is for use in machines. In weighing up all these factors, the teacher may reasonably conclude that his best course is to buy programmed books, and thus not tie himself down to programs from a single source. He can further reassure himself in his choice in the knowledge that the book (a) is mechanically reliable, (b) permits the programmer to vary the number of words and the amount of illustration from item to item (a facility not possessed by most of the cheaper machines) and (c) can be carried about and used anywhere at any time.

6. The superiority of the machine group in a study by Barcus and his colleagues in 1963 may be attributable to the interaction of the subject-matter and the mode of presentation. This linear program on reading and writing Spanish seems to have been largely devoted to practising and 'drilling' the skills of reading and writing. A study by Leith and Eastment in 1967 showed an over-all superiority for the book group, but the low ability subjects who constructed their

answers in the machine group were significantly better than their peers in the book group. These two studies may be saying the same thing, viz. the machine acts as an attention-focusing device, potentially useful for younger and less able students on certain – as yet to be clearly defined – kinds of learning tasks. Of the four studies in which branching programs were used, only one by Wallis and Wicks, in 1963, showed the machine presentation to be better, and here again the students (Junior Ratings, aged between 15 and 16 years, recruited to the Electrical Branch of the Royal Navy), although of average academic ability, might be said to have shown a lack of interest in academic studies by their very decision to leave school at the statutory minimum age of 15 years. Their choice of career also indicates a predominant interest in machinery and the kinds of intellectual problems associated with it.

7. The three branching studies in which no significant differences were found (Allender *et al.* (1965), Miller *et al.* (1965) and Stretton *et al.* (1967)) cast doubts on the frequently made claim that machines are pre-eminently suitable for presenting branching programs. The fact that the subjects were university students is perhaps of importance since it can be inferred that they would already possess good methods and habits of study. The mode of presentation might in this case be of relatively minor significance. The whole rationale of branching as it is seen in the present generation of machines and 'scrambled' textbooks has been cast into doubt by a number of studies. In one, Senter *et al.* in 1966, it was found that only about 6 per cent of the total possible 'wrong' branches were used (the program was Crowder's 'Arithmetic of Computers'). Kaufman in 1963 investigated the effects of varying the amount of remedial material available to the student and found no significant differences among the treatments either on post-test scores or completion times – with the implication that the 'students did not fully avail themselves of the material on the remedial frames'. Similar results were obtained by Duncan and Gilbert in 1967, except that in this case the original branching program took significantly longer to complete. A possible inference is that, until we can make full use of computers, the major variable is the quality of the original task analysis rather than the adaptive measures being currently built into programs and machines.

Two other studies that are relevant here are those of Biran in 1966 and Biran and Pickering in 1968. A branching book was 'unscrambled' by having all the remedial frames placed on the same page. In one experiment, the group reading the unscrambled version obtained higher post-test scores and completed the program in a shorter time; in the other, the post-test scores were not significantly different, but the completion time was again shorter for the unscrambled treatment. If, as Biran suggests, the act of searching through the scrambled book interferes with learning, then the branching machine has obvious advantages in that it relieves the student of this time-consuming chore. We are now brought back to asking whether, in fact, the Wallis and Wicks experiment is quite so relevant to the book versus machine controversy as the scrambled book may be an inferior presentation medium any way.

8. To revert to the other kinds of machines referred to in paragraph 3, we have ample evidence demonstrating their value. Morgan has devised a system, consisting of arrays of cards, a tape-recorder, microphone and 'posting box', for teaching reading to slow-learning secondary-school children. One of the advantages has been that the older child, embarrassed and anti-social because of his low ability in such a basic skill, has been able to take himself away from the view of his teacher and fellow-pupils during the difficult stages of acquiring the new skill. O. K. Moore's 'Edison Responsive Environment' instrument has been extensively used by Gotkin and McSweeney for developing a pre-reading skills program. The device, known as the E.R.E. or talking typewriter, consists essentially of a tape-recorder, slide projector, electric typewriter and a classroom chalk-board. The combination of these basically simple devices has produced a sophisticated teaching machine of considerable power. A similar but simpler approach has been used by Amswych for teaching the operation of the lathe to craft apprentices, where a program presented via a tape-recorder and headphones has been highly successful. The solution of many industrial training problems will probably be found in machine-based systems of this kind. Tobin, Biran and Waller have used tape-recorders, in group and individual situations, for presenting a program on basic electricity to primary school children. The 'audio' treatments were significantly superior with the low reading-ability subjects and the results lend support to the contention that the conceptual nature of much subject-matter is

well within the grasp of younger children; it is their imperfectly-developed reading skills that are holding them back. There are numerous other instances that can be cited to show how teaching machines of this kind can be used in group and individual situations for teaching subject-matter in which the oral element is important. Even where this is not the case, special-purpose machines have shown their value. Gunzburg and Watsham have developed and used such a device for teaching adult mental retardates. A correct answer choice by the subject is signalled by a buzzer (and/or a light) and the dispensing of two ball-bearings which can be exchanged at the end of the session for sweets or other rewards. A wrong choice leads to the loss of a ball-bearing. This basically simple electro-mechanical device can be used for presenting a wide range of programs dealing with basic mental and social skills and relieves the teacher of hours of repetitive drilling.

9. The program writer may also defend the use of machines as affording him information during the empirical testing of his materials. The student's inability to turn back, or look ahead, or alter his answer may give the writer greater control and enable him to plot the learner's path through a branching program and to locate errors in a linear sequence. It is arguable, however, that even these advantages are illusory since the item-analysis of post-test scores will show up the defective parts of the program just as effectively. Further developments in, for example, group teaching machines such as those used in Sheffield by Moore and in Loughborough by Leedham will no doubt add to the teacher's flexibility. The Didaktomat developed in Hungary is clearly of great promise in that it has the benefits of cheapness and can be assembled by secondary-school pupils despite its apparent complexity. Similar devices are being developed in the U.S.S.R. and can be used for teaching and testing, much in the style of the original Pressey machines, but with such additional benefits as provision for the instructor to observe each step of the pupil's progress and the automatic logging of the assistance and additional material required by the pupil. This, too, is claimed to be simple and inexpensive and can be made in the workshops of any school.

10. If, as seems reasonable to infer, the present generation of machines has little to offer over and above what can be achieved by a programmed book, then the next step forward must consist of

specifying more precisely the kinds of situations in which mechanical devices can perform operations that are outside the range of printed books. There is also a need to prepare teachers more thoroughly so that they can evaluate the evidence cited in favour of these devices and incorporate them into their armoury of professional skills. Perhaps, too, they will need to take cognizance of such work as Noble's 1967 study of children's perceptions of teaching machines and programmed learning – the children perceived the machine as being novel, active and 'young' while they saw the program as forceful and demanding like their teacher.

4 The feasibility of programmed television instruction*

S. K. GRYDE

There is little doubt that television is likely to have an increasingly important effect on education. It is already being used in many parts of the world as an important medium of instruction. However, many problems have to be solved before its full potentialities can be realized. In this paper the author considers the main problems in developing effective teaching by television and suggests some ways of tackling them. He suggests that basic to the development of T.V. as an instructional medium is the need to apply to its use the concepts developed in programmed instruction. In discussing this, he considers the key aspects of programming and reviews the findings of research on programming techniques. The paper is thus a useful source of information about educational television and programmed learning.

Programmed instruction

The essential elements of programmed instruction have been listed by Schramm. They are:

(a) An ordered sequence of stimulus items.
(b) Specific student response.
(c) Immediate knowledge of results.

* Reprinted and abridged from S. K. Gryde, 'The Feasibility of "Programmed" Television Instruction', *A.V. Communication Review*, **14** (1) Spring 1966, pp. 71–89.

(d) Small steps.

(e) Minimum errors.

(f) Gradual shaping of terminal behaviour.

(g) Self-pacing.

Of these the features that have greatest significance for this paper are: active responding by the learner, prompt feedback and self-pacing.

Television: an effective instructional medium

Gropper and Lumsdaine name three key advantages in using television as an educational medium. First, television can provide instruction for hundreds or thousands of students at the same time. This means economy because of the low cost of lesson preparation (prorated over large numbers of students) and the small number of teachers required. Second, by recording the lesson on tape or film, the content can be standardized nationally. In this way, high-quality lessons can be shared. Third, television allows the instructor virtually an unlimited choice of audio-visual materials in making his presentation.

Functional requirements of devices for presentation of programmed learning

In evaluating the ability of television to present programmed learning, it may be appropriate to establish a list of the general functions that may be provided for in the design of teaching machines, simulated teaching machines and systems of instructional instrumentation. Carpenter and Greenhill have prepared a list of the general functions performed by most teaching machines and devices:

(a) Provide for storage or organized programmed information.

(b) Provide for sequential, patterned or random access to stimulus materials or frames.

(c) Display stimulus material legibly and clearly.

(d) Permit use of a range of different content channels, signs and symbols.

(e) Provide for appropriate student responses relative to performance criteria.

(f) Present immediate feedback or reinforcement to the learner.

(g) Regulate the rate and repetition of learning cycles (or steps) for efficient learning. The student proceeds at his own pace.

(h) Record data on the essential phase of the stimulus–response–reinforcement cycle.

These eight functions are intended to achieve two interrelated objectives with programmed instruction, namely, the control of the conditions under which learning takes place and the accommodation of individual differences in the student's ability to learn.

How well does television meet these functional requirements? Television is a versatile medium. All other media of instruction can be used in conjunction with it or can be channelled through its system. Static visual materials, such as graphs and prints, can be stored, retrieved and presented in varied patterns and sequences by slides, filmstrips and transparencies. The material can be full-colour or black-and-white and the sizes of displays can be varied to accommodate the number of viewers. Dynamic visual stimulus materials can be easily stored, retrieved and displayed by motion pictures, 'live' television and videotapes. Audio stimulus materials can be presented by disc and tape-recorders and by radio.

There is no question but that television is adaptable to a wide range of content, from the very abstract to very concrete. The television instructor can show close-ups, motion and on-going processes, all of which are particularly valuable in teaching through demonstration. One of the most promising areas for the development of television for use with programmed learning is in its ability to combine the capabilities of several media. For example, written material, motion pictures, slides and sound recordings can be used as television material.

Three basic requirements of programmed television

The success of adapting programmed instruction to television will be determined by how well three requirements are met: self-pacing, feedback or reinforcement, and active response by the learner.

Requirement No. 1: Self-pacing: experimental findings

Carpenter and Greenhill approach the problem of adapting programmed instruction to television by stating – and then challenging – some very basic assumptions. The first assumption is that the student should be permitted to proceed through programmed materials at his own pace. In their discussion of self-pacing, Carpenter and Greenhill do not include learner control of the rate of development although this does interact with pacing. The student controls the pace at which the materials are presented, but the rate of development is a function of the program structure. Carpenter and Greenhill divide pacing into three categories: (1) self-pacing with unlimited time; (2) self-pacing with limited time; and (3) external pacing.

In their experiments, the results showed no substantial difference in performance among three pacing methods – self-pacing teaching machines; self-pacing programmed textbooks; and externally paced filmstrips. In another series of experiments, they presented the material on externally paced filmstrips. In this experiment, the base time was referred to as 100 per cent. and the groups were paced frame by frame through the programmed course, using times which corresponded to 80 per cent, 90 per cent, 100 per cent and 110 per cent of these base times for each frame. The results within this range of variations and external pacing showed no significant differences in student performance or in attitudes towards programmed learning. Externally paced study and self-paced study were equally effective. The experimenters determined that students of the population sampled have a wide tolerance for variations in pacing rate and that self-pacing was not necessarily the optimum rate.

Glaser indicates that self-pacing has been proclaimed as one of the substantial advantages of programmed self-instruction. It is an advantage if it de-emphasizes a lock-step curriculum and if it contributes to the notion that for different individuals learning can take varying amounts of time. Schramm is convinced that students like to pace their own learning.

From another point of view, however, programmed instruction can provide an opportunity for *not* permitting students to go at their own rate and, in fact, of forcing them to learn at a faster rate than they would choose. From their experiments with 30 subjects working for 13 minutes on a 20-item paired-associate task, Briggs, Plashinski and Jones found that the test scores of the automatically paced group were not significantly different from those of the self-paced group. Interestingly enough, the automatically paced group was less accurate on the first trial but equally accurate on later trials. The observation is that it takes a while for a subject to adjust to the auto-matic, externally paced procedure.

Guided pacing. Self-pacing data in mechanical-assembly experi-ments suggested to Maccoby and Sheffield that no purely *ad libitum* self-pacing method will be very successful. Unguided self-pacing results in such a great variety of stopping points that these cannot be regarded as accurately adjusted to the abilities or requirements of the student. The student ends up by adopting his own theory as to the best method of distributing demonstration and practice. Maccoby and Sheffield believe that some form of 'guided self-pacing' might be the most effective training method if self-pacing is at all feasible. 'Guided pacing' may be defined as a procedure by which a student is provided certain rules to follow in determining, during a demonstra-tion, when he should stop the demonstration and shift to overt prac-tice. In this manner, he could be made aware of the natural units of the task and he could also be instructed to attempt larger segments of demonstration with successive complete showings to let him see where the step fits into the total task. In the geometric-construction task, self-pacing – when used by superior students – was very effective. It is pointed out, however, that self-pacing is not always feasible even if it produces superior learning.

Maccoby and Sheffield state that 'self-pacing is not a genuine training procedure. It is a method of adjusting the distribution of demonstration and practice to the abilities of the learner.' In situ-ations that require self-pacing, *guided* self-pacing produces better learning than *ad libitum* distribution of demonstration and practice. These findings may help to explain why programmed lessons on television are effective, considering that each viewer has to fit his pace to that of the telecast. Briggs suggests the possibility that variable automatic pacing – slow at first and faster as learning trials progress – could be superior to self-pacing.

'The inherent difficulties in programming for television instruc-tion should not be glossed over,' says Lumsdaine. He feels that when individuals within the untrained student audience differ widely in ability, a good match between the program and the ability of the student in a fixed-paced group presentation cannot be achieved. The only way to reduce this mismatch would be (1) to develop lessons and present them to audiences homogeneous in ability and background;

(2) to try out these lessons on a strictly representative student audience under strict representative conditions of instruction; and (3) to exploit all of the results of research on fixed-paced group instruction.

Requirement No. 2: Feedback to the student

The second basic factor of programming that must be incorporated into televised instruction is rapid feedback; results should be given to the student immediately following his active response.

Confirmation function. An important aspect of programmed learning is that the program contains some confirming mechanism to let the student determine the correctness of his response. It is generally assumed that confirmation is reinforcing if the learner's motivation is intrinsic to the task being learned. Without enough confirmation, the student tends to lose the point of the long development and often fails to respond to the stimulus item at all; he may omit responses, misplace responses etc.

The method by which the feedback is provided to the student can vary, of course. Students may be given the correct answers for comparison with their own, or they may be told that their answers were correct or incorrect. Confirmation may be provided only after the student responds correctly or after any response (correct or not) is made. The student may be allowed repeat trials until he responds correctly, or he may be allowed only one trial regardless of whether his response is correct or not. Incorrect responses may be followed by additional prompting to facilitate correct responses. The television medium is capable of providing confirmation (reinforcement). However, as in the case of display and response functions, confirmation is influenced by the fixed rate of presentation. Since the television presentation progresses independently of the rate of student responses, the amount of time allotted to confirmation or feedback is uniform and invariable for all students. The opportunity for the student to compare his own constructed response with the correct response provided orally by the instructor or visually on the screen, for some students, may be reduced. There may be difficulty under the pressure of time for a student to decide how well his response matches the correct answer.

In programmed television instruction, the information which provides confirmation will follow opportunities for the students to respond, whether or not they have responded correctly. Confirmation may also tend to follow without allowing students sufficient time to rehearse a correct response following correction. However, at the present time, television does not have the capability of making adequate accommodation of individual differences.

Holmes feels that objections of students to the lack of *interaction* or *feedback* can be overcome through adequate planning and programming of the presentation. Meierhenry feels that these objections are based on a failure to use television properly and not on faults inherent in the medium. Students, however, may get along without this so-called interaction more readily than the teachers. The teacher who enjoys answering questions will miss the feedback that he is accustomed to. He will miss having his jokes laughed at and will miss seeing the light of understanding or perplexity cross the students' faces. In short, he will miss the personal contact that tells him how well his lesson is being received.

Methods for providing feedback to the instructor. In the developmental stages of a program, it is very important that the instructor be provided with immediate student response. This is necessary so that the instructor can adapt his materials to the needs and abilities of his students. He can repeat, restate or rephrase points when the students' responses indicate that they do not understand. Each successive revision of a programmed learning sequence should help to insure that each student's performance is brought closer and closer to the defined terminal behaviour, i.e. the training or educational objectives of the program. The most important aspect of a programmed learning sequence is that it provide constant feedback about its effectiveness. Of course, once the program has gone through a reasonable number of revisions after presentation to representative student audiences and is ready to be put on tape, feedback to the instructor becomes unimportant. Prior to this time, however, feedback to the instructor is vital.

There have been three techniques for providing feedback to television instructors. One of these techniques has been the development of two-way communication systems, permitting television instructors to ask questions of students who are watching the television presentation in distant classrooms. This two-way system allows the instructor to determine whether or not the students understand his presentation. When necessary, he can determine also what changes to make in his presentation to improve student understanding. Obviously, the weakness of this technique is that the system can be overloaded too easily by too many questions and may become ineffective. In addition, there is no visual feedback.

Recording devices. The second technique is that of using one of the various equipment systems. The Classroom Communicator designed by Carpenter and others was a device for providing rapid, accurate testing and for recording the responses of individuals in groups. The Film Analyser, a concurrent development by Carpenter, was able to record continuously a range of responses from individuals in groups consisting of a maximum of forty people. Reactions and other responses to various kinds of instructional informational programs could be accurately timed. When used with film, the records could be synchronized with the film as it was projected. A rating profile developed by Twyford provided a graphic representation of the continuous reactions of rating of an audience to a film or radio program as it was under way. Margulies reports that the Teleprompter Corporation has developed a device within an 'answerback' pushbutton control unit to permit each viewer throughout the entire closed-circuit television system to respond to multiple-choice questions shown on the screen. The programmer or lecturer can change his behaviour (alter the program) on the basis of the student's responses, which he can read from a percentage meter either at the lectern or at a television studio. This system is used at the U.S. Air Force Academy.

Recording procedures of this nature are adequate for purposes of sampling the understanding of the students in the presentation course of a given lesson unit. The recording device can even record the response of each individual student for later evaluation. But, like the two-way communication procedure, the recording of student responses during the lesson for testing purposes does interrupt instruction, and it reduces the time available for presenting additional lesson material. If the questions are asked at the end of a lesson, the instructor will not be able to point out the students' mistakes until the next lesson.

Pre-testing of television. A third technique that can affect the ability of television to provide teacher–pupil interaction is the pre-testing of lessons. Studies by Greenhill and Carpenter and Greenhill show that when students are able to view the production of pre-release phases of the film during preparation and are tested afterwards, the instructor is able to analyse the results and make important revisions of those portions of the film that failed to teach. The same methods have had an initial application to the preparation of effective television lessons. Gropper and Lumsdaine maintain that with the use of the lesson pre-testing method, the absence of student–instructor interaction is no longer a primary handicap. The television instructor can foresee student misunderstanding and forestall it, as well as build student understanding. Detailed tryout and revision procedures for television instruction are available and, when followed, will produce substantial improvement in lesson presentation to promote student understanding. These procedures are the same as those used in the tryout and revision of teaching machine programs. This method of program improvement is the main reason why programmed instruction is effective, and it must be used to make programmed television effective.

Requirement No. 3: Active response: overt versus covert response

The last major hurdle in adapting programmed instruction to closed-circuit television is the need of providing active student response. Learning responses may be divided into two general classes: First, there are *overt* responses which can be observed and recorded if desired. For example, in perceptual motor skills, responses and practice trials can be observed. The overt constructed response has traditionally been an important element in Skinnerian programming, and the multiple-choice selected response is an important element in Crowder programming. Second, there are the *covert*, or implicit or thinking, responses which are not readily observed. Some covert responses are reflected by overt reactions, and usually there are oral or written language responses.

Learning responses need not necessarily be overt and observable. They can be of the covert type, like thinking, deep concentration with covert symbolic and imaginative content, problem solving, the implicit raising of questions and the search for answers, or the implicit resolving of issues and conflicts. All of these kinds of behaviour are responses although they cannot be directly observed or they are often detected only with difficulty. Nevertheless, they may have a closer relationship to effective learning than many kinds of overt responses.

In research into the relative merits of overt and covert responding, a number of studies report no significant differences between covert or overt response modes. Gropper and Lumsdaine included in these experiments a television lesson on chemistry that required students to construct responses on a worksheet, completing sentences presented on the television screen. This was compared with an identical lesson in which the blanks had been filled in and which the instructor read twice while the students read silently. They also conducted a lesson on chemistry that required students to make active responses by completing sentences while the instructor paused as a question mark was flashed on the screen. Their conclusions were that although overt responding required more time than either reading or listening, it still may be worth while to require constructed written responses – if only to be able to get a record of the responses. This may be more important in television instruction than the amount of the material covered. It is this record of results which allows the programmer to revise his program. In their seventh report, Gropper and Lumsdaine reported that a learn-by-doing technique for programmed television lessons proved significantly better than the conventional television lecture presentation.

To conclude this point both the general criticism that television is too passive and the requirement of learning theory that calls for active student responses demand program types and formats that will insure the right kind and amount of responding at the right times during programs.

Programmed group instruction

By now it is quite evident that in attempting to build the three elements of instructional control into television lessons, a new approach which might be called programmed group instruction has resulted. The objectives, technology and methods of preparation of auto-instructional programs can be adapted to the preparation of group instructional programs via television. Television can provide for physical control over stimulus presentation, control the opportunity for the students to respond and control the occasion for providing feedback to the student. Students can be brought from an initial to a final behavioural repertoire which is larger and much more complex. Lesson materials can be reduced to small steps. Cues can be provided within these steps. The steps themselves can be sequenced to obtain the correct responses. Program goals can be identified, the intermediate steps to attain them can be developed and the whole program can be pre-tested to evaluate its adequacy.

Problems and procedures in programming for television

There are three key differences between auto-instructional and group instructional program presentation. Televised instruction proceeds at a fixed rate of presentation. It is prepared for simultaneous presentation to students in groups and is most often orally presented. Each of these factors, alone and in interaction with one another, puts constraints on the kinds of programs that can be written for televised presentation. Can these differences in presentation permit the development of programs that will produce acceptable rate of correct responding for individual students?

A successful program should produce a high percentage of correct responses. When the *same* program is prepared for all students, the cues within sequences and the sequences themselves may not be sufficient to elicit covert response from all students.

The *pressure* of the fixed duration of time established for display, response and confirmation imposed on all students may lead to a high frequency of student errors.

When material is presented orally, it becomes more difficult to learn because, once presented, the material can become available again only in the form of memory cues. The same material presented visually – printed words, for example – would remain on the television screen for a period of time. Even though the exposure time is the same for all students, at least the material remains on the screen as a directly available stimulus. *Oral presentation* of material presented to all students at a uniform fixed rate provides the least allowance of all for individual differences in student ability. Here, it would appear, the need for feedback would be the greatest.

Much more progress must be made before programmed *group instruction* will be able to accommodate individual differences. Evidence reported earlier in this paper has shown that efforts to program for groups varying widely in ability may backfire with low-ability students. The student may be hindered rather than helped by programmed material unless the material adequately prepares him to make correct responses.

Cuing

Cuing in programmed instruction is used to elicit a specific response. When the presentation is oral, cues to respond may be given by:

(a) Pausing or using a rise in voice inflection at the end of phrases or sentences.

(b) Flashing a question on the screen accompanied by a pause by the lecturer.

(c) Asking the student to respond, i.e. 'Say the answer on your worksheet.'

(d) Commenting in such a way that the comment may be both a prompt for responding and a cue for a particular response, i.e. 'How big a force . . .'

(e) Accompanying a work form with blank spaces to be filled in by the student.

(f) Having other students call out the answers.

(g) Using both visual and auditory cues. The cues for particular responses can be objects that the instructor is pointing to.

(h) Taking advantage of the ability of television to show motion and process. On-going processes should be pointed out and it should be remembered that while the burden of programmed instruction may be carried by the audio, the cuing of particular responses can be bolstered by the visual stimuli.

(i) Using demonstrations to illustrate verbal principles and to integrate the visual and oral presentation.

(j) Using demonstrations to elicit motor responses, such as having the students perform the procedures they see on the screen. This can be achieved by (1) providing the actual device to assemble or disassemble; (2) wiring, soldering and assembling electronic or mechanical components; and (3) performing laboratory procedures.

Fixed pacing

The lesson should be developed for, and presented to, audiences homogeneous in ability and background. The program for television presentation is presented by completing the following steps:

(a) Listing the lesson objectives, including facts and concepts students are expected to acquire.

(b) Developing the lessons and preparing an achievement test covering specific points in the lesson objectives.

(c) Trying the lesson over television or on film to a sample audience from the population of classes that will ultimately be taught.

(d) Giving the achievement test to the test audience.

(e) Discussing with the instructor and the television production personnel any weak points or areas of possible misconception.

(f) Analysing test results.

(g) Revising the lesson, using both the test results and television production analysis.

Orally presented material

Orally presented material requires careful structuring: Pauses must come at the ends of phrases or sentences that contain complete ideas or thoughts; otherwise the statements will probably not elicit the correct response. Very likely, not more than one completion within a single sentence or statement can effectively be made. If the oral presentation appears awkward, printed 'frames' may be used.

The accommodation of individual differences

Individual differences can be partially accommodated in the following ways:

(a) Gearing the program to the lowest common denominator.

(b) Permitting the least able students to respond with high frequency throughout the presentation. Conventional programming procedures should be used to achieve this.

(c) Selecting the duration for stimulus display response opportunity and for feedback of results that would allow for correct responding.

(d) Dividing the entire viewing audience into homogeneous sub-groups.

(e) Developing multiple-track programs in which the student selects his most comfortable pace. It may be feasible to show simultaneously three separate programs in which the student may move from the fast or advanced track at his own discretion.

It is assumed that television and programmed instruction have desirable potentialities to create effective learning opportunities for students. However, the assumption does not guarantee that the potentialities are exploited as fully as they should be in accord with the essential condition for learning and with the best-known theories and principles of learning. Unless they are used in this way, they cannot achieve their educational goals. Many of the demonstrable inadequacies in television and programmed instruction are not due to the limitation of the media themselves but to our inability to program materials for the maximum stimulation of learning responses. We must invent, develop and employ new production methods and new ways of using the media so that their potential for stimulating learning can be fully realized.

Equally important is the need for a task analysis of subjects, kinds of learning and learning behaviour. This analysis is needed in order to produce instructional materials for the media. Concentration on the *potential function* and not on the already demonstrated advantages of television and programmed instruction must be stressed because the greatest advantages can result only when the potentials are fully used.

Summary

A brief review of the literature establishes that programmed instruction has been tried out and has proved to be a very effective way of teaching. Previous research in instructional films has proved that people learn from films and that the amount of learning from films can be increased by the use of suitable procedures and methods either built into films or applied to their use. The research findings in the use of educational films can be extrapolated to educational television. This extrapolation may not be appropriate because in television the audio track tends to carry the message, and the pictorial channel merely illustrates or attracts attention. The opposite emphasis occurs in film.

Instructional television research has proved that students can learn as effectively from television as they can from conventional methods of instruction. The question was raised as to whether these two media, proven in their ability to teach, could be combined in order to provide programmed instruction to larger audiences. Criteria were established for an ideal approach to present programmed instruction materials. An analysis of the capabilities of television to meet these criteria was made, and the conclusion was reached that television met all but three of the requirements. It is quite evident that before television can present programmed material effectively, the features of self-pacing, feedback and active response from the student must be provided in some form.

Self-pacing: The self-pacing requirement may be resolved by (1) developing methods for preprogramming pacing rates for groups and (2) developing and presenting lessons to audiences homogeneous in ability and background. The major features of programmed learning are applicable in the group instruction situation.

Feedback to the student: Although television can provide knowledge of results to students – and with some measure of flexibility can control its presentation – television does not at present have the capability to adequately accommodate individual differences. Research in multiple-track programs may provide this desired capability.

Feedback to the instructor: The problem of providing feedback to the instructor may be readily solved by (1) providing a two-way communication system between the student and the instructor, (2) using an equipment system that allows each student to respond to questions shown on the screen and (3) pre-testing each lesson. On the basis of the student's responses, the instructor can revise his program. He can then anticipate student misunderstanding and forestall it. By successive revisions, the majority of questions will be answered in the presentation.

Active response: The two classes of response, overt and covert, were evaluated. Although the response need not be overt, learning was more efficient for students who made overt responses during the programmed television lesson. Covert responses cannot be recorded and measured to verify that they have occurred.

Problems arising because programmed television is prepared for simultaneous oral presentation to students in groups were reviewed. Techniques in program preparation to minimize these problems were suggested.

Additional study, carried out in analytic and systematic ways, is required to determine how the control of student behaviour by visual means can improve the effectiveness of instruction.

5 Strategy and tactics in programmed instruction*

E. STONES

This paper presents the view that questions such as whether or not to use machines or whether or not to use a branching or a linear mode are more appropriate to the tactics of program writing than to the strategy. A more fruitful approach is to develop a considered optimum strategy through the procedures of task analysis and only then to consider the implications in terms of hardware and the specific instructional mode.

No assumptions are made about the 'true' nature of a program but the view is taken that a program is a pre-prepared lesson which has been empirically validated.

It is argued that in all junior teaching and in much secondary teaching, entirely verbal programs are inappropriate. At these levels a program must therefore make use of integrated ancillary material.

A program could therefore be considered to have a central core which acts as a datum, which controls the learning activity of the children and which provides feedback.

Some material has no obvious 'best' sequence. Different children may have different strategies in the same learning situation. A model of a program to allow for different strategies is presented and its implications for programming discussed.

Tactical problems concerning the relating of ancillary material (including hardware) to the central datum are discussed, together with flexible approaches to frame writing.

This paper reports work in connection with the problems of the larger over-all procedures of programming, which I call strategy, and more specific procedures relating to such things as frame construction and response requirements, which I call tactics. The paper also makes suggestions and speculations for future developments. The work going on and the suggestions made are informed by the point of view that our attitude to programmed instruction at present should be to encourage the maximum of flexibility and open-mindedness of approach. At the same time we should attempt to incorporate

* Reprinted from E. Stones, 'Strategy and Tactics in Programmed Instruction', *Programmed Learning*, 5 (2), 1968, pp. 122–8.

relevant theory from behavioural research and studies of classroom teaching into our programming. Hence, although I take the view that a program is analogous to a pre-tested lesson, it is not suggested that we should merely take current classroom practice, refine it and translate it into programs. Rather, an interaction between the study of classroom events, behavioural theory and programming techniques will influence all three.

One of the most important common properties of programs and lessons is the fact that they are both self-sufficient. That is, both should supply all that is necessary for efficient learning. Most classroom lessons attempt to do this by a combination of verbal and non-verbal material and some sort of planned pupil activity. Although few lessons are entirely verbal, many of the currently available programs are. When non-verbal material is introduced, it is often brought in as ancillary material, rather than as part of an integrated and programmed sequence of learning experiences.

I prefer to consider the verbal material as the key element in the program which acts as a controller of the children's learning in a similar fashion to a teacher in the classroom situation. It can, in fact, fulfil many of the functions of the teacher. It can, for example, structure the learning situation: it can set goals: it can direct attention. It can make substantive statements about subject-matter: it can explain: it can solicit activity and responses from the children, and it can provide feedback. All these activities can be directed out from the controlling core of the program, which will generally be verbal, to other material which may be verbal or non-verbal. Explanations can relate to experimental procedures. The activity solicited can involve the pupils in verbal or non-verbal behaviour far more complex than filling the holes in a frame, or choosing one answer out of two or three. In such a program the child monitors his own performance by constant reference to the program datum.

Some programs currently being written are following these lines; especially, perhaps, those which are taking Nuffield type approaches to the teaching of maths and science. The stress in these programs is upon the formation of concepts and on the avoidance of 'mere verbalizing'.

The prototypical Skinnerian frame is particularly prone to mere verbalizing – or rote-learning: by which I mean learning without understanding. This is probably because of the too ready assumption of linearity in progressing from infra-human to human learning. Thus when the techniques of operant conditioning are applied to shaping up the responses in a sequence of Skinnerian frames, they may well shape up the language without necessarily developing the underlying concepts.

The approach I suggested above may avoid this danger but it could produce others. For instance, time might be wasted on quite unnecessary practical activity. It is also possible to engage in practical experience and still learn in a rote fashion. But probably the greatest danger is that in the desire to avoid 'mere verbalizing', the programmer might neglect the most powerful agent of concept formation, *viz.* language.

I regard man's use of language as the most important distinguishing feature of human learning. Although conceptual learning is not the sole prerogative of man, only in man does conceptual learning predominate. This is because language is of prime importance in conceptual learning. And one's total grasp of concepts and principles in a given field may be conceived of as one's knowledge about that subject.

There is a good deal of evidence now that the language of the teacher is one of the most important elements in the pupil's concept formation. There is also strong evidence that the pupil's own verbalizing can make his understanding more precise. Therefore, while we should make sure that when we introduce new concepts we provide the pupils with a sufficient number of concrete examplars and non-examplars of the concept, once they have had the experience we can move on and shift the emphasis from the practical towards the verbal. In junior school and in the lower secondary school, however, a relatively high proportion of practical work is likely to be necessary; later, in higher secondary and in further education, the instruction can become entirely verbal except when completely new and foreign concepts are introduced.

But at all levels language can play a similar role, and especially in two key particulars. In respect to feedback there is probably a good case for giving more than the bald correct response as confirmation. Intrinsic programmers do provide more. They explain why a given response is incorrect and there is no reason why linear programs should not do the same. We have some evidence that feedback which is more than mere confirmation improves learning and it seems to me that in addition to explaining the wrong answers in a multiple choice question, we should in certain circumstances explain the reasons for the correct answer, too. This sort of confirmation serves not only to add precision to an answer but would go some way towards answering the perfectly legitimate question which a student might ask after such an item: *viz.* 'Why?'

Frames such as these resemble some of those in Susan Markle's program (*Good frames and bad*, Wiley, 1964). The characteristics of such programs are that there will be few 'filling the hole in the cheese' frames; formal prompts will be minimal; the responses called for will be as varied as need be for the instruction being given. Feedback will at times be detailed explanation. The student may also be asked at times to justify or explain his answer in a short statement. The rationale of this tactic is based on the point made earlier, that when students have to verbalize their learning they learn better. This is not the overt–covert controversy rearing its head again. There is a world of difference between speaking or thinking one word answers and explaining in succinct terms which demonstrate the grasp of a principle or a concept. However, this is a field for further investigation.

I should now like to turn my attention to what I have called the strategy of programming. However, the over-all plan of the program and the more specific details are not independent. The frame structure will obviously be determined to some extent by the over-all strategy and vice-versa. But, in the past the connection between the two has been too rigid. Linear programs have had linear-type frames and branching programs have had branching-type frames. The distinction between linear and branching frames is tending to disappear and it has been suggested that the real distinction is not between linear and branching but between stimulus-centred and response-centred approaches.

From the point of view of strategy, however, traditional branching and traditional Skinner type programs are both linear. Both progress in an essentially unidirectional mode. It is true that the more sophisticated intrinsic programs seem to disprove this point of view, especially if washback is introduced. However, all the branches and remedial sequences etc. are related to a hypothesized best linear path through the material. In fact, of course, many currently available branching programs are minimally sophisticated and allow of little diversion from the mainline.

Two developments have helped to suggest ways in which the programmer-determined, strictly linear mode, may be modified. One is work like that of Mager and his associates and the developments in computer-based instruction. Mager's studies show that when students are told their expected terminal performance and given an instructor whom they can turn on or off at will, they generate their own information seeking strategies and learn as much as linear program groups but in half the time. They take less time because they do not seek information they do not need. They cannot do this in most currently available programs. Mager suggests we should be paying attention to 'Curriculum generating machines' as well as to programs and teaching machines.

Excursions into computer-based instruction have attempted to do this. The ideal program might be envisaged as one which acts similarly to the instructor in Mager's experiments. Starting with virtually unstructured material, the structure is gradually developed on the basis of an analysis of the student's responses. The strategy is generated, as in Mager's experiments, as a dialogue between the teacher and the student.

But there is a further important consideration which also bears on this question of teaching strategy. Some material has no obviously best sequence. And in fact it could well be that forcing the instruction into a unidirectional mould might give the pupils the wrong idea and make them see structure where none exists: or perhaps see a linear structure at variance to a real convoluted structure.

Material which might be in this category could probably be taken from most subject areas. The ones which occur to me are themes from history when one deals with single major topics such as Waterloo, or from geography when one deals with complex interrelationships of phenomena which cannot be strung out in a unidirectional chain without giving a distorted view of reality. Much the same can be said about subjects as diverse as ecology and poetry.

In attempts to program material such as this, two main requirements have been borne in mind. The program had to avoid imposing a unidirectional impress on inappropriate material: it also had, as far as possible, to allow the children to develop their own strategies as they work through the program. The latter requirement was also to be extended where possible to allow a pupil to skip with facility material in which he was already competent. Machine presentation was not to be a requirement but recourse to hardware would be made if it were seen to be essential at any point.

The strategy employed was developed in an attempt to cope with the problem of programming a specific historical event for junior children, namely the Great Fire of London.[1] The problem was that during the period of the fire there was a mass of activity, all important, all of interest and all happening at the same time. A unidirectional program would not have conveyed the idea of simultaneity. At the same time, it was desirable to give the children as much freedom as possible to follow their interests and generate their own strategies in the program.

The solution which emerged envisaged a program structure which might possibly be described as spiral. A schematic outline of the structure of the program is presented in Fig. 1. The key to the program is the Master Card which presents the main concept areas of the program. In this particular program the concepts are expressed in the form of questions. The concepts and the questions are generated by the normal processes of task analysis, but in addition, representatives of the target population are consulted to check the kind of question they do, in fact, ask. The Great Fire of London program makes use of such questions as: 'Why did the fire spread?' 'How do we know about the fire?' 'What was the firefighting equipment like in those days?'

The child enters the program by consulting the Master Card. Introductory material tells him what the program is about and then asks him what he would like to learn about first. The pupil then looks at the content questions and decides which of them he would like to investigate first. In the present design he is then routed from the Master Card by instructions linked with the questions. These instructions may well be merely a reference to a frame number. From the Master Card he goes to a Main Concept Card which corresponds to the concept area covered by the question he chose. In Fig. 1 these

[1] Developed in collaboration with Mr J. N. Fowles.

cards are labelled A, B, C and D. In the full program, of course, there could well be very many more than four such cards.

Each Main Concept Card is the point of departure for a linear sequence such as has been described earlier. That is, although it is a set of sequential material, it is not entirely verbal. There is a key verbal element which controls the sequence but the sequence in-

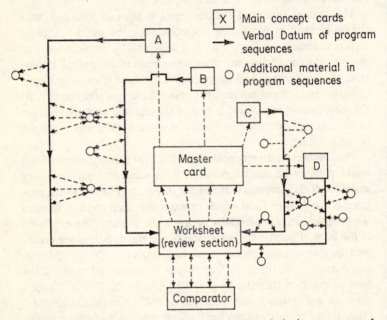

Figure 1. Schematic lay-out of a program for relatively unstructured material

corporates additional material and activity, *not as a matter of principle*, but when task analysis suggests it is appropriate. The frames, also, are of the type described earlier and within each sequence it is possible to make use of any of the techniques of branching or skipping as necessary.

When the child has completed this first sequence, he is routed to a review section of criterion frames. In Fig. 1, this is the Worksheet. In the Great Fire program the review items are presented in the form of a structured piece of prose which the child should be able to complete accurately if he has learned successfully from the related sequences. The child actually completes this review section on his own answer sheet so that he has a permanent record when he has finished. He then checks his performance against another card, which acts as a comparator, and then corrects his own sheet. Finally the Worksheet tells him to return to the Master Card and make another choice.

He continues in this way until he has worked through all the items on the Master Card. At the end he will have his own synopsis of the program on his answer sheet. In order to preserve the idea of simultaneity of occurrences or the idea of the equal importance of the different concept areas, the Worksheet is not envisaged as being in a sequential form but in some other form, for example, as a table or as a circle with segments consisting of the various review sections.

Problems can arise when the programmer wishes to make a cross reference from one sequence to another. It is necessary to assume that the child who is referred from sequence A to sequence B will not yet have done B. This problem can be coped with by siting the elements common to A and B in the additional material so that this material is common to both sequences. As an example in this particular program, a contemporary street map of London is common material for such sections as 'The King's Role', 'Pepys' Role' and 'Why the fire spread'. In Fig. 1, common additional material can be seen linked up with two sequences while other additional material is specific to separate sequences.

Pupils who enter the program completely naïve work through the whole program using an idiosyncratic strategy. Pupils of varying degrees of sophistication are able to do the same but have the additional facility of by-passing material with which they are familiar. Such pupils first check the Worksheet and attempt the criterion frames. They then move on to the Master Card but only work through those sequences related to the sections of the Worksheet they were unable to complete.

One interesting feature of this kind of programming is that it seems to provide a tool for checking the strategies which children generate when they have a choice. It is possible that one could treat other apparently more 'logically structured' material like this to see if children generate the same strategies as we provide for them.

Clearly the model presented with this paper can be developed. Whatever form the development takes it seems that the flexibility of attitude to the problems of strategy and tactics suggested is very important for the future development of programmed instruction.

6   C.A.I.: some problems and perspectives*

L. STOLUROW

To ardent programmers computer-based instruction is the crock of gold at the end of the rainbow. Their hope is to use a computer to generate teaching programs analogous to the teaching sequences generated in a teacher–pupil interaction. There is a high probability that such a teaching system will eventually be developed. However, the present state of the art is one not uncommon in computer technology: the hardware far outstrips the software in level of sophistication and potential for development. In the use of computer technology in teaching, as in other applications, we need to beware of the 'garbage in, garbage out' danger. Teaching programs are difficult to construct and, as Stolurow points out, there is as yet no definitive prescription for generating such programs. All the more need, therefore, to be cautious that we do not generate trivial programs for C.A.I.

In this paper, Stolurow discusses models of computer operation, some of the work currently going on, and makes projections for future developments.

To teachers in British schools discussion about C.A.I. may seem impossibly Utopian. However, this is a rapidly changing field and no educationist can really afford to ignore developments which have such potential for educational innovation.

There are three critical dimensions of computer-assisted instruction or of computer-assisted learning. First of all with the computer we

* Reprinted from L. Stolurow, 'C.A.I.: Some Problems and Perspectives' in W. Dunn and C. Holroyd, *Aspects of Educational Technology 2*, Methuen, 1969, pp. 501–8. The paper was made possible in part by a contract with the Office of Naval Research ONR N00014-67-A-0298-0003, monitored by Dr Glenn Bryan and Dr Victor Fields. Reproduction in whole or in part is permitted for any purpose of the United States Government.

have the opportunity to take seriously individualization or personalization of instruction. Perhaps personalization of instruction is a better term to use than individualization because individualization has sometimes been misinterpreted as the individual always learning in solitary confinement. The personality dimension involves prescription because this is an attempt to instruct under conditions where some responsibility is taken by the teachers, for they commit themselves to a position with respect as to how they want the instruction to take place. This is done by trying to determine the needs of the student and then to make a definite commitment as to how it is thought these needs are best handled. The over-all objective here of course is to optimize the learning retention and transfer of information.

The second dimension concerns the problem of selective media control. Do some individuals learn better from certain media? Are certain kinds of materials best presented through certain media? With computer assistance the media can be planned in advance to automatically control and present at a time when they appear to be best used.

The third dimension is multi-modal teaching. C.A.I., C.A.L. and a whole lot of combinations of letters are differently interpreted by different individuals but when it comes down to it, if computers are going to be used then maximum use must be made of them. This means that a rather broad teaching repertory must be used and not just a single orientation towards teaching which has grown out of programmed instruction. The latter is only really one of a number of orientations or modes of instruction which can be identified.

The initial mode, the most easily employed mode of a computer, is to use a terminal connected to a central processing system and to let the students engage in problem-solving activities where the problems are primarily scientific and mathematically orientated utilizing an available general purpose language, for example Fortran or Basic. Apart from finance very little involvement of the institution is required for this kind of application. The students can come along and learn how to interact with these devices and the same problems can be assigned by the faculty to all students because the onus is on the student to learn the language, to deal with the input and to determine whether or not he is getting satisfactory performance. The teacher is only concerned about whether or not the student has completed his homework.

The second mode can be thought of as drill-and-practice and here there is more commitment of staff. The staff has to make some decisions that at certain points in the language program the students are going to need some drill in the subjunctive cases or in certain inflexions. These are programmed much in the way in which one would lay out sequences for programmed instruction. The big problem is how much material to prepare so as to provide adequate practice to build up skill levels. The material is highly repetitive with highly structured kinds of experiences. In fact the structure is frequently generalized so that a wide variety of materials can be substituted in a single structure and thus allow the programmer to use essentially a fixed sequence of code to handle the problem. The coding however involves someone other than the student and so also with planning. The student in this case works with a system in his natural language (as opposed to computer language) and sees only what he has been programmed to see. So there is less onus on the student and more on the staff.

The third mode is called the inquiry mode. Historically, in computer business this is referred to as information retrieval. This is a historical and unfortunate separation of modes of use as certainly there are many conditions where it would be an advantage to have information retrieval facilities available while learning. In chemistry, the student may be asked to look up various things such as an atomic number on a periodic table of elements and there would be log values. Also one wants to think in terms of staff support, and information retrieval is an important staff support function and mode of use of a system so that the staff can gain some mileage out of these systems.

Simulation and gaming are sometimes not distinguished. Symbolic feedback has to be used in many pedagogical situations, but, obviously, the intention should be to move as closely as possible to the real situation and simulation is an attempt to do just that. The term 'gaming' is used to describe the situation where only certain properties of the situation are able to be captured and as a result, the situation is not as close to reality. In both cases the individual is asked to explore some complex set of ideas that might require a lot of frames to lay out in a linear or even a branching program. Both simulation and gaming are dynamic interaction models built into a system or process such that it is capable of coping with a wide variety of possibilities in terms of input and coping with the image of some kind of output to the student. Also some attempt is made to give direction and correction of his performance to the student. This means that, when a computing system is used in this fourth mode of simulation and gaming, a kind of programming economy is achieved because the general case is being programmed without having to lay out all the possible contingencies. There is a more general grasp of the problem area because it is formalized and represented in terms of a formal system – either a mathematical equation or a computer code.

Socratic instruction is regarded as a cut above the modes previously described only because it involves or can involve the management of these other modes through the actual utilization of these on the basis of student performance together with some prescriptive basis. In addition, of course, it would involve kinds of things more familiar in programmed instruction such as questioning the student and utilizing his answers as a basis for making some subsequent decisions. The decision might be to lead him to a game or it might turn him into a simulation or provide some problem-solving exercises.

The sixth and least developed, but hopefully the most to be developed, is the author mode when the concern is to provide an educational compiler where the computer will ease the job of the author by generating frames with minimal instruction. The author would specify the data base and that teaching was to be in the inductive mode or using a rule procedure and with these kinds of general prescriptions on the part of the author it would be ideal if the system could then take care of the rest of the process. This is obviously difficult. It can be done in certain highly structured areas. A few simple passes at it have been made in the area of symbolic logic where syllogisms both in the abstract and concrete form were generated. The system not only generates the syllogisms but also the correct response so that the system can judge the student's response to the syllogism. This can obviously be done in arithmetic and certain areas of mathematics but in areas of more abstract ideas the problems in the utilization of language and a generative grammar come into the picture. What has been dealt with, in a sense, is the problem of the generative grammar of instruction. What is wanted is the ability to generate instructional material from an instructional grammar.

At the risk of over-simplification three different levels of complexity or system design can be distinguished.

Stage one is a small system. The small system is extremely useful as a way of getting started, helping define problems and providing more opportunity to do experiments and control conditions. However, you soon find that one's appetite is whetted and one wants to get many students on-line, and if many teachers are to write programs then something simpler than high level compiler languages will have to be used. A medium-sized system starts providing these kinds of facilities. The system is no longer the toy or pet of the individual investigator but has become a tool for instruction generally and of course this means added responsibility. Ignorance about some of the decision processes to be implemented on a system is exposed because research with the small computer has typically been inadequate. Not all the problems are solved when one is dealing with the uneven environment with respect to resources. There is an embarrassment of riches with the computer but only poverty with respect to educational guidance that can be given to the larger educational and instructional community. Except for work in mathematics and the concepts of ruleg, notions about how we plan sequences are pretty idosyncratic and not well supported in terms of research. Now this is not bad but simply recognizing the state of the art.

The medium-sized systems are probably in the long run going to be the most widely utilized systems for developing the state of the art with respect to instruction. Most medium-sized systems really do not have the capability to exceed more than 50 terminals simultaneously. Now there is a capacity to go beyond that, to exceed 50, and there are some systems in use that do that – when one talks about thousands of users on-line. This frequently comes about because a variety of different people make use of a single terminal throughout the course of a day but if everybody sat down at all the terminals of most medium-sized systems and dialled up somebody would get a busy signal because they frequently have a ratio of about three terminals to the maximum number they can handle. At Harvard about 100 terminals are linked to the SDS 940 computer but at any moment in time there are only thirty-two available lines. That frequently does not get people into great difficulty but it does give some measure of the relative magnitude.

Large systems are being planned, in fact king-sized ones. The U.S. office recently asked two companies to propose a system design which would accommodate 100,000 students. These designs are still not exposed and it is going to be a little while before they are operational.

Turning to the problems of implementation in schools and universities, terminals can be introduced into the classroom to produce a kind of dynamic blackboard capability. During the lesson some kind of mathematical function may be discussed and the students may want to know what happens when a particular parameter is changed. They can individually read in through their own keyboard, insert a change in the parameter and see displayed on the cathode ray tube the particular function they are dealing with and the changes that take place as a result of the manipulation. This sort of thing can take place for quite complex problems in mathematics in a very short period of time so that one has an ability here to explore some concepts or ideas in a way which one couldn't do ordinarily when students have to be sent home to calculate for long hours and then come back. The students would perhaps have become lost in the detail and fail to gain the general sense of the problem. This is one kind of supporting activity which is a classroom kind of orientation.

The I.B.M. 1050 terminal is borrowed from the business industry and provides typewriter capability and hard copy, rear view projection screen and audio tape-recorder. Any of these media are capable of being played or utilized at any time. The point to be made is that not only is multi-media control being used to embed the concept or idea but in addition the console must be in a learning environment. Since such a console would be new the first thought is to put it in some closet or remote location and then have students go to it. One treats it as precious and locks it up. As long as this attitude prevails it is not going to be embedded in and part of the environment. It would be apart from, rather than part of, the instruction and this is a serious problem. What one wants to do is to build around the student not only the new gadgets but the old things that he is used to working with in a laboratory type of environment.

In the Philadelphia schools project GROW, the SAVI system with cathode ray tubes, has been installed in four schools. The C.R.T. capability is that of a television tube which maintains its television capability and by dial selection or by programming one could have a television series played by changing channels. By converting entertainment devices to education, presumably larger scale production would be obtained and therefore a cheapening of terminals. This has not taken place yet and really one of our critical problems is not the cost of the computer but the cost of the terminals. Once a multi-access system is started it does not take long for the cost of the new terminals to exceed the cost per student of the central processing unit. The time the central processing unit is actually engaged in interaction with the student is very trivial – it is a matter of seconds for maybe an hour of instruction and so one is not tying up much of the computer, but the terminals are expensive when multiplied fifty or one hundred or two hundred times.

There are and there have been some efforts to cut these costs but we in education are the step-children, we are disorganized. For industry I.B.M. recently announced a new terminal which was developed for some industrial application and allows a light-pen to be used on 120 points on a film projection surface. This gives another dimension of response for a young child who can point to any one of these places and the system will detect that. This is really great but why are we not seeing terminals designed for education? Why are they designed for industry and then brought over to the educator as second hand clothes? We are not seeing the interface between the student and the system taking the form that best suits it to our instructional requirements. By way of projection it is suggested that this is a dimension in which we will be moving hopefully in the future.

Turning from systems to concepts, it has been suggested that tutorial instruction is a managerial level of instruction employing a variety of other modes as kinds of sub-sets of available resources to be tuned in or out, or used as deemed most effective. Taking this as the point of departure, the sequence of requirements can be divided into three sets.

The first set is the pre-tutorial set. The purpose here is to achieve the best initial but provisional match between the characteristics of the student and the instructional resources of the system. Obviously this has to be an adaptive process not only within a course but within education generally as our ability to make these kinds of decisions improves. Systems do collect the kind of data which have not been available in the past and which would permit the kind of adaptation suggested and make it possible for us to move towards better and finer kinds of decisions.

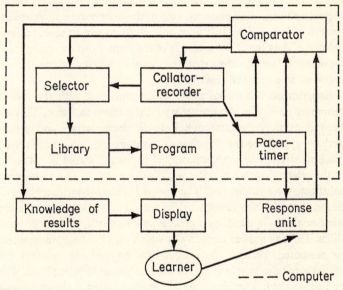

Figure 1

Although they were originally set up in the early sixties the set of functions shown in Fig. 1 still wear well with respect to the basic requirements of any teaching system live or computerized. One has to take into account these kinds of functions in order to be able to cope with the instructional problem. This means, of course, that one needs a computer language capable of handling each of these kinds of problem. If the language is at that stage of its development when it is incomplete and insufficient, this does not mean that it cannot be used but it means that some important functions are left out and in many languages there is no collative recorder function.

In planning for a language there are several steps involved. One that has most been neglected in educational technology is the development of an instructionally orientated language of our own that is independent of the machine but can be utilized by any machine language. Efforts have been started to code materials so that, in addition to our statements of objectives, we will have a list of basic kinds of materials or concepts. The idea is to have some very cogent way of representing a lot of information and have it coded in such a way that one can deal with the code sequences instead of the verbal sequences to examine patterns. One of the intentions is to reveal the pattern of instruction. It is very difficult to do when there is a large volume of data but if the contents of the frames can be symbolically represented then it seems that one can start looking at questions of sequence in a more efficient way.

Experiments have been made with sequencing with the idea of minimum change as the learner goes from frame to frame. This has been found to give maximum help to the poorer learner and one can perhaps appreciate the way that this is done through an interesting teaching strategy in histopathology. The learner would of course be at the teletype with rear view projector for slides. The slides are a substitute for a microscope. The learner is presented with an interrogation that asks him about what he sees. The student may be asked what he thinks is the disease process in a particular slide or series of slides. He may answer correctly in which case the next frame would be presented. Perhaps the learner may be confused however and choose wrongly. In this event the student would then be shown what he had selected. The idea here is that the student is shown visually what he thought it was so that he can examine his error before taking him back to the original and asking him to make another choice. The student is given visual support for his error and not just told that he is wrong. He is allowed to explore the error correcting technique.

Another dimension of the language is the provision for the student to make notes. The kind of provision which can be made is that the student at any time in the program may make the three number signs (three crossed hatches) and then type his note and comment and the computer will ignore this completely. It is not treated as a response nor processed.

In another approach to instruction the student is interrogated by a program called HEURISOL. It is called HEURISOL because we are trying to teach him a heuristic approach to problem solving. The idea is not to teach a particular way of solving a problem but a general way of going about mathematical problems. It is based upon some work of Polia who is a mathematics instructor at Stanford and who has suggested ways in which students might benefit if they were taught a particular kind of approach to problem solving.

The basic idea of HEURISOL is that the student is first asked what kind of problem it is. Is it a problem to solve or a problem to prove? He then goes on to what is unknown, what is to be proved, what are the given data? By interrogating him consistently over a set of questions he will eventually, in Polia's terms, become an intelligent problem solver, namely a person who engages himself in dialogue about the material he's interacting with in a consistent and intelligent way and the notion is to embed in his thinking the set of questions so that he becomes an habitué of these questions and uses them over and over again when he gets a problem.

Turning to testing, we have heard about multi-choice, true–false objective testing. Shauffenhauer and Messingill are doing research in this area and they are investigating a different kind of approach to testing in which the student is asked his confidence in a variety of possibilities. The student is shown an interrogation frame on the cathode ray display. The student reads the question. When he feels he is ready to respond he points his light-pen to the display to bring the response frame. On the response frame they provide four possible answers. The student may be confident that the first possibility is not correct. He reduces its probability to zero by communicating with his light-pen to the sign which is DEC (decrease) beside the alternative. This increases the probability of the other three answers because the maximum probability is proportioned over the set and when the student subtracts or decreases from one he merely adds to the others. The system records these responses.

The probabilities as he estimates them and his decisions, and alongside them the number indicating his score as the proportion of the total which is represented by his actions in relating his confidence in the alternatives – these are displayed to the student. Much more information is gained from the student by this procedure.

A final table representing the kind of summary is given in Fig. 2. Student 1 is a student who is maximally confident in one choice and minimally confident in another. However he is maximally confident in the wrong answer and so is coded as C, C being regarded as completely misinformed. The next student, student 2, has his confidence distributed but his maximum confidence 35 is next to the right answer and he is classified as P which is partially informed because

		Confidence				
		S_1	S_2	S_3	S_4	S_5
A N S W E R	Lincoln	0·00	0·20	0·25	0·20	0·00
	Harding*	0·00	0·35	0·25	0·15	1·00
	Harrison	0·00	0·30	0·25	0·30	0·00
	Adams	1·00	0·15	0·25	0·35	0·00
	Total Confidence	1·00	1·00	1·00	1·00	1·00
	Score**	0·00	0·54	0·40	0·18	1·00
	Interpretation	c	p	u	m	w

KEY: c = Completely misinformed
p = Partially informed u = Uninformed
w = Well-informed m = Misinformed
  * Indicates correct answer
  ** Log function

Figure 2. Confidence (probability) values of five students for illustrative example

his maximum confidence though in the right place was not very high. Student 3 is a student who is playing his bets. He doesn't know so he is going to cover everything. He has got 25 on everything so something has got to hit and he is coded as U, uninformed.

The point to be made is that one can see through this a way of extracting much more information from student behaviour than one gets from the usual devices employing true–false, multi-choice questions, when the student picks the right answer and lets it go at that. Using this method the author can have feedback on what is happening and whether or not his sequences are working.

In some area C.A.I. needs to be thought of in terms of a symbiotic relationship between research and instruction. We need not only to teach with systems in order to help justify them but our teaching has to be based upon a plan which is greater than just planned instruction – a research plan to extract information, to upgrade our ability to handle the complex problems these systems present to us. Somebody has asked what rules of decision are used by people who are using C.A.I.? The point being made was that the onus was being placed on the new technology. The onus has really been with us for a long time and it is just that we are now confronted with the reality that when we teach we have to be explicit about the rules of the game – we have to know what the contingencies are. Instruction can be regarded as the management of contingencies of if/then relationships. This gives us a rather explicit way of trying to set down on paper or in our minds, the way in which we have to start structuring our thoughts. We have been thinking more about global ideas, discovery learning, things of this sort which really don't help much when it comes to laying things out in a concrete manner for instruction and I believe that we now have to start looking at the fine grain of instruction.

The problem and the challenge is to make C.A.I. the effective system it can be and hopefully will be in the next few years.

7 An instructional systems approach to course development*

M. R. ERAUT

All too often programmed learning enthusiasts have failed to see the wood for the trees. In their concern with the finer details of programming techniques they lost sight of the over-all picture. In recent years,

* Reprinted from M. R. Eraut, 'An Instructional Systems Approach to Course Development' in *A.V. Communication Review*, 15 (1), 1967, pp. 92–100.

however, attention has been increasingly focused on the wider implication of programming. In some cases this has involved taking a whole course and scrutinizing it according to programming criteria. Other workers have drawn on the ideas of systems engineering and tried to apply them to course development. We have yet to see to what extent systems theory can be applied to problems of teaching. We also need to exercise caution to ensure that we are not mesmerized by the jargon and complicated diagrams which are the stock in trade of devotees of systems theory.

Nevertheless, it would be a serious mistake for educationists to ignore developments in this field. The paper chosen to acquaint the reader with some of the basic ideas of the 'systems approach' should introduce the concept to the uninitiated relatively painlessly.

Preface

The term 'system' is now fashionable, so I have used it. It also has the advantage of being definable in one's own terms. An alternative title for this paper could have been 'A Programmer's Approach to Course Development'. But while some people now define programmed instruction as a process for developing effective learning sequences, others still seem determined to define it in terms of the more prominent characteristics of the early programs, their authors and their advocates. Thus, the term 'programmed instruction' seems to convey different sets of connotations to different people, and I have temporarily discarded it as a barrier to effective communication.

This article is an attempt to summarize and to advocate a methodology for course development which has arisen in a number of centres over several years and to which many have contributed.

Introduction

A course can be considered as an instructional system. The components of the system are the learners, the instructor(s), the material(s), the machine(s) and the technicians. The input is the learners' initial knowledge, and the output is the learners' final knowledge. The purpose of course development is to design validated instruction that is guaranteed to convert any input meeting the input specifications to an output that meets the instructional system's output specifications. The output will normally be defined in terms of the standards of performance required for certain jobs or in terms of the entry requirements of the course that will follow. In either case, a guaranteed output is essential. We cannot allow failure on the job; nor can we expect the subsequent course to teach content that should have been taught in the preceding course.

The design of a validated instructional system is a complex and time-consuming process involving much research and development. It is unlikely that our 'prototype' will meet our output criteria, but

COURSE DEVELOPMENT

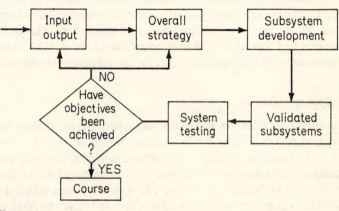

Figure 1

we can use information from its performance to revise the system and design a second that works better. We may have to design several versions before we finally have one that meets our specifications. Two essential requirements of this research and development process are:

1. We need a comprehensive test of the system's output so that we can assess the efficiency of the system.

2. We must be able to obtain sufficient data from the testing of the system to be able to pinpoint the deficiencies in our prototype and to suggest how revision could increase its efficiency.

The instructional system may be divided into several sub-systems, each with its own defined input and output, so that decisions about media and teaching techniques can be made at the sub-system level. Appropriate instructional strategies can be chosen for each content area, and scarce resources (expert personnel, expensive equipment etc.) can be allocated to the sub-systems which most need them. Each sub-system is revised until it meets the desired specifications; then the validated sub-systems are combined and the total system is tested. Further revisions may yet be necessary until the total system finally achieves the required effectiveness (Fig. 1). It can be noted in Fig. 1 that one 'feedback' arrow returns from System Testing to Input–Output and one to Over-all Strategy. Either input–output specifications need modifying, perhaps because students take too long to achieve the required performance level, or the over-all strategy must be changed by resequencing the sub-systems or, more probably, by raising the output specifications of a sub-system whose output is inadequate as input for the following sub-system.

Output specification

An output specification serves two main purposes: it defines the required effectiveness of the instructional system so that we know when we can stop revising; and it gives other people a complete, accurate and unambiguous description of what a student will be able to do when he finishes the course. The first component which the system designer must produce is a list of terminal objectives, each of which satisfies the following criteria:

1. It must describe what the learner will be required to do in order to demonstrate that he has reached the objective.

2. It must describe the important conditions given and/or restrictions under which the learner will be expected to demonstrate his competence.

3. It must indicate how the learner will be evaluated and specify at least the minimum standard of acceptable performance.

An objective which fails to meet these criteria cannot be used until it has been reformulated in more specific terms. A general objective such as 'the student will understand the concept of kinetic energy' may tell us a little about the subject-matter of the course, but it does not tell how we can prove that a student has achieved the objective;

and it will be given very different interpretations by different teachers.

The second component of an output specification is a post-test. Performance on this test will be the main criterion for evaluating the system and must, therefore, indicate whether the student has achieved all of the terminal objectives. To ensure that all the objectives are dealt with in the post-test, it is useful to construct a

INPUT—OUTPUT

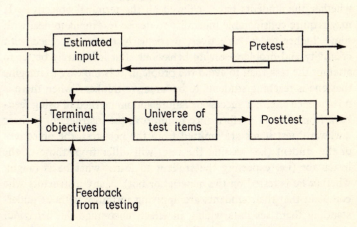

Figure 2

'universe' of all the test items relevant to those objectives; then, careful sampling of the universe of test items gives a number of alternative but equivalent versions of the post-test. Construction of the universe of test items may also lead to modifications of the statement of terminal objectives (notice the feedback arrow in Fig. 2), particularly if ambiguities are detected. Figure 2 also shows that feedback from student performance may lead to modification of the terminal objectives. The content of the course may be too great or too small; some of the criterion performances may be too easy or too difficult.

The third component of an output specification is the performance standard. Nothing less than 100 per cent could be tolerated on the post-test of a system for training airline pilots, and the system would be evaluated on the number of students who achieved the 100 per cent performance level. But most academic courses would gladly settle for something less, though it should not be much less. The U.S. Air Force has a 90/90 criterion – i.e. 90 per cent of the students must get 90 per cent of the post-test; and many courses of this standard have been developed. A lower standard would be liable to affect the input of the subsequent course. It should be emphasized that these post-tests are not designed to be easy or difficult, nor to discriminate between students: their sole purpose is to determine whether the students have achieved all the terminal objectives. It may require considerable ingenuity to devise test items to deal with some 'higher order' objectives, particularly those concerned with creativity and problem-solving behaviour. But it is surely better to attempt the task than to avoid the problem. It is too easy to imagine that one is teaching students to be 'creative thinkers' when there is no evidence of either success or failure and no method of using feedback from student performance to improve the instruction. If these 'awkward' test items are omitted from the post-test, the objectives of the student (i.e. passing the test) will differ from those of the instructor (i.e. expecting the student to learn 'what he is taught' whether he is tested on the material or not). Many instructors who complain that their students are applying formulae without understanding them set tests which, in effect, encourage the behaviour they are trying to extinguish. Often the student has a history of passing tests through the blind application of formulae and has little conception of what the instructor means by 'understanding'.

Input specification

An input specification can serve three main purposes. These include:

(1) Preventing students who don't have the necessary prerequisites from entering the course.

(2) Preventing students who can already pass the post-test from entering the course.

(3) Directing students who have already achieved some, but not all, of the course objectives to an appropriate place in the middle of the course.

Each of these functions requires a different form of pre-test. In the ideal situation, the input can be defined in terms of the output of a previous course, but this applies only in the rare case where the previous course is a validated instructional system. But in a typical academic situation, there is considerable variation in the learners' initial knowledge. The system designer has to estimate his input and write a pre-test to measure it. Data from the pre-test then leads to a revised estimate of the input (Fig. 2) and to a revised pre-test; this procedure may have to be repeated until sufficient information has been obtained for a final decision about the prerequisites a student must have to enter the course, and a pre-test has been developed to determine which students are to be admitted. Often the prerequisites will include competence in basic mathematics or language skills as well as relevant subject-matter knowledge.

Over-all strategy

The main advantages of dividing the system into several sub-systems are as follows:

1. Development of the latter parts of the course usually requires students who can perform competently on the earlier parts of the course. These students will not normally be available unless the earlier parts of the course have already been developed to criterion effectiveness. Thus, students who have been through validated earlier sub-systems are needed for the development of later sub-systems.

2. Directing semiproficient students into the middle of a course is much easier if the course contains several sub-systems, each with its own pre-test and post-test.

3. If some very slow students do not finish the course, they can go through it again without having to enter sub-systems whose content they have already mastered.

4. Decisions about media and teaching techniques can be made at the sub-system level. This greatly increases the flexibility of the system and leads to a more efficient allocation of personnel and resources.

The contents of the Over-all Strategy box in Fig. 1 are shown in

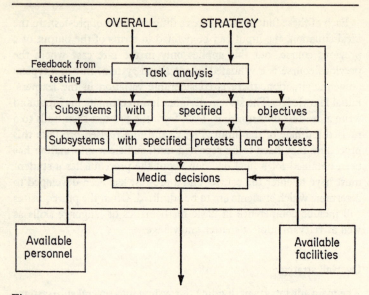

Figure 3

Fig. 3. The reader should note the feedback arrow from System Testing, which indicates that modifications of the task analysis may prove necessary.

Sub-system development

Figure 3 shows that the system designer enters the sub-system development stage with a number of sub-systems, each defined in terms of input and output with the appropriate pre-tests, post-tests and performance standards. Resources and personnel have already been allocated, and the designer is now ready to develop validated instructional sub-systems. The developmental process is summarized in Fig. 4. In the task analysis stage, the sub-system designer sequences the instructional content and chooses examples of the concepts and principles to be learned. Materials are then produced and tried out on individual students. Individual tryout usually shows up many deficiencies in the materials and in the task analysis. The revise–tryout–revise–tryout cycle may be repeated several times before proceeding to field test with a group of students under real-life conditions. If performance on the field test meets the specified criteria, our sub-system is ready for incorporation into the total system. Otherwise, further revisions are necessary until the field-test performance meets the required standard.

The only requirements for an instructional sub-system are that it can convert the given input to the required output. No assumptions are made about instructional techniques, but experience has shown that frequent active responding by the learner is essential to the

SUBSYSTEM DEVELOPMENT

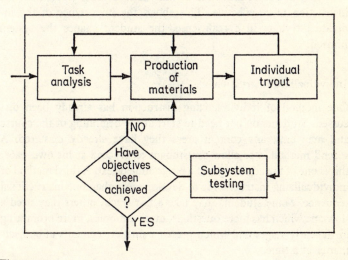

Figure 4

development of an efficient instructional system. There is considerable evidence that more learning takes place when a student is required to make a response, and system designers should proceed on the assumption that any subject-matter which the student does not immediately use in making an active response will not be effectively learned. After a student makes his response, he is usually shown the answer. In many cases, this motivates the student who realizes that he is gaining new knowledge, though often he knows that he is right and doesn't need to confirm his answer. For the same reason, it is important to keep the error rate low: students are discouraged by wrong answers, and asking them questions which they cannot answer is not an effective instructional method. A high error rate on a response is a reliable indicator of defective instruction.

Frequent student responding also provides the system designer with more comprehensive data. He may get many ideas about how and where to revise his system from analysis of the post-test data, but a continuous record of student responses during the learning process will be far more valuable in helping him to pinpoint instructional deficiencies. He can question the student about wrong responses and tutor him to determine what revision could make the instruction more effective. This shows the importance of the individual tryout; in a real sense, the student shapes the system himself.

Individualized instruction

One method of individualizing instruction has already been discussed. Students do not need to start at the beginning of the course and may omit any content areas they have already mastered. A second method is to allow the student to proceed at his own pace; this is one of the advantages of a programmed text. A third method of individualizing instruction is to develop more than one instructional sequence. Some students may take a fast track; others may need a slow one which has more questions, more examples, more prompting in the early stages and which presents smaller segments of subject-matter at a time.

However, tracking should be used only when the sub-system development has shown that it is needed. The most rational procedure is to develop a fully validated fast track using only the brightest students (perhaps the top 25 per cent) and then to adapt this track to students in the next ability range (perhaps the next 25 per cent). In places where the revised sequence is not significantly larger than the fast sequence, the former can replace the latter, but where the revised sequence is much longer, both are kept as alternative tracks. The longer sequence is then adapted to a third group of students, and a third track is added where necessary, and so on. In their final versions, some instructional systems may have as many as three tracks in places, while others need only one track throughout.

In all cases, however, the system must be developed to fit the student – and not on the basis of preconceived but unproven ideas.

FURTHER READING

H. Barrington, 'A survey of instructional television researches', *Educational Research*, **8** (1), 1965, pp. 8–25.

B. S. Bloom *et al.*, *Taxonomy of educational objectives 1: cognitive domain*, Longmans, 1956.

J. P. De Cecco (Ed.), *Educational technology*, Holt, Rinehart and Winston, 1964.

W. A. Deterline, 'Learning theory teaching, and instructional technology', *A.V. Communication Review*, **13**, 1965, pp. 405–11.

W. R. Dunn and C. Holroyd, *Aspects of educational technology 2*, Methuen, 1969.

H. C. Ellis, 'Evaluation: judging the effectiveness of programmes' in G. D. Ofiesh and W. C. Meiehenry (Eds.), *Trends in programmed instruction*, Department of Audiovisual Instruction and National Society of Programmed Instruction, 1964, pp. 207–9.

R. Glaser (Ed.), *Teaching machines and programmed learning 2: data and directions*, National Education Association, 1965.

G. L. Gropper and A. A. Lumsdaine, 'The use of student response to improve televised instruction', *Studies in televised instruction 7*, American Institute for Research in Education, June 1961.

P. I. Jacobs, H. M. Milton and L. M. Stolurow, *A guide to evaluating self-instructional programs*, Holt, Rinehart and Winston, 1966.

H. Kay, B. Dodd and M. Syme, *Programmed learning and teaching machines*, Penguin, 1967.

H. Kay, 'Programmed instruction' in E. A. Lunzer and J. F. Morris (Eds.), *Development in human learning*, Staples, 1968, pp. 386–411.

P. C. Lange (Ed.), *Programmed instruction*, The Sixty-sixth yearbook of the National Society for the study of education, Part 2, N.S.S.E., Chicago, 1967.

G. O. M. Leith, E. A. Peel and W. Curr, *A handbook of programmed learning*, University of Birmingham, 1964.

N. Mackenzie, M. R. Eraut and H. C. Jones, *Teaching and learning:*

an introduction to new methods and resources in higher education, UNESCO and I.A.U., 1970.

R. Maclean, *Television in education*, Methuen, 1968.

R. F. Mager and C. Clark, 'Explorations in student controlled instruction' in G. D. Ofiesh and W. C. Meiehenry (Eds.), *Trends in programmed instruction*, Department of Audiovisual Instruction and National Society for Programmed Learning, U.S.A., 1964, pp. 235–8.

R. F. Mager, *Preparing objectives for programmed instruction*, Fearon, 1962.

S. M. Markle, *Good frames and bad*, John Wiley, 1964.

G. Mialaret, *Psychology of the use of A/V aids in primary education*, Harrap/UNESCO, 1966.

A. Oettinger and S. Marks, 'Educational technology: new myths and old realities', *Harvard Educational Review*, **38** (4), 1968.

S. L. Pressey, 'A puncture of the huge "programming" boom?', *Teachers College Record*, **65** (5), 1964, pp. 413–18.

W. Schramm, P. H. Coombs, F. Kahnert and J. Lyle, *The new media: memo to educational planners*, UNESCO, 1967.

W. Schramm, *The research on programmed instruction*, U.S. Department of Health, Education and Welfare, 1964.

H. Schueler and G. S. Lesser, *Teacher education and the new media*, Washington American Association of Colleges for Teacher Education, 1967.

B. F. Skinner, *The technology of teaching*, Appleton-Century-Crofts, 1968.

B. F. Skinner, 'Teaching machines', *Scientific American*, November 1961, Offprint no. 461.

P. Suppes, 'Computers in education', *Scientific American*, **215** (3), 1966, pp. 207–20.

M. J. Tobin, *Problems and methods of programmed learning*, National Centre for Programmed Learning, School of Education, University of Birmingham, 1968.

Failure in learning

The problem of children who fail to learn adequately is one of the most difficult which teachers have to face. Often they are ill equipped by training to cope with the problem. All too often these children get much less attention than the more successful ones, whereas they really need more. The papers which follow should give an insight into the nature of the problem and methods for coping with it.

This section consists of one fairly lengthy paper by Cashdan which gives a comprehensive survey of the main questions in this field, and shorter papers by Wedell, Graham, and Rosenthal and Jacobson which deal with specific aspects. Wedell in dealing with perceptual motor difficulties analyses the interrelated factors which cause learning problems. Graham discusses aspects relating to language deficit. Rosenthal and Jacobson report on work which investigates the effect on children's learning of the teacher's expectancy.

Although these papers are specifically concerned with backwardness they all have great relevance for the teacher working with 'normal' children.

1 Handicaps in learning*

A. CASHDAN

This paper gives a comprehensive survey of the field of learning handicap. It deals with specific and general disabilities, with causative factors and with the application of research findings in practice. A very important suggestion is that children with learning difficulties have much greater potential than has usually been expected of them.

I. SOME GENERAL CONSIDERATIONS

Success and failure in learning are relative things. In a professional family a child who does not secure a university place may be regarded as dull; in another milieu the adolescent who can stumble haltingly through the sports page of the newspaper may be considered the bright one. Furthermore, terms such as dull, backward, subnormal, retarded – all frequently used in this field – have none of them a precise scientific meaning. In any particular study or discussion where precision is needed the terms have to be defined anew. For their meanings are affected not just by dictionary definition, but also by the population being studied, the point in time and the skill under consideration.

A child whose arithmetic is below average today might, ten years ago and with the same attainments, have compared favourably with his peers if, for example, standards have since risen. However, by today's standards, the child is backward. This is a descriptive statement, telling us that his attainments are below those of (say) half the population of children of his age. It should not be confused with a prescription – that is, with the decision as to how advanced in arithmetic children of that age *should* be. Looked at in wider perspective, standards in arithmetic might turn out to be anything from unnecessarily high to very low. So that by a more objective evaluation the 'backward' child we have been considering might be doing very poorly or quite well.

* Reprinted and abridged from A. Cashdan, 'Handicaps in Learning', in J. F. Morris and E. A. Lunzer, *Development in Learning: Contexts of Education*, Staples Press, 1969, pp. 165–94.

What constitutes a learning handicap is thus seen to be a question of social demands, both in the sense just discussed and in a further one also. Different skills acquire different valuations. Thus, in our society, literacy is highly prized but musical attainments, though approved of, are not considered essential. An educated man can cheerfully confess to an inability to sing in tune or play a musical instrument; if he could not read, his claim to be educated would be derided. So teachers make tremendous efforts to get children reading, but are relatively casual about musical performance. By the objective standard of what could be achieved given equal amounts of educational attention, the population as a whole is probably underfunctioning musically and overfunctioning in terms of literacy.

If a child has an intellectual handicap there are three aspects which need clarification: the severity of the handicap, how general it is and what progress or improvement is likely or possible. Progress and improvement will be dealt with at the end of this paper; for the present it is enough to point out that almost all children, however handicapped, make intellectual progress, though often not enough to change their standing relative to other children.

The severity of the handicap is normally defined by the use of standardized tests and the application of reasonable, albeit arbitrary, conventions. Thus at the junior-school age a child is considered backward if his attainments are below the average for children a year younger – say, a gap between chronological age and attainments of approaching two years. However, a gap of two years is obviously of lesser significance for older children (at age 6 a two-year gap produces a quotient of 67, whereas at age 15 this would be 87). So a better convention is probably that of standard score. Using this, one might call attainments one standard deviation below the mean (usually a quotient of 85) mild handicap, and those two deviations below average (70 or less) more serious.

The generality of the handicap may be estimated by comparing the child's performance at different skills, say reading and mathematics. More frequently, a poor showing on an intelligence test is held to indicate general limitation even if the child's scholastic showing is average at some skills. Estimates of general intelligence do, of course, show high correlation with school attainment, but there are some pitfalls in using the I.Q. as a sole, or even main, index of handicap.

Children who over-function in relation to their I.Q. may often be interesting problems but it would be slightly odd to describe them as cases of learning handicap.

However, the obverse – the child of average or superior intelligence who is under-functioning – frequently leads to muddled thinking. It does not follow that because a child's mental age is higher than, say, his reading age, he ought to be reading better. To claim this is to deny that abilities at particular skills depend on anything but a single general factor rather than on both general and specific ones. Or, to put the point in another way, one must beware of overrating the predictive powers of the intelligence test. Usually, the intelligence test is little more than a disguised set of tests of attainment so designed as to be rather less dependent on specific training than are ordinary attainment tests. Recently, this concept of retardation (M.A. higher than Attainment Age) has been further questioned in a factorial study by Curr and Hallworth. They found that although social variables such as adjustment, home background, delinquency, showed definite loadings on a backwardness factor (low I.Q.), this was not true for retardation: retardation is thus a statistical concept which has yet to prove its meaningfulness.

So far no mention has been made of emotional and motivational factors in learning. Much learning failure or difficulty is undoubtedly due to faulty attitudes and poor (or even negative) training. However, there seems little advantage in treating emotional and intellectual difficulties in learning in separate compartments. The implication is usually that intellectual difficulties are permanent and irremediable, whereas emotional blocks can be cleared up by suitable social, educational or medical treatment. Behind this lies the further assumption that intellectual powers are pure and 'given' but that everything else is acquired. But in practice emotional difficulties rarely melt away at speed and intellectual weaknesses can nearly always be at least partly reduced.

To conclude this section, one might suggest that a child has a learning handicap worthy of further investigation if at some socially valued skill he performs at a level below that of three-quarters or more of children of his age. This corresponds roughly to a quotient of 85. But there is great variability in normal development, a steady progress curve being probably the exception rather than the rule; so that one need not suspect any long-term difficulty if the child performs at a low level for a short period. But when the difficulty, general or specific, persists and the child falls back to a level two deviations below the mean (70 or less) one thinks in terms of serious handicap.

II. CAUSAL FACTORS IN LEARNING HANDICAP

1. Heredity and environment

It has been customary to divide the causes of handicap, particularly subnormality, into two groups, a variety of typologies being suggested. These include 'endogenous' and 'exogenous', 'pathological' and 'sub-cultural' and so on. Nowadays, most psychologists would probably prefer a threefold classification: inherited, due to physical pathology, and socially determined. But attempts, either in general theorizing or in particular cases, to apportion these causes can lead to arguments which are unfruitful and often irrelevant. To develop Hebb's point of view, we might say that practically no one has perfect hereditary endowment and no one at all receives absolutely ideal environmental support and stimulation. As many studies have shown, subnormal children are particularly likely to suffer adverse environmental conditions whether as primary or secondary factors in their condition. Certainly, recent thought favours an environmentalist approach, so that one is nowadays inclined to look at a child's social history at least as carefully as at hereditary factors. Among the severely subnormal, physical pathology can at times be demonstrated, though surprisingly often nothing obvious is found. Among the more mildly subnormal the position is quite different. In an interesting study, Stein and Susser found that among those E.S.N. children who showed physical abnormalities all social classes were represented, but of those who were 'clinically normal' none came from outside the 'demotic subculture'. Thus they see mental retardation in the clinically normal as a social phenomenon.

2. Pathological causes – minimal brain damage

This paper is not the proper place for a full discussion of the whole problem of brain damage, but it is important to note that alongside the generally increasing emphasis on cultural factors new information has also come to light on the pathological side. Essentially this consists of studies of children who are very nearly normal clinically but who nevertheless have suffered minor brain-damage either before or during the birth process. This, it is suggested, reveals itself only in very careful examination (if at all: the diagnosis may be largely presumptive). But children who have suffered in this way may exhibit long-lasting, if not permanent, learning disabilities and/or behavioural disturbances. Thus Stott, in a study embracing nearly two hundred subnormal and retarded children, found a significant correlation, which could not be explained in any other way, between maternal illness and stress during pregnancy and a passive, withdrawn, unsuccessful personality in the child, which he labels 'unforthcomingness'.

3. Early relationships

The importance of early relationships for healthy intellectual and emotional development no longer needs stressing. It is now well established, both through studies of animals and work with human infants, that where primary socialization is very delayed or inadequate, development can be difficult or stunted, though the effects are not necessarily completely irreversible, as was at first thought. Clearly, adequate earlier relationships form a substratum of confidence which makes it possible for the child to develop intellectually as well as emotionally. Without this, he is quite likely to have emotional and possibly also intellectual difficulties. In case of severe subnormality where laborious distinctions between mental illness and mental deficiency are apt to break down, it can be difficult to put much meaning into discussions of differential diagnosis. If the child makes no or very distorted relationships and at the same time shows little capacity for learning, either factor might be the primary one, though the conventional diagnosis is still likely to be subnormality. The recent growth of interest in autistic symptoms has somewhat blurred this picture, but Russell Davis has argued for some time that even without the presence of 'psychotic' symptoms, subnormality may often be the end product of a 'burnt-out' psychosis – the child having come through an early period of unbearable stress.

4. Stimulation and affection

As we have just noted, the child's early relationships with other adults, particularly the mother, set the tone for his whole emotional, and hence also intellectual, development. Hence the concentration on investigating the continuity and quality of the early mother–child relationship. This is often best approached indirectly by studying the mother's attitude to her child. But another major dimension of the mother–child relationship is what the mother actually does (or fails to do) with the child and the experiences, cognitive as well as emotional, with which she presents him. In a study of normal children in the first year of life Blank found stronger relationships between stimulation variables and development than between affectional measures and development. Whatever the reason for the subnormality, it seems likely that mothers of subnormal children may not provide enough or appropriate experiences for their children. This may be because of feelings of guilt or rejection, through a desire to protect the damaged infant from further strain, or through an inadequate appreciation of the child's special needs. It may also be through the sheer overwork and practical difficulties caused by having a handicapped child in the family.

5. Language and development

As ours is essentially a linguistic culture – as any advanced culture is bound to be – poor language development and control is likely to be both a cause and a sign of intellectual failure, whether mild or severe. Language training begins immediately after birth. By the time a child is ready for school the pattern of his development may be largely set. So the language training the child receives from those about him at home – again mainly the mother – is crucial. The mother is not responsible only for the child's diction, accent and vocabulary. She also teaches him (as she does in emotional relationships) what to expect of linguistic communication.

Bernstein suggests that in working-class subcultures language is frequently restricted to crude and essentially general uses. It is not used, as in the dominant culture, as a means of expressing and in fact creating fine shades of meaning, conceptual thinking and awareness of one's own status and feelings. Thus many children may come from a background which has doubly impoverished them. They may lack vocabulary, complex language structures and skill in using language; in addition, they may not expect to acquire sophisticated language skills, for they have not been trained to perceive them. As education at school becomes progressively more demanding linguistically, children from these subcultures may fall farther and farther behind. As many recent surveys have shown, the educational system progressively discriminates against the working-class child; this may not be just for reasons of social prejudice, but also because as he grows older he is increasingly less capable of meeting the educational demands made of him.

III. SPECIFIC DISABILITIES

Parents (and teachers) frequently describe children's difficulties in terms of difficulty or failure in one area only. The child is generally bright, and average at arithmetic, but is doing very poorly at reading. Such cases certainly exist, but they are much less common than first reports would indicate. More typically, the child turns out to be of below average intelligence and poor attainments generally. Frequently also, he is suffering from emotional problems and it can be very difficult to determine whether these have caused, or are consequent upon, the learning difficulty. In this section we shall look first at reading difficulties in general, then at the problem of highly specific reading disability; this will be followed by a brief examination of difficulties in arithmetic and other learning areas.

1. Backwardness in reading

Among the many cases of reading difficulty the most frequently quoted is low intelligence. However, the ascription of reading failure to low intelligence is less informative than it might seem. Children of low intelligence do mostly make poor progress at reading, but the link between the two may be as much associative as causal and one wants to examine the root causes of both. In older children, of course, it may be the poorness in reading which depresses the intelligence test score.

While it may never be possible entirely to separate acquired from congenital factors, one can nevertheless distinguish two rough aetiological groups. First, there are congenital and physical causes. Poor readers are likely to be less mature mentally than good readers. They will have poorer memories, retarded language development and weaker conceptual powers; though these may not be purely inherited or even congenital, they may be determined early in life. Poor readers are more likely also to have visual and auditory defects.

As Vernon suggests, very few children lack the visual perceptive powers needed for learning to read; these may in fact be present in many children by 2 years of age. Nor do many more lack the requisite auditory powers although the complex skills needed in the phonic analysis of words may be beyond many 7-year-olds – as Bruce has shown – at any rate without specific coaching. Naturally, the understanding of reading difficulties is linked with the proper analysis of reading skill – a task barely begun.

Untypical laterality patterns (left or mixed dominance) have often been blamed for reading difficulties, sometimes on rather slender evidence. Belmont and Birch recently found no association between left dominance or cross-laterality and reading difficulty, but they did find that poor readers showed greater confusion in right–left orientation (awareness of right and left on one's own body and on others). Similarly, in a recent survey of over 1,200 retarded readers by Cashdan, Pumfrey and Lunzer, no over-representation was found of children with mixed or left dominance; nor did these groups show either greater retardation or poorer response to remedial treatment. As Belmont and Birch point out, the difference between these and the earlier studies lies probably in the fact that the earlier studies used small, highly selected, clinical groups, whereas both their study and the Manchester survey are in effect population studies.

A second group of factors are social and educational. Many children do poorly at reading because they have been unlucky in their educational experiences. They may have missed school, had too many changes of teacher or been badly taught. Their difficulties are often increased by their being given worse educational facilities rather than specially favourable treatment. It has also been suggested that children who miss learning to read at the appropriate age may have greater difficulty in doing so later. But such difficulty may be less related to inherent difficulties (or critical learning periods) than to rigid and inflexible classroom procedures where children who miss an important process are not afterwards given a chance to learn it thoroughly.

But perhaps the most important in this group of factors is the social background of the child. Many children come to school with attitudes which are at best indifferent to school attainment and at worst positively hostile. The child has not had the background experiences which are prerequisites of learning to read, he has no proper expectation of what will happen at school and he sees no particular advantages to himself in making educational progress. If the teacher lays appropriate foundations for learning and supplies both the intellectual and motivational background that has not been given at home, the child may make good progress. If these are not supplied he is very likely to become retarded. Thus the home background and the school provision may be seen to be mutually interdependent.

The normal provision for helping retarded children is to set up small remedial classes or groups with anything from one to half a dozen or so children, each group being taught once or twice a week by a specialist remedial teacher who may have a special qualification for such work. Typically, the children make fairly good progress at first, perhaps improving their reading age by two years in a year of coaching. Early reports showed this with some satisfaction. However, since 1961 when Collins published the results of a careful study in this field, later followed by similar findings by Lovell, it became clear that much of this earlier optimism was not justified. Ignoring those studies whose methodology failed to stand up to Collins' scrutiny, the general consensus may be expressed as follows: the treated children make good initial progress but this improvement is not sustained. Moreover, control groups of untreated children recover spontaneously (though a little more slowly), so that they eventually attain similar levels to the treated children. It seems that the remedial teaching has little long-term effect on the children.

Three things seem to be necessary for successful remedial work: the children should be brought to an appropriate frame of mind emotionally; linguistic and perceptual skills should be strengthened where necessary; and appropriate systematic teaching should be given. Unfortunately, many remedial teachers seem to focus (often unwittingly) on one or two of these aspects to the detriment of the third. Some concentrate on building up appropriate attitudes and motivation without ever teaching systematically; others provide excellent formal teaching without really reaching the children. When more appropriate material has been designed, programmed instruction may be of particular value in remedial teaching; with taped material, auditory as well as visual skills can be built up. But here, too, teacher control will be very important, so as to allow for the child's background and current reactions.

Even when teaching satisfies all the above criteria, it is still not surprising that progress is not better sustained. The remedial teaching is often poorly integrated with the child's regular classroom experiences, and it is very rare for any attempt to be made to modify parental and home attitudes. Furthermore, the remedial teaching, owing to pressures on the service, is often discontinued before the child's reading skill is really firmly established. If all these factors could be adequately dealt with, remedial teaching would probably be much more successful than at present; but the cost of the service might then be so uneconomical that one would do much better by strengthening general classroom facilities and paying more attention to reading difficulties in the preparation of the ordinary class teacher.

2. Other difficulties

Difficulties in writing and spelling tend to be considered with reading problems, though it is not uncommon for a child who is a competent reader to spell badly or to show extreme clumsiness in his attempts to write and draw. In some cases these problems may be associated with emotional upset or hostility to school work, but commonly there may be minor perceptual difficulties, often allied with undiagnosed sensory loss (such as high frequency deafness). The child may also have developed bad habits, as perhaps in the case of children taught exclusively by look-and-say methods who have never appreciated the relationship of heard sounds to printed symbols.

Poor progress at arithmetic is particularly thought to be due to emotional factors. Sometimes, however, there is confusion between the acquisition and the practice of skills. Emotional difficulties may interfere more in a subject like arithmetic where the child is constantly being asked to learn new structures and processes, whereas once he can read he is, in most arts subjects, being asked to exercise an already learned skill. Failure in other school subjects has received relatively little attention, partly because the child who has successfully learned to read is not likely to show obvious and alarming retardation in other subjects, and if he does, social explanations are likely to be looked for (e.g. reaction to the teacher, father's hostility to the subject etc.); partly also for the reason given at the beginning of the chapter that much the strongest social pressures are for the acquisition of basic skill at reading and mathematics.

In all these specific disabilities boys are more strongly represented than girls, often in a ratio of two or three to one. At first sight this might appear to support a social hypothesis – the boy's characteristic response to stress is aggression, negativism and refusal, whereas girls are more docile and when under pressure react in other ways than by school failure. Such differences must be due in good part to differences in social training; at the same time it is equally well established that boys are far more susceptible than girls, especially early in life (right from the perinatal period), to illness and traumata. So that, on an organic hypothesis also, far more boys than girls would have suffered minor brain damage and might therefore have impaired learning abilities.

IV. GENERAL DISABILITY

1. Studies of learning in the subnormal

The last twenty years have seen an increasing volume of empirical studies of language development, learning, transfer and problem-solving in the subnormal, much of it carried out in this country as well as in the United States and the Soviet Union. Good reviews may be found in the works of O'Connor and Hermelin, and Clarke and Clarke.

Luria has stressed the subnormal child's difficulties in developing the regulative functions of language. Such children have much more difficulty than normal children in learning to use verbal signals to inhibit behaviour. In the classic experiment a child has to squeeze a rubber bulb when a red light is shown but remain still if the light is green. Normal children find it easier to inhibit the action if they say 'No!' aloud, but the subnormal have great difficulty in managing this.

O'Connor and Hermelin have extended this work and Bryant has carried out a series of interesting experiments. In summary, these workers find that subnormals can be helped by verbal instruction but that general instructions may not be much help and seem in any case to be quickly forgotten. Specific verbal instruction carefully adjusted to the needs of the situation does, however, help considerably; although, as Hurtig has demonstrated, the effect of the help may be to raise the level of performance in the particular setting, rather than to increase the child's general potential. O'Connor and Hermelin have also shown that subnormals' learning is often not mediated by implicit verbal structures. This makes their learning less stable and, paradoxically, in one experiment led to their being able to 'reverse' a response more readily than could normal children who had learned the initial response-set more thoroughly. As Bryant puts it, subnormal children 'are relatively incapable of abstracting general rules from learning specific instances'. They learn what is given but do not go beyond it. If, however, the original situation is such that the subnormal child's attention is inevitably drawn to general features of a display, Bryant showed that the learning can be more general.

In a review of learning studies Denny argues for a general defect of inhibition in the subnormal which results in particular difficulty in discrimination learning. House and Zeaman are more inclined to attribute these difficulties to an attention defect. The position is summarized in a recent short discussion by O'Connor in which he stresses that a variety of different types of study nearly all point to an 'input-deficiency'. This idea is linked with work which suggests that in the subnormal short-term memory traces decay quickly and that the consolidation of new learning by its transfer to the long-term memory store is thus particularly difficult.

Studies of vocabulary and language in the subnormal tend to confirm O'Connor and Hermelin's view that subnormal children have normal (if retarded) language structure and semantic skills, but that they are less likely to make spontaneous use of the language skills they actually possess – thus slowing up progress still further. This may reflect not just inherent defects but also the constricting effect of the unstimulating environments in which many such children are brought up, both in and out of institutions.

Birch and Lefford have suggested that intersensory skills – the ability to translate signals from one sensory (or motor) channel to another, say, in recognizing an auditory stimulus in visual form ('house' and a picture of a house) – represent a particularly advanced and uniquely human achievement. Failure or weakness in this area may be associated with brain damage, specific disabilities in learning or with subnormality. O'Connor and Hermelin have investigated these skills (which they term cross-modal coding) in the subnormal and find that where subjects are forced to code cross-modally they perform better than in like-modal situations; the forced coding may act as an extra pressure on the subject to attend and inhibit automatic, stereotyped response-tendencies.

On a more optimistic note, attention is drawn to the series of experiments on transfer reported by Clarke and Clarke, and Clarke and Cooper. They have been concerned to show that the ability to transfer learning both within a class, as in Harlow's work on learning sets, and between different classes also, is a major factor in human development. Their research findings indicate that subnormals possess good transfer abilities and that with suitable training they may use these to make unexpected progress. One point these workers make is that transfer is more likely if practice situations are complex and that simple practice may be worse than none at all. When these findings can be successfully applied to the education of the subnormal they may have far-reaching results; in this connection programmed instruction techniques may prove particularly valuable.

In general, one may say that the subnormal child's main weaknesses are in attention, set and cue-selection – in other words the subnormal child is poor at 'getting the hang of' what is wanted of him, and his input deficiency makes this initial stage in new learning particularly difficult to surmount. In addition, his lack of spontaneity, particularly marked in poor language use and representational thinking, means that he does very little to explore or make links himself. New knowledge has to be brought to him and the situation specially structured. But if this is done successfully the child can learn relatively well and retains his knowledge.

On the other hand subnormal children have been found to possess virtually all the skills and abilities enjoyed by non-handicapped children. Nor is there much evidence that their intellectual development proceeds along radically different or distorted lines in comparison with that of the normal. In fact, studies based on Piaget's analysis of child development show even very subnormal children progressing through the same stages and in the same order as he has set out in studying normal children, though they sometimes seem to cease developing at quite early stages. Thus the Piagetian studies provide better evidence of an 'arrest' in development than do traditional intelligence tests.

In conclusion, it should be emphasized that nearly the whole of the experimental work described in this section has been carried out on severely subnormal subjects (with I.Q.s usually below 55), often in institutions. It is tempting to expect that the strengths and weaknesses so far discovered may be paralleled in the less severely subnormal children in E.S.N. schools and classes, but on a smaller scale. On the other hand, it may be that the profile which is beginning to emerge in these studies is essentially that of the pathologically damaged child (for whom the Russians use the term oligophrenic) and the 'sub-cultural' cases may have a different pattern of function. Much more investigation is needed.

2. Psychotic and autistic children

At the beginning of this paper it was pointed out that emotional disturbance might well be highly relevant to intellectual dysfunction. In fact, as we have just seen, many of the difficulties of the severely subnormal could well be interpreted as at least partly due to poor motivation and an unwillingness to learn from others, amounting often to an avoidance of the whole social situation. Children who are severely mentally disturbed may exhibit some of these characteristics in a very extreme form. They show no affective contact with human beings, often appear deaf, are completely withdrawn and may exhibit other bizarre symptoms. Such children are sometimes referred to as schizophrenic or more frequently nowadays as cases of infantile or childhood autism. There is, however, considerable uncertainty as to the definition and aetiology of this condition. Creak was chairman of a working party which attempted to clarify the position by proposing a nine-point diagnostic list and suggesting that a child should exhibit most of these symptoms to be classified as a case of autism.

In terms of test performance autistic children are nearly always in the severely subnormal category, but they show signs, in the opinion of many clinicians, of 'islets' of normal or superior ability, suggesting that were the 'disease' cured, they would prove of at least normal intelligence. Attempted treatments have ranged in the educational field from the extremes of psychoanalytically derived therapeutic approaches to behaviouristically rooted conditioning methods. Improvement is usually slow and incomplete, though a few children make fairly good recoveries; these are usually the ones who have some speech, perhaps established in early life before the onset of the condition. Although small intensive studies provide useful insights, systematic surveys are badly needed. Without them we can only agree with Tizard that the widely differing prognoses in these children may reflect the fact that we are dealing under one title with a number of different diseases, some perhaps organic in origin, others due to pathogenic social experiences.

V. EDUCATIONAL TREATMENT

1. The application of research findings

The immediate application of any new research finding in classroom practice is fraught with dangers. For one thing, the new idea may soon be contradicted, or at least modified, by later research. Again a general finding may not be easy to apply to individual children, or may have much less generality than the teacher expects. Half-understood ideas also may do more damage than good. There is too the backwash danger – if the psychologist feels called upon to produce practical classroom ideas he may sacrifice basic long-term research in favour of hasty and meretricious analyses.

Nevertheless, there is by now a body of knowledge, particularly in dealing with the severely subnormal and with brain-damaged children, which is still only being applied in a small minority of schools and centres. In the case of the severely subnormal this is in part due to the lack of well trained personnel, but even in the E.S.N.

schools there is far too little experimental work. Books like Kephart's[1] are full of interesting suggestions, as for instance on the strengthening and development of basic motor skills. Even if some of these fail to justify themselves entirely they are still worth trying. Particularly useful might be a demonstration school or schools associated with a university department or research unit.

One general lesson may be drawn from research work, particularly from that done by the Clarkes and by O'Connor and Tizard. All their work shows that handicapped children can achieve more than has frequently been expected of them. The attempt to teach a discrimination or a skill is often abandoned after a few unsuccessful trials; but if a far greater number of attempts are made there can be surprising success. This is not to suggest, however, that poor learners should be given long periods of repeating impossible tasks, nor that their attitudes should be ignored. The much repeated idea that subnormal people positively like monotonous, repetitive work would probably soon be discarded if they were brought up from the beginning in a more permissive, creative and unregimented atmosphere. Such myths can so easily be self-perpetuating; for children tend to live up to what is expected of them.

2. Segregation and integration

Much thought has been given both in this country and elsewhere to the question of educational provision for children with learning handicaps. Schonell et al. have collected a number of descriptions and opinions on current practice in many countries. On the question of whether handicapped children should be integrated with their normal school-fellows or segregated in special schools, no clear-cut decision is possible. Some children need the protection of the special milieu and regime while many others would benefit from closer contact with normal children. The problems of rejection and of stigma are also rarely completely solved. The solution, as Tansley and Gulliford say, must lie in a whole range of different types of provision; but, whatever the setting, some children will need individually designed programmes coupled with individual and small group work. If the child is given the right kind of work in an atmosphere

[1] See Further Reading.

of acceptance, his need for individual attention will progressively lessen. But there is no doubt that the specialist teacher of handicapped children needs to be particularly strong at diagnostic work and to be provided with help from psychologists and medical personnel. The most common error is not to take the unsuccessful child sufficiently far back, and thus to restart with remedial work at a point where the child will still fail. Before progress can be made, fundamental skills and attitudes have to be securely established. In this context the Brooklands experiment in this country and Kirk's work in the United States on early education both demonstrate amply the gains that can be made if this lesson is properly applied.

2 Perceptual-motor difficulties*

K. WEDELL

In this paper the author considers some of the most important factors that contribute to learning failure. He analyses the component skills in learning tasks and explains their interrelationships. The discussions of the possibilities of compensation for physical impairment is of interest and importance to any teacher, especially the need for early diagnosis.

Teachers are often puzzled that certain children, who are obviously in some ways able, none the less inexplicably fail in one or other aspect of school work. A child may speak fluently on a topic but be quite unable to put his ideas down on paper. Another writes fluently but builds his words up with plausible but wrong phonic spellings. Yet another can read without difficulty but can barely form his letters in writing.

These and similar types of discrepant performance are familiar to most teachers who may ask, 'If he can do one thing why can't he do

* Reprinted and abridged from K. Wedell, 'Perceptual-Motor Difficulties', *Special Education*, 57 (4), December 1968.

the other?' These children's learning difficulties can often not be explained by absences from school, by 'emotional blocks' about particular subjects or even by poor teaching in the past, and so these discrepant performance levels seem to present a paradox.

Yet it is a paradox only if one assumes that children's abilities are *necessarily* all developed to the same level. Research on children with learning difficulty has increasingly shown that such an assumption cannot be made and that some of them have failed to develop some of the basic perceptual and cognitive skills on which learning, and particularly school learning, depends. These skills are usually referred to as 'readiness' skills and it appears that they can be selectively impaired. Because of this it is not surprising that a child may perform better at tasks of one kind than of another, since each may be associated with a different underlying skill or function. Language and perceptual-motor functions constitute two of the main groups of functions which have been found to be selectively impaired. This article is specifically concerned with types of perceptual-motor impairment and their consequences.

Perceptual-motor functions – a description

Perceptual-motor functions have usually been regarded as those which enable us to discriminate incoming information from our senses and which mediate in the organization of movement. Pattern discrimination and pattern copying are examples of tasks which depend on perceptual-motor skills, as are also the 'non-verbal' aspects of reading, writing and number work. 'Perceptual-motor' is only one of a number of terms which have been used to refer to the functions involved in these tasks and the variation in shades of meaning of each term reflects the variety of functions included under this heading.

Rather than attempting yet another definition it may be more helpful initially to list some of the component functions which appear to be involved in perceptual-motor performance. Consideration will then turn to the types of impairment which may be found. From this it will be apparent that, even within the area of perceptual-motor performance, discrepancies of achievement are found which can be attributed to a specific impairment of one or more of the component functions.

Table 1 lists the main functions involved in the performance of perceptual-motor tasks. We are concerned here only with the most specifically relevant functions. Personality and motivation, for example, are not included in the list. Although they undoubtedly affect perceptual-motor activity their influence is, of course, not specific to it.

Table 1. Some component functions of perceptual-motor performance

(1) Sensory systems   (2) Motor systems

         (3) Sensory-motor feedback

(4) Organization of sensation   (5) Organization of
     (Perception)   movement

         (6) Inter-sensory association

         (7) Attention

         (8) Concept formation

         (9) Memory and imagery

         (10) Awareness of body coordinates

Some components of perceptual-motor performance

Let us go through the list of component functions as they might be relevant, for instance, to the copying of a pattern. Clearly the child has to be able to see the pattern in order to be able to copy it. In other words, the sensory system (1) must be adequate. The sensory input from the receptors (ears, eyes etc.) then has to be 'organized'. The organization of sensation (perception) (4) may involve the 'grouping' of sensations occurring simultaneously or in sequence. Much of visual perception can be said to occur simultaneously. For example, almost any of the words on this page can be perceived at one glance. On the other hand, if the words were spoken, the perception of them would involve the 'grouping' of a succession of sounds.

Perception can be seen as involving both 'closure' and 'analysis'. 'Closure', for example, would refer to a child's seeing a group of letters as a word. The ease with which a child can do this is related, among other considerations, to the relative size of the gaps between letters and words (a fact of which some publishers of children's books do not seem to be aware). 'Analysis', on the other hand, refers to the ability to reorganize the grouping as, for instance, when the word 'an' and 'other' are identified in the word 'another'.

Often two or more types of sensation have to be organized at the same time (6), as when a child hears and sees a word being read.

The way in which sensations are organized is not yet fully understood but it is determined by a wide variety of functions. Four of these have been mentioned in Table 1. A child's conceptual framework (8) has an important effect on his perception. Luria (1961), for instance, has shown in a variety of experiments that young children's visual discrimination may be improved if they name what they have to discriminate. Memory and imagery (9) also influence the way sensations become organized. Span of attention (7) is particularly crucial to perception in children since it determines both the range and variety of sensations which a child can 'organize' and also the duration for which he can do this. Attention is itself affected by the child's conceptual structure. Any teacher knows that children attend better if they can understand.

So far we have considered the component functions involved in the way our sensations are organized and clearly, before a child can copy a pattern, he has to be able to perceive it. But the functions remaining on the list are also involved. Just as sense receptors (eyes, ears etc.) have to be intact so must the child have adequately functioning muscles (2) to carry out the movements involved in copying the pattern. However, he also has to be able to organize his movements (5).

The American psychologist Kephart distinguishes two levels of motor organization. The first level refers to the basic forms of motor coordination such as those involved in walking, running and grasping. These and others are the basic motor skills which an individual has to organize at a second and higher level in order to achieve a purposive action as, for example, the copying of a square or the writing of a letter or a word. Figure 1 shows attempts by two children, both aged 6, to trace a pattern and to copy it freehand and also to copy a sentence. The difference between the first child's achievements in the tracing and in the other two tasks illustrates the distinction between Kephart's two levels of motor organization.

This organization of movement usually involves the judgement of direction. It is generally assumed that an awareness of the coordinates of one's own body (10), front and back, up and down, left and right, forms the basis for such a judgement.

Sensory-motor feedback (3) remains to be mentioned. This refers to the way in which sensations resulting from our actions are used to control further actions. Our speech, for example, is very closely controlled by what we hear ourselves say. This has been demonstrated in experiments in which a slight delay has been introduced into people's hearing of what they themselves say and this has caused their speech to break down seriously. This and analogous types of

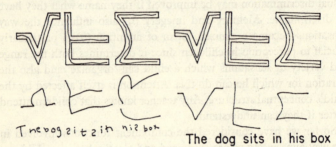

The dog sits in his box

Figure 1

feedback activity presumably occur between all the component functions all the time, and this can often be seen in action when a child makes mistakes and corrects them while copying a pattern.

The list of functions in Table 1 is largely based on conjecture. Knowledge of the relevant component functions is still slight. They have been presented in the form of a list rather than in the form of a diagram, since insufficient is known about how they interact and, indeed, about how they should be subdivided. It is certain, however, that the distinction between sensory and motor functions can only be made at a theoretical level, since in any one activity they are likely to be inextricably associated.

The consequences of impairment

What happens now if one or more of these functions are impaired? It is evident that some functions, if they are impaired, will preclude the normal functioning of others. If a child is blind he will not be able to develop visual perception. On the other hand, the sighted child may have difficulty in perceiving. Again, a child who cannot copy a pattern may at the same time show that his visual perception is unimpaired, by matching the pattern correctly. In other words, the interaction of the component functions at any one time can be seen as a kind of causal chain where impairment of the functions earlier in the chain affects functioning of later ones, but where the reverse does not always occur.

This statement is, however, only partly true. Impairment of any function will obviously affect 'feedback' processes. This is particularly true if impairment is seen in a developmental context. On the one hand, impairment of any function is likely to result in reduced or distorted experience which, in turn, will affect whether other functions develop adequately. The child who is poor at writing will not be able to strengthen his visual memory of words. On the other hand, a child will try to compensate for his impairment. For example, a child whose visual discrimination of words is poor will often try to read very quickly. By this means he can take in more words and so use a wider context from which to derive the meaning of a passage and to guess at the words he doesn't know.

Impairment of any one function has to be seen in the context of the other functions associated with it, both those which are impaired and those which are not. Those which are unimpaired will constitute the means by which an individual will attempt to compensate for his difficulties. Furthermore, impairment rarely precludes totally the operation of a function. A child who has difficulty in copying a diamond may manage to copy a simpler pattern such as a square. In addition, most follow up studies show that over a period of time children show improvement even in their impaired functions.

In the following section on the types of impairment and their consequences the above qualifications must be borne in mind. Impairment of a function is always relative. This fact has made any attempt at stating the incidence of perceptual impairment very difficult. Brenner, using criteria based on the extent to which performance on perceptual-motor tests was below performance on verbal tests, found an incidence of 6·7 per cent among 8-year-old Cambridge school children. This implies that in any class of forty children of this age range there may be about two who show some degree of specific perceptual-motor impairment.

Space does not permit full discussion of the consequences of impairment in each of the functions listed. Perception and motor organization are the main concern of this article and will therefore be dealt with in detail. Of the remaining functions mentioned, sensory and motor systems, attention and concept formation have been singled out for discussion, since defects in these have often been confused with perceptual-motor impairment. They will therefore be discussed first.

Sensory defects

It is surprising to find how well children with lesser degrees of sensory handicap often manage. This depends, of course, on several factors. A defect such as short sight may handicap a child when he has to copy from the blackboard but not when he is writing a composition. A child with partial hearing may be able to understand a familiar but not a new teacher. The effect of a moderate sensory handicap may therefore be variable but it may result in distorted perception and faulty concept formation. However, normally children are able to build up their concepts on the basis of their remaining unimpaired experience. This helps them to correct the organization of their defective sensation.

The success of this compensation will depend on the type of task and on its difficulty and familiarity. Gilbert, for example, found that inadequacy of eye movements affected early but not later stages of reading. Performance on various pattern discrimination and copying tasks was found to be only slightly related to visual defects by Abercrombie, Nielsen and Wedell. Children will tend to adapt to their sensory handicaps if these are constant. For example, the child with squint will gradually suppress one eye in order to avoid seeing double. If a handicap is not constant as in a case of alternating squint, adaptation may be harder. Haskell and Hughes, for example, found some evidence that children with alternating squints were poorer at pattern copying and visual discrimination tasks than children with constant squints.

Motor defects

Most of the points made about the effects of sensory defects apply also to motor defects but we have to distinguish between the direct and indirect effects of motor defects. Poor hand control, for example, will have a direct effect on a child's ability to copy a pattern although, as Fig. 2 shows, adaptation can be carried surprisingly far. These pattern copies were made by a 14-year-old athetoid boy who was able to build up his pencil copies with a succession of tiny strokes. The indirect effect of motor handicaps is likely to lie in the reduction of a child's experience of normal movement. The possible effect of

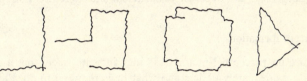

Figure 2

this on the ability to discriminate and reproduce patterns has been considered but in general it has been found to be slight. As with sensory handicaps this is likely to be due to individual differences in successful adaptation.

Attention defects

Kagan has pointed out that some children do badly on visual matching tasks because they do not attend for sufficiently long to consider all the possible alternatives. Similarly, a common cause of reading errors is failure to look at a word sufficiently long. In either of these situations, if a child's performance has been impaired by poor attention only, he is likely to improve it when helped to attend.

Katz and Deutsch have shown that some children who are poor at reading have difficulty in switching attention from sight to hearing and vice versa. They felt that this limited children's ability to associate sight and sound and this might be a cause of their poor reading.

Sensory defects may also affect children's attention to different types of sensation. Myklebust mentions that a deaf child is more likely to be distracted by peripheral visual stimulation since he cannot rely on hearing to check on what is going on around him.

Selective attention to particular types of sensation is also determined by development. A baby is preoccupied with its internal sensations such as hunger. The 1-year-old wants to mouth and touch everything he sees, while the 3-year-old will limit himself to touching what he sees. The 5-year-old is content to look and listen. This increasing attention to the 'distant' senses (vision and hearing) results from the fact that vision particularly takes on a kind of shorthand role, incorporating associations with other sensations. We say, for example, that a chair 'looks' hard and that a steak 'looks' tasty. In some children this pre-eminence of vision is not developed and results in disorganized and hyperactive behaviour and short attention span.

Concept formation

Failure on perceptual-motor tasks may indicate solely that a child does not adequately understand what he is required to do. Phillips and White suggest that children with physical handicap are particularly likely to have missed experiences and consequently not to have developed concepts which are assumed in some tasks. Schubert and Nielsen found that some children, who initially performed badly on pattern copying tasks, improved rapidly when they were given only a very few clues as to what was involved. The rapidity of their improvement indicated that the perceptual-motor skills involved in the tasks were intact.

The sensory, motor, attentional and conceptual defects summarized here show how perceptual-motor performance may be impaired, even though the component functions of perception and motor organization are intact.

Impaired organization of sensation (perception)

There are two main strands of research on perceptual impairment in children. One strand of research followed from the early work of Strauss and Werner, in which perceptual impairment was investigated as a diagnostic indication of organic defect in children. This hypothesis was, not surprisingly, never fully substantiated. However, the studies did demonstrate that there were some children who showed marked impairment of visual, auditory or tactile perception. The majority of studies were concerned with visual perception and particularly with perceptual 'closure'. Birch and Ayres showed that perceptual 'analysis' might also be impaired. Few of these studies related perceptual impairment to educational attainment.

This, by contrast, was the aim in the other main strand of research, in which the perceptual and perceptual-motor abilities of children with high and low educational achievement was compared. An important study by Goins found that only the early stages of reading achievement appeared to be directly affected by adequacy of visual perception. Vernon concluded from her review of the literature that adequacy of auditory perception affected some of the later stages of reading as well. This, of course, to some extent reflects the progression from 'Look and Say' to 'phonic' emphases in methods of teaching reading.

Little research appears to have been done on the effect of perceptual impairment on arithmetic achievement, although Brenner mentions that children showing perceptual impairment may have difficulty with number. Some of these children find that they become confused in trying to work out sums which are written out and so prefer to do them 'in their heads'. Presumably the difficulty lies partly in a failure to pick out, from the whole sum, the particular numbers which have to be combined in an operation.

One has to remember, of course, that visual and auditory perception are only two of a number of functions which must be involved in these basic areas of education attainment. Presumably, beyond the minimal levels of perceptual adequacy required, impairment of one function may be compensated for by other functions and particularly by language.

Gibson *et al.* have shown that in children between the ages of four and eight improvement of visual perception is apparent in those aspects which are critical in reading and writing. This may account for the finding that children may learn reading as a specific skill without showing improvement on other perceptual tasks. Examples of tasks on which these children have difficulty are the discrimination of line illustrations in books and, at later age levels, the understanding of maps and diagrams. Little work has been done on this but Smith mentions several studies showing a relationship between competence in technical subjects and performance on spatial tests at secondary age levels and above.

Two further aspects of perceptual impairment need to be mentioned. The first concerns perception of orientation, such as the discrimination of 'b' and 'd'. Here the difficulty lies not so much in the perception of the figure as in the discrimination of its orientation. While this type of discrimination difficulty is common in early normal development, most children appear to have overcome it by the age of 7 to 8.

Persistence of this difficulty has been attributed to an individual's poor awareness of his body coordinates or of his 'body image'. This is another term which has been used in a variety of ways. It does appear, however, that the ability to distinguish the spatial orientation of our environment in terms of up and down, front and back, left and right, depends on our ability to distinguish these directions with respect to our own body. The evidence on this point is still unclear since, as Ayres found, children who have demonstrable difficulty in the discrimination of spatial orientation may in fact be able to name their left and right hands without difficulty. However, this may be another example of how training in a specific task may not necessarily remedy impairment of an underlying function.

The second aspect of perceptual impairment refers to the situation where visual and auditory perceptions may themselves not be impaired but where there is an impairment in the association between the two functions. Belmont and Birch have shown that reading impairment may be related to difficulty in associating sight and sound. A further point of importance here is that, for adequate performance, the visual and auditory elements of a word have to be matched in their correct sequence. Difficulty may arise from the fact that, when a word is presented visually, it can be perused in any direction and starting from any point. As a result – and unlike sounds in a spoken word – the sequence in which letters may be visually perceived is not fixed.

Severe perceptual impairment has been thought to affect children's behaviour. Rimland suggested that the withdrawal of psychotic children may be the result of very severe perceptual impairment which makes it impossible for these children to organize their sensations sufficiently to make sense of their environment. Similarly, Cruickshank maintains that, in some children, distractibility is the result of a certain degree of perceptual impairment. Frostig found that, under the age of 7, perceptual impairment might affect a child's adjustment in school.

Motor organization

Children who are quite able to match patterns may yet have the greatest difficulty in copying them. For example, the child who failed to copy the pattern shown in Fig. 1 was quite able to distinguish it from others differing only slightly from it. This difference between level of perception and level of motor organization has perhaps been one of the most commonly noted forms of discrepancy in perceptual-motor achievement. Yet frequently researchers have ascribed perceptual impairment to children who have been poor at copy patterns when, in fact, the children's difficulty might be limited to poor motor organization. Anderson and Leonard have rightly pointed out, however, that copying a pattern demands more accurate visual perception than matching patterns and that the latter task does not assess visual perception at an appropriate level. Birch and Lefford found that pattern copying was more related to a child's ability to associate the 'look' of a pattern with the 'feel' of tracing it.

Impairment in children's motor organization has been demonstrated in numerous studies. In pattern copying, errors have been found particularly to involve angles, proportion and orientation. In basic educational attainments impairment has been found particularly in writing (see Fig. 1) and in the setting out of sums. With skilled teaching some children with motor organization impairment have learnt to write adequately, even though they may still have difficulty in copying patterns. However, when, at a later stage in schooling, speed of writing becomes important, level of performance may again deteriorate indicating that adequate writing is only achieved with considerable effort. Frequently this effort interferes with a child's attempts to express his thoughts in writing and so one finds the child who can express himself easily orally but only turns out the briefest compositions.

When difficulties in motor organization have been overcome in relation to writing, the impairment may emerge again when more complex levels of performance are required as, for example, in mechanical drawing.

Inadequate development of 'body image' may affect motor organization just as it may affect perception. This may show itself in reversals in writing or generally in incorrect movements. Many children show this difficulty in physical education when they move their limbs or their whole body in the wrong direction. Others have difficulty in everyday tasks such as laying the table, tying shoe laces, dressing and finding their way about a building or district. This impairment of motor organization in general can become very frustrating to children. Rubin and Braun found that motor organization defect was a major cause of maladjustment in some children. A contributory factor here is that these children show no obvious signs of physical handicap. Thus their companions see their poor performance in play as a sign of stupidity.

Follow up studies of children with motor organization impairment have shown that a proportion make considerable progress. It is not certain how far this improvement constitutes a lessening of impairment and how far successful compensation for it. Children certainly learn to compensate in a variety of ways, for example, by giving themselves verbal instructions or by finger tracing. Landmark describes a girl who in geometry slid her ruler over the paper until the angle 'looked right' before drawing her line. These compensatory knacks may be sufficient to achieve success at a lower but not at a higher level. How far a child is able to invent successful compensatory techniques depends upon the level of his other abilities and particularly on his desire to succeed.

Conclusion

The importance of perceptual-motor skills for educational and social adequacy seems to be generally substantiated. It is difficult, however, to generalize about the extent to which a particular type and degree of perceptual-motor impairment constitutes a handicap to a particular child. Severe defects of perception involving several senses may appear to constitute an almost totally crippling handicap, if one accepts Rimland's view of the causation of some forms of autism. However, the difficulty of applying the usual tests to these types of children has also made it difficult also to identify perceptual impairment as the determining cause of their condition. One could postulate that severe perceptual impairment, either visual or auditory, would have marked and generalized effects from infancy onwards in so far as it would severely limit the use which a child could make of its sensory experience. Short of this degree of severity the consequences of impairment may appear to be relatively limited, since normal life situations do not demand maximal efficiency and normal experience provides opportunities for compensation and specific learning. Children who find that a lesser degree of perceptual impairment is a handicap are likely to be those who have had insufficient help in the early stages of school learning, whose ability to compensate is limited because of low ability in other areas or who have gone on to a sphere of activity where a higher degree of perceptual skill is specifically required.

The consequences of impairment of motor organization are more easily identifiable. As has already been mentioned, they are more apparent to the child himself, who 'cannot make his hands do what his eyes see'. It is less easy for a child to compensate for his impairment. Sensory input can come through several senses but short of using 'props', such as using a ruler for drawing, the child with impaired motor organization has no way round his handicap. For the young child whose progress is assessed to a large extent on his motor adequacy both in the home, in skills such as dressing, and in school, in writing and number work, in skill at all kinds of games, and among his fellows, even moderate impairment of motor organization may be a major handicap and undermine self-confidence.

Early awareness of a child's perceptual-motor impairment in whatever form it appears is therefore important. The word 'awareness' rather than 'diagnosis' has been used because in the first instance it is usually the infant or even nursery teacher who notices that a child is having difficulty. Often a surprisingly small amount of extra help in building up one or other of the skills, which the remaining children in the class appear to pick up without effort, will enable the mildly handicapped child to maintain progress. It is just as important, however, for the teacher to notice when this type of help is not proving sufficient. At this point more extensive diagnosis is required and probably more intensive remedial help. Many remedial programmes are now available and a useful summary of them is provided by B. Van Witsen in *Perceptual Training Activities Handbook*, Teachers College Press. B. Bateman offers some interesting comments on their applications in 'Learning Disorders', *Review of Educational Research*, **36**, pp. 93–119.

3   Memory span and language proficiency*

N. C. GRAHAM

Other papers have discussed the importance of language in learning and the link between lack of competence in language and learning deficiency. This paper discusses what is implied when we talk about linguistic competence and suggests some possible factors associated with it. In particular, the author discusses the importance of short-term memory for competence. In the course of the paper the reader is introduced to some of the ideas of transformation grammar.

Many teachers are puzzled by the sometimes arbitrary boundary between what children with learning difficulties or very young children can understand and what they fail to understand in what is said to them and in what they are able or unable to express. Some recent factor analytic studies have identified components of cognitive processes such as perceptual speed, stimulus trace, its behavioural concomitant short-term memory and a sentence complexity. The experimental investigation of such factors as variables in cognitive tasks may shed some light on intellectual performance in general and on language performance in particular.

As yet the manner in which short-term memory limitations act to restrict cognitive functioning is still virtually unknown. The thinking and experimentation reported in this article are concerned with the relationships between what is sometimes called memory span which is usually very short in educationally subnormal (i.e. educable mentally retarded) children and the ability to process sentences of standard English in a limited number of tasks.

Human language and the accompaniments of language use constitute a phenomenon which has many, if not a multitude of facets. Language deficiency could have as many sources as there are component skills.

Much research interest has focused on the word as the unit of language and so a great deal of effort has been put into the study of

* Reprinted from N. C. Graham, 'Memory Span and Language Proficiency' in *Journal of Learning Disabilities*, 1 (11), 1968, pp. 644–8.

the size and nature of vocabulary as well as practical endeavour in the increase in extent and enrichment of the quality of children's vocabulary. This is all to the good. If children have the basic competence then it can only be to their benefit for the extent of their abilities to be increased. The flexibility, the range of applications of language, accuracy and quality can all perhaps be augmented by imaginative intensive teaching and well planned enrichment programmes including the creative use of language in an aesthetic sense.

This approach assumes basic competence. Without this, attempts to increase children's motivation to use language, to provide more language interpretable experiences and to involve language use in a wide range of different activities will fail. By giving more opportunities for failure, such programmes could destroy what confidence in the language process a child possesses at the outset.

We must, therefore, inquire into something of what may constitute at least one aspect of basic competence by asking what is the essence of human language. No matter how large a person's word vocabulary might be, we would not grant him basic competence if he could not string words together in acceptable ways to say things for which no one word exists and to understand such utterances by other people when he hears them. One of the characteristic features of language is that what we can say is not limited by our repertoire of single words (vocabulary). Words can be combined in certain acceptable ways to refer to a multitude of situations, experiences and concepts, however unusual, novel or complex in a creative or non-stereotyped way. I could utter words in random order and convey some meaning. I could say 'cat, dog' and something could be conveyed. I could say 'chase, cat, dog' and increase the information, but if I want to refer to one particular event, I must re-order the words in one of two ways, 'cat, chase, dog' or 'dog, chase, cat'. To specify the event even further, I can add 'a' or 'the' *before* each of the two nouns and indicate whether the event is in the past or is going on now, e.g. 'The dog chased a cat'. It would not do just to let the words tumble out in any order as, for example, 'a the chase cat 'd dog' and hope that the particular thing I wish to refer to would be communicated. We could also say 'A cat was being chased by the dog' which means roughly the same.

Furthermore, there is a sense in which we know what we want to say in advance of having said it. We seem to be able to think of a situation or concept or event *in toto* all at once and then to represent this in terms of a sequence of words one after another in time. It has been said that in order to be able to do this one of the characteristics of the language process is a kind of unconscious planning by which the order of the words is controlled. This is best illustrated by a sentence containing a relative clause: 'The man who sat on the chair was tall.' Presumably, before we utter this phrase we have it in mind to refer to the tallness of the man but we can insert another, subsidiary statement in the middle. It looks as if, in desiring to say something, we manufacture a plan which can be added to and manipulated as we go along. This plan governs the selection of appropriate words, and determines and controls the order in which we utter them. Now, the plans that we are able to manufacture are not personal, private idiosyncratic ones. The plans must correspond to similar plans which other people are able to make. The plan-making abilities we all have in common constitute the grammar or syntax of the language. The plan-making process can be described in a rather pedestrian fashion, in terms of a detailed system of rules. Some linguists have been trying to draw up such a system by which a plan-making device could operate. It is possible that in the course of learning our language we have acquired a set of ready-made plans which we draw on whenever we want to say something and to the extent that some persons' language forms are highly stereotyped and inflexible (e.g. Bernstein's restricted code users ?) this may be so. But there are so many different sentence forms, and so many different ways of stringing words together that it is not feasible for even the human brain to store them all, decide as quickly as it does which particular plan is appropriate and retrieve it from the store. Furthermore, such a hypothesis would deny the essential creativity of language. Not only poets and novelists are creating new sentence forms. All of us frequently use a sentence form which we individually have (*a*) never used before, and (*b*) never heard before. Where did it come from ?

It is both more plausible and more economical psychologically to think of the language planning capability in terms of a system of operating rules so highly practised that they operate at great speed and automatically produce plans appropriate to what we want to say.

instructions are received. Further instructions as to what can be done to the simple plan produced so far *can* be received. For instance, the simple instruction to combine the signal for 'past' with the signal for 'bite' would produce a signal which stands for 'bit'. At this stage, the plan could be used to say something, e.g. 'The dog bit the man.' Alternatively, other things may be done to transform the plan. There are strict rules governing the process. For example, it may be decided to make the simple statement into passive and utter it as 'The man was bitten by the dog'. Or something might be inserted, e.g. 'The dog that chased the cat bit the man.' The plan produced by these further, more complex instructions (called 'transformational rules') will enable the speaker to keep track of what he was going to say about the dog and the man while he is manufacturing a plan to make this aside about the dog chasing the cat. Obviously, much of this could be going on simultaneously but some things must occur before others and in any case quite a lot of 'work' or computation goes on which takes up a certain amount of time (measured, of course, in small fractions of a second). For each and every sentence an appropriate plan with its attendant rules could be inferred from what we know of the relationships among the words of sentences in English (or any other language). The number of rules which would be necessary to do this would be quite large as language is so complex.

In some way or other, all proficient users of a language must have acquired the same set of rules. They must have done this on the basis of the body of language to which they have been exposed. It is said (e.g. Lenneburg 1966) that most children have acquired the basic system of rules by the time they are about 4 years old, though of course vocabulary, the stock of concepts and skills in using the rules goes on improving for a very long time after that.

Now the question arises, what if children somehow fail to acquire all or some of the rules ? In this case some sorts of sentences would be beyond their ability to produce and possibly also understand. They would be deficient in language. Certain sentences spoken to them would fail to convey their full meaning. On the other hand, some other deficiency might interfere with the operation of the system. One such deficiency is in what might be called memory span; the ability to receive a number of signals in a row, retain them and then immediately reproduce them in the correct order. Seven such signals is the normal adult capacity of memory span but with some children and with all very young children it is much less.

Work done by the author suggests that memory span does operate as a restriction both on the ability to repeat sentences and to comprehend them. Thus a child who can only receive and reproduce accurately two signals in a row (digits, letters or single words) has greater difficulty in reproducing meaningful eight-word sentences than a child who has a span of say five such signals at whatever age and independently of intelligence test scores. This assumes that the words used in the sentences and the situation represented have been chosen for their familiarity to the children.

An interesting facet of the work is that restricted memory span will interfere with the 'processing' of one kind of sentence and not with another. For instance, many children with a span of only two items could easily repeat the sentence 'There is a bird flying in the air' but would have great difficulty with the sentence 'The dog that chased the duck is black' although both contain only eight words. This suggests that the plan governing the first is easier to construct or takes less time to construct than the plan for the second. This is borne out by the relative complexity of the tree diagram which one would have to draw to describe the structure of the respective sentences.

The procedure for testing repetition of sentences ability was very simple. Twenty-four different sentence types were used, e.g. negative, passive, question, relative clause and so on. Each sentence was eight words long and contained vocabulary drawn from Dale's list of easy words. Subjects were trained in the idea of repeating things accurately and then were given one sentence at a time in a normal speaking voice. What they said as a reproduction was carefully recorded and deviations from total accuracy noted. A scoring system was devised which took account not only of the number of words right but also the correctness of the order. Memory span was tested by presenting for repetition strings of words which were not sentences, ranging in length from two to six words. The words for this test were drawn at random from the sentences used. The average of a number of trials with this material was recorded as a subject's memory span. A comparison of performance on the two tasks revealed the relationship described above. Memory span restricts the range of sentence types which can be used with these subjects who were drawn from Special Schools for the Educationally Subnormal (aged 7–9), Primary Schools (aged 5–7) and Nursery Schools (aged 4–5).

Similarly when a test of comprehension of the same sentences was constructed and administered, memory span was clearly related to ability to perform on certain sentences and not others. The form of the test was multiple choice with four pictures so constructed that the correct choice among them could only be made if the child was able to obtain and hold all the information contained in each sentence after hearing it spoken only once as in the repetition test.

As would be expected of recognition as opposed to a production or recall task, more sentences were correctly comprehended than were recalled with 100 per cent accuracy. However, the order of attainment of the subjects and the order of difficulty of the different sentence types were significantly correlated.

This line of inquiry begins to establish how and why memory span (or immediate memory) plays the important role in language it has long been suspected to have. The observation that very young children and older subnormal children are deficient in this respect has been made many times over. With the advent of a type of linguistics which enables us to pose the right questions and the development of psychological techniques for putting the questions, further inroads into this complex area of language performance and language competence can be expected and are being made.

4 Levels of expectancy and the self-fulfilling prophecy*

R. ROSENTHAL and L. JACOBSON

One of the commonest practices in English education is the categorization of children. We still have the 'grammar-school child' and the 'secondary-modern-school child', we also have the 'Newsom child'.

* Reprinted and abridged from R. Rosenthal and L. Jacobson, *Pygmalion in the Classroom*, Holt, Rinehart & Winston, 1968, pp. 174–81.

In a very large number of schools we have A, B, C and D children. We have children who have been ascertained E.S.N. and we have 'high flyers'. In recent years another group has been identified: the 'Disadvantaged'. In England most of these children are from the schools of decaying inner ring urban areas, often including disproportionate numbers of children of non-English backgrounds.

This paper examines the way in which the use of such labels sets up attitudes in teachers and experimenters which help to produce the results expected. This effect is a self-fulfilling prophecy. Thus if a teacher thinks a child is an 'A' child he is likely to produce 'A' results for that teacher even if he is really a 'C' child in disguise. The paper examines the widespread nature of this phenomenon. We have an old saying 'Give a dog a bad name', which is closely related to this problem.

All teachers who have low levels of expectancies for 'C' or 'D' or 'Newsom' children could read this paper with particular advantage.

The central idea flowing from our research is that one person's expectation for another's behaviour could come to serve as a self-fulfilling prophecy. This is not a new idea, and anecdotes and theories can be found that support its tenability. Much of the experimental evidence for the operation of interpersonal self-fulfilling prophecies comes from a research program in which prophecies or expectancies were experimentally generated in psychological experimenters in order to learn whether these prophecies would become self-fulfilling.

The general plan of past studies has been to establish two groups of 'data collectors' and give to the experimenters of each group a different hypothesis as to the data their research subjects would give them. In many such experiments, though not in all, experimenters obtained data from their subjects in accordance with the expectancy they held regarding their subjects' responses. Quite naturally, some of the experiments involved expectations held by the experimenters of the intellectual performance of their subjects.

In addition to those experiments in which the subjects were humans, there were studies in which the subjects were animals. When experimenters were led to believe that their animal subjects were genetically inferior, these animals performed more poorly. When experimenters were led to believe that their animal subjects were more favourably endowed genetically, their animals' performance was superior. In reality, of course, there were no genetic differences between the animals that had been alleged to be dull or bright.

If animal subjects believed to be brighter by their trainers actually became brighter because of their trainers' beliefs, then it might also be true that school children believed by their teachers to be brighter would become brighter because of their teachers' beliefs. Oak School became the laboratory in which an experimental test of that proposition was carried out.

Oak School is a public elementary school in a lower-class community of a medium-size city. The school has a minority group of Mexican children who comprise about one-sixth of the school's population. Every year about 200 of its 650 children leave Oak School, and every year about 200 new children are enrolled.

Oak School is a streamed school, with fast, medium and slow learning streams in each grade. Reading ability is the primary basis for streaming. The Mexican children are heavily over-represented in the slow stream.

On theoretical grounds it would have been desirable to learn whether teachers' favourable or unfavourable expectations could result in a corresponding increase or decrease in pupils' intellectual competence. On ethical grounds, however, it was decided to test only the proposition that favourable expectations by teachers could lead to an increase in intellectual competence.

All of the children of Oak School were pre-tested with a standard non-verbal test of intelligence. This test was represented to the teachers as one that would predict intellectual 'blooming' or 'spurting'. The I.Q. test employed yielded three I.Q. scores: total I.Q., verbal I.Q. and reasoning I.Q. The 'verbal' items required the child to match pictured items with verbal descriptions given by the teacher. The reasoning items required the child to indicate which of five designs differed from the remaining four. Total I.Q. was based on the sum of verbal and reasoning items.

At the very beginning of the school year following the schoolwide pre-testing, each of the eighteen teachers of grades one to six was given the names of those children in her classroom who, in the academic year ahead, would show dramatic intellectual growth. These predictions were allegedly made on the basis of these special children's scores on the test of academic blooming. About 20 per cent of Oak School's children were alleged to be potential spurters. For each classroom the names of the special children had actually been chosen by means of a table of random numbers. The difference between the special children and the ordinary children, then, was only in the mind of the teacher.

All the children of Oak School were re-tested with the same I.Q. test after one semester, after a full academic year and after two full academic years. For the first two re-tests, children were in the classroom of the teacher who had been given favourable expectations for the intellectual growth of some of her pupils. For the final re-testing all children had been promoted to the classes of teachers who had not been given any special expectations for the intellectual growth of any of the children. That follow-up testing had been included so that we could learn whether any expectancy advantages that might be found would be dependent on a continuing contact with the teacher who held the especially favourable expectation.

For the children of the experimental group and for the children of the control group, gains in I.Q. from pre-test to re-test were computed. Expectancy advantage was defined by the degree to which I.Q. gains by the 'special' children exceeded gains by the control-group children. After the first year of the experiment a significant expectancy advantage was found, and it was especially great among children of the first and second grades. The advantage of having been expected to bloom was evident for these younger children in total I.Q., verbal I.Q. and reasoning I.Q. The control-group children of these grades gained well in I.Q., 19 per cent of them gaining twenty or more total I.Q. points. The 'special' children, however, showed 47 per cent of their number gaining twenty or more total I.Q. points.

During the subsequent follow-up year the younger children of the first two years lost their expectancy advantage. The children of the upper grades, however, showed an increasing expectancy advantage during the follow-up year. The younger children who seemed easier to influence may have required more continued contact with their influencer in order to maintain their behaviour change. The older children, who were harder to influence initially, may have been better able to maintain their behaviour change autonomously once it had occurred.

Differences between boys and girls in the extent to which they were helped by favourable expectations were not dramatic when gains in total I.Q. were considered. After one year, and after two years as well, boys who were expected to bloom intellectually bloomed more in verbal I.Q.; girls who were expected to bloom intellectually bloomed more in reasoning I.Q. Favourable teacher expectations seemed to help each sex more in that sphere of intellectual functioning in which they had excelled on the pre-test. At Oak School boys normally show the higher verbal I.Q. while girls show the higher reasoning I.Q.

It will be recalled that Oak School was organized into fast, medium and slow streams. We had thought that favourable expectations on the part of teachers would be of greatest benefit to the children of the slow stream. That was not the case. After one year, it was the children of the medium stream who showed the greatest expectancy advantage, though children of the other streams were close behind. After two years, however, the children of the medium stream very clearly showed the greatest benefits from having had favourable expectations held of their intellectual performance. It seems surprising that it should be the more average child of a lower-class school who stands to benefit more from his teacher's improved expectation.

After the first year of the experiment and also after the second year, the Mexican children showed greater expectancy advantages than did the non-Mexican children, though the difference was not significant statistically. One interesting minority-group effect did reach significance, however, even with just a small sample size. For each of the Mexican children, magnitude of expectancy advantage was computed by subtracting from his or her gain in I.Q. from pre-test to re-test, the I.Q. gain made by the children of the control group in his or her classroom. These magnitudes of expectancy advantage were then correlated with the 'Mexican-ness' of the children's faces. After one year, and after two years, those boys who looked more Mexican benefited more from their teachers' positive prophecies. Teachers' pre-experimental expectancies for these boys' intellectual performance were probably lowest of all. Their turning up on a list of probable bloomers must have surprised their teachers. Interest may have followed surprise and, in some way, increased watching for signs of increased brightness may have led to increased brightness.

In addition to the comparison of the 'special' and the ordinary children on their gains in I.Q. it was possible to compare their gains after the first year of the experiment on school achievement as defined by report-card grades. Only for the school subject of reading was there a significant difference in gains in report-card grades. The children expected to bloom intellectually were judged by their teachers to show greater advances in their reading ability. Just as in the case of I.Q. gains, it was the younger children who showed the greater expectancy advantage in reading scores. The more a given grade level had benefited in over-all I.Q. gains, the more that same grade level benefited in reading scores.

It was the children of the medium stream who showed the greatest expectancy advantage in terms of reading ability just as they had been the children to benefit most in terms of I.Q. from their teachers' favourable expectations.

Report-card reading grades were assigned by teachers, and teachers' judgements of reading performance may have been affected by their expectations. It is possible, therefore, that there was no real benefit to the earmarked children of having been expected to bloom. The effect could very well have been in the mind of the teacher rather than in the reading performance of the child. Some evidence was available to suggest that such halo effects did not occur. For a number of grade levels, objective achievement tests had been administered. Greater expectancy advantages were found when the assessment was by these objective tests than when it was by the more subjective evaluation made by the teacher. If anything, teachers' grading seemed to show a negative halo effect. It seemed that the special children were graded more severely by the teachers than were the ordinary children. It is even possible that it is just this sort of standard-setting behaviour that is responsible in part for the effects of favourable expectations.

The fear has often been expressed that the disadvantaged child is further disadvantaged by his teacher's setting standards that are inappropriately low (Hillson and Myers; Rivlin). Wilson has presented compelling evidence that teachers do, in fact, hold up lower standards of achievement for children of more deprived areas. It is a possibility to be further investigated that when a teacher's expectation for a pupil's intellectual performance is raised, she may set higher standards for him to meet (that is, grade him tougher). There may be here the makings of a benign cycle. Teachers may not only get more when they expect more; they may also come to expect more when they get more.

All teachers had been asked to rate each of their pupils on variables related to intellectual curiosity, personal and social adjustment, and need for social approval. In general, children who had been expected to bloom intellectually were rated as more intellectually curious, as happier and, especially in the lower grades, as less in need of social approval. Just as had been the case with I.Q. and reading ability, it was the younger children who showed the greater expectancy advantage in terms of their teachers' perceptions of their classroom behaviour. Once again, children of the medium stream were most advantaged by having been expected to bloom, this time in terms of their perceived greater intellectual curiosity and lessened need for social approval.

When we consider expectancy advantages in terms of perceived intellectual curiosity, we find that the Mexican children did not share in the advantages of having been expected to bloom. Teachers did not see the Mexican children as more intellectually curious when they had been expected to bloom. There was even a slight tendency, stronger for Mexican boys, to see the special Mexican children as less curious intellectually. That seems surprising, particularly since the Mexican children showed the greatest expectancy advantages in I.Q., in reading scores and, for Mexican boys, in over-all school achievement. It seemed almost as though, for these minority-group children, intellectual competence may have been easier for teachers to bring about than to believe.

Children's gains in I.Q. during the basic year of the experiment were correlated with teachers' perceptions of their classroom behaviour. This was done separately for the upper- and lower-stream children of the experimental and control groups. The more the upper-stream children of the experimental group gained in I.Q., the more favourably they were rated by their teachers. The more the lower-stream children of the control group gained in I.Q., the more unfavourably they were viewed by their teachers. No special expectation had been created about these children, and their slow-stream status made it unlikely in their teachers' eyes that they would behave in an intellectually competent manner. The more intellectually competent these children became, the more negatively they were viewed by their teachers. Future research should address itself to the possibility that there may be hazards to 'unwarranted', unpredicted intellectual growth. Teachers may require a certain amount of preparation to be able to accept the unexpected classroom behaviour of the intellectually upwardly mobile child.

There are a number of alternative 'theories' available to account for our general findings. One such class of theories, the 'accident' theories, maintain that artifacts are responsible for the results obtained, that there is really nothing to explain. The problems of test unreliability (see pp. 429–463) and of pre-test I.Q. differences were discussed and found wanting as explanations of our results. The possibility that teachers treated the special children differently only during the re-testing process itself was considered. The patterning of results, the fact that a 'blind' examiner[1] obtained even more dramatic expectancy effects than did the teachers, teachers' poor recall of the names of their 'special' children and the fact that the results did not disappear one year after the children left the teachers who had been given the expectations, all weaken the plausibility of that argument. Most important to the tenability of the hypothesis that teachers' expectations can significantly affect their pupils' performance are the preliminary results of three replications all of which show significant effects of teacher expectations. These replications also suggest, however, that the effects of teacher expectations may be quite complicated and affected both as to magnitude and direction by a variety of pupil characteristics and by situational variables in the life of the child.

It might reasonably be thought that the improved intellectual competence of the special children was bought at the expense of the ordinary children. Perhaps teachers gave more time to those who were expected to bloom. But teachers appeared to give slightly less time to their special children. Furthermore, those classrooms in which the special children showed the greatest gains in I.Q. were also the classrooms in which the ordinary children gained the most I.Q. The robbing-Peter theory would predict that ordinary children gain less I.Q. where special children gain more I.Q.

On the basis of other experiments on interpersonal self-fulfilling prophecies, we can only speculate as to how teachers brought about intellectual competence simply by expecting it. Teachers may have treated their children in a more pleasant, friendly and encouraging

[1] i.e. an examiner who did not know which children were in the experimental group.

fashion when they expected greater intellectual gains of them. Such behaviour has been shown to improve intellectual performance, probably by its favourable effect on pupil motivation.

Teachers probably watched their special children more closely, and this greater attentiveness may have led to more rapid reinforcement of correct responses with a consequent increase in pupils' learning. Teachers may also have become more reflective in their evaluation of the special children's intellectual performance. Such an increase in teachers' reflectiveness may have led to an increase in their special pupils' reflectiveness, and such a change in cognitive style would be helpful to the performance of the non-verbal skills required by the I.Q. test employed.

To summarize our speculations, we may say that by what she said, by how and when she said it, by her facial expressions, postures and perhaps by her touch, the teacher may have communicated to the children of the experimental group that she expected improved intellectual performance. Such communications together with possible changes in teaching techniques may have helped the child learn by changing his self-concept, his expectations of his own behaviour and his motivation, as well as his cognitive style and skills.

It is self-evident that further research is needed to narrow down the range of possible mechanisms whereby a teacher's expectations become translated into a pupil's intellectual growth. It would be valuable, for example, to have sound films of teachers interacting with their pupils. We might then look for differences in the way teachers interact with those children from whom they expect intellectual growth compared to those from whom they expect less. On the basis of films of psychological experimenters interacting with subjects from whom different responses are expected, we know that even in such highly standardized situations, unintentional communications can be incredibly subtle and complex. Much more subtle and much more complex may be the communications between children and their teachers, teachers not constrained by the demands of the experimental laboratory to treat everyone equally to the extent that it is possible to do so.

The implications of the research described herein are of several kinds. There are methodological implications for the conduct of educational research. There are implications for the further investigation of unintentional influence processes especially when these processes result in interpersonally self-fulfilling prophecies. Finally, there are some possible implications for the educational enterprise, and some of these will be suggested briefly.

Over time, our educational policy question has changed from 'who ought to be educated?' to 'who is capable of being educated?' The ethical question has been traded in for the scientific question. For those children whose educability is in doubt there is a label. They are the educationally, or culturally, or socio-economically, deprived children and, as things stand now, they appear not to be able to learn as do those who are more advantaged. The advantaged and the disadvantaged differ in parental income, in parental values, in scores on various tests of achievement and ability, and often in skin colour and other phenotypic expressions of genetic heritage. Quite inseparable from these differences between the advantaged and the disadvantaged are the differences in their teachers' expectations for what they can achieve in school. There are no experiments to show that a change in pupils' skin colour will lead to improved intellectual performance. There is, however, the research described here to show that change in teacher expectation can lead to improved intellectual performance.

Nothing was done directly for the disadvantaged child at Oak School. There was no crash program to improve his reading ability, no special lesson plan, no extra time for tutoring, no trips to museums or art galleries. There was only the belief that the children bore watching, that they had intellectual competencies that would in due course be revealed. What was done in our program of educational change was done directly for the teacher, only indirectly for her pupils. Perhaps, then, it is the teacher to whom we should direct more of our research attention. If we could learn how she is able to effect dramatic improvement in her pupils' competence without formal changes in her teaching methods, then we could teach other teachers to do the same. If further research shows that it is possible to select teachers whose untrained interactional style does for most of her pupils what our teachers did for the special children, it may be possible to combine sophisticated teacher selection and placement with teacher training to optimize the learning of all pupils.

FURTHER READING

A. M. Clarke and A. D. B. Clarke, *Mental deficiency*, London, Methuen, 1966.

J. E. Collins, *The effects of remedial education*, Edinburgh, Oliver and Boyd (for University of Birmingham Inst. of Education, 1961).

J. C. Daniels and H. Diack, *Progress in reading*, University of Nottingham Inst. of Education, 1956.

J. C. Daniels and H. Diack, *The standard reading tests*, Chatto and Windus, 1958.

M. Deutsch, 'The role of social class in language development and cognition', *American Journal of Orthopsychiatry*, **35** 1965, pp. 78–88.

J. W. B. Douglas, *The home and the school*, London, MacGibbon and Kee, 1964.

J. McV. Hunt, *Intelligence and experience*, New York, Ronald Press, 1961.

N. C. Kephart, *The slow learner in the classroom*, Columbus, Ohio, Merrill, 1960.

A. R. Luria, *The role of speech in the regulation of normal and abnormal behaviour*, London, Pergamon, 1961.

J. M. Morris, *Standards and progress in reading*, London, Newnes with N.F.E.R., 1966.

N. O'Connor and B. Hermelin, *Speech and thought in severe subnormality*, London, Pergamon, 1963.

R. Rosenthal and L. Jacobson, 'Teacher expectations for the disadvantaged', *Scientific American*, April 1968, pp. 19–23.

A. E. Tansley and R. Gulliford, *The education of the slow learning child*, London, Routledge, 1960.

M. D. Vernon, *Backwardness in reading*, London, C.U.P., 1957.

The evaluation of learning

The papers in this section are concerned with the evaluation and assessment of learning. Thus, although they are concerned with problems of testing they do not deal with such things as intelligence tests or personality tests or tests used in clinical conditions. Nor is the aim to explain principles of test construction. Rather the papers deal with wider issues, what might be called the general rationale of achievement testing.

The first fairly lengthy contribution by Connaughton surveys the main problems of test usage and considers some of the key problems connected with public examinations in Great Britain in the light of test theory. The short paper by Willmott complements this, referring specifically to problems of testing at GCE level. Glaser raises an important and quite fundamental question: should tests measure students' grasp of a given unit of learning, or should they be more concerned with producing a rank order of students according to their performance?

By and large, public examinations in Great Britain take the latter approach for granted. Willmott, for example, shows how GCE grades are decided in this way. Stones, on the other hand, argues for a more widespread adoption of tests which assess units of learning and are not concerned with ranking students. He suggests that tests should be viewed more as monitoring devices of students' learning than instruments of quality control.

1 The validity of examinations at 16-plus*

I. M. CONNAUGHTON

This paper comprises a comprehensive discussion of most of the aspects of test procedures and the particular problems of British public examinations. As may be seen, these examinations suffer from a number of weaknesses. Many of these weaknesses have been well understood by test theorists for several years but are only recently receiving serious attention from other educationists. The problem of validity is particularly important and gets a good deal of attention from the author.

This examination of test procedures is augmented by extensive discussion of research findings in respect of the various aspects of test theory. Many problems could be ameliorated by the adoption of more objective testing techniques. Unfortunately there is still a considerable body of teacher resistance to such techniques. It does seem, however, that this resistance is diminishing, which may help the development of more reliable and valid types of test.

Increasingly nowadays, a child's educational career and even the kind of employment he eventually obtains depend upon how well he performs in a series of examinations. The General Certificate of Education Ordinary level examination (GCE 'O' levels) and the Certificate of Secondary Education Examinations (CSE) are particularly influential, since they are the last secondary-school examinations available to most pupils before they leave school, and passes in at least two or three subjects in these examinations are now demanded by many employers and educational establishments before they will even consider an applicant for employment or further education (*Careers for School Leavers*, 1967).

Considering their importance and influence, relatively little is known about the efficiency or accuracy of these examinations and the review which follows has therefore been prepared with the aim of describing and evaluating the empirical evidence available on them – especially their reliability (their consistency) and validity (the extent to which they achieve their aims). First, however, before the research

* Reprinted and abridged from I. M. Connaughton, 'The Validity of Examinations at 16-Plus', *Educational Research*, 11 (3), 1969, pp. 163–78.

evidence on the examinations is reviewed, the topic of discussion will be defined.

Purposes of examination procedures

In educational usage, the term 'examination', or 'test', usually refers to a series of questions or tasks designed to measure the knowledge or skill of an individual. Such measuring devices can serve a variety of purposes. Morris, for example, classifies the purposes of examination procedures under four headings: (a) to maintain standards; (b) to act as an incentive to effort; (c) to serve as an administrative device; and (d) to provide a tool for social engineering. Pilliner lists somewhat different but related purposes: 'To the student, they are a stimulus and a goal. To the teacher they feed back information about the effectiveness of his teaching and hence serve as feedback. To society at large they furnish a guarantee of competence in those examined to perform the tasks demanded of them by the jobs or professions they take up.' Finally, to take one more example, the *Encyclopaedia Britannica* (1955) lists three specific purposes: to measure attainment, for diagnosis and for the prediction of a candidate's probable future performance in some course of study or training. In other words, an examination may possibly be designed to fulfil one or more of a wide variety of purposes or functions and it is important, therefore, to be as specific as possible about the essential functions of a particular examination.

Types of examination

Written, oral and practical examinations are the best known forms of assessment. Of these the written examination is the most popular. The essay form of written examination, widely used in England, is difficult to score consistently and has been supplemented in America by the objective test which is easier to score quickly and accurately. Instead of being asked to write a long answer to an essay topic, in an objective test the candidate has to give a short answer to a specific question. The multiple-choice test is probably the most popular form of objective test. In it, the examinee is presented with a series of items, or questions, each of which aims to measure a specific objective, and the examinee has to select his answer to each item from a number of possibilities presented to him. The other forms of examination – oral and practical tests – are generally included in subjects where such skills need to be assessed – for example in French and Physics. In recent years, variations on these traditional forms of examination have begun to be tried out. One of the most interesting of these is continuous assessment of coursework, an assessment of work performed by the examinee during his school year, which may include all three types of assessment mentioned above. At university level there have also been experiments with procedures in which papers consist of a selection from a larger number of questions which have been made available to the candidates beforehand. 'Open-book' procedures in which the candidates can take texts into the examination room have also been tried out.

Assessment procedures

Examinations may be internal, conducted by the students' own school and teachers; external, conducted by an outside examining board, as in the General Certificate of Education (GCE), or internal with external moderation, allowing the examinations to be set and marked internally but the results being moderated by external assessors. The latter procedure is followed in universities and it is now being introduced into fifth-form secondary school examinations, especially the Certificate of Secondary Education (CSE).

Preparation of an examination

Examinations require careful thought and construction if they are to be effective measuring instruments. Pidgeon, for example, lists eight separate steps which ought to be followed when an examination is being prepared.

(1) Identification of purpose (Specify the aim(s) of the examination).

(2) Development of the plan or 'blueprint' (Outline the objectives of instruction).

(3) Development of the detailed specification (Define the sylla-

bus or content area within which the expressed objectives are to be achieved).

(4) Preparation of appropriate items.

(5) Review and editing of items.

(6) Preliminary trial and item analysis (Pre-test questions on pupils similar to those who will take the actual, final, examination).

(7) Final selection of items.

(8) Organization of questions and their reproduction for use (Plan the lay-out of the paper).

These procedures are recommended in order to ensure that if the final examination is properly administered (i.e. the same procedures are followed by all teachers using the examination), then the results should be *reliable* and *valid*. These two terms are further defined below since they are most important attributes of examinations, and the review of research which follows later in this paper is mainly concerned with studies of these aspects of the GCE and CSE.

Reliability is concerned solely with the consistency or accuracy with which a test measures whatever it does measure. There are various ways in which reliability may be calculated (for example mark re-mark, test re-test), each of which takes account of different sources of error in a test score. It is therefore essential that the method used to derive any reliability coefficient should be clearly described. The estimation of clearly labelled components of error variance is the most informative outcome of a reliability study. However, this approach is not yet prominent in reports on tests. In the more familiar reliability studies the investigator obtains two measures and correlates them, or derives a correlation coefficient by applying one of several formulas to part or item scores within a test. Thus the maximum reliability coefficient obtainable is $1 \cdot 00$ and the minimum is 0. A reliability coefficient of above $0 \cdot 9$ is therefore often regarded as satisfactory. 'Low' reliability is less easy to specify, but a coefficient of $0 \cdot 5$ or less is generally looked on as suspect.

Validity is concerned with the extent to which a test measures what it is intended to measure and it is more important than reliability in that, even if a test is highly reliable, if it is not valid, then it should not be used. Like reliability, validity is a relative concept and if the question is asked about any particular test: 'Is this test valid?' the answer should be in the form of another question: 'Is it valid for what?' For example, for tests measuring existing knowledge or level of performance it is usual to refer to *content validity*. A test is a valid measure of achievement if the items it contains adequately cover the subject-matter to be tested. If a teacher wishes to measure pupils' ability to apply their knowledge in new situations but writes test questions which only require memory for facts, the test will have low content validity. *Predictive validity* refers to the association between the scores on a test and future behaviour. Tests used in the 11-plus, for example, will have validity if the scores on them can be shown to be closely related to future performance in secondary schools. *Concurrent validity* refers to the association between test scores and some other measure collected at the same time. The validity of a test of artistic ability might be demonstrated by comparing the test scores with teachers' judgements of the pupils' ability. *Construct validity* – sometimes used with ability or aptitude tests – is demonstrated by evidence that the test behaves in the intended or expected way. It might be argued, for example, that a *valid* test of musical appreciation would clearly distinguish between those who had received a musical education and those who had not. Evidence that this occurred would support, but not prove, the validity of the test. Another aspect of validity is concerned with the *comparability* of examinations from school to school and area to area, and it is particularly important for nationwide examinations such as the CSE and GCE to be similar in standards of grading and assessment. Up to the present time, however, research workers have shown greater interest in concurrent validity than in the other types listed above. As with reliability, co-efficients of correlation are frequently used to indicate validity. Such coefficients are often said to be 'high' when they are above 0·6 and 'low' when they are less than 0·3. These values are thus somewhat lower than those set for 'high' and 'low' reliability coefficients.

If an examination has been successfully prepared and administered in line with the criteria outlined above, then it should, finally, be found to have at least some of the characteristics of a 'good' examination, in the fairly broad sense, outlined by Wiseman and briefly described by Pilliner.

'(1) The content should consist of a representative sample of every aspect of the domain in which achievement or potential is to be assessed.

'(2) The procedure should be organized to impose as little stress as possible on the candidates so that each "should do himself justice".

'(3) The content and organization should make possible the consistent evaluation of the achievement or potential of each candidate.

'(4) The final outcome of the procedure should be the placing of candidates in a rank order, or in ordered categories, valid in respect of some acceptable criterion. Frequently the criterion is present achievement or potential success, or both, as defined explicitly, or accepted implicitly in a given culture.

'(5) The influence of the procedure on the work of pupils or students preparing for it, and on their teachers, should be educationally beneficial.'

Of course these standards are seldom, if ever, achieved, even in such widely used examinations as the CSE and GCE 'O' levels, but efforts to meet them are increasingly being made, as will be indicated by the review which follows.

The GCE 'O' level and CSE examinations

The GCE began in 1951, and the CSE in 1965. In summer 1965, 449,000 pupils took 'O' levels, and the same number took them in 1966; in the CSE the numbers of examinees increased from 66,000 in 1965 to 141,000 in 1966, indicating a very quick and wide acceptance of this new examination. Both examinations are meant to assess past achievement. The GCE examinations are also meant to predict future academic attainment (Ministry of Education, 1960) and are intended to be taken by pupils in the top 20 per cent of the ability range (see Diagram 1). The CSE examinations are designed to be taken by pupils in the 40th–80th percentile of the ability range (see Diagram 1). The GCE is a pass–fail examination. The CSE, however, has five grades – grade 1 being comparable to an 'O' level pass and grade 4 being the grade expected to be obtained by a candidate of 'average' ability. Both the CSE and GCE are individual subject examinations and the certificates list the subject(s) in which a candidate has satisfied the examiner.

GCE 'O' levels, like the School Certificate, have always been set by external examining boards (of which there are now eight), each of which operates on a national scale, and the examinations have changed little over the years. For academic subjects they usually

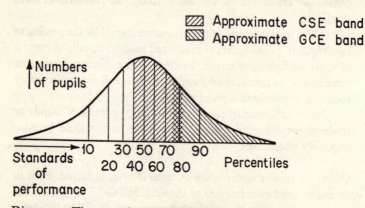

Diagram 1. The normal curve of distribution of ability
From *Secondary School Examinations Council (1963), p. 113*

consist of written papers, and in some instances a practical or performance test. Generally, the written papers are of an essay type and the examinee has to give answers to, or write essays on, a number of topics chosen from a larger number offered. In recent years, some objective test papers have also been introduced by several boards. One or two boards have also begun to try out continuous assessment of schoolwork on a small scale (University of London, 1967; Joint Matriculation Board, 1967; *Sunday Times*, 1968). The examinations of practical subjects are similar and are usually in two sections, written paper(s) and practical test. Papers and practicals vary in the time allowed, from as little as 30 minutes (French aural, for example), up to a whole school day (Art practical, for example). Generally, however, most papers seem to have a time limit of about 2½ hours.

The syllabuses for the GCE examinations are normally prepared by the appropriate subject committees, most of whose members are practising teachers. New syllabuses cannot be introduced without at least two years notice (in the JMB) and it may take up to five years to produce an actual examination based upon a new syllabus. The examinations are usually set by chief examiners in each subject and the papers are scrutinized by a moderator (or reviser) who comments on such matters as ambiguity of wording. In some boards, a third individual called 'the assessor' actually takes the paper in order to see that the questions asked are capable of solution in the time allowed. The subject committee is then asked to comment on the drafts and it is its responsibility to approve the final version of the paper.

The papers and practical pieces are marked according to the marking and weighting schemes prepared by the Chief Examiners and the examiners' panel. Usually, all examiners have to send in samples of the scripts they have marked so that they can be checked. The marks are standardized by discussion and by reference to the standards of previous years. Borderline cases generally have their scripts re-marked by Chief Examiners, although this practice varies from board to board. Finally, an Awarding Committee considers the work of candidates who have been reported by their schools as suffering from ill-health during the examination.

The CSE examinations are set by fourteen regional boards and tend to be more 'experimental' than the GCE examinations. For example, they are available in three modes: mode I, in which syllabuses and papers are usually set and marked by the boards; mode II, in which syllabuses are proposed by individual schools or groups of schools, but the examinations are set and marked by the boards: and mode III, in which syllabuses and examinations are set and marked by the schools themselves, subject to the moderation of standards by the examining boards. In mode I, objective tests are fairly widely used in the written examinations, and most boards have included 'continuous assessment' of coursework as part of both their academic and practical examinations. The CSE mode I examinations (used by over four-fifths of the schools taking CSE) therefore often consist of a written paper, a practical test and coursework. The examining boards usually prepare and assess mode I examinations in a similar manner to the GCE boards, although coursework is assessed by the teachers and moderated by the boards on a much wider scale than among the GCE boards. In general, therefore, the policies of the CSE and GCE boards are fairly similar, but the roles of the moderator and the teacher are more important in the CSE than in the GCE. The CSE system also appears to make greater use of research than the GCE system.

Research on academic subjects

Essays are still the most widely used type of assessment in the GCE if not the CSE. There are two main forms of essay test, the subject-matter essay test and the composition test. The essential differences between the two are that the content of the subject-matter test is fairly fixed (for example, solve specified mathematical problems), whereas the content of the composition test is not, and abstract literary qualities such as 'style' and organization are very important in the marking of composition tests, whereas they are supposedly of little importance in subject-matter tests. Although British studies have not always distinguished between these two types of essay examination, both have been investigated.

In the United Kingdom the first systematic comparison of any importance of the marks of examiners was made in the 1930s and it showed that chance played a large part in the results obtained on a wide variety of subjects ranging from School Certificate Latin to University Mathematical Honours. For example, when average School Certificate History scripts were re-marked by the same men after twelve to nineteen months, the examiners had changed their minds about pass, fail and credit classifications in ninety-two cases out of 210. It was stated in the report on the survey that boards of examiners were better than individuals in these matters but they were still far from perfect. Little attempt appears to have been made to revise the School Certificate or GCE examinations in the light of this knowledge. Nor did the GCE boards show much interest in putting into practice the results of research into selection at 11-plus in which Wiseman, for example, found that combined marking by three or four examiners could increase the reliability of the composition essay mark.

However, what GCE reports there have been, have described some interesting results. For instance, Daniels investigated the reliability and validity of three types of specially prepared 'ordinary' level GCE geography papers: (*a*) an objective-type paper, (*b*) a paper requiring pupils to interpret tabulated statistics, diagrams and maps and (*c*) an ordinary essay-type paper (three questions out of eight to be answered). He found that the essay-type paper was the most valid (concurrent validity) in that it had a correlation by itself of 0·72 with the criterion (teachers' estimate of geography ability). This correlation was so high that it suggested that the essay could have been used as the sole assessment without greatly reducing the validity of the examination results.

In contrast with this finding, later studies have raised serious questions about the reliability and validity of essay papers in actual examinations in use at present. For example, the 1965 English Language examinations of the Joint Matriculation Board and three other boards were compared when pupils from twenty-three schools took two of the examinations. It was found that the average performance on the paper for which pupils had not prepared was about half a grade below that achieved in the JMB examination. Unfortunately, the report did not indicate whether this variation was due to examinee variability, examiner variability or both. However, some indication of the influence of marker variability is given in a later part of the report. The JMB examination was analysed further and it was found that paper B was 'easier' for the examinees than papers A and C, and that candidates of similar ability to those taking the A and C papers obtained better grades on B. Inter-board differences in marking standards were also found when JMB and London University examinations were compared in Latin, French and Biology.

Other GCE studies have largely concentrated on the problem of the effectiveness of multiple marking. In one study, Lindley analysed the marking of an 'O' level French paper by thirteen examiners. There were two questions in the paper, both compulsory, question two having a stricter marking schedule than question one. Each script was marked three times by three different examiners. The results indicated that, as might be expected, there was smaller variation between the examiners in their marking of question two than in their marking of question one. The analysis also indicated that the standards of some examiners varied more than the standards of others. Another study analysed in the 1964 'O' level English

Composition examination of the Cambridge Board. The GCE Composition scripts of a representative sample of 500 boys and girls were marked independently by three markers and by a fourth marker who applied a code of penalties for mechanical errors. A candidate's mark was the total of three impression marks each out of ten and a mark out of ten for mechanical accuracy. The researchers found firstly that their marks were more reliable than the marks of the Cambridge Board, and secondly that their marks were more valid since they agreed more closely than the Board marks with an independent estimate of the pupils' ability to write compositions.

In the CSE a study of the reliability and validity of English examinations was conducted in 1964 by the Southern Board among 450 candidates. Three written tests were used: (a) Essay, (b) Comprehension paper, (c) Literature and special topics. The validity criterion was the average mark obtained on six essays. The papers were marked by rapid impression marking by four examiners. Agreement between markers was low for the Essay paper, higher for the Comprehension paper and highest for the Literature paper, and the correlation of the examination as a whole with the criterion was 0·75. The report concluded that: 'the greatest progress on the evidence of this trial examination would come from a greater consensus among English teachers as to what constitutes good writing and good understanding'.

The evidence reviewed above suggests that subject-matter essay tests tend to be marked more reliably than composition essays, but both need to be marked carefully if they are to have satisfactory reliability. The composition test in particular needs to be marked at least twice if the marks are to have reliability of 0·7 or more. The reliability of examinees is largely unexplored. The evidence on validity indicates that concurrent validity is often almost as high as marker reliability.

The objective test

Some interest is now being shown in objective tests, partly because they are easier to mark reliably and quickly than essay tests. Two major categories of objective test items are commonly identified; short answer items and multiple-choice items. The first category covers test items to which the examinees respond by writing a word, phrase, number or symbol. The other category refers to test items which clearly state or imply the alternatives, so that the examinee's task is simply to indicate which alternative he regards as the correct or best answer. True/false, multiple-choice, matching, classification and rearrangement items belong in this category. Unfortunately the type of objective test being reviewed is rarely mentioned in research reports, some of which are summarized below.

One of the few studies of objective GCE-type tests was reported recently by D. G. Lewis. Multiple-choice 'objective' tests of ability in Physics, Chemistry and Biology were constructed and administered to 191 boys who had previously taken the JMB examinations in these same subjects. The tests were constructed to assess (a) basic knowledge, (b) comprehension and application and (c) evaluation, along the lines of the Bloom Taxonomy. The results were factor analysed and the analysis suggested that although the category of 'evaluation' was an important aspect of the ability tests, this ability was not being assessed in the 'ordinary' level examinations.

In contrast with the GCE, there have been several studies of actual and experimental objective CSE examinations. The North Regional Examinations Board, for example, has published two papers on the mark re-mark reliability of their examiners in the 1965 CSE examinations of Geography and Physics-with-Chemistry. The 'objective' paper from each examination was re-marked. In both cases there was a mark re-mark reliability of 0·93 to 0·99 between the two marks awarded by the same examiner.

Three further studies reviewed an experimental Mathematics examination developed in the South Western CSE Board. In the first project, a twenty item 'multi-facet' test, each item with five true/false choices, was administered to 1,125 children in ten grammar and thirteen secondary modern schools. The test had an internal consistency reliability of 0·92 and validity correlations with term tests, scores on leaving certificates and so on ranged from 0·3 to 0·7. Next, 917 children sat for three different types of Mathematics examination: (a) traditional, (b) multiple-choice, (c) true/false/don't know. The 'traditional form' was found to be the hardest for the children and the true/false/don't know form was the easiest. Reliability ($r = $ 0·92 to 0·97) and validity (against teachers' forecast grade [$r = 0.51$ to 0.68]) were high for all forms of the test but lowest for the multi-facet test.

Finally, Taylor set a revised version of the multiple-choice test under three different instructions to three random samples of a total of 830 pupils of average and above average ability. The aim of the instructions was to dispose the pupils so as (a) to inhibit tendency to guess, (b) to be neutral towards guessing and (c) to encourage it. Analysis of variance of scores showed there to be no significant effect attributable to instructions. However, there were fewer 'omits and unfinished' items than would be expected by chance arising from the inhibiting instructions (a), the level expected by chance from the neutral instruction (b) and more from the instructions encouraging guessing (c).

The results given above and evidence from American studies indicate that well-constructed objective tests can have high internal consistency and mark re-mark reliability (up to r of 1.00) and acceptable concurrent validity ($r = 0.5$ or better).

Coursework and school-based examining

These two forms of assessment are considered together because, so far, there is little evidence of their effectiveness, and also because they are both 'new' types of assessment involving internal assessment by teachers. They have been introduced into the CSE on a large scale in an attempt to overcome some of the difficulties arising from the use of completely external examinations, and they are now beginning to be tried out in GCE examinations for the same reasons (*Sunday Times*, 1968).

Of the CSE studies which have mentioned coursework, few have discussed it thoroughly. One two-phase study of Science took place in 1963 and 1964. The 1963 examinations (Practical and Scientific Thinking paper) were set and marked externally. The 1964 examinations included a Facts and Principles paper and an assessment of coursework, both set and assessed by teachers. The report concluded that 'it is clear that appropriate records over at least a whole year are necessary to assess coursework more satisfactorily, and ways of organizing the records need to be developed'. A later study, this time of History, concentrated on one particular aspect of coursework, the personal topic, defined by the authors as 'the work in History which a candidate, entered appropriately for the CSE examination, has chosen to undertake and to offer as part evidence of his attainment in History'. The most interesting conclusions of this report were that 'time must be allowed for the development of improved techniques in guiding, overseeing, marking and moderating' and 'there is a need for teacher guidance concerning the choice and subsequent oversight of personal topics as well as the desirability of a precision in marking them' (mark re-mark reliability $= 0.65$ to 0.69). Thus both the Science and History reports stressed the need for the development of techniques of assessment which can be applied successfully over a period of time.

The examinations described so far have gradually tended to progress from those completely set and marked by external examiners to those partially set and marked by teachers. In school-based examinations, of which mode III CSE examinations are an example, the teachers set and mark the complete examinations with the aid of external moderators who can revise the grading up or down but cannot change the pupils' order of merit.

An interesting investigation of this type of examining was made by the JMB in 1964. An attempt was made to devise a method by which GCE 'O' level awards could be based on school assessments. Ten schools in Leeds entered 479 candidates for a special English Language examination and each of the schools assessed their own pupils' work over a year and did not use a final examination. Twenty examinees from each school (including the top and bottom pupils) had five samples of their work sent to a moderator as a check on standards. In the event, 91.5 per cent of the sample 'passed' (the schools' normal rate was 87 per cent). A later paper, after reviewing the reliability of an 'ordinary' JMB English Language examination ($r = 0.70$) concluded that 'there is good reason to believe that the awards made in the Leeds experiment are at least as satisfactory as those arrived at by traditional methods'. The later report also noted that the evidence indicates that 'methods of equating standards from school to school must be employed'.

More recently, the West Yorkshire and Lindsey CSE Board studied school-based English and school-based Physics in two sets of two schools. In the English study the final grade was derived from the grades in each of three sections: (*a*) two written papers, (*b*) oral English and (*c*) coursework, and the oral English and coursework were assessed throughout the year. The oral English was found to be difficult to assess but according to the report, 'a reassuring feature of the exercise was the patent reliability of assessment by experienced teachers'. Unfortunately little statistical evidence is presented in support of this judgement. The Physics study was in two parts. In the first part, pupils from two schools were assessed on their performance on four examination sections: objective test, essay test, practical test and coursework. The writers concluded that 'the experiment as a whole was successful but the practical test was difficult to organize and should, in future, be assessed as part of the coursework'. In the second part of the study, one of the schools used only coursework, which determined 60 per cent of the marks, and a written examination which determined 40 per cent. The correlation between coursework and teachers' estimates was very high ($r = 0.88$) and the over-all correlation of the examination with the criterion was 0.86. The final conclusion on both the English and Physics experiments was that, 'it is possible for teachers to produce assessments which are as reliable and valid as any examinations which may emanate from external sources'.

The evidence so far available on coursework and school-based examining indicates that new methods of assessment need to be developed if full advantage is to be taken of the benefits of school-based examinations. It appears to be especially difficult to include reliable and valid oral and practical sections in such examinations at the moment.

Content and predictive validity of academic examinations

So far the review has concentrated on the concurrent validity of examinations largely because the greatest information is available about these aspects of the GCE and CSE. However, some interest is gradually beginning to be shown in other attributes of these examinations, including content and predictive validity.

For example, in the GCE, Crossland and Amos analysed 'O' level Biology, General Science, Chemistry and Physics papers for the period 1948–64 and categorized the questions under four headings: (*a*) acquisition of facts, (*b*) interpretation of facts and drawing of conclusions, (c) application of scientific principles to new situations and (d) designing and planning of experiments. In all four subjects (especially Biology) it was found that the examinations placed the greatest emphasis on the acquisition of facts (34 per cent to 93 per cent of marks) and the least on the interpretation of results (0 per cent to 25 per cent of marks). The authors suggest that, on this evidence, 'scientific method is virtually ignored in "O" level science courses'. This conclusion is in agreement with that hypothesized by Lewis in the paper mentioned earlier.

As far as content validity of CSE examinations is concerned, Eggleston reviewed the science syllabuses of nine of the boards and concluded that 'the demand for a consideration of abilities other than the ability to recall facts . . . is almost unanimous'. However, he also found that coursework assessment left something to be desired, as far as specification of objectives is concerned and suggested that 'to reap the benefits of coursework assessment a two-dimensional structure will have to be devised according to the same rigorous rules which the American test setters apply to objective tests'. As yet, unfortunately, there is little published evidence on what is actually assessed in CSE examinations. The Yorkshire Board, however, analysed their 1967 mode I Geography examination using Bloom's categories and found that 'the examination has not so far encouraged the development of abilities other than the ability to recall facts'. This Geography examination is now being revised in the light of this knowledge. A number of other boards (particularly the South East Regional Examination Board) are also producing examinations based on blueprints but reports on the efficiency of these examinations are not yet readily available.

There is even less evidence available on the predictive validity of either the CSE or GCE 'O' level examinations. This is rather surprising in the case of the GCE examinations since they were originally designed to be predictive of future academic attainment. However, although there have been few predictive studies, there have been some intriguing studies of variables affecting performance (or non-performance) in the GCE.

For example, a recent book by Douglas gives an interesting account of the relation between social class and GCE success.[1] The

[1] Douglas, Ross and Simpson, *All Our Future*, Peter Davies, 1968.

report describes a longitudinal study of the secondary education, up to the fifth form, of a nationally representative sample of 5,000 pupils, all born in the same week in March 1946. It was found that, 'differences in measured ability explained only part of the social class differences in "O" level results. Among the pupils of high ability, the proportion of the upper middle class achieving a good certificate (passes in at least four subjects covering three or more of the four main academic fields) is twice that of the lower manual working class, and discrepancies in achievement are even greater at the slightly lower levels of ability. For instance, the upper middle class are three times as likely as the lower working class to achieve a good certificate if their ability is at the borderline level for grammar school admission, and thirteen times as likely to achieve a certificate of some sort if they are of just below average ability.' The report also comments that, 'in the population as a whole, as well as in the selective schools, the middle-class pupils have retained almost intact their historic advantage over the manual working class'. Some additional evidence on the GCE, CSE and school leavers is given in the annual *Statistics of Education* publication of the Department of Education and Science.

Discussion

In spite of the difficulty experienced in marking them reliably, essay tests will no doubt continue to be used in secondary school examinations. There are a number of reasons why this should be so, the main one being that the essay test requires the student to show an achievement – skill in written expression – which is not required by an objective test. The objective test also tends to take longer to prepare than an essay test. However, there is a great deal of evidence, from studies in America and in Britain that objective tests can be valid measures of attainment and can, for example, assess writing ability just as validly as, and more reliably than, essay tests. It is unfortunate, therefore, that teachers appear to dislike objective tests. Fortunately this distaste appears to be lessening gradually, and it seems likely that, as time goes by, objective tests will become more widely used in the CSE and GCE than they are at present.

The lack of study of oral and practical tests is rather surprising considering the number of years they have been in use. It is all the more surprising when considered in the context of well-verified findings from the armed forces and industry. In both situations it has been found that the interview (or oral test) adds very little extra information to that provided by written tests, unless it is well structured and performed by a team of interviewers. Practical tests of all types have also often been found to be more trouble than they are worth. However, oral and practical tests should not be dismissed out of hand since they may indicate skills which are important in some courses. Their inclusion in coursework may be one way of establishing their utility.

The strongest points in favour of coursework and school-based examining are that the assessment may be made by an examiner (the teacher) who knows the pupils, who can assess them over a period of time, and can make use of different types of examination as often as he feels they need to be used. The main problems are: the difficulty of calibrating standards from school to school and teacher to teacher; the possibility of teachers leaving before the assessments are completed; and the danger of the teacher's assessments being influenced by his feelings about the pupil. The system may also become too complicated and time-consuming if care is not taken to think out the procedure to be followed before the assessment begins. In addition, the pupils may feel that they are under pressure for too long if they know that they are being assessed throughout their last year or two at school. The small amount of evidence so far available concerning these objections is reassuring, but clearly more work needs to be done.

Thus, although the research studies reviewed in this article indicate that the CSE and GCE examining boards are increasingly aware of the difficulties of assessing pupils fairly, the findings also suggest that there are still a number of aspects of these examinations, which would benefit from further study and improvement. For example, the reliability of markers of coursework assessments is very difficult to establish at the moment, particularly in mode III CSE assessments. Examiner and examinee reliability indices are also difficult to estimate for written examinations, especially when candidates have a wide choice of questions from which they can select the few they wish to answer. In fact, at the moment, in some examinations, the range of choice is so wide that pupils can choose a combination of questions which has not been attempted by anyone else – thus making it impossible to estimate the reliability of that particular set of questions. There is also the problem that even if the reliability of the separate examination sections (written paper, practical test and so on) can be established, the varying inter-correlations of the various sections makes it quite difficult to calculate an 'over-all' reliability for the examination, particularly if a complicated weighting scheme is used when the marks in the various sections are added together.

This problem of 'weighting' is, of course, an aspect of content validity of examinations, and really, there is a greater need for information on the validity of the CSE and GCE – especially content, predictive and construct validity – than there is for evidence on reliability. For instance, many boards attempt to award varying percentages of marks to the different examination sections (e.g. practical test 35 per cent, written paper 40 per cent, coursework 25 per cent). Apart from the fact that boards (and schools) tend to apply different 'weights' to the 'same' subjects, there is also the difficulty that accurate 'weighting' of examinations is difficult to achieve on such an *a priori* basis, especially when the examination sections are of unknown reliability. Greater emphasis on this aspect of content validity, and also on the 'goal-orientated' approach to content validity, as described earlier in this paper, would aid in the clarification and justification of the 'weighting' procedures used by the boards. The content-validity aspect of examinations will probably, therefore, be quite closely studied in the coming years. There is still little sign of progress, however, in the study of predictive and construct validity. No doubt, progress in these directions is hindered by the difficulty of establishing adequate criteria and theories of assessment. However, if we are to obtain an adequate perspective on examinations, and their influence on education, then at some time these wider aspects of validity should be reviewed, including, for example, the influence of socio-economic differences in attitudes to education and tests, the effect of test-form factors (e.g. essay versus multiple-choice tests) on test scores and last, but not least, the influence of such variables as stress and anxiety on achievement.

The need for further research into and information on all aspects of the validity of examinations has been emphasized, because it is increasingly clear that examinations such as the CSE and GCE *do* have a strong influence on the training that a child receives at school, and if the aims and effects of these examinations are not known, then it is difficult to specify clearly the aims of education, at least in secondary school. 'In the past, the tendency has been to see (examinations) as isolated to some extent from the system, rather like industrial quality control tests occurring at various points in a production line. Up to a point, the analogy serves. But in the educational process, not only is a very large proportion of the product tested, but also the effects of the test on the product are considerable, and apt to spread to the untested remainder.'[1] Educationists therefore encourage the growth of such aspects of examining as teacher-based assessment (mode III CSE), specification of objectives, coursework and so on at least partly because it is hoped that such approaches to examining will help the teacher who uses them to develop his curriculum on the basis of the feedback he receives from them about his students' standing in the skills and knowledge being assessed.

Probably the best-known proponent of this view that 'evaluation is a form of educational intelligence for the guidance of curriculum construction and pedagogy' is the American psychologist Jerome S. Bruner. He holds that measurement without understanding is pointless, and that, to be effective, curriculum evaluation must contribute to a theory of instruction.

'If it does not, then it cannot contribute to the aims of the educational enterprise. Those aims centre upon the problem of assisting the development of human beings so that they make use of their potential powers to achieve a good life and make an effective contribution to their society. . . . The task of understanding how human beings can, in fact, be assisted in their learning and development is the central task of a theory of instruction, and techniques of evaluation derive from it in the same way that the practice of medicine derives from the medical sciences.'

[1] See Further Reading, A. E. G. Pilliner.

2   Reliability and the GCE examination*

A. S. WILLMOTT

In this paper the author discusses some of the problems of testing as they affect a specific examination, the London GCE. As may be seen, the tests used have many shortcomings. However, although the author refers to the practice of determining grades by ranking, he does not query its appropriateness. The reader might care to consider this in the light of the contribution by Glaser on criterion and norm referenced tests.

The examinations of the General Certificate of Education (GCE), in common with other predominantly 'essay' tests, are obviously not the most accurate measurements of ability. Many factors contribute to the degree of unreliability and it may be worth while to comment briefly on some of the more obvious ones.

A. The GCE consists, *ipso facto*, of a series of 'long answer' papers, in each of which the candidate is required to illustrate or explain some aspect of his subject in essay form. In scientific and technical subjects, the essay is often supported by diagrammatic work (sketch, maps, graphs, drawings of apparatus etc.) and calculations which, while contributing to the total assessment of the candidates, will not be discussed as a separate entity here. Because only a few 'long answer' questions can be attempted in the limited examining time available, only a small facet of each candidate's potential achievement is tested. This topic selection factor itself produces a large increase in unreliability since a different, but parallel, paper might easily contain questions solely on topics with which the candidate was less familiar.

B. As Section A implies, the end of the GCE examination period (in the case of the University of London, this is a bi-annual event falling in January and June each year) produces a monumental number of examination scripts for urgent marking. How is the marking done

---

* Reprinted and abridged from A. S. Willmott, 'Reliability and the GCE Examination', *International Newsletter*, **V**, September 1968, Education Testing Service, pp. 24–7.

and when? The University of London employs some 2,000–3,000 examiners (most of whom are school teachers or university lecturers) who each, during the main examinations in the summer, mark some 400–500 scripts in a period of three to four weeks. Standardizing, coordinating and correlating the work of so many examiners is a formidable task, and, inevitably, scope remains for the emergence of unreliability yet again.

C. Almost all of the GCE examinations contain more questions than the number a candidate is required to answer, in order to provide a reasonable choice. This factor of selection or choice effectively permits each candidate to choose his own examination within the scope of the particular paper.

D. The GCE examination results are usually reported in the form of grades, each of which covers a range of marks. The marks which the grades represent are usually expressed in percentages, though, in practice, the range is not 0–100. In one examination, for example, the range of marks may be only 15–65 (a maximum range of 50 marks) and this narrower range reduces considerably the discrimination between candidates. Therefore, as the final marks are expressed as integer values between 0 and 100, two candidates whose final marks were separated on the wider 0–100 range might well be awarded the same mark on a 15–65 range. Compensation for the loss of discrimination provided by the narrower scale is provided to a certain extent by the very fact that a grade, not an individual final mark, is awarded. The means of expanding the mark ranges lies in the hands of the examiners who set, mark and devise the marking schemes for the papers unless, for some reason, these distributions are juggled statistically to fulfil some previously designed criteria. It should be remembered, however, that the differences in range from one examination to another do not affect the grade allocation, since these are awarded on a percentage basis, i.e. the top 10 per cent (approximately) are awarded grade A, the next 10–15 per cent (approximately) are awarded grade B etc.

These, then, are some of the many factors which contribute to the unreliability of the traditional system of GCE examinations in Great Britain at the moment. One may wonder what is being done to eliminate, or at least to reduce, the more obvious of these contributions.

The University of London is fully aware of the need for reliability in the GCE examination system and of the various deficiencies which reduce reliability in the traditional examining pattern. It is engaged, at the moment, on several investigations aimed at increasing the reliability of the system. The major step in this direction is the introduction of multiple-choice objective test papers into the traditional system. This is not the appropriate place to detail the advantages of multiple-choice testing, but listed briefly below are a few of the advantages which particularly commend objective testing to the University of London:

(1) Greater coverage of the syllabus (seventy items per seventy-five minutes).

(2) Consistency of marking (and the additional advantage afforded by machine scoring).

(3) Elimination of selection/choice of questions (the paper is worked from beginning to end).

(4) Pre-testing of items (reliable pre-test statistics make possible the construction of sound final papers from the pre-tested items).

The University of London's present practice at Ordinary level is to replace the traditional three-hour paper in a given subject by a multiple-choice paper of one hour's duration, together with a two-hour traditional paper so that the total length of examining time remains unaltered. As experience is gained, we will know more precisely what proportion of objective testing is needed and may adjust this proportion accordingly.

The problem presented by choice in the traditional GCE examination pattern has been investigated at the University of London only very recently. Nevertheless, it is worthwhile examining a hypothetical example to give some measure of a problem presented by the traditional papers. Let us suppose that a traditional paper contains ten questions and of these the candidate must answer five. The number of possible combinations of questions is 252 though this number spirals when one includes the candidates who answer only four (or even three) questions. How many different combinations is one to expect? How many candidates attempt each combination? How does the reliability of each combination vary? How does the mean score on the examination vary for each combination? These and other questions have been partially answered. One particular paper, for example (set at GCE Advanced level in the summer of 1967), did offer ten questions from among which the 1,800 candidates who took the paper were asked to select and answer five. From the 1,800 candidates emerged 245 different combinations of questions but only 192 of these different combinations came from candidates who had answered all five questions. The discrepancy, some fifty-three combinations, was produced by those who answered only two, three or four questions.

3 The measurement of learning outcomes: some questions*

R. GLASER

This paper raises an issue which is of fundamental importance in the assessment of learning. Should tests be designed to discriminate among individuals so that a rank order of students' performance can be drawn up, or should testing concentrate on the evaluation of group performance after instruction according to some absolute criterion? Generally speaking tests and examinations in Great Britain are concerned with ranking students. This applies to most school examinations, to all selection examinations and to GCE examinations, although in the latter case some might consider that this is not so. And yet this approach to testing is arguably quite inappropriate to the assessment of learning following a course of instruction.

This paper examines the rationale of the two approaches to testing and suggests that we need seriously to reappraise our approach to the assessment of learning.

Achievement measurement can be defined as the assessment of terminal or criterion behaviour; this involves the determination of the characteristics of student performance with respect to specified

* Reprinted and abridged from R. Glaser, 'Instructional Technology and the Measurement of Learning Outcomes: Some Questions', *American Psychologist*, **18**, 1963, pp. 519–21.

standards. Achievement measurement is distinguished from aptitude measurement in that the instruments used to assess achievement are specifically concerned with the characteristics and properties of present performance, with emphasis on the meaningfulness of its content. In contrast, aptitude measures derive their meaning from a demonstrated relationship between present performance and the future attainment of specified knowledge and skill. In certain circumstances, of course, this contrast is not quite so clear, for example, when achievement measures are used as predictor variables.

The scores obtained from an achievement test provide primarily two kinds of information. One is the degree to which the student has attained criterion performance, for example, whether he can satisfactorily prepare an experimental report, or solve certain kinds of word problems in arithmetic. The second type of information that an achievement test score provides is the relative ordering of individuals with respect to their test performance, for example, whether Student A can solve his problems more quickly than Student B. The principal difference between these two kinds of information lies in the standard used as a reference. What I shall call criterion-referenced measures depend upon an absolute standard of quality, while what I term norm-referenced measures depend upon a relative standard.

CRITERION REFERENCED MEASURES

Underlying the concept of achievement measurement is the notion of a continuum of knowledge acquisition ranging from no proficiency at all to perfect performance. An individual's achievement level falls at some point on this continuum as indicated by the behaviours he displays during testing. The degree to which his achievement resembles desired performance at any specified level is assessed by criterion-referenced measures of achievement or proficiency. The standard against which a student's performance is compared when measured in this manner is the behaviour which defines each point along the achievement continuum. The term 'criterion', when used in this way, does not necessarily refer to final end-of-course behaviour. Criterion levels can be established at any point in instruction where it is necessary to obtain information as to the adequacy of an individual's performance. The point is that the specific behaviours implied at each level of proficiency can be identified and used to describe the specific tasks a student must be capable of performing before he achieves one of these knowledge levels. It is in this sense that measures of proficiency can be criterion-referenced.

Along such a continuum of attainment, a student's score on a criterion-referenced measure provides explicit information as to what the individual can or cannot do. Criterion-referenced measures indicate the content of the behavioural repertory, and the correspondence between what an individual does and the underlying continuum of achievement. Measures which assess student achievement in terms of a criterion standard thus provide information as to the degree of competence attained by a particular student which is independent of reference to the performance of others.

NORM-REFERENCED MEASURES

On the other hand, achievement measures also convey information about the capability of a student compared with the capability of other students. In instances where a student's *relative* standing along the continuum of attainment is the primary purpose of measurement, reference need not be made to criterion behaviour. Educational achievement examinations, for example, are administered frequently for the purpose of ordering students in a class or school, rather than for assessing their attainment of specified curriculum objectives. When such norm-referenced measures are used, a particular student's achievement is evaluated in terms of a comparison between his performance and the performance of other members of the group. Such measures need provide little or no information about the degree of proficiency exhibited by the tested behaviours in terms of what the individual can do. They tell that one student is more or less proficient than another, but do not tell how proficient either of them is with respect to the subject-matter tasks involved.

In large part, achievement measures currently employed in education are norm referenced. This emphasis upon norm-referenced measures has been brought about by the preoccupation of test theory with aptitude, and with selection and prediction problems; norm-referenced measures are useful for this kind of work in correlational analysis. However, the imposition of this kind of thinking on the purposes of achievement measurement raises some question, and concern with instructional technology is forcing us towards the kind of information made available by the use of criterion-referenced measures. We need to behaviourally specify minimum levels of performance that describe the least amount of end-of-course competence the student is expected to attain, or that he needs in order to go on to the next course in a sequence. The specification of the characteristics of maximum or optimum achievement after a student has been exposed to the course of instruction poses more difficult problems of criterion delineation.

THE USES OF ACHIEVEMENT MEASUREMENT

Consider a further point. In the context of the evaluation of instructional systems, achievement tests can be used for two principal purposes. First, performance can be assessed to provide information about the characteristics of an individual's present behaviour. Second, achievement can be assessed to provide information about the conditions or instructional treatments which produce that behaviour. The primary emphasis of the first use is to discriminate among individuals. Used in the second way, achievement tests are employed to discriminate among treatments, that is, among different instructional procedures by an analysis of *group* differences.

Achievement tests used to provide information about *individual* differences are constructed so as to maximize the discriminations made among people having specified backgrounds and experience. Such tests include items which maximize the likelihood of observing individual differences in performance along various task dimensions; this maximizes the variability of the distribution of scores that are obtained. In practical test construction, the variability of test scores is increased by manipulating the difficulty levels and content of the test items.

On the other hand, achievement tests used primarily to provide information about differences in treatments need to be constructed so as to maximize the discriminations made between *groups* treated differently and to minimize the differences between the individuals in any one group. Such a test will be sensitive to the differences produced by instructional conditions. For example, a test designed to demonstrate the effectiveness of instruction would be constructed so that it was generally difficult for those taking it before training and generally easy after training. The content of the test used to differentiate treatments should be maximally sensitive to the performance changes anticipated from the instructional treatments. In essence, the distinction between achievement tests used to maximize individual differences and tests used to maximize treatment or group differences is established during the selection of test items.

In constructing an achievement test to differentiate among *individuals* at the end of training, it would be possible to begin by obtaining data on a large sample of items relating to curriculum objectives. Item analysis would indicate that some test items were responded to correctly only by some of the individuals in the group, while other items were answered correctly by all members of the group. These latter 1·00 difficulty level items, since they failed to differentiate among individuals, would be eliminated because their only effect would be to add a constant to every score. The items remaining would serve to discriminate among individuals and thus yield a distribution of scores that was as large as possible, considering the number and type of items used.

On the other hand, if this test were constructed for the purpose of observing *group* instead of individual differences, the selection of items would follow a different course. For example, where instruction was the treatment variable involved, it would be desirable to retain test items which were responded to correctly by all members of the post-training group, but which were answered incorrectly by students who had not yet been trained. In a test constructed for the purpose of differentiating groups, items which indicated substantial variability within either the pre- or post-training group would be undesirable because of the likelihood that they would cloud the effects which might be attributable to the treatment variable.

In brief, items most suitable for measuring individual differences in achievement are those which will differentiate among individuals all exposed to the same treatment variable, while items most suitable for distinguishing between groups are those which are most likely to indicate that a given amount or kind of some instructional treatment was effective. In either case, samples of test items are drawn from a population of items indicating the content of performance; the particular item samples that are drawn, however, are those most useful for the purpose of the kind of measurement being carried out.

There is one further point which must be mentioned, and that is the use of diagnostic achievement tests prior to an instructional course. It appears that, with the necessity for specifying the entering behaviour that is required by a student prior to a programmed instructional sequence, diagnostic assessment of subject-matter competence must take on a more precise function. This raises the problem of developing an improved methodology for diagnostic achievement testing. In this regard, researchers using programmed instructional sequences to study learning variables point out that prior testing influences learning, and that this effect must be controlled for in determining the specific contribution of programming variables. In an instructional sense, however, the influence and use of pre-testing is an important variable for study since it is not the terminal criterion behaviour alone which dictates required instructional manipulations, but the differences between entering and terminal behaviour. Furthermore, pre-testing of a special kind may contribute to 'motivation' by enhancing the value of future responses; there is some indication that this may be brought about by prior familiarity with future response terms or by permitting some early aided performance of the terminal behaviour eventually to be engaged in.

In conclusion, the general point is this. Test development has been dominated by the particular requirements of predictive, correlational aptitude test 'theory'. Achievement and criterion measurement has attempted frequently to cast itself in this framework. However, many of us are beginning to recognize that the problems of assessing existing levels of competence and achievement and the conditions that produce them require some additional considerations.

4 The evaluation of learning*

E. STONES

This paper raises the question of the place of examinations in a system of instruction. Instead of examinations being virtually isolated from teaching it is argued that they should be integrated with teaching in an instructional system. The desirability of clearly stated instructional objectives serving both teaching and testing is discussed and the view is proposed that criterion-referenced tests are more appropriate to the instructional system envisaged.

Examples of research and innovation in the field of medical education are discussed. However, the principles involved are of general application to teaching at all levels and in any subject.

In the report of work at Illinois, reference is made to the use of a computer to monitor student test performance. While this is not a practical proposition at the moment in British schools, classroom records and progress charts could provide a monitoring function albeit less sophisticated than the computer service.

Problems of assessment and the evaluation of student learning are currently being given more attention by teachers and students than at any other time. University teachers have expressed their concern at the shortcomings of traditional methods, students have protested and in some cases torn up their question papers. The shortcomings of conventional examining methods are well documented and a convenient recent symposium is to be found in *Universities Quarterly* (1967). This present paper suggests some possible approaches to the evaluation of student learning which could help to improve present procedures. What I am suggesting is akin to what is sometimes called 'continuous assessment', although the general line of the argument also bears on other methods of evaluation.

It seems to me most appropriate that we take a view of evaluation which may be summed up in the phrase: *diagnosis – prescription – evaluation*. This view suggests that the teaching model involves, in the first instance, an examination of the capabilities of the student when he enters: this is diagnosis. The question we ask is, has the

---

* Reprinted and abridged from E. Stones, 'The Evaluation of Learning', *British Journal of Medical Education*, 3, 1969, pp. 135–42.

student got the prerequisite capabilities for embarking on the learning in question? If he hasn't, then it really is a mistaken policy to get him to embark on it. Once we are satisfied that the student is ready for the instruction we start him on an appropriate course. This is prescription. Finally we check to see if learning is satisfactory. This is evaluation. The process does not, of course, end there; often the end of the course becomes the starting point for the next. Thus the evaluation test for Course A should relate closely to the diagnostic test for Course B.

Norm- and criterion-referenced approaches

Such an approach raises immediately one of the most important questions in evaluation: the question of test reference. We ask, is the criterion of competence in the subject under scrutiny related to a set of norms drawn from a typical population, or is it related to an objective standard of attainment? That is, do we give a test, score it, arrange the students in rank order and then decide on pass, credit, distinction and so on? Or do we decide beforehand on certain skills and concepts which we expect the students to have, devise a test to test these attributes and then score students' performance according to the extent to which they demonstrate their grasp of those skills and concepts? The difference between these two approaches is quite fundamental. In norm-referenced evaluation the discriminative power of the test instrument is all-important and will often take precedence over its other functions. In instruments related to an objective criterion, discrimination will be unimportant and individual items in the instrument will be selected for reasons other than their power to discriminate.

The most obvious practical difference between the two approaches is that norm-referenced measures will emphasize grading of students and the production of a rank order of examinees, while criterion-referenced measures will not be concerned with ranking but will emphasize the achievement of pre-determined standards. In norm-referenced evaluation, examiners will probably have some notion of what constitutes a pass, or average, or distinction performance which they carry in their heads and which may lead to their working on a scale roughly following a normal distribution. Performance here is related to the performance of the group, and one student's distinction depends on the non-distinction of the rest of the group. Criterion-referenced assessment is different. Theoretically all students could reach distinction level, or all could fail. Since performance is related to an objective pre-determined criterion, however, it is not enough for an examiner to conceive of an intuitive pass mark – say 50 per cent – whenever he attempts to assess student performance. Nor is it enough for him to observe and perhaps record student performance, and then to rank on this performance and finally to decide on cutting scores to determine pass, fail or other categories.

In general, most public examining bodies and universities adopt a norm-referenced approach to assessment. However, much can be said for considering criterion-referenced methods as the most appropriate approach to evaluation. The consequences of deliberately, overtly and systematically adopting a criterion-referenced approach are important, and in part, point up the essential difference between this approach and the norm-referenced approach. Clearly if an objective criterion is to be used, it is essential to decide on the criterion before devising the evaluative instrument. In other words, one must specify precisely the objectives of instruction before deciding how to assess whether in fact the objectives have been achieved. *Precisely* is emphasized because syllabuses and schemes of work are rarely noted for their precision. It is useful in this context to borrow an expression from the jargon of programmed learning, and specify objectives in *behavioural* terms – that is, state unequivocally what the student must be able to *do* at the end of instruction. It is of little use to say as one syllabus in sociology said recently that the examination will expect the student to be able to show an awareness of some of the concepts – for example, *role, status* – used in sociology. This is of little use because we are given no idea how we would discriminate between a student who shows an awareness and one who doesn't. Nor is it much help to say that a medical student 'will be expected to appreciate the wholeness of his patient. . . .' Objectives expressed in this form are impossible to evaluate. What is needed is an explicit unequivocal statement of what is meant by the *wholeness* of the patient, and just what is meant by *appreciate*.

Evaluating objectives

The question of objectives is probably the crux of the matter. The problem is to suggest ways in which objectives may be made more amenable to evaluation than is usually the case. I should like here to refer to two systems of classification which have been very influential in the educational field. They are the *Taxonomy of Educational Objectives* edited by Bloom,[1] and the suggested taxonomy of learning types proposed by Gagné. Both help us to analyse our teaching objectives and our evaluative instruments. The Bloom taxonomy, whose main headings are set out in Table 1, is the work of a group of American psychologists. It has been developed over a number of years and was submitted to considerable scrutiny before publication. It cannot, of course, be considered to be an absolute and definitive statement, but it has achieved considerable prestige since publication. The system puts objectives into two categories: those of a conceptual nature into the so-called *cognitive domain* and those of an emotional nature into the *affective domain*. It is not merely a classification according to type: it is a taxonomy, which implies a definite set of relationships. In this case, it is a hierarchical classification. Objectives at the first level are subsumed in the second; the first and second in the third, and so on, so that in the cognitive domain the sixth level, that of evaluation, is a category superordinate to the remainder. Thus, in the cognitive field, the higher one moves in the hierarchy, the more complex the intellectual skills needed to cope with concepts at that level.

The value of this taxonomy is that it provides a key by which one can assess the level of functioning of any evaluative device. It is possible to do this assessment after the device has been constructed, but this is rather pointless and ideally it should be done before. If one approaches evaluation in this way, one must determine, ideally before instruction and certainly before evaluation, the proportions of the course which relate to the different categories. Testing level six of the cognitive objectives *ipso facto* involves testing objectives at all preceding levels and it would be plausible to argue that, in a terminal examination, test items should mainly cover the higher level objectives.

[1] See Further Reading.

Table 1A. System of classification[1]

I. The cognitive domain

1.00 *Knowledge*

1.10 Knowledge of specifics
    1.11 Knowledge of terminology
    1.12 Knowledge of specific facts
1.20 Knowledge of ways and means of dealing with specifics
    1.21 Knowledge of conventions
    1.22 Knowledge of trends and sequences
    1.23 Knowledge of classifications and categories
    1.24 Knowledge of criteria
    1.25 Knowledge of methodology
1.30 Knowledge of universals and abstractions in a field
    1.31 Knowledge of principles and generalizations
    1.32 Knowledge of theories and structures

2.00 *Comprehension*
    2.10 Translation
    2.20 Interpretation
    2.30 Extrapolation

3.00 *Application*

4.00 *Analysis*
    4.10 Analysis of elements
    4.20 Analysis of relationships
    4.30 Analysis of organizational principles

5.00 *Synthesis*
    5.10 Production of unique communication
    5.20 Production of a plan, or a proposed set of operations
    5.30 Derivation of a set of abstract relations

6.00 *Evaluation*
    6.10 Judgement in terms of internal evidence
    6.20 Judgement in terms of external criteria

---

[1] Abstract from *A Taxonomy of Educational Objectives*, Bloom *et al.*, 1956.

The logic of a taxonomic analysis suggests that, in general, abilities tested early in a course will be subordinate to those tested at the end of the course and will be subsumed by them. Thus it seems that testing during the course of a given unit of instruction is redundant *if one is solely concerned with assessing*. If, however, one is testing to evaluate learning then a different situation exists. The results of testing subordinate skills are tremendously useful to the

Table 1B. System of classification[1]

II. The affective domain		
1.0	*Receiving (attending)*	
	1.1	Awareness
	1.2	Willingness to receive
	1.3	Controlled or selected attention
2.0	*Responding*	
	2.1	Acquiescence in responding
	2.2	Willingness to respond
	2.3	Satisfaction in response
3.0	*Valuing*	
	3.1	Acceptance of a value
	3.2	Preference for a value
	3.3	Commitment
4.0	*Organization*	
	4.1	Conceptualization of a value
	4.2	Organization of a value system
5.0	*Characterization by a value or a value complex*	
	5.1	Generalized set
	5.2	Characterization

[1] Abstract from *A Taxonomy of Educational Objectives*, Krathwohl *et al.*, 1964.

student and teacher as feedback giving an indication of the efficacy of their efforts and a diagnosis of the readiness of the student to proceed to the next unit of instruction.

Monitoring function

Looked at in this way, the continuous evaluation of students' learning resembles a monitoring device rather than a screening device and this monitoring function is probably the most important function that continuous evaluation can perform, even though it may not necessarily provide a yardstick of student capability at the end of the course. It is, of course, perfectly possible to decide that some of the objectives lower in the hierarchy should be used in assessment, even though they may be subsumed by the objectives in higher categories. It is also possible, and most likely, that some sub-units of a course may be self-contained and discrete so that they can be assessed before the end of the course. The essential factor is that, in either case, an awareness of the different categories of objectives will enable a tutor to prepare an evaluative instrument which adequately covers the objectives of the course. Table 2 suggests a way in which this can be done. This matrix is a suggested plan of an examination in science, showing the allocation of questions to different levels of the taxonomy. As a salutary first exercise in using a taxonomy it is revealing to subject an existing test to analysis using a matrix like this to see into which category the items fall. It is quite remarkable how a disproportionately large percentage of items in many tests tends to fall into the lowest levels of the taxonomy and tests nothing more than specifics in the cognitive domain.

It is possible to submit evaluative instruments to another test. One can take a somewhat broader view and consider the kinds of learning being tested. This approach follows the suggestion of the American psychologist R. Gagné and is set out in Table 3. Are we testing simple response learning? Or the chaining of responses? Or concepts? And so on. The learning of motor skills will be at the lower levels, but it is important to be careful that we are not testing at this level when we think we are testing at the conceptual level. This can all too easily happen when a student is asked to give a definition or asked a question in the same form as he has been taught earlier. All too often the familiar situation or the familiar question evokes the familiar (correct) response without understanding. This is testing at the lowest levels. It may well be considered necessary, and in some cases desirable or unavoidable, to test at this level. The essential thing is of course to be aware of what we are doing and apply a systematic analysis to the construction of our evaluative instruments. Table 3 presents an approach to such an analysis. It refers specifically to an objective test, but it could clearly be applied to a variety of situations. It provides a method of analysis which can help us to determine the types of learning involved in various test items.

It is one thing to decide to test this or that kind of learning, or to test at this or that level in the taxonomy, it is another thing to be sure that a test does, in fact, do what it purports to do. That is, is the test valid? And, concomitantly, is it reliable?

Table 2. Two-axis chart of specifications for a final examination in natural science – term I[1]

Objectives[2] / Course content	Knowledge	Comprehension (translation, interpretation, extrapolation)	Application	Analysis	Total
1. Perception, symbolization and the methods of science	5	5			10
2. The cell-structure and function; cell principle spontaneous generation and biogenesis	5			5	10
3. Sexual reproduction in animals and plants; human reproduction and sex hormones	4	6			10
4. Cellular reproduction: mitosis	4	6			10
5. Meiosis; chromosomes and genes	3	3	4		10
6. Monohybrid cross		4	6		10
7. Dihybrid cross		3	3	4	10
8. Blood group inheritance; heredity in man		4	6		10
9. Linkage and crossing-over	3	3	4		10
10. Sex determination and sex linkage	1	1	2	6	10
Total	25	35	25	15	100

[1] From De Cecco (1968). [2] See Bloom (1956).

Validity

Validity has several forms, but the one I urge as being most appropriate is content validity as related to the stated objectives of a course of instruction. Such a test is valid if it adequately measures the degree of achievement of the aims and purposes of instruction. In the last analysis, validity is probably a subjective matter. A consensus view of validity is preferable and is probably the most fruitful approach to the production of an evaluative instrument at present. Using this approach, one would build a test to a clearly stated set of behavioural objectives using an analytical approach such as the Bloom taxonomy, then one would subject this instrument to scrutiny by a number of experts, and finally one would try it out several times with revisions between each trial.

Reliability

The question of reliability is also important. By reliability is meant the extent to which an evaluative instrument will produce the same pattern of scores with the same population on two different occasions. To be of any use an instrument must be very reliable, otherwise one can have no confidence that the pattern of results obtained on one occasion is a true measure of student ability. Reliability can be increased by using objective methods of testing and by increasing the number of individual sub-items in a given instrument. It should be stressed, however, that reliability on its own is not enough. Validity is the important thing. An objective test of students' understanding of geology could be extremely reliable, but absolutely invalid and useless as a test in anatomy.

Problems and possibilities

Two specific accounts of assessment taken from the field of medical education provide concrete examples of current problems of testing and outline possible future approaches. The first is taken from a *Lancet* article by Bull[1] who reports an investigation into the final

[1] G. M. Bull, 'An examination of the final examination in medicine', *Lancet*, 2, pp. 368–72.

Table 3. Chart for planning tests, based on Gagné's classification of learning types[1]

Learning types Instructional objectives	Signal learning	Stimulus-response learning	Chaining	Verbal association	Multiple discrimination	Concept learning	Principle learning	Problem solving
1. Define and illustrate performance assessment in terms of auxiliary and terminal performances								
2. Describe and illustrate the relationship of performance assessment to other components								
3. Distinguish and illustrate the differences between absolute and relative standards of performance								
4. Describe and illustrate the disadvantage of using relative standards in performance assessment								

5. Describe and illustrate three important results of using absolute standards							
6. Define and illustrate validity in terms of instructional objectives and test items							
7. Define reliability in terms of consistency							
8. Define objectivity in terms of scoring and illustrate its use in scoring essay and objective tests							
9. Describe the relationship between task analysis and test preparation							
10. Construct two essay questions which follow the guidelines							

[1] From De Cecco (1968).
Empty cells will contain numbers indicating number of items for each objective and learning type.

medical examination. He found that the essay component of this examination was extremely unreliable and suggested that it be abandoned or considerably modified. On the other hand he found the *viva* element of the examination fairly reliable. However, this finding does not imply that the *viva* is a good test. Indeed, although it was supposed to test factual knowledge, it had a very low correlation with the objective test. In all probability the *viva* was an invalid test of factual knowledge. It might, however, be a valid test of certain personality characteristics and these characteristics might well be desirable attributes in medical students. The problem is that the examiners had not at that time examined and isolated the factors they were examining. If the *viva* is to be used, then it would seem that a thorough analysis along the lines suggested in the taxonomy should be made to attempt to identify the objectives of the *viva*.

One important question is raised by this investigation. To what extent should different evaluative instruments highly correlate? I suggest that there is a lot to be said for having low correlations between different measures. Low correlation implies that the different instruments are assessing different skills and this is probably desirable.

The other account of evaluation is taken from a report of a medical course which tackles some of the problems raised by the *Lancet* article. The course in question was the medical course of the University of Illinois College of Medicine. Preliminary studies found that, in the then current system of student examination, grading and promotion not only failed to provide evidence of student achievement of the most important goals of medical education, but actually jeopardized their attainment by exacerbating tendencies towards fragmentation of learning, by focusing student attention on esoteric or trivial detail, and by intensifying unhealthy competition among students for grades.

The next stage was to develop a set of coherent and comprehensive institutional goals and standards in terms of which student progress could be assessed. The resulting behavioural objectives were then categorized into the cognitive, affective and skill domains, and methods of assessing each were explored. It was decided to assess cognitive and some skill goals by objective written examinations and to use practical laboratory and clinical examination to measure other psychomotor skills. Habits and attitudes were to be assessed by systematic accumulation of anecdotal records. The general approach followed lines similar to those referred to earlier. Tests used later in the course sampled skills acquired earlier and subsumed by the later skills.

Many new approaches to assessing competence were developed and old methods extended. These sought to face the student with problems and situations as near as possible to real life situations. Exercises based on a variety of visual and aural material required the student to demonstrate competence in a wide variety of skills rather than merely answering pencil and paper tests on the subject.

In addition to the developing of new types of test items, the objective minimum passing standards are predetermined. It is thus, in principle, possible for all students to pass or to fail. In addition, results of students' performance on the tests are continuously monitored by computer analysis. Students and teachers are thus able to have running information about their performance and teachers have continuous feedback about the way in which their evaluative instruments are functioning.

Future developments in Great Britain

I consider that evaluation of learning should develop along these lines. We have relatively little experience of this kind of approach in Great Britain. Continuous assessment, which is the nearest approach, tends to consist mainly of weekly or fortnightly quizzes or essays. This approach is not really satisfactory. In the first place the instruments are often poor. As has been repeatedly shown essays have many shortcomings as test instruments. The objective tests seldom make use of their full range of possibilities and often test at the lowest conceptual levels. Furthermore, the intervals of testing are often arbitrary and unrelated to the achievement of sub-tasks in the system of education objectives. What is needed is a system of evaluation planned to assess the achievement of clearly enunciated behavioural objectives; a system which provides for the evaluation of learning at key points in the course when a given module of instruction is complete; a system which provides feedback to students and staff and thus facilitates the continuous monitoring of their performance. Such a system would enable tutors to detect and correct deficiencies in their teaching, thereby improving instruction and student perform-ance. Improvement in student performance, the knowledge that all students could achieve excellence, the fact that they could be clearly informed about course objectives and given detailed diagnostic infor-mation about their learning achievements would all tend to improve student motivation.

The elements of this system of evaluation should simulate actual practising situations as closely as possible. They should be integrated as closely as possible with the actual teaching program and be seen as a natural part of it, being at least as much value to the student as to the tutor.

If these aims can be achieved, then I think we shall have a program which exemplifies a model of continuous evaluation – namely, a situ-ation in which student evaluation is an integral part of a teaching program.

Summary

The evaluation of learning has traditionally relied heavily on essay type tests given at the end of term or academic year. Usually assess-ment of a student's learning makes use of norms of attainment drawn *post hoc* from the scores of the test population. The efficacy of such methods is being increasingly questioned. An alternative approach to the evaluation of learning is suggested, which replaces norm-referenced assessment by criterion-referenced evaluation. The im-portant consequences of such an approach – namely, the necessity for clearly enunciated instructional objectives – is discussed. Suggestions are made for the marrying of criterion-referenced evaluation and the precise specifying of instructional objectives in order to produce a system of teaching in which evaluation becomes a monitoring device for student learning.

FURTHER READING

B. S. Bloom *et al.*, *Taxonomy of educational objectives 1: cognitive domain*, Longmans, 1956.

R. L. Ebel, *Measuring educational achievement*, Prentice Hall, 1965.

H. C. Ellis, 'Evaluation: judging the effectiveness of programmes' in G. D. Ofiesh and W. C. Meiehenry (Eds.), *Trends in programmed instruction*, Department of Audiovisual Instruction and National Society of Programmed Instruction, 1964.

J. A. Lauwerys and D. G. Scanlon (Eds.), *Examinations*, The World Year Book of Education, 1969, Evans for University of London Institute of Education and Teachers College, Columbia University, 1969.

C. H. McGuire, 'An evaluation model for professional education – medical education' in *Proceedings of the 1967 invitational conference on testing problems*, Educational Testing Service, Princeton, N.J., 1968.

D. Pidgeon and A. Yates, *An introduction to educational measurement*, Routledge and Kegan Paul, 1969.

A. E. G. Pilliner, 'Examinations', *University of Edinburgh Bulletin*, 4 (9), 1968.

A. E. G. Pilliner, 'Purposes of examination procedures' in H. J. Butcher (Ed.), *Educational research in Britain*, U.L.P., 1968.

J. M. Stalnaker, 'Suggestions for improving essay questions', *Educational Measurement*, American Council on Education, 1951, pp. 516–28.

Universities Quarterly, 21 (3), 1967.

R. C. Whitfield, 'Improving examining at sixteen plus', *Educational Research*, 10 (2), 1968, pp. 109–13.

S. Wiseman (Ed.), *Examinations and English education*, Manchester University Press, 1961.

Name Index

Subject Index